MAKING THE CASE

MAKING THE CASE

FEMINIST AND CRITICAL RACE PHILOSOPHERS ENGAGE CASE STUDIES

EDITED BY
HEIDI GRASSWICK AND
NANCY ARDEN McHUGH

SUNY PRESS

Published by State University of New York Press, Albany

For information, contact State University of New York Press, Albany, NY
www.sunypress.edu

Library of Congress Cataloging-in-Publication Data

Names: Grasswick, Heidi Elizabeth, 1965– editor. | McHugh, Nancy Arden,
   editor.
Title: Making the case : feminist and critical race philosophers engage
   case studies / edited by Heidi Grasswick and Nancy Arden McHugh.
Description: Albany : State University of New York Press, 2021. | Includes
   bibliographical references and index.
Identifiers: LCCN 2020023773 | ISBN 9781438482378 (hardcover : alk. paper) |
   ISBN 9781438482385 (pbk. : alk. paper) | ISBN 9781438482392 (ebook)
Subjects: LCSH: Social justice—Case studies. | Feminist theory. | Racism.
Classification: LCC HM671 .M346 2021 | DDC 303.3/72—dc23
LC record available at https://lccn.loc.gov/2020023773

10 9 8 7 6 5 4 3 2 1

Contents

Acknowledgments

Many people have helped make this volume possible. Much of the early impetus for our thinking about the value of in-depth casework for feminist and critical race philosophers came from our involvement in the National Endowment for the Humanities Summer Seminar on Feminist Epistemologies, organized by Nancy Tuana and Shannon Sullivan in 2003. The two of us met there and started collaborating in a range of ways at that seminar. Many of the conversations that took place there and the longstanding relationships forged among the participants have been crucial to each of us and our ongoing commitment to the development of philosophical tools to support social-justice work. Another important locus of inspiration has been the community of FEMMSS (Feminist Epistemologies, Methodologies, Metaphysics, and Science Studies). This organization has provided continual support, critique, and engagement that has made today's versions of case-engaged philosophical work viable and strong. This volume also benefitted from having a series of papers presented PechaKucha-style at the 2016 SRPoiSE (Consortium for Socially Relevant Philosophy of/in Science and Engineering) that was a collaboration with the Center for Values in Medicine, Science, and Technology at the University of Texas at Dallas. This venue tested several of the papers in their early stages and allowed for conversation between presenters themselves and between presenters and the audience.

We appreciate the time, energy, and patience of all of the contributors as this volume developed, and we are grateful for their willingness to share their ideas on an underexplored yet critical topic in philosophy.

We also want to acknowledge the support of our families throughout this project. Without them (both humans and animals) we would not be the philosophers and teachers we are today, nor would we have the energy and strength to see lengthy academic projects such as this one through to their completion.

Introduction

HEIDI GRASSWICK AND NANCY ARDEN McHUGH

The Use of Cases and Case Studies: Philosophy and the Contributions of Feminist and Critical Race Philosophy

What it means to use cases and case studies in one's scholarship and research varies tremendously across fields. Case histories in medicine focus on the course of disease, diagnosis, and treatment of one particular individual and are taken to hold crucial pedagogical value for medical education; case studies in political science may draw conclusions about political behavior from an in-depth study of a few different historical cases. As Mary Morgan (2014) has pointed out, even what gets labeled as a *case study* varies between disciplines. *Making the Case* brings together new works by established and emerging feminist and critical race theorists, primarily philosophers, who engage specific case studies and/or analyze case-based methodologies. In doing so, the volume seeks to demonstrate the depth and breadth of work in this area while highlighting the distinct approaches that feminist and critical race philosophers have pursued when it comes to case-study work. We use the term *feminist and critical race philosophies* (and *philosophers*) throughout in order to identify work of feminist and critical race theorists that engages with the tools, practices, and theories of philosophy.[1] Feminist and critical race philosophers employing casework such as that represented in this volume have also reflected on the role of casework within philosophy, including both its challenges and its potential.

Historically, much of the discipline of philosophy has shied away from employing cases and case studies, seeking instead to provide abstract

1

and decontextualized analyses, particularly in the case of those philosophers who are trained in the analytic tradition. Some of the hesitancy of philosophers to use or develop case studies stems from a conception of good philosophical analysis as necessarily abstract and removed from the messiness of life's complexities. Many philosophical works seek to clarify the concepts and frameworks that lie behind our everyday interactions with the world and each other, with a goal of allowing us to understand and articulate the core concepts that cut across the particularities of individual cases. Relatedly, many philosophers see themselves as seeking to identify and articulate ideals that form worthy goals for human beings or offering paradigms that serve as ideal schemas from which we can better understand the world. Such philosophers focus their attention on such lofty questions as, What is the ideal of justice? the good? truth? knowledge? Sometimes, philosophers have then gone on to apply their ideal schemas to particular cases, such as has been done in the field of applied ethics. Yet, increasingly, numerous philosophers who are concerned with making philosophy relevant to understanding our current situations have found such a model of the application of a philosophical theory or ideal to be an inadequate way of engaging with cases and have questioned the value of developing philosophical theories and ideals in the abstract. These theorists' commitment to working with cases can be understood as a form of nonideal theorizing (see Corwin Aragon's contribution to this volume), through which the philosophizing begins with the specific situations at hand and builds from there. Feminist and critical race philosophers have been central to this trend. In this volume, we draw attention to the ways in which cases and case studies have become important methodological tools for the specific work of feminist and critical race philosophers. The individual chapters that follow showcase the wide variety of forms and uses of case studies that feminist and critical race philosophers engage; taken as a collection, they highlight certain common themes and methodological choices that are distinctive (though not exclusive) to feminist and critical race philosophy.

Trends toward Case Studies in Philosophy

In spite of philosophy's history noted above and the persistence of certain pockets of resistance, it would be a mistake to characterize contemporary philosophy as inherently resistant to casework. Several trends within various areas of current philosophical discourse can be identified that lend themselves to the encouragement of casework.

First, the move toward naturalizing epistemology, which began with W. V. O. Quine (1969) but has developed in a variety of directions, can be read as offering strong encouragement for the use of cases and case studies within philosophy. Naturalized epistemologists claim that we cannot determine the ideals of knowledge without taking seriously how we actually engage (as humans) in knowledge seeking (Kornblith 1994). This requires looking at how we know things, and cases can provide observations and descriptions of this. According to naturalists, the normative claims of epistemologists that elevate certain propositions to the status of knowledge cannot be answered without close attention to describing our epistemic capacities (psychological and social) and those circumstances within which we engage in inquiry. Relatedly, the historicist turn in philosophy of science that began with Thomas Kuhn (1962) encouraged the study of actual cases of scientific development to inform one's philosophy of science and ensure that it is based on such evidence of how science has actually been done.

Second, as Lorraine Code notes in this volume, there has been a certain "thawing" between the two schools of continental philosophy and Anglo-American analytic philosophy. This thawing has resulted in more possibilities for a mixture of approaches and a recognition that there are philosophical things to learn about the world through the careful investigation of cases, including the use of narrative and literary styles of theorizing that historically found a more natural home in continental philosophy while meeting sharp rebuke from epistemologists of the analytic tradition.

Third, there is a growing movement of philosophers of science interested in producing socially relevant philosophy of science (see, for example, Fehr and Plaisance 2010). Socially relevant philosophy of science entails attending to the ways that philosophy of science "contributes to public welfare and collective wellbeing" of societies by taking up the epistemological and ethical issues of science that arise within our struggles to develop, interact with, and use science (SRPoiSE).[2] Careful attention to cases is a crucial tool in undertaking socially relevant philosophy of science, and several contributions to this volume offer examples of how to do this from the perspective of feminist and critical race philosophies, especially the chapters by Sean Valles, Carla Fehr, Lacey Davidson and Mark Satta, and Sergio Armando Gallegos-Ordorica.

Fourth, feminist philosophers and critical race theorists have for the last thirty years increasingly been pressing on the problems of philosophical methods that fail to attend to the socially located specificities of oppressed people. Here, the criticism has been that by ignoring the specifics of situations in attempts to engage in abstract theorizing, philosophy runs the danger of generating theories that have little to do with "lives on the ground" and can be a distraction from the hard realities of those lives. It also runs the risk that specific theories created within philosophy and the problems they focus on bear a closer resemblance to the lives of and challenges faced by those in dominant and mainstream epistemic locations while ignoring the lives of people who are oppressed or otherwise margin-alized in society. Reflecting on philosophy and its attraction to the abstract, the universal, and the ideal at the expense of the concrete, the situated, and the present, feminist and critical race philosophers have argued that philosophy itself can contribute to structures of domination by ignoring its own situatedness. This theme comes out in many of the contributions to this volume. What has become apparent in these criticisms is that in spite of the activity of theorizing at times being presented as though it is disconnected from real-world cases, the authors' situations and experiences shape the problems taken up and the frameworks formed such that the theory is never as removed from real-world situations as it purports to be. The pressure stemming from these oppression-focused criticisms of abstract methodology has contributed to a certain opening within philosophy, an opening through which case-study analysis has thrived.

Characteristics of Case Use in
Feminist and Critical Race Philosophies

Given their critiques of abstract methodology, it is no surprise that feminist and critical race philosophies have been major contributors to contemporary case-study work. The contributions to this volume demon-strate the impressive range of ways in which feminist and critical race philosophers are making use of cases. In many instances, the authors are employing now-well-developed concepts from feminist and critical race epistemologies to understand particular cases. For example, concepts such as epistemic injustice and epistemologies of ignorance offer incisive ways of understanding how oppression is playing out in specific circumstances. In other instances, the authors are providing new analyses of the demands of responsible research involving cases, integrating ethical and epistemic concerns, and carefully developing understandings of what kinds of knowledge can be generated from the study of cases. While the selections featured here demonstrate the plethora of ways in which feminist and critical race philosophers are engaging casework, they also make evident certain features that are characteristic of casework done from feminist and critical race perspectives.

Perhaps most importantly, we see that feminist and critical race philosophers are very deliberate in the *kinds* of cases that they choose to work with. They are motivated to engage cases that focus on elements of marginalized and oppressed peoples' experiences. Attention to the details of such cases can reveal the complexity of how domination and injustices play out. In the process, feminist and critical race philosophers often use cases to demonstrate how knowledge and epistemological frameworks play a role in such domination. They are not just attracted to case studies because such studies offer more details than abstract theory and can be more empirically grounded as a result. Rather, they acknowledge that the very choice of the case study one works with can make a difference in the type of understanding generated because the cases selected determine where the epistemological attention is directed. What we see in the work of feminist and critical race philosophers is an illustration of just how important the use of case studies can be for revealing aspects of oppression and marginalization that would otherwise be hidden from view, falling outside the scope of existing philosophical frameworks that were not drawn up with an eye toward explaining such experiences.

Our Definition of Cases and Case Studies

In formulating this collection of works, we have been very deliberate in taking a broad conception of what constitutes a case and, correspondingly, a case study or case-analysis methodology. This breadth is in keeping with feminist and critical race philosophers' willingness to use a variety of methodological and conceptual tools to attain their goals of identifying the structures, practices, and experiences of various forms of oppression while taking seriously the need for those tools to be well grounded in experiences. What we take to be common to the idea of case-engaged work is a commitment to the epistemological value of employing *thickly described* cases in one's analyses.

The contributions presented here vary widely in the ways in which they can be understood as engaging with cases. Lorraine Code's chapter, for example, argues for the epistemological value of narrative in its ability to capture the nuances of an individual situation. For Code, this includes fictional narrative and literature, which can at times serve as extremely rich tools for revealing the pervasive effects of oppression as well as offering contrasting imaginings of a different social world. In this regard, we do not restrict our definition of *case studies* only to the use of actual historical and contemporary examples, although it must be stressed that the epistemic value of literary examples will be a direct function of how well these cases resonate with lived experience and existing evidence while also using creative scope to emphasize certain aspects of human conditions and situations. Gaile Pohlhaus's chapter uses a case from her own personal experience (a case of nonfictional narrative) as a philosopher in an interdisciplinary group to reflect on larger questions concerning the situatedness of philosophers themselves, how they come to understand problems of interest to them, and how they might be missing the relevance of situation. ShaDawn Battle's chapter, on the other hand, provides an analysis of the murder of Michael Brown and other Black men by police officers through the literary lens of James Baldwin's *Blues for Mister Charlie*. She thus combines the fictional with the all too real.

In a different mode, many other chapters in this collection use a social-scientific model of a case study, through which a case is taken to provide evidence either disrupting or supporting particular knowledge claims or larger epistemic frameworks. All the pieces in this volume use case studies to highlight various forms of injustice, and, in so doing, they illuminate the ways in which the philosophical use of case studies has the potential to serve an important function in dismantling dominant epistemic, scientific, social, and political structures. Thus, the right sort of case study can play a key role in social change and the remediation of injustices.

Crucially, although we have taken a broad view of what constitutes cases and case studies, we do not mean to include every type of example that a philosopher might draw on. A hypothetical example that is *thinly* described to illustrate a philosophical point clearly falls outside the scope of case-based methodology and can represent exactly the kinds of problems of abstract philosophical method that many of the case analyses employed within this volume seek to avoid through their careful attention to *thickly* described cases. Furthermore, this volume specifically attends to the kinds of uses of cases and case analyses that feminist and critical race philosophers have found helpful in their epistemic goals of revealing the details and contexts of oppression and marginalization and developing potential solutions to conditions of injustice.

Contents and Organization of This Collection

The analyses in this volume represent a distinctive composition of cases. Traditionally, cases in philosophy, especially those drawn from science, medicine, and policy, have started their analyses from the perspective of dominant knowers. Feminist and critical race theorists inside and outside of philosophy have consistently critiqued this fault since at least the late 1980s. For example, Guyatri Spivak's ([1988] 1994) "Can the Subaltern Speak?" marked a turning point in this area. Her paper, which examines the *sati* suicides of Indian widows, is also a scathing critique of what academia attends to. She argues that white academic subjectivity actively erases the subjectivity of nondominant knowers even when it claims to be reflecting or focusing in on the experiences of oppressed groups. The chapters in this volume largely start their theorizing about cases from the perspectives of nondominant knowers. The frameworks employed and the insights provided in these chapters are robust and critical. Importantly, they present an opportunity for readers to examine specific social effects of epistemic practices that have largely been unrecognized.

Making the Case is divided into three parts. The first section, "Theoretical and Methodological Perspectives on Case Studies," engages some of the epistemological and ethical challenges that arise from the use of case studies inside and outside of philosophy and the ways that these affect social-justice claims and outcomes.

The second section, "Critiquing the Practice: The Case of Philosophy," analyzes and assesses philosophy's own practices for their ability to impede or further social justice. These chapters not only seek a reshaping of philosophical practice, they also call upon philosophy to be significantly more intentional in recognizing the responsibilities involved in case-engaged research.

The final section, "Case Studies for Social Justice," offers a series of case studies: the murder of Black men by police, the impacts of settler-colonial epistemologies, the epistemology of HIV transmission, the Mexican Genome Diversity Project, and the death of Matthew McCain in a North Carolina jail. The chapters utilize a set of shared tools from feminist and critical race philosophies and demonstrate the ability of case-engaged philosophical work not only to reveal what frequently goes unnoticed or unexamined but also to highlight the ways in which these tools can drive and frame social-justice responses.

Part 1: Theoretical and Methodological Perspectives on Case Studies

The use of case studies to generate theoretical knowledge and understanding brings with it epistemological questions concerning the status and consequences of such knowledge. As many have noted, though case studies can be very informative with respect to the case at hand, it is not immediately clear when or how the knowledge they generate can be applied from one context to the next (Morgan 2014; Crasnow, this volume), nor is it clear the ways in which they can move broad social-justice goals forward. The chapters in this first section in particular take up epistemological and methodological challenges that stem from the use of case studies and highlight the ways in which epistemological and methodological practices have broad and specific impacts on social justice.

The first chapter, Corwin Aragon's "Building a Case for Social Justice: Situated Case Studies in Nonideal Social Theory," focuses on social theory and locates the importance of case-study use within the larger project of nonideal theorizing. Nonideal theorizing seeks to begin with "the messy, unjust reality of our actual world" and, through such critical engagement with the actual world, builds theory that helps us understand how to make that world more just (Aragon 26, this volume). In contrast to ideal social and moral theory (Aragon uses the work of Rawls as his foil), in nonideal theorizing, ideals are not posited theoretically at the outset and then applied to the world to see if they obtain, but rather the theorizing itself occurs through critical engagement with actual social practices, or what Sally Haslanger (2012) has called an ameliorative philosophical analysis. Case-study work will be crucial in this regard. Aragon recognizes that there are several different types of case studies, each with advantages and disadvantages. He articulates three types: nonideal hypothetical case studies (which include fictionalized accounts that are informed by social conditions), nonideal experiential accounts of lived experiences of social injustice, and social-scientific case studies that provide evidence that identifies systematic social phenomena. He draws on the strengths and weaknesses of these in order to articulate the parameters for building the kind of *situated* case studies that will be helpful to the project of nonideal theorizing and its ability to facilitate social change to benefit marginalized groups.

Aragon's methodological requirements for situated case studies speak to the issue of how case studies are selected, while Sean Valles's chapter, "The Coupled Ethical-Epistemic Model as a Resource for Feminist Philosophy of Science, and a Case Study Applying the Model to the Demography of Hispanic Identity," speaks to how methodologies are selected and how they have significant outcomes for social policy. His chapter both outlines a theoretical framework to guide feminist methodological choices and demonstrates the joint epistemic and ethical impact of methodology selection through his case study of the United States census. Valles argues in favor of Nancy Tuana's "coupled ethical-epistemic" model of analysis (Tuana 2010), a model that allows for "jointly examining the ethical features and evidentiary features of a scientific case study" (Valles 47, this volume). He then puts this model to work, building on his 2015 paper with Katikireddi by developing four questions for researchers to employ to help them understand the ethical-epistemic implications of research methodologies, practices, and policies (Katikireddi and Valles 2015). Using his expanded ethical-epistemic model, Valles goes on to examine the case of the collection practices of the US census, assessing the ethical-epistemic significance of the two-question-format collection tool through which individuals must self-report race and ethnicity data on their census forms. He compares this to a combined one-question format, pointing out numerous ethical and epistemic concerns with the current two-question method that are illuminated by the ethical-epistemic framework. Valles concludes that instead of treating race and ethnicity as two independent questions on the 2020 census, a combined race-ethnicity question that places *Hispanic* as an ethnicity category "alongside racial categories" would best meet ethical-epistemic standards (66).

It is clear that feminist and critical race philosophers have frequently turned to case studies to make visible the ways in which social practices have failed to achieve their stated goals and ideals of social justice and objective knowledge, failures for which nondominant groups have often paid the price. In her contribution "Feminist Science Studies: Reasoning from Cases," Sharon Crasnow focuses on feminist science studies and its very effective use of case studies to demonstrate evidence of androcentric and sexist bias within numerous scientific studies. However, she notes that epistemological problems remain concerning what exactly the case studies show, and these problems can dull the force of such feminist work. According to Crasnow, such problems stem from an undertheorization of case-study methodology. For example, if one views a case study as providing a piece of evidence used to offer inductive support for the claim that science is value laden and biased, as a single case it offers only a very weak inductive argument. Such cases of androcentric bias can then reasonably be dismissed as outliers without challenging the idea of objective science being value neutral. Instead, Crasnow takes a deeper dive into the epistemological issues of case-study work to help strengthen an appreciation of the significance of feminist science criticism. To do this, she draws on some of the recent work on case-study methodology to articulate how the feminist case studies should be understood as providing a stronger challenge to the appropriate role of values in science. Crasnow employs both Hasok Chang's conception of the relationship between cases and our philosophical accounts as a process of "epistemic iteration" between the abstract and the concrete and Mary Morgan's strategies for how to take what we learn from one case and move it to another site. Crasnow uses the work of Chang and Morgan to engage two cases of feminist work in science studies (Elizabeth Anderson's study of the role of values in divorce research and Elisabeth Lloyd's study of the research on female orgasm) in order to develop a more robust understanding of the epistemological significance of the case studies found in feminist science studies.

Part 2: Critiquing the Practice: The Case of Philosophy

While the chapters in the previous section assess the theoretical value and practical implications of case studies, those in this section turn their analyses inward by reflecting upon how the habits, theories, and practices of philosophy itself can either further or impede social justice. Thus, the discipline and practice of philosophy becomes the locus of the cases in this section. Philosophy is examined in action, whether that be examining how reviewers have responded to published philosophical work, how philosophers have interacted with members of other disciplines, or how philosophers have responded when questioned about their professional responsibilities. While the field of philosophy in general has not been particularly invested in reflecting upon either what biases are incorporated into its practice or what are or should be the outcomes of philosophical activity, feminist and critical race philosophies have been very active in doing so. In particular, they have provided robust critiques of the norms and standards of the field, not only for its lack of attention to race, gender, sexuality, ability/disability, class, and location but also for how the discipline has ignored the situated nature of its own practices and likewise ignored the responsibilities that arise from its research. For example, Charles Mills's 1997 book, *The Racial Contract*, served as a watershed moment by explicitly raising much-needed questions about philosophy's failure to understand itself as a discipline that has participated in silencing and marginalizing socially and politically disenfranchised groups. Mills's book highlights how US culture exists under a racially dominated state of ignorance and demonstrates how philosophy has been complicit in furthering this agenda. The lack of engagement by philosophers on "matters related to race" (Mills 1997, 18) has been enabled by the tendency in mainstream epistemology to analyze hypothetical examples that are distant from the material conditions of people's lives, what Lorraine Code (1987) has called thin narratives.

Code's body of work, from her initial book, *Epistemic Responsibility* (1987), through to her 2006 book, *Ecological Thinking*, presents a lineage of critical evaluation of the functioning of contemporary mainstream philosophy. She brings to the forefront philosophy's inability to reflect upon its practices and identify to what it does and does not lend attention. In her contribution to this volume, "The Power and Perils of Example: 'Literizing Is Not Theorizing,'" Code returns to her initial work in this area and further points to the limitations of a common form of philosophizing that ignores the situated nature of the practice of philosophy.

Code begins her chapter by taking up the case of how her own early work was received. She reexamines the hostile response *Epistemic Responsibility* received in the late 1980s from those entrenched in the abstract methods of contemporary analytic epistemology and considers what this reception reveals about the framework of analytic epistemology. She argues that narrative, including literary narrative, can offer a richness and attentiveness that is necessary for substantive understanding, especially in developing an understanding of the lives of the nondominant. She views her work in *Epistemic Responsibility* as well as much of her later work as contending that, contrary to the orthodox approach of analytic epistemology, knowing well cannot be done "without fleshed-out, situated-populated examples conveying a sense of the lived implications of the questions and circumstances that generated them" (102, this volume).

Code intentionally employs a broad understanding of case study, using the terms *extended examples, narrative,* and *examples* interchangeably. She does this to challenge the conception of a *case* or an *example* as a thin articulation used to develop a narrow understanding of the work of epistemology. As she states, if the valued epistemic framework is built on theorizing the simple case of "the cat is on the mat," we will not develop an epistemology that will move us toward epistemic responsibility. Instead, she articulates the shift in our view of knowledge that results when we take seriously the value of fleshed-out examples embedded in both literature and rich narrative descriptions of particular real-world cases. This shift requires an acceptance of uncertainty and an attitude of humility on the part of the knowers, recognizing that exactitude is often sacrificed through the development of such rich forms of understanding. Drawing on a variety of specific philosophical uses of examples throughout her chapter, Code demonstrates how "examples specific in their discursive positioning . . . perform the function of contesting epistemic commitments to 'a view from nowhere' " (123).

In "What Philosophy Does (Not) Know," Gaile Pohlhaus takes up similar themes concerning the failure of philosophy and philosophers to recognize the situatedness of their own frameworks, arguing that philosophers need to become more reflective about who they are and what kind of knowledge they are able to generate. Pohlhaus conceptualizes the activity of knowing as involving "epistemic movement," and she is concerned with cases where knowers can at times get stuck within a certain framework (disciplinary or otherwise) that can prevent the development of rich understanding. Pohlhaus works with two cases in order to illustrate her points. First, she uses an experiential case, offering an extended description of her personal experience of bringing her philosophical framework to the table in an interdisciplinary group discussion. Pohlhaus takes herself to be someone who strives to maintain a clear awareness of her own situatedness and its effects on her philosophizing. With this in mind, she experiences puzzlement when, in this interdisciplinary discussion about the extension of (human) rights to primates, her philosophical concern that such a move in effect centers a rights framework on humans are met with accusations that her concerns "come out of nowhere." This experience provokes her reflection on a kind of epistemic "discoordination" within the group, stemming from differences in their rhetorical spaces (Code 1995), that cause her discussants to fail to see the pertinence of her points. Importantly, through this experiential case, Pohlhaus identifies a distinct value of the epistemic movement practiced in philosophy: philosophers "move toward considering the conceptual conditions that enable epistemic activity," and this "provides an opportunity for reflecting on whether the conventions governing our epistemic movement are in line with our avowed commitments" (135, this volume). In her second case, Pohlhaus focuses on the forum of philosophy conferences, analyzing how their specific rhetorical spaces, complete with expectations of presentation, questioning, and levels of agreement and disagreement, can lead to nondominant groups having more difficulty getting their objections heard and understood as relevant. Pohlhaus argues for the epistemic value of explicitly acknowledging the specifics of the rhetorical space within which our epistemic movement is happening. She uses both of her cases to demonstrate the importance of identifying the process of reorienting oneself such that "what at first appears unintelligible, misplaced, or irrelevant can become intelligible, well placed, and relevant" (140, this volume).

While the previous two chapters reflect upon the lack of awareness of the situated nature of philosophy, Carla Fehr's contribution, "Doing Things with Case Studies," turns to a consideration of how philosophers have failed to think seriously about what is *done* with case studies when they engage them philosophically. In particular, Fehr is concerned with the responsibilities philosophers have when their case studies are what she calls socially significant case studies. These are case studies that reveal or "trade on injustices or harms faced by individuals or groups of people in fairly direct ways" (Fehr 155, this volume). While many feminist and critical race philosophers have found that case studies can be particularly useful for making visible the manifestations of the particularities of the social injustices facing specific groups, Fehr is concerned about the relationship between the academic employing the case study and the subjects and stakeholders of socially significant case studies. She argues that when a philosopher makes the choice to take up and develop a socially significant case study, moral demands follow to take action in working toward the alleviation of the social injustice in question, in order to avoid objectifying the subjects of the case study in problematic ways. As Fehr notes, when academics employ such socially significant case studies, they and their careers benefit from the significance of the injustice itself. For Fehr, it is not enough to simply unearth the workings of these injustices for a philosophical and academic audience through discipline-based conference presentations and publications, which is what philosophers tend to do. To avoid engaging in objectification, more must be done with the case study, through taking action oneself or, at a minimum, by finding ways to put one's work and insights in the hands of those who are well placed to work toward the elimination of the injustice. Fehr also argues that, in addition to the ethical dimension of how an academic selects, develops, and "does things" with socially significant case studies, there is an epistemic dimension to this work. Activities such as disseminating one's work to the case study's subjects, various stakeholders, policy makers, and other nonphilosophers more closely connected to the circumstances of the case, as well as collaborating with these groups, can provide various checks on the assumptions behind one's research and offer further epistemic resources for the research itself.

Part 3: Case Studies for Social Justice

In her landmark 1990 book *Black Feminist Thought*, Patricia Hill Collins develops Black feminist epistemology explicitly as a tool of social justice and social change for oppressed groups, especially for Black women. As she describes in subsequent editions, Black feminist thought is "committ[ed] to justice, for one's own group and for other groups" (Collins [1990] 2000, 31). This sentiment is endemic in many areas of feminist philosophy, especially feminist epistemology, where the explicit goal of harnessing its tools to drive social change has been frequently enlisted.

The case studies in this section build upon decades of this work, making use of now-well-developed concepts from feminist and critical race theory such as epistemologies of ignorance and epistemic injustice to understand a range of cases that present immediate and dangerous injustices that are in urgent need of attention and action. These chapters offer strong examples of how contemporary feminist and critical race philosophers are taking philosophical analysis to places previously unexamined by philosophy, allowing these places to be interrogated and reshaped in the service of social-justice goals. The cases in these chapters build upon a set of shared theoretical underpinnings to illuminate the potentially deadly nature of social and bureaucratic systems that function through and further epistemologies of ignorance and epistemic injustice. ShaDawn Battle's contribution, "Singing the 'Blues' for Black Male Bodies: Epistemic Violence, Non-alterity, and Black-Male Killings," makes this startlingly clear.

Battle's chapter builds upon work in epistemologies of ignorance and epistemic injustice to read the 2014 murder of Ferguson, Missouri,

Black teenager Michael Brown by police officer Darren Wilson through the lens of James Baldwin's 1964 play *Blues for Mister Charlie*. Initiating her argument from a postcolonial perspective rooted in Frantz Fanon's *Black Skin, White Masks* (1952), Battle combines this theoretical underpinning with Charles Mills's epistemology of ignorance and Kristie Dotson's (2011) conception of epistemic violence to argue that "Baldwin's fictional protagonist, Richard Henry, and the late Michael Brown are victims of epistemic violence insofar as they are silenced and spoken for by white racist authority as overdetermined variations of the nonhuman" (181, this volume). A critical aspect of Battle's chapter in her alignment of Brown's murder with the murder of Richard Henry in Baldwin's play is that she shows just how scripted and predictable Michael Brown's murder and the murders of entirely too many Black men and women are in the late twentieth and early twenty-first centuries. Following Mills, she shows that the racial contract, its epistemology, and its deadly consequences are alive, flourishing, and, importantly, also traceable if we are willing to lend our attention to them. She concludes that the importance of detailing this sort of case analysis lies in "liberating Black male bodies from the white-supremacist social imaginary of them as a non-Others" (182, this volume) and in exposing racist epistemic practices that normalize and enable the murder of Black men and women.

On a similar trajectory, in her chapter "Land(point) Epistemologies: Theorizing the Place of Epistemic Domination," Esme Murdock positions her argument intentionally from the perspective of Black feminist epistemologies and Indigenous epistemologies to make clear how mainstream epistemic positionalities view their starting points as neutral ones for knowing the world, when they actually are "compromised in particularly colonial ways" that enable a "settler-colonial epistemological framework" (213, this volume). This dominant framework amounts to a kind of epistemic violence, providing a privileged understanding of settlers by prioritizing their sovereignty over the land and erasing "Indigenous socioecological systems" (213, this volume). Contesting this dominant framework, Murdock provides a case analysis of the contestability of what counts as evidence in the Bedouin people's attempt to protect their land in the Naqab Desert from Israel. She argues that the ways in which land and relationship to land are interpreted "can function as a site of both epistemic domination and epistemic decolonization" (213, this volume). Like Battle's chapter, Murdock's also makes clear the practical and political consequences of epistemic violence. This type of violence enables social systems of domination to operate in ways that are normalized and appear functional yet are highly dysfunctional and frequently deadly.

The frameworks of epistemic injustice and epistemologies of ignorance also shape the practices of science and medicine. In "Epistemology and HIV Transmission: Privilege and Marginalization in the Dissemination of Knowledge," Lacey J. Davidson and Mark Satta employ feminist and critical race philosophies to examine research findings and case studies on HIV transmission, tracing the ways that research is disseminated and interpreted by medical and lay audiences. They work to identify patterns of epistemic harms that are replicated in, and sometimes addressed by, communities who are significantly affected by HIV. To do so, they frame and explicate a specific type of epistemic injustice that they describe as a "structural-linguistic epistemic harm," which identifies "the structure of the language and the accompanying social practices" as the locus of the epistemic harm (259, this volume). They argue that the concept of structural-linguistic epistemic harm is vitally relevant for understanding the epistemology of HIV transmission because the social practice of linguistic exchange that involves seeking to know another person's HIV status "harms askers because they are less apt to receive the best information with which to make an informed risk assessment, and it harms those asked because it encourages either giving epistemically suspect answers or risking social consequences by providing a more informative response" (259, this volume).

Sergio Armando Gallegos-Ordorica's chapter, "*Mestizaje* as an Epistemology of Ignorance: The Case of the Mexican Genome Diversity Project," also takes up concerns with medical research, the formation and dissemination of knowledge, and epistemic harm. The chapter examines the influence of the study of genetics, specifically how the social policies of the Mexican government, including their goal of nation building through "race mixing," or *mestizaje*, shaped the Mexican Genome Diversity Project (MGDP) and its goals of understanding diabetes, hypertension, and obesity in Mexican communities. Gallegos-Ordorica argues that the concept of *mestizaje* functioned as an epistemology of ignorance by creating a false view of a "unifying and homogeneous Mexican identity" (272, this volume). This understanding of Mexican identity was employed in collecting samples and interpreting the results of the MGDP, which in turn led to a "racialized picture of the Mexican population that helped to perpetuate the myth of a homogeneous nation" (272, this volume). Gallegos-Ordorica wants to find avenues for resisting this state of ignorance that has harmed

Amerindian groups and the Mexican working class, both of whose health is poorly accounted for by the MGDP. He develops José Medina's (2013) arguments for "insurrectionist genealogies" and contends that creative work can provide beneficial epistemic friction that can begin to counter the outcomes of the MGDP. Gallegos-Ordorica points to projects by artists and writers who resist the homogenization of Mexican identity through their creative "reappraisal and retelling" of Mexican history and their active reconstruction and challenging of Mexican mestizo identity (283, this volume).

The volume's final chapter, by José Medina and Matt S. Whitt, "Epistemic Activism and the Politics of Credibility: Testimonial Injustice Inside/Outside a North Carolina Jail," builds upon Medina's previous work on epistemic resistance to develop the concept of epistemic activism. Medina and Whitt provide an analysis of the epistemic structures and physical conditions of the Durham County Detention Facility in North Carolina and the ways these led to the death of Matthew McCain in January 2016 while detained in this facility. They also make clear the ways that people who were incarcerated in the facility and their allies, through the Inside-Outside Alliance, worked to resist these epistemic structures to raise awareness of the conditions in the facility and of the death of Matthew McCain. As Medina and Whitt argue, particular epistemic structures are designed to obscure knowledge of and diminish the credibility of dominated epistemic subjects. Carceral structures are among those most pernicious in generating epistemic harm. Medina and Whitt argue that this is especially the case with jails, because they occupy a unique position in the carceral system in that they sequester people who have not been proven guilty of a crime—i.e., they are presumed innocent—but are still treated as carceral subjects whose credibility is significantly diminished and are thus considered to be unreliable epistemic agents. Medina and Whitt frame the pathways through which the social and institutional structures of jail intentionally diminish the credibility of people who are incarcerated and show how these dominated epistemic actors and their allies have worked to actively and successfully resist this mode of oppression. Thus, an account that wishes to document both how people are epistemically harmed and oppressed and how they resist such epistemic domination must provide a robust framework that makes clear the complexity of interactions, social structures, and contexts.

The chapters in this volume present a cohesive argument for and demonstration of the value and impact of case-engaged research in feminist and critical race philosophies. At times, chapters share similar theoretical frameworks, especially those in the third section of the book whose focus is on epistemic injustice and epistemologies of ignorance. These last chapters demonstrate the valuable range through which these frameworks can be employed. Yet each piece is comprehensive in itself and can function theoretically and practically as an independent paper for use in scholarship as well as in advanced undergraduate and graduate coursework. From the works in this collection, we can see how contemporary feminist and critical race philosophers are developing ways of working through the complex methodological issues that come with using case studies to generate knowledge and understanding and how they are using the tools of casework to extend the range of philosophical analysis, putting it into the service of social-justice work in novel ways.

Notes

1. Where appropriate, we refer to *feminist and critical race theorists/theories* to explicitly recognize the broader theoretical resources that come from feminist and critical race theory. Critical race theory has a long and rich history outside of philosophy, starting in the late 1980s. In a similar vein, feminist philosophy is in many ways a subfield of feminist theory, especially that which emerges from the social sciences.

2. See, for example, the special issue of *Synthese* (volume 177, no. 3, 2010), the website presence of the Consortium for Socially Relevant Philosophy of/in Science and Engineering (https://www.srpoise.org), and the Joint Caucus of Socially Engaged Philosophers and Historians of Science (https://www.jointcaucus.philsci.org).

References

Code, Lorraine. 1987. *Epistemic Responsibility*. Hanover, NH: University Press of New England.

———. 1995. *Rhetorical Spaces: Essays on Gendered Locations*. New York: Routledge.

Collins, Patricia Hill. [1990] 2000. *Black Feminist Thought: Knowledge, Consciousness, and the Politics of Empowerment*. 2nd ed. New York: Routledge.

Dotson, Kristie. 2011. "Tracking Epistemic Violence, Tracking Practices of Silencing." *Hypatia* 26 (2): 236–57.

Fehr, Carla, and Kathryn S. Plaisance. 2010. "Socially Relevant Philosophy of Science: An Introduction." *Synthese* 177 (3): 301–16.

Haslanger, Sally. 2012. *Resisting Reality: Social Construction and Social Critique.* New York: Oxford University Press.

Katikireddi, S. Vittal, and Sean A. Valles. 2015. "Coupled Ethical-Epistemic Analysis of Public Health Research and Practice: Categorizing Variables to Improve Population Health and Equity." *American Journal of Public Health* 105 (1): e36–e42.

Kornblith, Hilary, ed. 1994. *Naturalizing Epistemology.* 2nd ed. Cambridge: Massachusetts Institute of Technology Press.

Kuhn, Thomas S. 1962. *The Structure of Scientific Revolutions.* Chicago: University of Chicago Press.

Medina, José. 2013. *The Epistemology of Resistance: Gender and Racial Oppression, Epistemic Injustice, and Resistant Imaginations.* New York: Oxford University Press.

Mills, Charles W. 1997. *The Racial Contract.* Ithaca, NY: Cornell University Press.

Morgan, Mary S. 2014. "Resituating Knowledge: Generic Strategies and Case Studies." *Philosophy of Science* 81 (5): 1012–24.

Quine, W. V. 1969. "Epistemology Naturalized." In *Ontological Relativity and Other Essays*, 69–90. New York: Columbia University Press.

Spivak, Gayatri Chakravorty. [1988] 1994. "Can the Subaltern Speak?" In *Colonial Discourse and Post-colonial Theory: A Reader*, edited by Patrick Williams and Laura Chrisman, 66–111. New York: Columbia University Press.

SRPoiSE (The Consortium of Socially Relevant Philosophy of/in Science and Engineering). n.d. "Home." SRPoiSE. Accessed July 25, 2020. https://www.srpoise.org.

Tuana, Nancy. 2010. "Leading with Ethics, Aiming for Policy: New Opportunities for Philosophy of Science." *Synthese* 177 (3): 471–92.

PART 1

THEORETICAL AND METHODOLOGICAL PERSPECTIVES ON CASE STUDIES

Chapter 1

Building a Case for Social Justice
Situated Case Studies in Nonideal Social Theory

CORWIN ARAGON

Introduction

The purpose of social theory is to help us shape a more just world. However, much social theory, "ideal theory," obfuscates features of injustice and, consequently, offers an incomplete account of both how our world operates and what we should do to seek greater justice within it. Critical social theory, in contrast, directly addresses persistent and widespread injustice and, in doing so, develops normative guidelines more responsive to actual injustice. This alternative method for doing social philosophy, employed in much feminist philosophy and critical philosophy of race, has recently gained in popularity, albeit under a new moniker: *nonideal theory*. Despite nonideal theory's increasing popularity, its underlying methodology has received less philosophical attention than has the criticism of ideal theory that motivates the shift in approach. One particular area of needed attention is in developing the starting points of nonideal philosophical analysis. Nonideal theorizing is supposed to begin from the world as it actually is—or, more precisely, from an account of the world as it actually is—but nonideal theorists have yet to provide a methodology for articulating these starting points. In this chapter, I offer such a methodology; specifically, I argue for a *situated* methodology of building case studies for nonideal theorizing.

This argument proceeds in two parts. First, I articulate a situated methodology of nonideal theorizing. I start by identifying the method of nonideal theory as ameliorative and critical theory building, or *theorizing*. Then, drawing on criticisms of ideal theory, I enumerate methodological principles for performing the method of nonideal theorizing. Second, I explain what a situated methodology requires of nonideal case studies and what is methodologically valuable about well-formulated nonideal case studies. I examine three different types of nonideal case studies—abstract hypothetical, experiential, and social scientific—and argue that each accentuates a different methodologically valuable feature of an account of the world as it actually is. I suggest that situated case studies should work to incorporate all three of these valuable features, and I conclude by developing a preliminary list of methodological priorities for building situated case studies for nonideal theorizing.

A Methodology for Nonideal Theory

All social theory provides answers to questions about how our social reality is and ought to be structured.[1] Critical social philosophy, such as feminist philosophy and critical philosophy of race, is particularly concerned with questions about our social realities including existing injustice, what should be done to remedy it, and who is responsible for doing so. How we answer any one of these questions will impact our answers to the others, as our understanding of the social world affects what we find unjust about it, and, in turn, our understanding of injustice will affect what we believe we should do to remedy it.

These questions can be roughly sorted into three categories: onto-logical, epistemological, and moral. Social ontology considers what things exist socially and the specific character of their existence. Social epistemol-ogy considers what it is that we (do and do not) know socially and the processes by which we come to know (or not know) these things. Social morality considers how our social world ought to be structured and our moral responsibilities to work toward such a structuring.[2]

Nonideal social theory offers a systematized and cohesive set of answers to questions of social reality, knowledge, and responsibility to guide us in shaping a more just world. But how should we go about building such a theory? Or, more specifically, how should we use philosophical analysis to provide answers to the ontological, epistemological, and moral questions generated by the existence of structural injustice?

THEORY, METHOD, METHODOLOGY, EPISTEMOLOGY

These questions about how to build nonideal social theory are methodological. They are questions about how we should perform philosophical analysis to satisfy our own theoretical and pragmatic ends. One way to answer these two methodological questions is to articulate a set of principles to guide us in performing such an analysis. Philosophers, however, are often less than explicit about the specific methodological commitments and aims that guide our analyses. And we often conflate four related but importantly distinct concepts: theory, method, methodology, and epistemology.[3] This conflation may lead us to confuse the philosophical project at hand, leave unexamined the underlying reasons for favoring some answer or method over another, or fail to see our own preclusion of possibly important philosophical questions or answers. To avoid these issues, I will disaggregate these four concepts.

A *theory* is a systematic and comprehensive understanding of some set of phenomena that serves some particular purpose. "Good theories," according to Sally Haslanger, "are systematic bodies of knowledge that select from the mass of truths those that address our broader cognitive and practical demands" (2012, 226). A good *social* theory provides a systematic understanding of the ontological, epistemological, and moral dimensions of our social world to aid us in meeting the epistemic and practical demands involved in shaping a more just world.

A *method*, on the other hand, is "a technique for (or way of proceeding in) gathering evidence" (Harding 1987, 2). Researchers, depending on their discipline, will gather evidence for their claims using different techniques, such as the scientific method, mathematical modeling, ethnographic observation, and so on. Social theory utilizes the method of social *theorizing*, or theory building, which is a method of formulating systematic relationships among empirical and normative claims to articulate and defend a specific view of how the social world ought to be structured.

But *methodology* aims to answer a prior question: What should guide us in the adoption and practice of some particular method of analysis? Theresa Tobin explains, " 'methodology' refers to criteria for what constitutes a good . . . method and our views about how to develop methods that satisfy these criteria" (2009, 146), and "the success of any methodology will be measured by how capable it is of generating methods that facilitate our theoretical and political goals" (147). In other words, a methodology articulates the aims and values of an analysis in order to select starting assumptions and methods for performing that analysis.

Finally, an *epistemology* is a view of what we know and how we know it. Epistemologies articulate the kinds of reasons that offer sufficient justification for taking some particular belief to be true and, relatedly, how we should determine the epistemic authority that we should afford to different knowers (Jaggar 2008). Methodologies and epistemologies can be quite similar, as both provide criteria for attributing authority to some claims (and claim makers) rather than others. But we can still distinguish the two by focusing in on their distinct aims: the former articulates the criteria for building the system of claims that comprise our theory, while the latter articulates the criteria for judging whether those claims are true.

Is nonideal theory a theory, a method, a methodology, or an epistemology? I take it that what theorists call nonideal theory is a mixture of all four. A *nonideal theory* is a specific account of the way that the social world works and how we ought to structure it. The *method* of nonideal theory is a particular way of going about building, or theorizing, this theory. The criteria that determine selection of the starting points of analysis and guide the activity of nonideal theorizing comprise a *nonideal methodology*. And a *nonideal epistemology* focuses on the actual epistemic processes through which we come to know (or not know) about our shared social world and by which this knowledge is shared (or silenced).

Though much of this chapter makes claims that appear theoretical or epistemological, my main project is to articulate the methodological commitments that should guide nonideal theorizing. The hope is that this methodology will help to build better nonideal social theories (theories of social ontology, epistemology, and morality).

Nonideal Theorizing as Critical Method

Nonideal theorizing begins with the messy, unjust reality of our actual world and works to articulate a theory to help in working to make it more just. In this way, nonideal theorizing is a method of ameliorative philosophical analysis (Haslanger 2012). Ameliorative analysis is distinguished from other philosophical methods in part because it explicitly draws on normative inputs to guide the analysis. Sally Haslanger explains: "On this approach . . . we begin by considering more fully the pragmatics of our talk employing the terms in question. What is the point of having these concepts? What cognitive or practical task do they (or should they) enable us to accomplish? Are they effective tools to accomplish our (legitimate) purposes; if not, what concepts would serve these purposes better?" (2012, 223–24). An ameliorative method begins by questioning the reason for performing the analysis in the first place, locating the purposes that we aim to realize, and evaluating those purposes.

At this point, we might ask: what are the specific purposes of non-ideal theorizing? The straightforward answer to this question is to seek a more just world. The more robust answer to this question comes from the tradition of critical social theory.

Critical social theory is, in the words of Karl Marx, "the self-clarification of the struggles and wishes of the age" (as cited in Fraser 1985, 97). It "begins with the assumption that current conditions are unacceptably unjust and a commitment to understand and remedy that injustice" (Haslanger 2012, 22). In this way, critical social theorizing (the method of critical social theory) is normatively and epistemically situated in actual movements of social resistance and, consequently, locates its judgments and norms in a particular sociohistorical moment. As Iris Marion Young explains, "Critical theory presumes that the normative ideals used to criticize a society are rooted in experience of and reflection on that very society, and that norms can come from nowhere else. . . . The philosopher is always socially situated, and if the society is divided by oppressions, she either reinforces or struggles against them. With an emancipatory interest, the philosopher apprehends the given social circumstance not merely in contemplation but with passion" (1990, 5–6). Critical theorizing is normatively situated in actual social movements by committing itself to working to ameliorate the injustices they name and pursuing the "unrealized possibilities" for greater justice already seen in those movements (Young 1990).

Critical social theorizing also is committed to further developing the epistemic frameworks embedded in actual social movements. In this way, critical social theory is "epistemically situated" (Haslanger 2012, 23): it aims to develop conceptual schemas and systems of belief that will aid resistance to injustice. Moreover, the epistemic situatedness of critical theorizing means that the theorist adopts the specific pragmatic ends of contemporary resistance movements and continually attempts to aid in the realization of those ends in building the ontology, epistemology, and morality of their theory. The theorizer does not position themselves as an "abstract subject" or "'neutral' observer" (Haslanger 2012, 24), nor do they aim to address "an audience made up abstractly of all reasonable persons from the point of view of any reasonable person" (Young 1990,

13). Instead, they situate their theorizing in the normative and epistemic demands of the critical social movements of a particular sociohistorical moment.

CRITIQUE OF IDEAL THEORY

Nonideal theorizing, however, is not the predominant method of building theory in social philosophy; as Elizabeth Anderson states, "This method is unorthodox" and "is usually regarded as derivative of ideal theory" (2010, 3). Moral, social, and political philosophy often proceeds from the assumption that our normative principles must be located through ideal theorizing and that nonideal theory merely answers questions about how to practically realize these principles.[4] On this assumption, ideal theory does the heavy philosophical lifting, while nonideal theory is left with the merely practical task of implementation.

But what really makes ideal theory ideal? Charles W. Mills (2005, 166) helpfully distinguishes among three different senses of the concept of ideal. The first, "ideal-as-normative," identifies the "uncontroversial background normative sense of the ideal" that is involved in all moral philosophy, namely that of working toward normative, prescriptive, or evaluative ideals. The second, "ideal-as-descriptive-model," identifies the sense of *ideal* involved in describing a model that picks out "the crucial aspects" in a generalized description of some phenomenon/a (366). All descriptive models involve some level of abstraction and, thus, are ideal in this sense (366). The third, "ideal-as-idealized-model," identifies the sense of *ideal* relevant to ideal theorizing: "For certain *P* (not all), it [is] possible to produce an idealized model, an exemplar of what an ideal *P* should be like" (167).

Ideal theorizing is not unique in providing normative judgments, prescriptions, or principles, as all moral philosophy does this (ideal-as-normative). Neither is it unique in analyzing some set of phenomena from a simplified description of those phenomena (ideal-as-descriptive-model); we can have abstraction in our theorizing without idealization (O'Neill, 1987). Rather, ideal social theorizing is ideal in the sense that it bases its theorizing in ideal-as-idealized-models of social agency, moral reasoning and social epistemology, and social practice.

No recent figure has been more central in shaping the method of ideal theorizing than John Rawls. In *A Theory of Justice*, Rawls (1999b) attempts to identify and explain "the principles of justice that would regulate a well-ordered society" under conditions of "strict compliance" (8), where these principles are those that would be agreed to by free and equal signatories to a social contract within a hypothetical, idealized, and fair initial-choice situation (9–10). *A Theory of Justice*, originally published in 1971 and revised in 1999, and Rawls's later restatements of his theory of justice as fairness (1985, 1999a, 2001, 2005) offer an archetype of ideal theorizing. Considering Rawls's impact, we can see his ideal method not as an idiosyncratic outlier in contemporary social and political philosophy but, rather, as a central influence of much of the discipline.[5]

In the critique that follows, I draw on representative claims made by Rawls to exemplify broader assumptions made in ideal theorizing. However, I am not attempting to offer a fatal methodological critique of Rawls's theorizing—I do not have the space in this chapter to adequately develop Rawls's view, let alone a full methodological critique.[6] Nor am I claiming that Rawls's methodological assumptions or analytic methods are common in contemporary social theorizing. Rather, the purpose of drawing on Rawls's claims is to develop an explanatory foil that will help me to identify methodological principles for nonideal theorizing.

IDEALIZED SOCIAL ONTOLOGY

Ideal theorizing assumes an idealized social ontology. First, ideal theorizing assumes an idealized picture of the basic structure of society. For example, Rawls begins with an understanding of society as a "fair system of social cooperation among free and equal citizens" (1985, 231), structured by publicly recognized rules and procedures that all members could rationally agree to and that work to the mutual advantage of all involved (2001, 8–9). Second, ideal theorizing assumes an idealized version of the social subject. In Rawls's theory, for example, citizens are presumed to "engage in mutually beneficial social cooperation over a complete life" and "be moved to honor its fair terms for their own sake" as equals (2001, 19). Third, ideal theorizing assumes an idealized version of the social processes that shape interaction among the members of an ideal society. Citizens in Rawls's well-ordered society, for example, have "a normally effective sense of justice," which "enables them to understand and apply the publicly recognized principles of justice, and for the most part to act accordingly as their position in society, with its duties and obligations, requires" (2001, 9).

However, an idealized social ontology obscures features of our actual social world that are salient to an ameliorative analysis. Specifically, an idealized social ontology obfuscates (a) the existence of systematic social inequalities, (b) the constitutive role of the social in the individual subject, and (c) the unintentional reproduction of inequality in our social processes.

Our social world is characterized by persisting injustices that are at least potentially theorized as organizing features of the basic structure. For example, consider Michelle Alexander's (2012) claim that the contemporary US criminal justice system functions through the mass incarceration of black Americans as the "new Jim Crow." Alexander argues that US society is built upon an underlying racial caste system that, in the era of "colorblindness," takes the form of mass incarceration. If we take this argument seriously, then we should at least entertain the possibility that enduring racialized inequalities in the criminal justice system are not isolated failures of the American legal system to equally protect the basic rights of black Americans; rather, we should examine whether or not the American legal system is, at its core, a system of racialized social control. By adopting an idealized social ontology, "we risk leaping to the conclusion that any gaps we see between our ideal and reality must be the cause of the problems in our actual world, and that the solution must therefore be to adopt policies aimed at directly closing the gaps" (Anderson 2010, 4). In diagnosing actual injustice as mere failures to meet ideal theoretical principles, we run the risk of misdiagnosing the problems that plague us by misunderstanding their causes (4). In particular, we run the risk of treating underlying structural issues as isolated failures of the nonideal world to fully realize the principles of justice discovered through ideal theorizing.

Moreover, actual social subjectivity is largely mediated by identities, systems of belief and value, and structural constraints that are tied to one's social location. An idealized social ontology encourages us to think of social agents (for the purposes of formulating principles of justice) as entirely unencumbered by the contingent realities of their social locations, like the parties to Rawls's "original position" (explained below). But facts of social location might be (a) constitutive of, and thus not easily bracketed from, social subjectivity and (b) salient to an ameliorative analysis. Let's return to the argument given by Alexander that I mentioned above. If Alexander is right that US society has been and continues to be organized by a system of racial caste, then one's position in that system will significantly shape their life options, what they believe about themselves and value in their world, and what kinds of treatment they will receive from others. For this reason, one's racial identity is likely to at least partially mediate their understanding of actual injustice and their relationship to it. Thus, an idealized social ontology, in positing an idealized social subject detached from sociohistorical contingency, obscures potentially salient features of social subjectivity by assuming away the possible constitutive character of social location.

Finally, there may be ways in which social inequalities are systematically reproduced in social processes that cannot be recognized by a method of theorizing that assumes an idealized model of those processes. At least potentially, some of the injustices that exist in our world are built into the everyday and even well-intentioned actions that many people perform as part of normal social practice (Young 1990, 2000, 2011). For example, if Mills is correct in claiming that "white supremacy is the unnamed political system that has made the modern world what it is today" (1997, 1), then the contemporary social situation is shaped around the systematic reproduction of conditions of nonwhite subordination. The systematic reproduction of social subordination in the absence of deliberate institutional design or individual failure will go unacknowledged in the idealized models of social practice that ideal theorizing assumes. Consequently, certain pressing issues of injustice will not even arise in the process of ideal theorizing (Anderson 2010; Mills 1997, 2005, 2007a, 2007b, 2009).

IDEALIZED SOCIAL EPISTEMOLOGY

Ideal theorizing also assumes an idealized social epistemology. First, ideal theorizing assumes an idealized version of the epistemic subject, who discovers principles of justice independent of the influence of social and historical contingency. For example, Rawls posits an idealized social epistemology grounded in the justificatory device of the "original position" (1985, 1999a, 1999b, 2001, 2005) as the appropriate basis for identifying principles of justice. Subjects in the original position decide upon these principles from behind a "veil of ignorance," which hides from their reasoning facts about their own social location, their own particular values and beliefs, and even facts about their actual society (1985, 1999a, 1999b, 2001, 2005). Second, ideal theorizing assumes an idealized knowledge base, or idealized set of epistemic resources, upon which we can draw in making decisions about how society ought to be structured. In Rawls's (2001) theory, for example, the parties to the original position must reach agreement by drawing on the same epistemic resources; "the veil of ignorance achieves this result by limiting the parties to the same body of general facts . . . and to the same information about the general circumstances of society" (86–87), such as "the presently accepted facts of social theory" (87) and facts of the "circumstances of justice" (84). Third, ideal theorizing assumes an idealized understanding of the social processes of knowledge formation (with respect to principles of justice). According to Rawls, the restrictions imposed by the veil of ignorance answer the "problem of justification" (1999b, 16) under circumstances of "reasonable pluralism" (2001, 84): they provide a "suitably general point of view" (2001, 85–86), "removed from and not distorted by the features of the all-encompassing background framework, from which a fair agreement between free and equal persons can be made" (1985, 235). Epistemic justification for the principles of justice can only be found through a process "abstract[ed] from and not affected by the contingencies of the social world" (1985, 236), and this justification is objective, as it is based neither on cognitive biases or shortcomings nor in insufficient or inconsistent understandings of the social world.

However, an idealized social epistemology obfuscates features of how it is that we actually come to know, or, perhaps more importantly, come not to know, things about our social world. Specifically, ideal theorizing obscures facts about (a) the role of the social in shaping the epistemic subject, (b) the role of the social in shaping social knowledge, and (c) barriers to knowledge systematically built into social epistemic processes.

Actual epistemic subjects are situated in a wide-reaching complex of social relationships that affect what it is that they come to know. The central insight of feminist epistemology is that knowledge is socially situated: the various social roles that we occupy shape a system of norms and expectations that in turn affect what it is that we know (Anderson 2017). In other words, actual human beings are always situated epistemic subjects whose knowledge of the world is partly influenced by the roles, norms, and expectations that define their social situations. Ideal theorizing assumes that situated knowledge cannot provide appropriate justification for claims about social injustice or how to remedy it, since it is necessarily dependent upon social and historical contingencies.

Moreover, actual epistemic subjects never know a complete set of uncontested facts about their social world. It is unclear whether or not there will ever be a set of presently accepted facts of social theory, as all social theory is contested. But even if there were such a set of presently accepted facts, actual epistemic subjects may never actually know all these facts. Actual epistemic subjects always depend upon partial, incomplete, and sometimes inconsistent worldviews. Ideal theorizing insists that these facts about actual social epistemology are irrelevant with respect to understanding the process by which we should justify principles of justice.

Finally, our actual social epistemic processes are characterized by a number of systematic barriers to knowledge. At least since Marx and Engels, social systems of power have been thought to create barriers to social knowledge. Feminist epistemologists and critical philosophers of race have expanded the class-based claims of Marx and Engels to examine how gender and race function to shape and maintain systematic biases. And a growing body of literature on epistemic injustice and epistemologies of ignorance (Anderson 2012; Dotson 2011, 2012, 2014; Fricker 2007; Medina 2013; Mills 1997, 2005, 2007a, 2007b; Sullivan and Tuana 2007) has illuminated social forces that systematically obscure facts about our present social situation in order to maintain its unjust structure. Ideal theorizing views barriers to knowledge as undercutting the possibility of objective justification for claims about social justice, and, consequently, it must leave these barriers out of the descriptions of its processes of epistemic justification.

IDEALIZED SOCIAL MORALITY

Ideal theorizing also assumes an idealized social morality. First, ideal theorizing assumes that understanding justice requires an understanding of the functioning of a morally perfect society. For example, Rawls assumes that we must begin our theorizing with "strict compliance theory" (2001, 13). According to Rawls, to determine principles of justice in strict compliance theory, "we ask in effect what a perfectly just, or nearly just, constitutional regime might be like, and whether it may come about and be made stable under the circumstances of justice . . . and so under realistic, though reasonably favorable, conditions" (13). Second, ideal theorizing assumes that a just society is comprised of moral agents who exercise their agency in an ideal manner. In Rawls's theory, strict compliance assumes that the members of society rationally act on their two moral powers to pursue their own conception of the good in their private lives while pursuing the realization of the principles of justice in their shared public life (8–9). Importantly, these agents are economically rational and not swayed by the "special psychologies" of envy, spite, extreme risk aversion, or a will to dominate (87). Third, ideal theorizing assumes that all members of the just society perfectly understand and fulfill their obligations of justice. Rawls's citizens, for example, are guided by their sense of justice and their recognition of the rational justification of the principles of justice. Given this characterization of the members of the ideal society, we can understand those idealized agents to perfectly fulfill their social responsibilities.

However, idealized social moralities, such as Rawls's, obfuscate morally salient facts about our actual social world and, consequently, inform inadequate theories of justice and responsibility. Specifically, an idealized social morality obscures (a) the way moral thinking about justice actually works, (b) the nonideal moral motivations of actual agents, and (c) the nonideal social conditions that give rise to noncompliance or partial compliance.

In assuming that we can only come to know what justice is and what it requires of us by examining what would be a perfectly structured society, ideal theory "misunderstands how moral thinking works" (Anderson 2010, 3). Moral thinking arises from the recognition of certain moral problems, not primarily from the recognition of a failure to realize some moral ideal. Anderson claims, "We recognize the existence of a problem before we have any idea of what would be just or more just" (3). We do not have to know the ideal to be able to work to make the world a better place; "knowledge of the better does not require knowledge of the best" (3). Presupposing that we must first understand the ideal society to understand justice reverses the order of our moral thinking and potentially obscures helpful resources for thinking about justice and for better realizing it in our nonideal world.

Moreover, an idealized social morality that relies upon an idealization of the exercise of moral agency offers a theory of justice that might be completely ineffectual for actual moral agents. "A system of principles that would produce a just world if they regulated the conduct of perfectly rational and just persons," Anderson asserts, "will not do so when we ask human beings, with all our limitations and flaws to follow them" (2010, 3–4). Idealized moral agents are not subject to the "motivational and cognitive biases" (4) of actual agents, and, thus, many of the kinds of actions that actual agents perform and that result in injustice are not explained or accounted for in ideal theory. In addition to this theoretical concern, we might also wonder about the possibility of actual agents' ability to even approximate, let alone regularly exercise, the idealized capacities of the agents of ideal theory (Mills 2005, 168).

Finally, by assuming that all members of society perfectly fulfill their social obligations, ideal theory reduces all questions of responsibility to questions of civic duty. If we can conceive of what is morally required of the citizens of an ideal society, then we can fully understand their obligations of justice. But in the actual world, characterized by persistent and widespread injustice, there may be remedial responsibilities that extend beyond the duties of citizenship. In the same way that some issues of justice are likely to go unrecognized by ideal theory (Anderson 2010; Mills 1997, 2005, 2007a, 2007b), some questions of remedial responsibility are likely to go unasked.

A Situated Methodology

By adopting an ideal-as-idealized-model starting point for theorizing the social, ideal theorizing relies upon a set of assumptions that prevents it from examining potentially salient ontological, epistemological, and moral characteristics of the contemporary social world. Consequently, ideal theorizing is likely to obfuscate or ignore theoretically significant features of our social world as well as render inadequate the theories it builds to the theoretical task at hand—namely, explaining how to understand and remedy existing injustice. These issues are methodological rather than theoretical: the problems lie in the way that ideal theorizing precludes consideration of facts about the actual world because these facts do not cohere with an assumed ideal-as-idealized-model of the world.

But my critique is not meant to condemn or reject all ideal theory; again, that is a project beyond the scope of this chapter. Rather, the critique is meant to provide an explanatory foil for the method of nonideal theorizing. Drawing on that critique, I can now articulate a situated methodology of nonideal theorizing.

First, a situated methodology must begin from the nonideal conditions of our actual world. Nonideal theorizing should start from the facts of pervasive and persisting injustices, ideological barriers to understanding these injustices, and insufficient accounting of our responsibilities to remedy these injustices. Second, a situated methodology is guided by the specific normative aims of critical social theory:

1. To articulate a social ontology that describes the way that social structures and social agents function in the actual world to reproduce injustice and highlights theoretical resources for understanding social resistance and transformation

2. To articulate a social epistemology that describes the epistemic processes of our actual world, paying special attention

to the epistemic actions that harm individuals as knowers and to the epistemic barriers to understanding and accepting responsibility to remedy injustice

3. To articulate a social morality that describes the character of existing structural injustices, identifies the agents responsible for remedying these injustices, explains the basis of their responsibilities, and guides them in meeting those responsibilities

This methodology is not only nonideal—beginning from facts about the actual, nonideal world—but also critical—normatively and epistemologically situated in movements of social resistance.

Situating Case Studies for Nonideal Theory

My situated methodology gives the nonideal theorist a starting point and a set of guiding values for building a nonideal social theory. More concretely, this methodology captures what social theory can do to aid our actual, ongoing struggles to remedy injustice. However, it does not yet provide us with the material we need to begin this analysis; this can only be provided by case studies. In this penultimate section, I explain how the situated methodology I have mapped guides the formulation of situated case studies for nonideal theory.

CASE STUDIES: WHAT THEY ARE AND WHAT WE WANT THEM TO BE

According to Tobin and Jaggar (2013, 414), "A case study is a detailed investigation of an instance of something in a specific context." They continue, "Inherent in the idea of a case study is the idea that it represents some wider class of cases, so cases are investigated not simply in their own unique particularity but with the thought that studying them will shed light on other cases." Informed by the conception offered by Tobin and Jaggar, I take a case study for social theorizing to be (1) a detailed description of some particular state of social affairs that (2) provides the substantive starting point for philosophical analysis and (3) a basis for wider generalizations about the way that our social world ought to be structured. I will call these three features the (1) descriptive, (2) substantive, and (3) prescriptive elements of a case study.

All social theorizing, ideal or nonideal, builds its analysis from some kind of case study. Though ideal theorizing brackets many of the features of real-world states of affairs, it still draws on a model of the social world. In this way, even ideal theorizing bases its analysis in case studies, namely ideal-as-idealized-model case studies. These case studies offer (1) descriptions of idealized social conditions, subjects, and practices; (2) a substantive formulation of the features of our social lives assumed to be of primary importance and an elimination of the contingent features taken to be irrelevant from the perspective of justice; and (3) the basis for generally applicable principles for making our own world more ideal.

My critique of ideal theorizing identified theoretical limitations of ideal-as-idealized-model case studies: they rely on descriptions of social conditions and social subjects that substantively obscure or eliminate features of the present structure of social reality salient to ameliorative analysis. At best, these obfuscations limit the prescriptive efficacy of analyses that begin from those case studies; at worst, they provide justification for social practices that exacerbate and sustain existing injustice.

Nonideal case studies avoid these limitations by describing actual unjust social conditions in which the substantive details of the case are gathered from critical social movements, with the hope of performing an ameliorative analysis that offers effective prescriptive guidance for those movements to combat injustice. The question then arises, How should these case studies be formulated to meet these methodological aims? I answer this question with a set of methodological criteria that I draw from an examination of three common kinds of case study used in nonideal theorizing.

ABSTRACT HYPOTHETICAL

Nonideal abstract hypothetical case studies describe a hypothetical situation that is informed by actual social conditions by abstracting details of the case from generalized features of the social conditions to be examined. The case is informed by some understanding of a set of social conditions that need to be addressed, but it is formed as a hypothetical scenario to isolate the salient features of those conditions. The abstraction involved here, even though it is used to generate a hypothetical case, is not an idealization—the case study is meant to reflect an abstracted view of actual social conditions rather than a hypothetical case of idealized social conditions. Abstract hypothetical case studies are empirically informed fictionalized accounts of the present social situation; in some cases, social theorists draw directly from literary fiction to formulate their cases.

Consider, for example, Miranda Fricker's (2007) use of the stories of Marge Sherwood from Anthony Minghella's *The Talented Mr. Ripley* and Tom Robinson from Harper Lee's *To Kill a Mockingbird* in her book *Epistemic Injustice: Power and the Ethics of Knowing*. Fricker draws on the experiences of these two fictional characters to articulate a specific set of social phenomena to be examined in her analysis of epistemic injustice. Marge Sherwood and Tom Robinson have in common the (fictional) experience of being silenced and dismissed in their attempts to share their knowledge. Fricker draws out of these two stories a conception of testimonial injustice that explains how some knowers are harmed *as knowers* by suffering credibility deficits due to systematic identity prejudice. These fictional stories provide not only a simplified description of a nonideal social situation but also a substantive framing of the issue from which to draw out these illuminating conceptions.

The methodological strengths of these types of nonideal case studies are that they are simultaneously abstract enough to bring the substantive contours of the case study into focus and not so abstract as to completely detach the descriptions they offer from actual social conditions. The hypothetical nature of the case studies allows the theorist to shape them in a manner that highlights specific features that are especially salient for the analysis at hand. In other words, the abstraction brings clarity to the substantive features of actual social conditions by abstracting away from other complicating features. But the abstraction involved does not undermine the analogical reasoning necessary to allow the case study to be helpful for understanding actual social conditions. The hypothetical case studies of Marge Sherwood and Tom Robinson are not so far abstracted from actual social experience that they undermine the ability of the theorist to draw more generalizable claims from the analysis.

However, abstract hypothetical case studies run the risk of obscuring salient aspects of our social processes through abstractions or hypothetical reasoning. In their potential to conceal facets of our social reality, abstract hypothetical case studies may undermine the analogical reasoning upon which they rely.

EXPERIENTIAL

Nonideal experiential case studies offer a view of the lived experience of social injustice. These experiential accounts can be based in personal testimony, stylized narratives, or other forms of artistic expression. Experiential case studies, insofar as they typically address the emotional and phenomenological aspects of being harmed by unjust social practice, can be especially powerful in their depictions of the substantive features of the case. In contrast to abstract hypothetical case studies, experiential case studies frame their descriptions in personal terms.

Ta-Nehisi Coates's *Between the World and Me* (2015) provides an experiential case study that exhibits the strengths of this kind of nonideal case study. Coates, in writing a letter to his son about what it means to be a young black man in the United States, shares a number of concrete examples of the impact of race on his experience of the so-called American Dream and of the fear and terror he saw in his community. Perhaps one of the most powerful moments of the book is found in Coates discussing the fear, rage, and "the old gravity of West Baltimore" (77) he felt in reading that his friend, Prince Carmen Jones, was shot and killed by a Prince George's County police officer. In Coates's story, we engage with a narrative about the lived experience of being a member of a community that is a too-regular target of lethal police violence: the fear of recognizing that "this could have been me, and holding you—a month old by then—I knew that such loss would not be mine alone" (76); the pull of the gravity of a social reality that "condemned me to the schools, to the streets, to the void" in finding that even though "Prince Jones had made it through, . . . still they had taken him" (77); a growing rage in the recognition "that Prince was not killed by a single officer so much as he was murdered by his country and all the fears that have marked it from birth" (78). From his experience, Coates derives powerful, even if unsettling, conclusions about the social control of black bodies and about the need for struggle.

The methodological strength of experiential case studies is primarily found in their ability to directly engage the phenomenological experience of being oppressed. Experiential case studies provide for a fuller description of the harms of unjust circumstances by explicitly articulating this phenomenological experience. Phenomenological experience rooted in personal testimony is likely to highlight specific forms of harm—such as the fear, rage, and "gravity" experienced by Coates—that hypothetical cases may have greater difficulty capturing. Experiential case studies are especially good at bringing the humanity of victimization to the forefront of philosophical analysis.

However, experiential case studies run the risk of overgeneralizing the experience of some, potentially distorting the experience of or silencing others. Moreover, experiential case studies may encourage a pernicious form of experientialism that undermines their ability to address systematic injustice.

SOCIAL SCIENTIFIC

Nonideal social-scientific case studies draw on empirical findings in anthropology, psychology, sociology, and other social sciences to offer an evidenced account of the present social situation. This account is more generalizable than that provided by an experiential case study, as it is based in findings that identify broader and systematic social phenomena. It also provides a concrete description of at least some of the causal mechanisms behind ongoing injustice.

The Imperative of Integration by Elizabeth Anderson (2010) offers a strong social-scientific case study for racialized injustice in the United States. Anderson draws on recent research in sociology and social psychology in particular to identify and frame deep racialized inequalities within the material and symbolic systems of the contemporary US context. Anderson argues that racialized segregation is the underlying cause of these inequalities, and she draws this conclusion from the case study she has built. Specifically, Anderson argues that segregation causes spatial, capital-mediated, and state-mediated material inequalities among black and white Americans (23–43). She also argues that segregation causes pernicious and self-reinforcing forms of group stigmatization (44–66). Anderson's arguments are rooted in an in-depth social-scientific case study that synthesizes findings in multiple disciplines to provide rich material for philosophical analysis.

The methodological strength of social-scientific case studies lies in their ability to provide evidenced depictions of the systematic character of social injustice. Social-scientific case studies offer the fullest description of a social situation, in particular by identifying some of the possible underlying causal mechanisms of injustice. By highlighting these causal mechanisms, social-scientific case studies provide nonideal theorists with a view of the ways that injustice is sustained, and, through analysis of these case studies, nonideal theorists can locate mechanisms for social change.

However, social-scientific case studies are likely to disregard the phenomenological experience of the social processes they describe. In relying upon social-scientific case studies, we potentially lose sight of important aspects of social experience that are not easily quantifiable, measurable, or empirically demonstrable.

SITUATED CASE STUDIES

I offer the discussion above to draw attention to the methodologically valuable features of well-formulated nonideal case studies. These case studies provide the material for nonideal theorizing to realize situated methodological aims. They also pursue those aims in gathering the evidence for the formulation of the case study in the first place. Since these case studies aim to realize the values of situated methodology, both in their formulation and in the theorizing they enable, I call them *situated case studies*.

As suggested by the discussion above, situated case studies should provide an account of the world that (a) highlights salient features of actual states of affairs, giving their contours shape and definition, by abstracting from a complete description without becoming detached from the real-world conditions of the case; (b) takes seriously the phenomenological dimensions of injustice by working from the lived experiences of those that suffer unjust burdens in the case at hand; and (c) provides a broad description of the case backed with empirical evidence of its systematic features. At the same time, they should not (a) overlook features of a real-world situation that would lead the case study to lose track of what is salient about the case to actual resistance movements; (b) overgeneralize or automatically validate the experiential claims of some in a manner that distorts the experience of or silences others; or (c) ignore features of the case that are not easily quantifiable or empirically demonstrable.

I offer these observations as a loose set of guidelines for thinking through the formulation of the starting points of nonideal theorizing. To make these guidelines more methodologically concrete, I also offer the following list of methodological criteria for crafting situated case studies. Situated case studies should be:

1. Empirically adequate. Situated case studies should provide a rich descriptive account of the situation to be analyzed, highlighting the complex interrelations of its features.

2. Nonarbitrary. Situated case studies should not arbitrarily include or, more importantly, exclude aspects of actual social conditions that are salient to an analysis of injustice.

3. Applicable. Situated case studies should allow for analysis that shapes theoretical conclusions that apply to more than just the isolated case at hand.

4. Experientially grounded. Situated case studies should directly engage the lived experience of those individuals living in the situations they describe.

5. Specific. Situated case studies should draw on the expressed claims of actual social movements to emphasize analysis of the more substantive features of the situations they describe.

While this list of criteria is not technically derived from my earlier analysis of the three kinds of nonideal case study, it offers a set of standards for working to craft case studies that capture the strengths and minimize the weaknesses that analysis highlighted.

Conclusion

Drawing on a critique of the idealized starting assumptions of ideal theory, I articulated a set of methodological aims that should guide nonideal theorizing. These aims require nonideal theorizers to start from claims about the actual world, situated in contemporary social movements, to build social ontologies, epistemologies, and moralities that will aid these movements in resisting injustice. These methodological values should also guide us in crafting the starting points of our analysis: the case studies that nonideal theorizers adopt ought to work from and enable theorizing toward understandings of the world that facilitate effective social resistance. To build these case studies, nonideal theorizers should seek to realize the valuable features of the three different types of case study—abstract hypothetical, experiential, and social scientific—while also minimizing their shortfalls. To aid in the project of building situated case studies, I enumerated a set of methodological criteria. Together, the methodological aims of the second section and the methodological criteria of the third section of this chapter comprise a nonideal methodology for building a case for social justice through nonideal theorizing.

Acknowledgments

A previous version of this chapter was presented as "Seeking Justice Through Nonideal Theory: A Philosophical Method for Social Change" at "In the Unjust Meantime: A Conference in Honor of Alison M. Jaggar." I wish to thank all the participants of this conference for their helpful feedback. I also want to thank Annaleigh Curtis and Barrett Emerick for their constructive criticism of an earlier version of this chapter. And I appreciate the fruitful discussion of the paper's topics I had with Katherine Gasdaglis, Brian Kim, and Alex Madva. Finally, I want to thank the editors of this volume, Heidi Grasswick and Nancy McHugh, for their careful readings and suggestions for improvement on an earlier draft.

Notes

1. Following John Rawls (1985, 1999a, 1999b, 2001, 2005), I assume that questions of justice are primarily about the "basic structure" of society rather than the specific moral character of the lives of the individuals that comprise that society.

2. Though I am using the term *morality* in a somewhat-unconventional manner, my use is meant to capture the distinction between interpersonal or interactional morality, on one hand, and institutional or structural morality, on the other. For a helpful way of distinguishing these two different aspects of moral analysis, see Young (2011, 73).

3. Sandra Harding, in a discussion of feminist method and methodology, offers distinctions among *method*, *methodology*, and *epistemology* to help analyze a uniquely feminist method of research (1987, 2–3). Discussions of nonideal theory often run together not just these concepts but also the concept of theory, so I add it to Harding's set of distinctions.

4. Consider, for example, Rawls's description of the roles of ideal and nonideal theory in his *The Law of Peoples*: "Nonideal theory presupposes that ideal theory is already on hand. For until the ideal is identified, . . . nonideal theory lacks an objective, an aim, by reference to which its queries can be answered" (1999a, 90).

5. See Mills (2005, 169; 2009, 161).

6. For fuller methodological critiques of Rawls's ideal theory, see Mills (2007a, 2009) and Schwartzman (2006).

References

Alexander, Michelle. 2012. *The New Jim Crow: Mass Incarceration in the Age of Colorblindness*. Rev. ed. New York: New Press.

Anderson, Elizabeth. 2010. *The Imperative of Integration*. Princeton, NJ: Princeton University Press.

———. 2012. "Epistemic Justice as a Virtue of Social Institutions." *Social Epistemology: A Journal of Knowledge, Culture and Policy* 26 (2): 163–73.

———. 2017. "Feminist Epistemology and Philosophy of Science." Edited by Edward N. Zalta. *Stanford Encyclopedia of Philosophy*. https://www.plato. stanford.edu/archives/spr2017/entries/feminism-epistemology/.

Coates, Ta-Nehisi. 2015. *Between the World and Me*. New York: One World.

Dotson, Kristie. 2011. "Tracking Epistemic Violence, Tracking Practices of Silencing." *Hypatia* 26 (2): 236–57.

———. 2012. "A Cautionary Tale on Limiting Epistemic Oppression." *Frontiers: A Journal of Women's Studies* 33 (1): 24–47.

———. 2014. "Conceptualizing Epistemic Oppression." *Social Epistemology: A Journal of Knowledge, Culture and Policy* 28 (2): 115–38. https://www.doi. org/10.1080/02691728.2013.782585.

Fraser, Nancy. 1985. "What's Critical about Critical Theory? The Case of Habermas and Gender." Special issue on Jürgen Habermas, *New German Critique* 35 (Spring–Summer): 97–131.

Fricker, Miranda. 2007. *Epistemic Injustice: Power and the Ethics of Knowing*. New York: Oxford University Press.

Harding, Sandra. 1987. "Is There a Feminist Method?" Introduction to *Feminism and Methodology*, edited by Sandra Harding, 1–14. Bloomington: Indiana University Press.

Haslanger, Sally. 2012. *Resisting Reality: Social Construction and Social Critique*. New York: Oxford University Press.

Jaggar, Alison M. 2000. "Ethics Naturalized: Feminism's Contribution to Moral Epistemology." *Metaphilosophy* 31 (5): 452–68.

Jaggar, Alison M. 2008. "Introduction: The Project of Feminist Methodology." In *Just Methods: An Interdisciplinary Feminist Reader*, edited by Alison M. Jaggar, vii–xi. Boulder, CO: Paradigm.

Jaggar, Alison M., and Theresa W. Tobin. 2013. "Situating Moral Justification: Rethinking the Mission of Moral Epistemology." *Metaphilosophy* 44 (4): 383–408.

Medina, José. 2013. *The Epistemology of Resistance: Gender and Racial Oppression, Epistemic Injustice, and Resistant Imaginations*. New York: Oxford University Press.

Mills, Charles W. 1997. *The Racial Contract*. Ithaca, NY: Cornell University Press.

———. 2005. " 'Ideal Theory' as Ideology." *Hypatia* 20 (3): 165–84.

———. 2007a. "Contract of Breach: Repairing the Racial Contract." In *Contract and Domination*, by Carole Pateman and Charles W. Mills, 106–33. Cambridge: Polity Press.

———. 2007b. "The Domination Contract." In *Contract and Domination*, by Carole Pateman and Charles W. Mills, 79–105. Cambridge: Polity Press.

———. 2009. "Rawls on Race/Race on Rawls." *Southern Journal of Philosophy* 47 (S1): 161–84.

O'Neill, Onora. 1987. "Abstraction, Idealization and Ideology in Ethics." *Royal Institute of Philosophy Supplement* 22 (September): 55–69.

Rawls, John. 1985. "Justice as Fairness: Political Not Metaphysical." *Philosophy and Public Affairs* 14 (3): 223–51.

———. 1999a. *The Law of Peoples with "The Idea of Public Reason Revisited."* Cambridge, MA: Harvard University Press.

———. 1999b. *A Theory of Justice.* Rev. 2nd ed. Cambridge, MA: Belknap Press of Harvard University Press.

———. 2001. *Justice as Fairness: A Restatement.* Edited by Erin Kelly. Cambridge, MA: Belknap Press of Harvard University Press.

———. 2005. *Political Liberalism.* Expanded ed. New York: Columbia University Press.

Schwartzman, Lisa H. 2006. "Rawlsian Abstraction and the Social Position of Women." In *Challenging Liberalism: Feminism as Political Critique*, 55–73. University Park: Pennsylvania State University Press.

Sullivan, Shannon, and Nancy Tuana, eds. 2007. *Race and Epistemologies of Ignorance.* Albany: State University of New York Press.

Tobin, Theresa W. 2009. "Globalizing Feminist Methodology: Building on Schwartzman's *Challenging Liberalism*." *Hypatia* 24 (4): 145–64.

Tobin, Theresa W., and Alison M. Jaggar. 2013. "Naturalizing Moral Justification: Rethinking the Method of Moral Epistemology." *Metaphilosophy* 44 (4): 409–39.

Young, Iris Marion. 1990. *Justice and the Politics of Difference.* Princeton, NJ: Princeton University Press.

———. 2000. *Inclusion and Democracy.* New York: Oxford University Press.

———. 2011. *Responsibility for Justice.* New York: Oxford University Press.

Chapter 2

The Coupled Ethical-Epistemic Model as a Resource for Feminist Philosophy of Science, and a Case Study Applying the Model to the Demography of Hispanic Identity

Sean A. Valles

Introduction

This chapter will illustrate how the "coupled ethical-epistemic" model of analysis functions as a tool for feminist philosophy of science. The model was developed by Nancy Tuana (2010, 2013; Tuana et al. 2012) and then elaborated on by Katikireddi and Valles (2015). It provides a framework for jointly examining the ethical features and evidentiary features of a scientific case study. First, the chapter will describe the model. Second, it will articulate how the model promotes existing goals for feminist philosophy of science. Third, it will apply the model to a particular case in demography, the disputed two-question format for collecting self-reported race and ethnicity data in the US.

This chapter does not seek to propose *the* appropriate model for doing feminist analyses of science case studies but rather to present *a* model for such analyses, one which has been developed to facilitate uptake by practicing scientists and to directly impact scientific practices. It is a model that promotes thoroughness without sacrificing usability, a model that has implicitly manifested feminist values and promoted feminist goals. This chapter will make explicit the previously implicit reasons that the coupled ethical-epistemic model is a feminist model while also illustrating the model's efficacy as a tool for feminist philosophical analysis with a case study.

Coupled Ethical-Epistemic Analysis

Nancy Tuana created the coupled ethical-epistemic model as a tool for her collaborative work with a team developing models for climate-change risk management and has worked to develop it in subsequent years (Tuana 2010, 2013; Tuana et al. 2012). She has also surveyed feminist literature on climate change, citing her publications on the coupled ethical-epistemic model, but without showing how the model itself is a feminist tool for analysis (Tuana 2015).

The model is a response to the observation that certain scientific problems involve intertwined ethical and evidentiary features. However, adjusting one's analytical tools to incorporate ethical and evidentiary features and their connections (to suit the nature of the problems) risks pushback from scholars seeking to protect science's objectivity. Tuana preempts this criticism, arguing that such adjustment actually makes the science *more* objective by allowing previously hazy or tacit scientific features to come into focus. Coupled ethical-epistemic issues arise in science in a variety of ways. There are often, for example, value decisions embedded in research models and methods that go unquestioned and often unappreciated. These can both be ethically significant and have consequences for what is (and is not) known. Thus, rendering these values transparent and examining their coupled ethical-epistemic significance creates an important and often-underappreciated resource for more-objective science (Tuana 2013, 1957). The reference to "objective science" ties the model's rationale to a perennial debate in feminist philosophy of science: the nature of scientific objectivity. This was a central point of contention during the so-called science wars of the 1990s, which featured battles between postmodernist and cultural studies scholars espousing science's cultural contingency and modernist scholars defending science's purported universality and rationality. While at first glance it might seem contrary to objectivity to mix epistemic analysis with ethical analysis, Tuana argues that quite the opposite is true. When we carefully make transparent the values that are involved in our scientific practices, we make our science more objective. We cannot simply value nothing—even choosing to research a certain topic is an expression of what one values—and the only way to clearly examine and critically debate those values is to make them visible and to scrutinize them with a comprehensive analytic framework. The coupled ethical-epistemic framework provides this.

S. Vittal Katikireddi and I adapted Tuana's framework to show how it can be used to clearly and rigorously analyze complex cases in public health. Our work grew out of a series of meetings between Katikireddi and I about our shared interest in equitable public-health research practices, which both of us had written about previously; Katikireddi had written from an epidemiologist's perspective (Katikireddi et al. 2013), and I had written from a philosopher's perspective (Valles 2012). We adopted Tuana's model of coupled ethical-epistemic analysis to structure our paper and each provided a case study of how the model can aid analysis of different policy-relevant public-health sciences: Katikireddi provided the case of the Scottish Index of Multiple Deprivation, a system for geographically identifying underserved populations, while I provided the case of the so-called gay blood ban, a long-standing rule of the US Food and Drug Administration (FDA), partly revised in 2015, that forbade blood donations from men who have ever had male-male sexual contact.[1] This chapter will continue expanding the model's range of applications to policy-relevant science outside of the previously explored public-health and environmental contexts.

To build upon Tuana's model, Katikireddi and I (2015, e40) specified the model to ask that users answer four questions and proceed with their scientific practices only after they have answered these questions and considered the significance of their answers:

1. What are the chosen variables' strengths and weaknesses for evidence gathering and analysis?

2. What are the chosen variables' ethical strengths and weaknesses?

3. How will the chosen variables' strengths and weaknesses for evidence gathering and analysis affect ethical issues?

4. How will the chosen variables' ethical strengths and weaknesses affect evidence gathering and analysis?

We created these four questions in an effort to more easily operationalize Tuana's general model in public-health practice. We intentionally did not provide rules for what ought to be valued above what else. Instead, the model simply encourages practitioners to (a) explicitly consider the ethical impacts and evidentiary features of their work (rather than letting either or both go unspoken), (b) recognize that these features are interrelated (rather than, for example, considering evidentiary issues now while bracketing ethical issues for consideration "later"), and (c) finalize their planned scientific practices only after they have spelled out and confronted the ethical impacts, the evidentiary impacts, and the dynamics between those impacts.

While our 2015 paper applied the method exclusively to the design of public-health variables, the model is applicable to other aspects of research design in public health and other scientific contexts. It is a tool for making difficult research-design choices when the choices made have potential ethical consequences in addition to the research's inevitable epistemic consequences. It also works retrospectively as a tool for science-studies scholars to evaluate and critique previous research designs.

Coupled ethical-epistemic analysis is a flexible framework that rests on two key assumptions. First, scientific practices have both ethical and evidentiary features that each require consideration and analysis. Second, the ethical features and evidentiary features of scientific practices should not be evaluated in isolation from each other. These commitments are nonrestrictive and should be amenable to scientific practitioners with a wide range of values and methodological priorities. This framework is, in fact, so nonrestrictive that its value as a specifically feminist analytic tool is something that is not obvious at first glance. In the next portion of this chapter, I will articulate in detail how coupled ethical-epistemic analysis qualifies as a feminist framework. I will then apply the framework to a case study in demography as an illustration of how the framework works in practice. I argue that the coupled ethical-epistemic model is a valuable tool for performing feminist case studies because it facilitates the pursuit of three aims previously highlighted by feminist philosophers of science as being among the goals of feminist philosophy of science.

Promoting direct engagement with scientific practitioners during critiques in order to advance social welfare is a goal of feminist philosophy of science that is advanced by the coupled ethical-epistemic model. Sarah Richardson's (2010, 338) essay on the relationship between feminist philosophy of science and socially relevant philosophy of science contends, "Engaged case study work and interdisciplinarity have been central to the success of feminist philosophy of science in producing socially relevant scholarship."

The crux is the meaning of *engaged*. Many philosophy-of-science case studies are neither engaged nor socially relevant. Autobiographically, my previous career interest of untangling the causal metaphysics in Newtonian physics was neither engaged with scientific practice nor socially relevant.

Carla Fehr (2012) provides a detailed argument for why feminist philosophy of science should overcome any reluctance to fully engage with scientific communities, even if those communities have been judged problematic by feminist analyses. She argues this in the context of evolutionary psychology, a field that has drawn a great deal of criticism from feminist philosophers of science for using inadequate research methods to reach conclusions that are sometimes deeply socially troubling—for example, see Elisabeth Lloyd's (2001) analysis of Randy Thornhill and Craig Palmer's hypothesis that the behavioral trait "men raping women" is evolutionarily adaptive or the indirect byproduct of other adaptations. Fehr elaborates that her case studies are enriched by actual engagement with the community of evolutionary psychologists, which led her to the feminists within the community. Creating dialogue with the practitioners—rather than examining science from a distance—"offers an opportunity to advance central research programs within feminist philosophy and science studies" (Fehr 2012, 66). Staying closely engaged with the people and practices of the science, as Fehr does within the evolutionary-psychology community, also promotes the additional feminist goal of seeking to help improve the practices identified as problematic.

Engagement requires going beyond writing single-author case studies for science-studies audiences. The coupled ethical-epistemic model has been developed in only a few venues, but its short history is defined by engagement between philosophers and science practitioners, particularly Tuana's integration of the model into an interdisciplinary team's large-scale climate-research project (Tuana et al. 2012) and Katikireddi (a public-health scholar) and I (a philosopher) publishing our interdisciplinary project in a leading public-health journal (Katikireddi and Valles 2015).

Attending to causal complexity is a second goal of feminist philosophy of science that is advanced by the coupled ethical-epistemic model. The purported virtue of simplicity is tied to assumptions that hierarchies of dominance and unidirectional control are the standard. By contrast, Helen Longino (1995) notes that valuing "complexity of relationship" in representations of causation is a theme in many feminist contexts. After Thomas Kuhn (1977) had offered simplicity as a universal theoretical virtue in science, Longino offered complexity as a feminist counterpoint.

Models prioritizing simplicity "mimic social relations of domination" and thus "naturalize these relations" (Longino 1995, 393–94).

That is, the logic of causal simplicity is embedded in an unspoken circular rationalization. A preference for social hierarchies of domination makes some scholars prefer similar sorts of relationships in nature. This preference leads them to see more of such relationships and then to use those observations as a justification for the naturalness of the original social hierarchies. One goal of feminist models of science-studies analyses is to identify and unsettle arrangements where patriarchal social domination and science serve to prop each other up. Longino shows that embracing complexity is one way of shaking up these relationships. Meanwhile, some scientists do recognize the limitations of simplicity as a theoretical virtue, as indicated by the emergence of scientific journals devoted to complexity (*Journal of Complexity*, *Ecological Complexity*, etc.).

Given the core feminist interest in identifying and responding to oppression, identifying causal complexity allows us to uncover indirect and incidental benefits and harms. The coupled ethical-epistemic framework is designed to analyze and respond to causally complex systems—originally, climate-change models used for purposes such as clarifying the risks of strategies for combatting climate change (Tuana et al. 2012). Moreover, the ethical-epistemic model itself is complex in the sense that it rejects the "model involving causal relations going only in one direction" targeted by Longino (1995, 393) and instead offers a model where the ethical and the epistemic exist in a reciprocal, bidirectional relationship, and neither is treated as primary. Coupled ethical-epistemic analysis is a tool that is designed for contending with complex decisions about how to design research variables when faced with the pivotal question that arises during research design and subsequent analyses of the design (Which variable(s) should be used in this research?). However, coupling ethical analysis and epistemic analysis and treating their relationship as complex and reciprocal treads into the contentious territory of science-values disputes.

Recognizing the interrelation of ethics/values and evidence is a third goal of feminist philosophy of science that is advanced by the coupled ethical-epistemic model. Elizabeth Anderson (1995, 32–33) reports the oft-heard worry that allowing values to play prominent roles in science "would allow inquiry to be infected by wishful thinking: people would feel entitled to infer from the fact that they wanted something to be true that it was actually true." In other words, the concern is that letting our value judgments interact with evidentiary judgments could allow our desires (about what ought to be in the world) to tip the scales when we weigh the evidence about what is in the world. At its most insidious, this worry can lead to shutting out feminist critiques that seek to undermine, revise, or replace science that rests on problematic social assumptions, such as the ones highlighted by Longino (1995), discussed above. Efforts to keep values out of science thus preempt values-motivated efforts to investigate and ameliorate problems in that science, even if that science already rests on reprehensible values.

Even among those who accept that values play some legitimate roles in science, there is dispute about how expansive their roles should be. In critiquing Heather Douglas's (2009) advocacy of limited roles for values in science, Matthew Brown (2013) highlights a premise shared by many of those who seek such limited roles: "the lexical priority of evidence over values." Making a similar point using the alternate phrasing "lexical priority of truth," Daniel Hicks describes the premise as the view that "ethical and political values have a legitimate role to play only after evidence had done as much work as it could" (2014, 3281).

Alternatively, drawing on Donald Davidson's work to advance a general thesis of the holism of facts and values, Sharyn Clough (2003, 115) points out that evidence and values are tightly connected in "our web of belief." It is not as if beliefs about evidence are only connected to the outside world while beliefs about political values are only connected to our inner lives. Beliefs are beliefs, and are, of course, formed partly in response to empirical evidence: "Our scientific theories and our beliefs about oppression and justice are not merely relative to our feminist conceptual schemes; they are justified by the evidence and they are true" (Clough 2003, 127).

The coupled ethical-epistemic framework neither commits to nor rejects Clough's holism. More broadly, the model shares her position that, as a matter of methodology, certain relations cannot be neatly cleaved apart: evidentiary concerns-ethical concerns, science-values, and description-prescription. The ethical and the epistemic must be confronted together. The following case study will illustrate how the coupled ethical-epistemic model analyzes a case, yielding valuable insights about the current dispute over whether the US should replace its standard federal system for collecting self-reported race and ethnicity data, which is currently formatted as two independent questions: one regarding race and another regarding ethnicity.

Introduction to a Case Study:
Collecting Hispanic Ethnicity Data Separately
from Race Data in the US

The planning process for the 2020 decennial US census began making headlines starting in 2017 due to the chaotic development and rollout of the draft text of the census form to be sent to most US households. In that text, a question about citizenship was inserted, but it lacked any cogent basis in public policy or methodological needs. Instead, it looked suspiciously like an attempt by the hard-line xenophobic Trump administration to intimidate noncitizens from identifying themselves to the federal government, thus intentionally undercounting noncitizen residents to reduce the amount of federal population-based resources allocated to communities with large proportions of residents who are noncitizens (Gedeon 2019). The hectic and apparently malicious effort ended up being rejected by the Supreme Court. This episode shifted attention away from a complex and philosophically rich social science and policy debate, predating the Trump administration, about how to redesign the *Hispanic* classification, partly in order to reduce undercounting. Tentative plans to implement these major changes in 2020 were jettisoned by the Trump administration in favor of minor tweaks (Gedeon 2019). Setting aside the way the 2020 census turned out, the theoretical and practical conversations about the *Hispanic* classification have intensified in the process and will not end anytime soon.

In preparation for the 2020 census, the United States Census Bureau deliberated about whether and how to revise its race and ethnicity classification system, paying special attention to whether race data and ethnicity data should continue to be collected using two independent questions: "Is this person of Hispanic, Latino, or Spanish origin?" and "What is this person's race?" (Race and Hispanic Origin Research Working Group 2014; Compton et al. 2013). The Census Bureau refines and reformats its demographic data collection questions on a regular basis, within the limits of its mission and legislative mandates. For example, the 2000 census moved the Hispanic-ethnicity question so that it precedes the race question because experimental data indicated that this would "yield the lowest non-response rate for the Hispanic/Latino ethnicity question and the lowest rate of reporting 'other race' by Hispanics and Latinos in the race question" (Smith et al. 2010, 623–24). After conducting the 2010 Census Race and Hispanic Origin Alternative Questionnaire Experiment

(AQE), testing potential new formats for 2020, and collecting input from stakeholders, the Census Bureau determined that the net evidence favored a single question that combines the two previously independent questions—"What is Person 1's race or origin?"—asking respondents to tick all of the boxes that apply in a single list that includes *Hispanic, White, Black*, and so on (Race and Hispanic Origin Research Working Group 2014, 15). The Census Bureau report shies away from directly advocating for this "combined" format, calling for more data to be collected (Race and Hispanic Origin Research Working Group 2014), and the Census Bureau's follow-up 2015 National Content Test that evaluated new race formats in a representative sample of 1.2 million US households agreed that this would be "the optimal question format" (Mathews et al. 2017, 84) as long as respondents are given detailed checkboxes where they can elaborate on what they mean when they select any given racial or ethnic category (e.g., *Asian*) by marking one or more subsidiary checkboxes (e.g., *Chinese* or *Filipino*). The data are compelling:

> The appeal of this change is apparent in every area of the AQE results. First, the large-scale survey shows that Hispanic item non-response to the race question shrinks dramatically when the combined approach is used. Second, the telephone re-interviews show that Hispanics' self-reporting is more reliable (i.e. consistent) when a "Hispanic" checkbox is combined with the other [Office of Management and Budget] categories. Finally, focus groups revealed that the combined approach seemed to make most sense to respondents, both Hispanic and non-Hispanic, and equally importantly, it seemed fairer and more symmetric. (Race and Hispanic Origin Research Working Group 2014, 19)

Shifting around these boxes in census paperwork—or declining to do so—has far wider repercussions than one might imagine. The Census Bureau's decisions for how to carry out federally mandated race and ethnicity data collection set the standard for demographic data practices outside the government, including in health researchers' surveys (Smith et al. 2010). Because of census agencies' effects on day-to-day practices for demographic data collection, their decisions drastically shape societies' abilities to monitor and respond to disparities (Valles 2016) and even influence populations' self-identification practices through repeated exposure in routine paperwork (Spencer 2014). This shapes the structure of the knowledge available to us and determines our possible responses to that knowledge.

The current two-question format leaves the United States with an unusual system for classifying race and ethnicity, compared to other national systems. First, it retains its use of race concepts even after some other peer nations have abandoned race concepts, generally in favor of ethnicity concepts, which emphasize overall sociocultural affiliation rather than race's narrow focus on (self-reported) ancestry, as it has been applied in the census.[2] Second, it officially collects both race data and ethnicity data. There are five official US races: White, Black or African American, American Indian or Alaska Native, Asian, and Native Hawaiian or Other Pacific Islander. Apart from race, there is also one official US ethnicity: " 'Hispanic or Latino' refers to a person of Cuban, Mexican, Puerto Rican, South or Central American, or other Spanish culture or origin regardless of race" (Humes, Jones, and Ramirez 2011, 2). By international contrast, New Zealand, the UK, and Canada use only ethnicity concepts (Valles 2016; Callister et al. 2007; Statistics Canada 2013). Many European governments instead distinguish between populations on the basis of some measure of immigration status or country of origin (Jacobs et al. 2009). In this light, it should come as no surprise that the peculiarities of the system create special issues for the sole recognized ethnic group, Hispanics, whose members must navigate the US racial classification system in addition to the *Hispanic* question.

Hispanic is ethnic rather than racial in nature. The distinction can be fuzzy, but for official US purposes " 'Hispanic or Latino' refers to a person of Cuban, Mexican, Puerto Rican, South or Central American, or other Spanish culture or origin regardless of race" (Humes, Jones, and Ramirez 2011, 2), while the five recognized races are defined as "having origins in any of the original peoples of" a particular region (3). But *Hispanic* is not really an ethnicity; it is a panethnicity. It lumps together many different ethnicities under the definition articulated in the US census: Native Basque-speakers from Spain, Cubans of West African descent, and bilingual Quechua-and-Spanish speakers from Peru—all must decide whether they choose to identify under the Hispanic or Latino (or, to use the gender-neutral term, Latinx) panethnicity once they begin residing in the US. Since the term *Hispanic* is a uniquely American designator for lumping together disparate populations (as described below), it creates a variety of identification quandaries. For example, a newly arrived Mexican immigrant might only—in some sense—become a self-identifying Hispanic by virtue of checking the "Hispanic" box on a patient-intake form in a hospital waiting room.

In Valles (2016), I review some limitations of the utility of the *Hispanic* label for epidemiological research, showing how it serves some important social goals, especially providing collective political power to minority communities, but also creates problems for undertaking health-equity research. As illustrated in the article, the *Hispanic* variable is difficult to operationalize in public-health contexts, making it a primary reason why there is a lingering, three-decade debate over the "Hispanic paradox"—data indicating that Hispanics, on average, seem to have unexpectedly good health despite socioeconomic disadvantages. Efforts to resolve this paradox are impeded by confusion over the boundaries of the *Hispanic* label and how to interpret Hispanic data in light of the inevitable heterogeneity within a panethnic category. There are very real consequences for how we operationalize US race and Hispanic ethnicity data collection methods. In the case of the Hispanic paradox, the most worrisome consequence is that the conceptual ambiguity leaves us unable to answer even basic questions related to Hispanics' health needs, including whether they have better-than-average, average, or worse-than-average life expectancy (Valles 2016).

The question of how to format the race and ethnicity question involves complex epistemic questions and complex ethical questions that are further complicated by the fact that these issues are interrelated. This case's complexity, its relevance to social welfare, and the pressing need to nevertheless choose some research variable(s) together make it a prime candidate for coupled ethical-epistemic analysis, which the following sections will provide, organized according to the schema of the four questions offered in Katikireddi and Valles (2015).

What Are the Chosen Variables' Strengths and Weaknesses for Evidence Gathering and Analysis?

According to Cristina Mora (2014), the *Hispanic* panethnicity label was intentionally designed in the 1960s and 1970s to include ambiguity in its definition: "Ambiguity was a critical element of this new Hispanic field. Activists, media executives, and census officials never really defined who Hispanics were, nor did they argue definitively that characteristics like language, place of birth, or surname made Hispanics Hispanic. Instead, they reiterated that, above all, Hispanics were Hispanic because they shared a common set of values and a common culture. The stakeholders used descriptors like hardworking, religious, and family-oriented—adjectives that could be applied to any group—to describe the unique characteristics uniting Hispanics" (156). This ambiguity should make us skeptical of the *Hispanic* concept in certain scientific contexts. Yet the ambiguity is not a sufficient reason to immediately reject *Hispanic* as epistemically inadequate for all scientific purposes. Racial and ethnic concepts' chief scientific purpose is tracking social inequities, and a racial/ethnic population with marginal social status merits scientific attention to monitor the effects of that marginality. The Hispanic grouping and anti-Hispanic bias are firmly entrenched in the US, and an ethnic label is thus necessary to track the consequences of discrimination against the population, even when the population is ambiguously defined (Valles 2016).

In a further weakness of the two-question version of Hispanic identity, the Hispanic population is failed by the US demographic classification system at a hugely disproportionate rate compared to non-Hispanics. In the 2010 US census data, 37% of those self-identifying as "Hispanic" also ticked only the "Some Other Race" box to describe their racial identity (Humes, Jones, and Ramirez 2011). This indicates that a large portion of the Hispanic population found the US racial scheme to be inadequate for their self-identification preferences. Even more strikingly, among the total 19.1 million people who identified their race as only "Some Other Race," 97% of those respondents were Hispanic (Humes, Jones, and Ramirez 2011). This is a disproportionate burden for the Hispanic population, insofar as it is a burden for a group's demographics to be misconstrued and hence its social needs misappraised. A Census Bureau study of "churn" in how individual people responded to race and ethnicity questions in the 2000 census versus the 2010 census further illustrates the disproportionate burden that the current race and ethnicity classification system places upon Hispanics. Those switching their self-identifications back or forth between "Hispanic; Some Other Race" and "Hispanic; White" made up 37% of the total cases of "churn" between all race/ethnicity identifications (Liebler et al. 2014, 29). It is troubling to see that a huge chunk of all US racial/ethnic identity "churn" consists of Hispanics trying to determine whether "White" or "Some Other Race" best describes them.

In sum, there are two epistemic weaknesses in using the two-question version of the *Hispanic* variable (a panethnicity separate from race). First, the *Hispanic* variable is a recent construction with fuzzy boundaries. However, that is an epistemic weakness shared by any attempt to measure the *Hispanic* variable. Second, Hispanics disproportionately struggle to find appropriate labels in the current two-question format of the *Hispanic* variable, but less so in the alternative one-question format. Demographic methods rely on the ability of respondents to self-identify.

What Are the Chosen Variables' Ethical Strengths and Weaknesses?

The initial process of defining the *Hispanic* variable as a separate demographic concept was motivated by the goal of promoting social justice, and it has served that end. Beginning in the 1960s, community activists began gathering support from social scientists, the government, and the media for collecting more-nuanced data on the population that had previously been identified by having Spanish surnames (Mora 2014; Humes and Hogan 2015). Responding to the calls for a new demographic variable to track and ameliorate the experiences of US residents with roots in Spanish-speaking countries, a 1976 congressional mandate dictates "Spanish origin or descent" demographic data must somehow be collected in the census (Rumbaut 2006). United by a common panethnic label legitimized by the government, Hispanics have gathered social power that would otherwise be unavailable to their disparate minority groups. For example, few US political candidates are interested in the Honduran vote, but most are interested in the Hispanic vote. However, switching to a one-question format that lumps Hispanic panethnicity and race together would still serve that same purpose—the key is just that *Hispanic* must exist as a US demographic variable in some form or another.

Despite having served ethically important sociopolitical purposes, a fundamental ethical weakness of the *Hispanic* variable in the two-question format (a panethnicity independent of race) is that this version of the variable is a poor reflection of how people in the relevant populations prefer to be identified. As a Pew Research Center survey report summarizes, "When it comes to describing their identity, most Hispanics prefer their family's country of origin over pan-ethnic terms" (Taylor et al. 2012, 2). The mismatch between self-identification preferences and available demographic choices is a serious ethical weakness unique to the current two-question format used. It even contradicts one of the explicit "principles" the Office of Management and Budget (1997, 58782) used in the most recent major overhaul of race and ethnicity data collection: "Respect for individual dignity should guide the processes and methods for collecting data on race and ethnicity; ideally, respondent self-identification should be facilitated to the greatest extent possible." This emphasis on self-identification has guided demographic data collection in recent decades, with observer-reported race and ethnicity data collection (once standard) treated as a disfavored last resort (Ulmer, McFadden, and Nerenz 2009). A single-question format is more consistent with self-identification preferences, yielding the empirical result quoted above: more Hispanics finding ways to self-identify their racial identities, increased consistency in those responses over time, and higher satisfaction among the respondents (Race and Hispanic Origin Research Working Group 2014, 19).

In sum, the creation and continued use of the *Hispanic* variable plays a vital social-justice purpose, and it cannot be jettisoned. Survey questions involving the *Hispanic* variable can be reformatted while still serving this ethical goal. The two-question format in particular is problematic because it disrespects community members' self-identification preferences. Respecting those preferences is a keystone ethical commitment of contemporary demography.

How Will the Chosen Variables' Strengths and Weaknesses for Evidence Gathering and Analysis Affect Ethical Issues?

The challenges in collecting and interpreting data on Hispanic populations are troubling because disproportionately vulnerable subpopulations are most harmed by problems therein. Among US residents, those who have origins in Spanish-speaking countries are disproportionately more likely to be immigrants. This makes it particularly ethically problematic to apply a demographic concept that is peculiar to the United States. As a National Research Council volume puts it, the "catchall label [of *Hispanic* or *Latino*] has a particular meaning only in the U.S. context in which it was constructed and is applied, and where its meaning continues to evolve" (Rumbaut 2006, 18). This means that, by default, immigrants from Argentina, Cuba, Mexico, and so on are forced to accept or reject a panethnic label that they have most likely never previously used to identify themselves. If respect for self-identification is a guiding principle, then the idiosyncratically American *Hispanic* label is not well suited for the measurement of a population in which 35% of the members are foreign born (López and Patten 2015).

As articulated by M. Anne Visser (2014, 246–47), the current US race/ethnicity classification system "does not accurately approximate the informal patterns of identity operating among the populace and may result in the disempowerment of segments of the Hispanic population and by implication the Hispanic population as a whole." According to a Census Bureau survey (Humes and Hogan 2015), Hispanics over the age of twenty are more likely to report being "Some Other Race" if they are noncitizens (41%) than if they are citizens (34%). This indicates that the racial categories are accepted more and more over the passage of generations. Meanwhile, the burden of disrespect and alienation from being asked to self-identify with terms and concepts at odds with one's identity is disproportionately placed on noncitizens, a socially vulnerable group.

The problem of large numbers of "Some Other Race" responses among Hispanics motivated the Census Bureau's aforementioned reappraisal of its racial and ethnic classification system. According to a Census Bureau report, "Some Other Race" was supposed to be a "small residual category" (Compton et al. 2013, 8). It generally works as intended for non-Hispanics (0.2% identify their race as only "Some Other Race"), but it does not work this way for self-identified Hispanics (as noted above, a massive 37% identify their race as only "Some Other Race"; Humes, Jones, and Ramirez 2011, 6). According to the Census Bureau, such a high proportion of "Some Other Race" reports is inherently a sign of a poorly designed system (Compton et al. 2013, 8).

By contrast, Nancy López (2013, 432) disagrees that high rates of "Some Other Race" reporting among Hispanics is a reason to alter the race and ethnicity classification system: "As a sociologist of racial, ethnic and gender stratification, I see the phenomenon of 'some other race' as an empirical and analytical goldmine. For example, the 2010 Census identified very unique responses to the race question among Latinas/os. . . . These variations in responses to the race questions should not be construed as a problem or as 'inaccurate' or 'not reliable.' Rather, these differences reflect the reality that Latinos are racialized in very different ways."

In other words, examining the varying rates of "Some Other Race" identification among Hispanics of different generations, national origins, and other groupings gives us a lens for examining Hispanic subgroups' diverse perceptions of how they fit into the US racial schema, which can be cross-referenced with data on their social welfare. López (2013, 430) goes on to argue that the racial data and the ethnic data are both needed since racial discrimination and ethnic discrimination have different causal "pathways." That is to say, independently tracking self-reported Hispanic status and self-reported racial identity gives us two dimensions of data, each of which is informative. For example, if a subpopulation retains the *Hispanic* label over a ten-year period but increasingly reports a *White* racial identity, this could be interpreted as a signal that its members retain a distinct cultural or national-origin identity but increasingly see themselves as accepted members of the dominant US racial group.

Contra López's suggestion that racial experiences and ethnic experiences should be teased apart, Hana Brown and Jennifer Jones (2015, 182) warn that driving a methodological wedge between the study of ethnicity (including panethnicity) and the study of race reinforces a misguided split among social scientists: "The panethnicity-racialization divide is both a symptom and a cause of the chasm between race and immigration scholarship . . . the division is one consequence of the broader scholarly assumption that race and ethnicity constitute distinct analytical concepts rather than folk ones." Collecting both race data and ethnicity data on Hispanic populations allows us to split what would otherwise be lumped together, but Brown and Jones point out that this split may rest on dubious assumptions and also do more harm than good to research strategies.

Nancy López (2013) is concerned with the fact that lived race and lived ethnicity have distinct meanings that merit separate data collection because demographic categories are crucial for the monitoring of discrimination.[3] She cites a passage by Census Bureau officials Karen Humes and Howard Hogan (2009, 111) that states "there is no firm distinction between 'race' and 'ethnicity,' as both are dimensions in group identity. Groups currently considered 'ethnic' or 'national' were once viewed as separate 'races.'" Unlike López, Humes and Hogan seem to take the self-identification standard to be a conceptually prior constraint on methodological disputes; we can debate how to achieve the goal of monitoring discrimination, but it is imperative that we work within the framework of respecting people's self-identifications: "The ultimate goal should be to develop a racial and ethnic classification system that will allow the multi-cultural population to self-identify their heritage in the most meaningful manner possible, yet will still provide the critical data needed for the enforcement of civil rights laws and monitoring equal access" (127). López rightly draws attention to the racial and ethnic classification system's goal of monitoring discrimination. But demographic categories that are poor reflections of self-identification are also weakened as tools for performing the necessary discrimination monitoring. Even if racial discrimination and ethnic discrimination are distinct phenomena, categories that fail to reliably measure the population of interest are unable to serve the ethical goal of monitoring discrimination in that population. An epistemic weakness leads to an ethical weakness.

In sum, the epistemic features of the case feed into ethical issues in several ways. The use of the US-specific concept *Hispanic*, in any format, burdens the population's large proportion of foreign-born members. But the two-question format of the *Hispanic* variable has one major strength due to epistemic-ethical feedback: it allows tracking of both ethnic discrimination and racial discrimination. However, keeping racial and ethnic discrimination data separate reinforces the problematic divide between racial-discrimination scholars and ethnic-discrimination scholars. An added weakness of the two-question format compared to the one-question format is that the two-question format's failure to align with respondents' self-identification impedes the rigorous monitoring of discrimination against Hispanics regardless of the race-versus-ethnicity methodological questions.

How Will the Chosen Variables' Ethical Strengths and Weaknesses Affect Evidence Gathering and Analysis?

The epistemic problem of people shifting between "Hispanic; Some Other Race" and "Hispanic; White" in the 2000 to 2010 censuses is an indication that Hispanics are not given checkboxes that reflect their racial/ethnic self-identification preferences, an ethical problem (Liebler et al. 2014). As Katikireddi and I (2015) argue in our coupled ethical-epistemic analyses of public-health cases, behaving disrespectfully ("even unintentionally") toward a population undermines any attempts to collect future data from that population. Since contemporary demographic data collection is by default done via asking multiple-choice questions and hoping for a complete and truthful answer, such data collection necessarily depends on trusting relationships between practitioners and the populations served. As noted in the above citation of Spencer (2014), day-to-day paperwork routinely confronts US residents with the request to locate themselves within the official racial and ethnic classification system. When that classification does not reflect a population's preferred self-identification practices, it yields repeated signals of disrespect from the government and perhaps from the other data collectors using that classification system. Undermining the relationships between data collectors and the populations served through disrespect is an ethical problem that also creates dire long-term epistemic risks.

As noted in the previous section, Humes and Hogan (2009, 2015) are sanguine about replacing the two-question format for race and ethnicity data collection with a single-question format. López's (2013, 430) opposition to collapsing the two-question format is motivated by her view of how to prioritize the trade-offs between two aspects of the coupled ethical-epistemic model—the ethical impacts of epistemic practices versus the epistemic impacts of ethical practices: "Over the last four decades the 'gold standard' for the collection of racial and ethnic data is collecting self-identified data whenever possible; however, the gold standard needs to also consider the importance of the collection of race and ethnicity data that allows civil rights organizations and researchers to monitor and assess race and ethnic discrimination as distinct pathways of inequality." Humes and Hogan (2009, 127) make "meaningful" measurement the first priority and treat metrics' usefulness (for monitoring discrimination) as secondary—in other words, they seek to maximize meaningfulness within the boundaries of adequate utility. López seeks the reverse, taking the ethical need to monitor racial discrimination and ethnic discrimination as the primary goal while arguing that accordance between classifications and self-description preferences must simply be adequate.

In sum, the two-question format disrespects Hispanics' self-identification, undermining trusting relationships between researchers and the population. The desirability of the one-question versus two-question format partly hinges on whether one prioritizes respect for self-identification practices or the need for separate racial and ethnic data.

Summary of the Analysis

Epistemic Strengths and Weaknesses

- The *Hispanic* variable is a recent construction with fuzzy boundaries.

- Hispanics disproportionately struggle to find appropriate labels in the current two-question ethnicity-race system.

ETHICAL STRENGTHS AND WEAKNESSES

- A *Hispanic* label allows Hispanics to wield collective social power.

- Treating *Hispanic* as a panethnicity separate from race is disrespectful of community self-identification preferences.

EPISTEMIC FEATURES' EFFECTS ON ETHICAL FEATURES

- A US-specific panethnic *Hispanic* concept is especially burdensome for the large subpopulation of immigrants, an especially socially vulnerable group.

- Gathering separate race data and Hispanic-ethnicity data allows us to track distinct types of experiences, including different types of harms from discrimination (ethnic discrimination and racial discrimination).

- Gathering separate race data and Hispanic-ethnicity data reinforces a methodological and disciplinary split between race scholars and ethnicity scholars, which hampers the development and application of effective responses to social inequities.

- Hispanics' difficulties with locating themselves within the current racial-ethnic classification system reduces the system's efficacy in monitoring discrimination.

ETHICAL FEATURES' EFFECTS ON EPISTEMIC FEATURES

- Disrespecting community self-identification preferences leads us to collect poorer data.

- How one prioritizes two ethical considerations—respecting self-identification preferences versus monitoring ethnic discrimination and racial discrimination as separate harms—inclines one to accept or reject the epistemic strategy used by the current two-question format for race-ethnicity data collection.

This coupled ethical-epistemic analysis compiles reasons for and against switching to a combined (one-question) format of race and ethnicity data collection. Seeing those reasons compiled and organized in this framework sharpens our focus on the ethical considerations, the epistemic considerations, and the considerations arising from mutual interactions.

One highlight of this analysis is that it shows why leaving Hispanics in their current demographic self-identification limbo undercuts the ethical and evidentiary benefits of collecting demographic data: self-identification data that poorly reflects self-identifications is epistemically weak; epistemically weak data is a poor foundation for ethical social policies such as government antidiscrimination programs. Based on the above analysis, I contend that future US censuses should use a combined race-ethnicity question format that places the *Hispanic* category alongside racial categories, unless contravening evidence emerges in the meantime. It is regrettably too late to do so in the 2020 census.

This is a case study in which marginalization and oppression are obvious and inextricable risks, a case that calls out for analysis using a methodology designed to help us understand and manage those risks. Demography of race and ethnicity concepts is more than the science of populations and identity—it is the science that determines minority groups' visibility and invisibility. Minority social policies of all sorts hinge on which minority populations we make visible through our data-collection practices. Further illustrating this point, potential Hispanic-classification changes were accompanied by a set of proposed revisions to include the addition of a new category, "Middle Eastern and North African (MENA)," at the urging of community advocacy organizations who contend that lumping these populations into the *White* category (as is the current practice) is a disservice to the communities (Race and Hispanic Origin Research Working Group 2014). Generating this demographic category will make it possible to routinely track the well-being of a cluster of populations that those advocacy organizations, Census Bureau experts, and focus groups all agree should not be designated as simply *White*. Among many other benefits, recognizing *MENA* as a category in the census and for other government purposes has the potential to monitor hiring discrimination and other matters of social welfare in an era characterized by Islamophobia, anti-Arab discrimination, and other associated forms of bigotry. So much hinges on the way we operationalize racial and ethnic categories.

Next Steps for the Coupled Ethical-Epistemic Framework

This chapter has explored the intellectual kinship between two philosophical methodologies, feminist philosophy and coupled ethical-epistemic analysis. They overlap through shared interests in advancing more socially responsible science: (1) promoting social welfare through working "in the weeds" and engaging with scientific practitioners; (2) recognizing the complexities of ontology, causation, and power in the real world; and (3) rejecting attempts to assert a bright line between the normative and the descriptive activities of science. Feminist philosophy of science was never just about improving how we manage gender issues in science. Rather, it is (among other things) a project of identifying and remediating the sorts of problematic power relationships that give rise to sexist inequities and other oppressions.

The coupled ethical-epistemic model and feminist philosophy of science both promote direct engagement with scientific practitioners during critiques in order to advance social welfare. In the case study analyzed above, this means engaging with the empirical research on Hispanic classification and with the policies founded upon that research. It is good that the Census Bureau continually collects, assesses, and reassesses the evidence and then refines policies accordingly (even if this process can be overridden by external political forces). I apply the coupled ethical-epistemic model here to support that evidence-assessment process, imploring policy makers and demographers to pay due attention to the feedback loops and unintended consequences that can transfer back and forth between evidentiary considerations and ethical considerations. Race and ethnicity experts' commitments to good evidence and to ethical conduct are each commendable, but even the most well-intentioned experts remain highly vulnerable to ethical and epistemic missteps if they are not vigilant for ethical-epistemic interactions.

This case study has—hopefully—illustrated the utility of coupled ethical-epistemic analysis for performing case analyses that mitigate science's oppressive potential and expand its liberatory potential. This is in keeping with this volume's gathering of two branches of philosophy with overlapping liberatory interests—feminist philosophy and critical philosophy of race. Most essentially, experts in intersectional theory have explored the connections and dynamics between race and gender (among other features), and intersectional theory is indeed beginning to get attention in the philosophy-of-science literature, long after feminist philosophy took root there (Bright, Malinsky, and Thompson 2016). The goal of this chapter is simply to show how coupled ethical-epistemic analysis furthers goals previously articulated in feminist philosophy of science. Moreover, it seeks to show the value of the coupled ethical-epistemic model to feminist philosophers and science practitioners who are interested in a user-friendly tool that helps to make analyzing complex, socially relevant scientific cases more manageable without dismissing their complexity. I have offered an analysis of the two-question *Hispanic*-classification debate as evidence that the tool can be useful. The hope is that the audience of this volume will find it a promising candidate as a model for feminist analysis of scientific research.

Notes

1. A few months after the paper was published, the FDA (most likely coincidentally) announced its intention to make the rule less restrictive.
2. See Afshari and Bhopal (2010) on trends in the use of racial versus ethnicity terminology in the medical literature. Curiously, while the ratio of racial to ethnicity language used to be higher outside the US than in the US, that trend flipped in the 1970s. As of 2005, even though ethnicity language is used somewhat more frequently than racial language across the globe, racial language is more common in the US that outside of the US.
3. See, for example, Harris and Sim (2002) on shifting racial identities and "lived race" experiences.

References

Afshari, Reza, and Raj S. Bhopal. 2010. "Ethnicity Has Overtaken Race in Medical Science: MEDLINE-Based Comparison of Trends in the USA and the Rest of the World, 1965–2005." *International Journal of Epidemiology* 39 (6): 1682–83.
Anderson, Elizabeth. 1995. "Knowledge, Human Interests, and Objectivity in Feminist Epistemology." *Philosophical Topics* 23 (2): 27–58.
Bright, Liam Kofi, Daniel Malinsky, and Morgan Thompson. 2016. "Causally Interpreting Intersectionality Theory." *Philosophy of Science* 83 (1): 60–81.
Brown, Hana, and Jennifer A Jones. 2015. "Rethinking Panethnicity and the Race-Immigration Divide: An Ethnoracialization Model of Group Formation." *Sociology of Race and Ethnicity* 1 (1): 181–91.

Brown, Matthew J. 2013. "Values in Science beyond Underdetermination and Inductive Risk." *Philosophy of Science* 80 (5): 829–39.

Callister, Paul, Robert Didham, Deborah Potter, and Tony Blakely. 2007. "Measuring Ethnicity in New Zealand: Developing Tools for Health Outcomes Analysis." *Ethnicity and Health* 12 (4): 299–320.

Clough, Sharyn. 2003. *Beyond Epistemology: A Pragmatist Approach to Feminist Science Studies.* Lanham, MD: Rowman and Littlefield.

Compton, Elizabeth, Michael Bentley, Sharon Ennis, and Sonya Rastogi. 2013. *2010 Census Race and Hispanic Origin Alternative Questionnaire Experiment Final Report.* Washington, DC: United States Census Bureau.

Douglas, Heather E. 2009. *Science, Policy, and the Value-Free Ideal.* Pittsburgh, PA: University of Pittsburgh Press.

Fehr, Carla. 2012. "Feminist Engagement with Evolutionary Psychology." *Hypatia* 27 (1): 50–72.

Gedeon, Joseph. 2019. "As Census Approaches, Many Arab Americans Feel Left Out." Associated Press, April 13, 2019. Accessed May 7, 2019. https://www.apnews.com/a25b5d977a5049d6a9038a536cc7129a.

Harris, David R., and Jeremiah Joseph Sim. 2002. "Who Is Multiracial? Assessing the Complexity of Lived Race." *American Sociological Review* 67 (4): 614–27.

Hicks, Daniel J. 2014. "A New Direction for Science and Values." *Synthese* 191 (14): 3271–95.

Humes, Karen, and Howard Hogan. 2009. "Measurement of Race and Ethnicity in a Changing, Multicultural America." *Race and Social Problems* 1 (3): 111–31.

———. 2015. "Do Current Race and Ethnicity Concepts Reflect a Changing America?" In *Race and Social Problems: Restructuring Inequality*, edited by Ralph Bangs and Larry E. Davis, 15–38. New York: Springer.

Humes, Karen R., Nicholas A. Jones, and Roberto R. Ramirez. 2011. *Overview of Race and Hispanic Origin: 2010.* Washington, DC: United States Census Bureau.

Jacobs, Dirk, Marc Swyngedouw, Laurie Hanquinet, Vèronique Vandezande, Roger Andersson, Ana Paula Beja Horta, Maria Berger, Mario Diani, Amparo Gonzalez Ferrer, Marco Giugni, et al. 2009. "The Challenge of Measuring Immigrant Origin and Immigration-Related Ethnicity in Europe." *Journal of International Migration and Integration* 10 (1): 67–88.

Katikireddi, Srinivasa Vittal, Martin Higgins, Katherine Elizabeth Smith, and Gareth Williams. 2013. "Health Inequalities: The Need to Move Beyond Bad Behaviours." *Journal of Epidemiology and Community Health* 67 (9): 715–16.

Katikireddi, S. Vittal, and Sean A. Valles. 2015. "Coupled Ethical-Epistemic Analysis of Public Health Research and Practice: Categorizing Variables to Improve Population Health and Equity." *American Journal of Public Health* 105 (1): e36–e42.

Kuhn, Thomas S. 1977. "Objectivity, Values, and Theory Choice." In *The Essential Tension: Selected Studies in Scientific Tradition and Change*, 320–39. Chicago: University of Chicago Press.

Liebler, Carolyn A., Sonya Rastogi, Leticia E. Fernandez, James M. Noon, and Sharon R. Ennis. 2014. *America's Churning Races: Race and Ethnic Response Changes between Census 2000 and the 2010 Census*. Washington, DC: United States Census Bureau.

Lloyd, Elisabeth A. 2001. "Science Gone Astray: Evolution and Rape." *Michigan Law Review* 99 (6): 1536–59.

Longino, Helen E. 1995. "Gender, Politics, and the Theoretical Virtues." *Synthese* 104 (3): 383–97.

López, Gustavo, and Eileen Patten. 2015. *The Impact of Slowing Immigration: Foreign-Born Share Falls among 14 Largest U.S. Hispanic Origin Groups*. Washington, DC: Pew Research Center.

López, Nancy. 2013. "Killing Two Birds with One Stone? Why We Need Two Separate Questions on Race and Ethnicity in the 2020 Census and Beyond." *Latino Studies* 11 (3): 428–38.

Mathews, Kelly, Jessica Phelan, Nicholas A. Jones, Sarah Konya, Rachel Marks, Beverly M. Pratt, Julia Coombs, and Michael Bentley. 2017. *2015 National Content Test Race and Ethnicity Analysis Report*. Washington, DC: United States Census Bureau. https://www.census.gov/programs-surveys/decennial-census/2020-census/planning-management/final-analysis/2015nct-race-ethnicity-analysis.html.

Mora, G. Cristina. 2014. *Making Hispanics: How Activists, Bureaucrats, and Media Constructed a New American*. Chicago: University of Chicago Press.

Office of Management and Budget. 1997. "Revisions to the Standards for the Classification of Federal Data on Race and Ethnicity." *Federal Register* 62 (210): 58782–90.

Race and Hispanic Origin Research Working Group. 2014. *2020 Census: Race and Hispanic Origin Research Working Group Final Report*. Washington, DC: United States Census Bureau.

Richardson, Sarah S. 2010. "Feminist Philosophy of Science: History, Contributions, and Challenges." *Synthese* 177 (3): 337–62.

Rumbaut, Rubén G. 2006. "The Making of a People." In *Hispanics and the Future of America*, edited by Marta Tienda and Faith Mitchell, 16–65. Washington, DC: National Academies Press.

Smith, Felicia D., Meghan Woo, and S. Bryn Austin. 2010. "'I Didn't Feel Like Any of Those Things Were Me': Results of a Qualitative Pilot Study of Race/Ethnicity Survey Items with Minority Ethnic Adolescents in the USA." *Ethnicity and Health* 15 (6): 621–38.

Spencer, Quayshawn. 2014. "A Radical Solution to the Race Problem." *Philosophy of Science* 81 (5): 1025–38.

Statistics Canada. 2013. *Ethnic Origin Reference Guide, National Household Survey, 2011.* Statistics Canada.

Taylor, Paul, Mark Hugo Lopez, Jessica Hamar Martínez, and Gabriel Velasco. 2012. *When Labels Don't Fit: Hispanics and Their Views of Identity.* Washington, DC: Pew Research Center.

Tuana, Nancy. 2010. "Leading with Ethics, Aiming for Policy: New Opportunities for Philosophy of Science." *Synthese* 177 (3): 471–92.

———. 2013. "Embedding Philosophers in the Practices of Science: Bringing Humanities to the Sciences." *Synthese* 190 (11): 1955–73.

———. 2015. "Climate Change through the Lens of Feminist Philosophy." In *Meta-philosophical Reflection on Feminist Philosophies of Science,* edited by Maria Cristina Amoretti and Nicla Vassallo. Cham, Switzerland: Springer International.

Tuana, Nancy, Ryan L. Sriver, Toby Svoboda, Roman Olson, Peter J. Irvine, Jacob Haqq-Misra, and Klaus Keller. 2012. "Towards Integrated Ethical and Scientific Analysis of Geoengineering: A Research Agenda." *Ethics, Policy and Environment* 15 (2): 136–57.

Ulmer, Cheryl, Bernadette McFadden, and David R. Nerenz. 2009. *Race, Ethnicity, and Language Data: Standardization for Health Care Quality Improvement.* Washington, DC: National Academies Press.

Valles, Sean A. 2012. "Heterogeneity of Risk within Racial Groups, a Challenge for Public Health Programs." *Preventive Medicine* 55 (5): 405–8.

———. 2016. "The Challenges of Choosing and Explaining a Phenomenon in Epidemiological Research on the 'Hispanic Paradox.'" *Theoretical Medicine and Bioethics* 37 (2): 129–48. https://doi.org/10.1007/s11017-015-9349-1.

Visser, M. Anne. 2014. "Two Plus Two Equals Three: Classification Error and the Hispanic Undercount in United States Census Surveys." *American Review of Public Administration* 44 (2): 233–51.

Chapter 3

Feminist Science Studies

Reasoning from Cases

SHARON CRASNOW

Introduction

Much research in feminist science studies has been informed by the analysis
of cases, and much feminist philosophy of science is either engaged in
or built upon such analysis. These case studies have illustrated a variety
of ways gender bias can distort scientific knowledge, such as excluding
women as researchers or subjects of research, relying on presuppositions
about gender that are either explicitly or implicitly exclusionary, or asking
questions that grow out of interests that do not align with the interests
of women or other nondominant groups. Despite the widespread use of
case studies in these ways, the question of how case studies improve the
understanding of science in feminist science studies or more generally
contribute to our understanding of science has been underexplored. This
is not surprising for a variety of reasons, some having explicitly to do with
feminist research and some related to the methodology of case studies.

First, in relation to feminist goals, as cases were first explored, the
most pressing need seemed to be to establish the reality of sexist bias in
many areas of scientific research. There were skeptics who needed evidence
to be convinced. But even clear-cut examples of bias may be dismissed
as bad science or outliers. One result is that feminist researchers have
been motivated to produce yet more examples—more case studies—to
accumulate evidence of androcentrism in different areas of science of

interest to feminists, thus documenting the extent of sexist bias while increasing the sample size. Second, general worries have been articulated about what epistemic work case studies are able to do, raising questions about the value of the evidence they produce. It is not obvious how case studies contribute to knowledge production. Through a case study, we learn a lot about the case investigated, but what more, if anything, do we learn? There has not been a clear body of methodological literature or a widely accepted theory to rely on for an account of how we learn from cases. Although case studies are used in many disciplines—political science, sociology, anthropology, and others—even within these disciplines an understanding of their epistemic function has been limited and their value is often questioned.[1]

There is, however, some recent work that addresses the epistemology of cases, and I draw on some of that research in what follows.[2] Among other things, this work reveals that there is no single way that case studies contribute to knowledge, but rather there are multiple points of contribution. I argue that by exploring how cases function in feminist science studies and philosophy of science we can expand our understanding of how case-study research produces knowledge relevant to both feminist research and philosophy of science more generally.

I begin by reviewing the role that case studies play in revealing sexist bias. Sarah Richardson (2010) worries that this emphasis on bias has a negative effect on feminist science studies through reinforcing the traditional conception of science as value free. I examine her concern and argue that case studies that uncover bias are typically doing other epistemological work as well. In the next section, I discuss Hasok Chang's notion of "epistemic iteration," which provides a tool for thinking about case studies and their role in knowledge production. Using Chang's idea, I consider an exemplary case study: Elizabeth Anderson's discussion of the research of Abigail Stewart et al. on divorce. I turn next to Mary Morgan's identification of three epistemic strategies used with case studies in order to develop a framework for understanding how knowledge from one site might be transported to others. I use both Morgan's idea about strategies and Chang's epistemic iteration to look at Elisabeth Lloyd's extended case study of research on the female orgasm. I conclude that the analyses of these examples using the resources from Chang and Morgan show how feminist case studies can do more than expose bias or convince skeptics that such biases can distort science.

Sexism and Gender Bias in Science

Sarah Richardson (2010, 346) gives the following overview of a common approach in feminist science studies: "The case study has been the traditional format for philosophical work on gender bias in science. The author presents a methodological critique of gender bias in a particular scientific research program, theory, or explanatory framework. He or she shows how gendered practices or assumptions in a scientific field prevented researchers from accurately interpreting data, caused inferential leaps, blocked the consideration of alternative hypotheses, overdetermined theory choice, or biased descriptive language." Richardson argues that this story emphasizes the role feminist scholarship plays in revealing bias and de-emphasizes other contributions feminist philosophers of science and science-studies scholars make to understanding science. She argues that uncovering bias is viewed as "legitimate" feminist work, especially in camps that are not always sympathetic to feminist approaches, since it reveals bad science—biased science is bad science. This work thus both is consistent with and reinforces a traditional ideal of science as value free. Feminist values motivate the critique of value-laden science, but that critique can in turn serve as a motivation for researchers to double down on their efforts to achieve the value-free ideal. Equating values with bias in this way results in a tension between the feminist goals motivating the critique and the value-free framework. Confining feminist concerns to negative critique and denying them a positive role in knowledge production resolves this tension, but at the cost of downplaying or even denying a legitimate role for egalitarian and liberatory values of feminist research. Richardson's concern is that "privileging the problem of bias relies on an idealized, progressive picture of science—in which unbiased, value-neutral science is the ideal" (355).

While Richardson acknowledges that outing particular instances of sexist assumptions or other modes of sexism in scientific research can be valuable, she seeks to direct us to ways feminist examinations of science challenge the value-free ideal more trenchantly. She points to feminist scholarship that aids in alternative framing of research questions, that revises concepts through which we understand the objects of inquiry, or that models interdisciplinary or community-based approaches. These and other such contributions have sometimes been misunderstood as anti-science when measured against the value-free ideal, whereas uncovering bias is the aspect of feminist science-studies research that is most easily digestible because it does not really challenge that ideal.[3]

However, how to argue that case studies support the legitimacy of values in these other roles is not obvious. One reason for this has been a lack of clarity about how case studies do epistemic work. How we learn from cases has been underexplored in the philosophy-of-science literature and in the disciplines in which case studies are employed. Both the focus on bias and the undertheorization of case-study methodology are connected to the persistence of the traditional value-free ideal. While this ideal acknowledges the legitimacy of exposing bias, it also creates resistance to other sorts of feminist critique. The value-free ideal is part of the legacy of logical empiricism that seeks to give an account of scientific reasoning as an analysis of interconnected propositions ultimately supported by fundamental empirical facts (also expressed as propositions). There are two results of this approach relevant to our discussion—one having to do with empirical content, and the other with the forms of reasoning: (1) values can play no role in this analysis because they are not thought to be empirical, and (2) reasoning must be analyzed as either inductive or deductive since these are the only allowable relations between propositions.

It is the second of these that pushes analysis of case-study research toward the logical-empiricist model. That model suggests that we take cases to be providing inductive support for empirical generalizations or theories. The case is the particular instance from which the general conclusion is to be drawn. It is difficult not to come to the conclusion that such support is weak, at best. An approach in which cases are not thought of as confirming through providing evidence for inductive conclusions but rather viewed as serving as tests of hypotheses can provide an alternative to viewing cases as less-than-optimal evidence in inductive arguments. However, such an approach really does not offer a better understanding of the epistemic work of case studies. Treating cases as tests only allows us to treat them as weak tests, since the failure of the case to conform to the hypothesis or theory only tells us that something in our set of beliefs needs to be revised, not what to revise.[4] Thus cases appear to be either evidence in bad inductive arguments or weak tests. If cases are more robustly epistemically useful, then they must be so in some other way. The challenge is to understand how.

Elisabeth Lloyd poses a version of this challenge for her extended case study of research on the female orgasm. She notes that her "book should be seen as a case study on how biases and background assumptions can affect the practice of science. But one may ask, 'So what?' What difference does it make that this particular topic seems to attract deficit scientific explanations?" (Lloyd 2005, 18). While she offers several answers to this question, the answer most directly related to what we learn about the nature of science from case studies is that the case provides evidence that androcentric bias does sometimes occur—a relatively weak conclusion evoking Richardson's worry, since it is a conclusion consistent with the value-free account. I argue that Lloyd's case study—and good case studies, generally—provides greater epistemic leverage than this.

The Problem with Cases

In order to see how great epistemic leverage is possible, we should first clarify why reasoning from case studies appears to be a problem. Joseph Pitt frames this as a dilemma in the history and philosophy of science: "On the one hand, if the case is selected because it exemplifies the philosophical point being articulated, then it is not clear that the phil-osophical claims have been supported, because it could be argued that the historical data was manipulated to fit the point. On the other hand, if one starts with a case study, it is not clear where to go from there—for it is unreasonable to generalize from one case or even two or three" (Pitt 2001, 373). I start with the first horn of Pitt's dilemma, since this is the particularly worrying one for feminist critique. If we do a case study, what is to prevent us from reading it through the philosophical point that we are trying to make, selecting the case and its interpretation accordingly? If we are thinking of the case in this way, not only are we engaging in bad induction by generalizing from one case study (the second worry) but we may also be guilty of cherry-picking—choosing our evidence to fit our preferred philosophical theory. In fact, the use of cases in feminist philosophy of science could be and has been criticized for committing both epistemic sins.[5]

Hasok Chang (2012a) suggests that Pitt's dilemma should be dissolved by thinking about the relationship between case studies and the philosophy of science in a different way. To illustrate, he refers to his own work on the invention of temperature (Chang 2004) and the discovery that water is a compound rather than an element (Chang 2012b), two cases from the history of science. He proposes that the relationship between the cases and our philosophical accounts should be thought of as a relationship between the concrete and the abstract rather than as inductive reasoning from the particular case to a general conclusion. When we use cases, we employ abstract ideas in order to understand what is concrete, but we also learn from examining the concrete episodes and use what we learn to revise and improve the abstractions used in the analysis. Thus, the two issues, fitting the case study to the theoretical account and using the case study to theorize, are intertwined. Chang refers to this process of working back and forth between the abstract and the concrete as *epistemic iteration*.[6]

Pitt's worries about case studies result, in part, from the false belief that we must reason either from the case to the philosophical point or from the philosophical point to the case. Chang's analysis (2012a) takes us through the horns of the dilemma with an alternative approach. If the case is a concrete episode of the philosophical abstraction, we are not bound by the inferential directionality that Pitt's description implies. Thus, Chang rejects the dichotomy and claims instead that we go back and forth between the philosophical point and the case. We alter our description of the case as we see it through the theoretical framework and alter the philosophical analysis in response to the specifics of the case as we go.

Chang proposes this account to shed light on the relationship between the historical analysis of cases in science and the contribution such analyses might make to philosophy of science; his idea of epistemic iteration also provides a tool for understanding how we learn from cases in feminist science studies. In his examples, Chang is particularly interested in the development and clarification of new scientific concepts, challenges to background assumptions, the reframing of problems, and proposals for alternative hypotheses, all of which he describes as part of epistemic iteration. As we shall see, these are all elements of good feminist case studies, as well.

Anderson and Feminist Values

Anderson's (2004) analysis of Stewart et al.'s (1997) research on divorce is such a case study. Anderson offers an abstract understanding of the role of values in scientific inquiry in the first part of her article and expands our understanding of what the interplay between science and values can accomplish through a detailed analysis of the case in the second half. Thus her method can be read as following the general outline of epistemic iteration suggested by Chang.

Anderson begins with an exploration of the value-free ideal. She follows Hugh Lacey (1999) in distinguishing between the impartiality and neutrality of scientific theories. A scientific theory is *impartial* if noncognitive (moral or political) values play no role in its acceptance, and it is *neutral* if it neither presupposes nor supports any moral or political values. Anderson's main focus is on neutrality. She notes that the two concepts are logically independent: a theory could be impartially supported by evidence that presupposed values (for example, if the concepts through which the data were classified were value-laden concepts) and be judged a better theory than its rivals, perhaps because it was more fruitful. Or an impartially supported theory might provide better support for one set of values than another.

There are two sorts of neutrality: presupposition neutrality and implication neutrality. Consequently, Anderson asks both whether it is possible that presupposing values can shape research in a way that systematically improves the science and whether science can reveal that some evaluative judgments are better supported than others. Anderson considers two arguments that are typically used to support the claim that neither of these two types of nonneutrality can produce good science. The first is psychological and addresses presupposition neutrality. The claim is that when values are presupposed, they prevent an impartial assessment of the evidence. That is, any science that presupposes particular values will be distorted by those values. She argues that this conclusion follows only if these values are held dogmatically. A value is held dogmatically if it is not subject to revision based on empirical evidence and so not supported in the same way as beliefs about matters of fact. Presupposing values only prevents impartiality if values are always held dogmatically—a view that depends on the idea that there is a difference between values and facts in this respect. If values can be and are revised when confronted by empirical evidence, then they function no differently than background beliefs, and hence they should be no more problematic. As we shall see, Anderson argues that at least some values are revisable based on experience and so not held dogmatically.

The second type of argument is instrumentalist. Evidence cannot be relevant to determining whether our ultimate or most basic values are right or wrong since ultimate values cannot be argued for. Evidence, then, is only useful for determining the *means* to achieve ultimate values but not for determining which values should be realized. However, Anderson objects that if we were to take this view seriously, it would mean that it would never be possible to have evidence for our value judgments that something was bad or good. On the contrary, Anderson argues that our experience can and does provide evidence that supports such evaluative judgments. She thinks this is particularly clear for our emotional experiences. Emotional experiences are "affectively colored experiences of persons, things, events, or states of the world" (Anderson 2004, 9). As such, emotions are signals of, and hence evidence for, the features of the world that are salient for us as subjects of these emotions, and, consequently, they serve as indicators of what we value—or, put another way, as evidence for value judgments.

To make this clearer, Anderson (2004, 9) considers what we require of evidence: "To count as presenting evidence, a mental state must a) have cognitive content, b) be independent of what it is supposed to be evidence for, and c) be defeasible—accountable and hence responsive to the way the world is." Emotions meet all three requirements according to Anderson. They have cognitive content—they represent the world as having certain features. For example, the awe felt when viewing the California redwoods represents them as splendid (Anderson 2004, 9). Emotions are independent of what they are evidence for in the sense that they are not self-confirming. I may love someone in part because I perceive that they are worthy of my love, and that love may die if they engage in behavior that repels me. Emotions are also defeasible as evidence in that they are responsive to reality—emotional responses alter in response to our experiences. Anderson concludes that values are not science free, since value judgments function like empirical hypotheses in that they are responsive to evidence, and because values are not science free, science is not neutral.

The idea that good science must be neutral is thus dependent on a notion of values under which they are never empirically supported and are always held dogmatically, and so when science presupposes values, they will always drive the inquiry toward a preordained conclusion. In addition, according to this view, science cannot imply values, because they are not amenable to evidence—again, because they are held dogmatically and, consequently, prevent proper assessment of evidence. But in both circumstances, it is the belief that values can only be held dogmatically that is the problem. Anderson concludes that the insistence on neutrality is misconceived because of this incorrect view about values. Many values are indeed responsive to evidence, particularly the evidence of our emotional experiences, and they also play a positive epistemic role in that they enable the identification of features salient to scientific investigation—the features of the world that matter to us.

Anderson next turns to the examination of a specific case: Stewart et al.'s research on divorce. Her stated goal is to use the case to construct a model of the "bidirectional influence of facts and values" that her philosophical argument from the previous section suggests is possible (Anderson 2004, 11). This bidirectionality involves values shaping the research while remaining responsive to the evidence. Her analysis of the case serves as a concrete instance of the abstract philosophical account, but, at the same time, it provides the opportunity for revising and improving on that abstraction.

While Anderson does not explicitly define what she takes to be feminist values, I will treat them as values that both are informed by and promote an awareness of how power relations may be distributed along lines of gender with the goal of redressing inequalities that result through that distribution. Minimally, such values require a commitment to considering whether gender makes a difference to the research. Anderson's case study provides an examination of how such values function at eight stages of Stewart et al.'s research: background interests give rise to the research questions, the framing of those questions, the understanding of the object of inquiry, the making of decisions about what data to collect, the generation and sampling of data, the analysis of the data including the choice of technique for analysis, the decision about when to end data analysis, and what conclusions are drawn.[7]

I focus primarily on just one of these stages: Anderson's discussion of how values affect the conception of an object of inquiry. In the study of divorce, there are a variety of such objects that need to be considered, but prominent among these are "divorce" and "family." Stewart's research team acknowledges these objects of inquiry as "thickly" described—that is, these concepts include both factual and value aspects. Anderson notes that, for example, the feminist values incorporated in the concept of divorce used by Stewart's team differ from those incorporated into Judith Wallerstein's earlier research on divorce (Wallerstein and Kelly 1980; Wallerstein, Lewis, and Blakeslee 2000). Feminists challenge the traditional model of the family in which spousal roles are aligned with parental roles. Relative to such traditional values, divorce is a disruption of that alignment and, as such, is construed as negative. Because feminists challenge many of the features of traditionally gendered family roles and generally have a more flexible conception of family, Stewart et al.'s conscious incorporation of feminist values led to an approach to divorce that did not include this presupposition.

This difference in value orientation is reflected in the key concepts through which the objects of inquiry are understood. In Wallerstein's research, divorce is conceived of as a loss or trauma, in part because of the traditional conception of family underlying the research. Stewart's team, in contrast, took divorce to be a process of adjustment to a new state rather than a traumatic disruption of a preferred state. As a result, there are at least two important differences between Stewart's team's understanding of divorce and that of Wallerstein. First, divorce is not treated as a one-time event with an aftermath but rather as an ongoing life adjustment. Second, the process of adjustment is open ended, allowing for both positive and negative effects.

The analysis makes it clear that both examples of research on divorce incorporate values. It is not that one is value free and the other value laden. The value presupposition that the traditional family promotes well-being for children (and for parents) results in a conception of divorce as a traumatic event in Wallerstein's research. Alternatively, the feminist conception of family that Stewart's team is working with does not require the alignment of spousal and parental roles and, as a result, is open to seeing divorce as potentially neutral or positive.

Since Wallerstein's framing of divorce as a trauma or loss calls for researchers to focus on the negative, these differing values also shape differences in data collection and analysis. The feminist values that undergird Stewart et al.'s research allow the possibility that the traditional framework is not always the best configuration for everyone—that alternative approaches may be more fulfilling and provide greater likelihood of well-being given the differences among people. Stewart et al.'s approach is thus open to collection of a wider variety of data, making it more empirically robust. This result supports the philosophical argument against implication neutrality: some values lead to science that better exemplifies cognitive values such as empirical adequacy, consistency, fruitfulness, and others.

In addition, the question of whether divorce can have positive and not only negative effects is open to empirical scrutiny. Anderson's account of how experience provides evidence for values is relevant here. The question of how good or bad divorce might be is subject to the evidence of experience—the emotional experiences of those researched. Stewart's team's conception of the objects of inquiry allows for both negative and positive experiences to count as evidence for the effects of divorce, and so the way the team conceptualizes the objects of inquiry allows for a consideration of the all of the evidence (unlike Wallerstein's approach, which focuses only on the negative effects). Thus, the case also illustrates how research can presuppose feminist values nondogmatically.[8]

As part of his account, Chang (2012a, 111) argues that once abstract ideas are generated out of cases, they need to meet two criteria, cogency and applicability:

> Once an abstract idea has been generated, it needs to show its worth in two different ways. First of all, its cogency needs to be demonstrated through further abstract considerations and arguments. This is where philosophy takes up the reins again, to examine carefully what has been generated through historiographical necessity. If the abstract idea is deemed to be cogent in itself, its range of applicability needs to be checked. This can only be done by . . . the framing of various other concrete episodes, with history in the driving seat again. An abstraction becomes general only when it has been applied widely. Successful application functions as confirmation, but without the presumption of universality in what is confirmed.

Although Chang does not specifically define *cogency* and *applicability*, his usage indicates that an abstraction is cogent if it is philosophically coherent and able to provide understanding. An abstraction is applicable if the analysis it offers can be transported usefully to other cases. Abstractions from cases are shown to be cogent—coherent and able to provide understanding—through philosophical argument and further abstract consideration of specific cases.

Anderson begins by using philosophical arguments to criticize the claim that science is neutral. These philosophical arguments lay the groundwork for her analysis of the divorce case study, but they only show the possibility of value presupposition and implication in good science (its nonneutrality). Her analysis of Stewart et al.'s research shows that values not only possibly but actually do work in science in these ways. The abstract philosophical point is illustrated and worked out through the detailed analysis of the case, and the cogency of Anderson's approach is partially demonstrated in this way.

Anderson's analysis of the Stewart et al. case also begins to address the second of Chang's criteria, applicability. Although she is only considering one case, as she works back and forth between the case and her philosophical analysis, she models what it is to apply the framework. We see the concrete example of the differences that the value assumptions underlying the concept of divorce make. The understanding of how such assumptions work to shape research is made clearer through treating the case as an episode of the philosophical abstraction and can be used in future analysis of other cases.

Chang's idea of treating a case as an episode works in this way. The success of the application of the philosophical framework offers good reason to think that the framework will aid in understanding other similar cases, as well, but also gives us guidance in how to use the framework—including suggestions about what might count as a similar case that come from the local context—that is, what aspects of the case should be scrutinized. These clues may, in turn, aid in understanding how we can take knowledge from one case and use it elsewhere. As we shall see, the discussion of Lloyd's extended case study of research on female orgasm shows similarities to Anderson's work. Just as Anderson analyzes the way that values affect the understanding of the object of inquiry (divorce), Lloyd explores the way that values shape the understanding of the object of inquiry (female orgasm) in the various research programs that she examines.[9]

Anderson's abstraction of the research process gives those interested in understanding the role of values in science specific points in the research process at which to conduct the examination. This is not an inductive argument in support of the role of values in science. Rather, Anderson fleshes out an abstraction about knowledge production through this concrete episode, which in turn offers an opportunity to clarify and extend the abstraction. The analysis of the case reveals its usefulness, and that usefulness becomes evidence of its adequacy and suggests its further applicability. I now turn to Morgan's work as a way of understanding applicability more clearly.

Morgan: Three Generic Strategies

As we see in the discussion of Chang and as I have argued through the use of Anderson's case study, it is not particularly helpful to think of learning from case studies as induction. The focus of Anderson's case analysis is not the logical structure of the reasoning, nor does she make a sharp distinction between empirical facts and nonempirical values—hangovers from logical empiricism. Morgan (2014) offers another approach to thinking about how cases give researchers epistemic leverage that similarly escapes those bonds. She frames the question in the following way: What allows us to take what we learn from a case and move it to another site—to "resituate" it? Morgan proposes three epistemic strategies that she calls "generic" in two senses: they are not only used with cases, and they are not specific to any particular discipline. She describes these three different strategies as follows: (1) stepping-stones or bridges, (2) ladders, and (3) representative or typical. I will only consider the first two strategies.

Stepping-stones involve taking local knowledge and directly applying it to some other location—think of crossing a stream by going from stone to stone. This local-to-local transfer of knowledge "relies on establishing sufficient similarity between the contexts, events, elements, and causal processes between two sites to allow the resituating of the findings from one domain to another" (Morgan 2014, 1015). This may be accomplished as a step-by-step comparison of the similarities in the two sites, or it might be more like a "bridge" where, in addition to the point-by-point comparison, there is an overarching argument about the similarity of the two cases—that they are of the same sort in some fundamental way.

The second strategy moves from one case to another through extracting or abstracting what are taken to be key elements of the case. In this process of abstraction, they are "decontextualized" (Leonelli 2009, 2011) and described through more general contexts. Morgan characterizes this process as going up a ladder to the abstraction and then back down to the new case or cases—often, since the concepts are abstracted, they are able to function in multiple cases. Again, she cautions that abstraction is not induction; the move is not from the particular to the general, nor is it even an inference, although it bears some similarity to generalization in that the abstract concepts are available for multiple sites since they are decontextualized. Because abstraction makes the concepts more widely available, it may look as though this is a more powerful strategy than the stepping-stones strategy. However, Morgan points out that in order to abstract up the ladder, one needs to have paid close attention to the original site—the concepts have to fit with, or be similar enough to, the details of the case from which they are extracted (the account must be accurate), and it is very easy to get them wrong. Additionally, once we go up the ladder, we still need to get back down if the abstraction is to be useful. That also means that a detailed comparison of the similarities between the various sites and the original site must be carried out.[10]

Using Morgan's strategies to analyze Anderson's case study of divorce research, it appears that at least one aspect of Anderson's work functions as a variation of the "ladder up" approach, Morgan's second strategy. Anderson takes features of the case—for example, the way that values shape the understanding of the objects of inquiry—and abstracts a framework for analyzing how those values direct research to focus on some aspects of the object of inquiry rather than others. Her comparison of Stewart et al.'s research with Wallenstein's reveals how values—what matters to the researchers—shape data collection and the relevance of evidence differently. Stewart's team's research takes factors to be relevant that differ from those Wallenstein's does primarily because the value assumptions underlying the concept of divorce are not shared. The fact that Anderson is comparing two approaches to research with different value assumptions but on the same topic (divorce) informs the abstraction, allowing her to isolate differences in how the values shape the questions, produce alternative understandings of the object of inquiry, lead to different decisions about what data to collect, and so on.

Chang's iterative element also appears in the analysis. Anderson does not move from the concrete features of the case to abstraction directly but rather uses the stylized (abstract) account of the stages of research. In addition, she uses an abstract *philosophical* argument about the possible interactions between science and values focusing on the claim that science should be neutral. The philosophical analysis presents the possibilities—how values can affect research—but the analysis of the two cases of divorce research is used to establish an actuality—how values did function in these cases: for Stewart, values function positively; for Wallenstein, negatively. The successful use of the philosophical analysis thus both depends on and is supported by the case study. Anderson's framework shapes her analysis, but then the value of the framework as an abstraction is vindicated by the analysis. This apparent circularity does not undermine the account, since the dependency and support are of different types. The philosophical argument establishes the possibility that good science can violate both presupposition neutrality and implication neutrality. But it is the case study that provides evidence that this is not just a possibility but an actuality.

The case study also shows how the abstract can be made concrete. As Morgan (2014) notes, the ladder-up strategy decontextualizes key features of the case—in the example that I have used, the role values play in how the object is conceived—but the question of how and where it is legitimate to "take the ladder back down" is problematic, precisely because of the decontextualization. What we know about one episode does not necessarily tell us what we need to know to understand another. But what we do learn in the case study is the details of the case—what belongs to the context—and such details tell us what similarities to look for that will allow us to make our way back down to a new case. Any increase in understanding that results from a successful analysis of the case must also include an awareness of what matters when we attempt to transport that understanding elsewhere, what is and is not relevant in the new context. Thus, the case study aids in understanding how to identify the limits of abstraction, as well.[11]

Lloyd: Research on the Female Orgasm

Anderson's case study focuses on a comparison of two approaches to a particular research topic. While she uses previous research as a contrast to highlight Stewart's team's commitment to explicitly feminist values, the analysis is circumscribed by the specifics of the two cases that she compares. Lloyd's (2005) analysis of research on the female orgasm is a more extended case study that looks at many research programs that she comes to see as sharing specific commitments she finds problematic. The two analyses differ in that Anderson, in looking at how different value commitments affect the results of research, starts from the values and works out to the implications of those values, whereas Lloyd begins with the results—different evolutionary accounts of female orgasm—and investigates what the values are that lead to the results.

Lloyd is working primarily at two levels of abstraction. The broadest is defined by subject matter—research on female orgasm—and it is for this reason that I treat the entire work as a case study of that subject. The more fine-grained level is the examination of the individual approaches. These might each be thought of as cases; however, since Lloyd's purpose is to investigate the nature of the body of extant research on this subject, I identify the case in relation to that project. It is the entire field that is the object of study, and the various approaches are studied in that context. As we shall see, Lloyd groups the approaches together in order to make claims about features the approaches share. She examines each with enough specificity to note their similarities and differences. Individuation of a case—what a case is a case of—is relative to the goal of the research. Lloyd's aim is to explore the extent to which sexist and other unwarranted assumptions create problems for research on this topic, and for this reason I treat the work as a case study of research in the field.

Lloyd proceeds by examining all evolutionary accounts that were available at the time. She does not cherry-pick examples and so avoids one of the concerns that Pitt raises about the use of case studies. Of central concern to Lloyd is why a theory with good evidence in support of it—the byproduct account proposed by Donald Symons in 1979—should be rejected in favor of theories that have less evidential support. Symons's (1979) account, unlike the others Lloyd looks at, proposes that the female orgasm does not serve a direct role in evolution but rather is similar to male nipples in that it is a remnant of the similar biological development of males and females—a byproduct. This is the only account among the twenty-one she explores that is not dependent on the biases and background assumptions that she argues are problematic for the others.

Lloyd discusses the twenty-one evolutionary accounts in enough detail to discern features that lead to her grouping them into four types: pair-bond accounts, a catchall "other" category consisting of various other evolutionary accounts (non-pair-bond and female-centered accounts), a byproduct account, and sperm-competition accounts. To organize her analysis, she identifies central requirements that any evolutionary account must meet: (1) the trait must actually exist, (2) a connection between genetics and that trait must hold, (3) that connection must be specifically between the genetic reproductive success and the trait, (4) the mechanism through which the link occurs must be found, (5) an historical account of how the current trait came to be as it is has to be presented, and (6) all the assumptions in the account should be tested against the available evidence (Lloyd 2005, 47–48). These are features that are applicable to all evolutionary explanations and not specific to explanations of female orgasm. These requirements provide a means to identify the background assumptions of the particular accounts. The pair-bond accounts, for instance, offer a different type of mechanism through which female orgasm brings about genetic reproductive success compared with sperm-competition accounts. All evolutionary accounts make assumptions relative to these six requirements. For example, in order to meet the requirement that the trait actually exists, assumptions need to be made about its identification. The final requirement is that all such assumptions need to be responsive to the available evidence. Through examining the assumptions made in each account—for example, assumptions about the mechanism through which the trait under consideration is linked to genetic reproductive success—Lloyd identifies the problematic background assumptions that result in inadequate consideration of the evidence.

How does Lloyd's examination of the individual approaches lead to her conclusion that sexist and other unwarranted assumptions are problematic for the broader case of evolutionary theorizing about the female orgasm? I will focus on only one of the sites at which assumptions may come into play: identification of the mechanism through which the trait is linked to reproductive success. At the particular level, Lloyd's analysis uses a strategy that looks very much like Morgan's stepping-stones strategy. She begins her discussion of pair-bond accounts with a detailed analysis of the account given by Desmond Morris (1967). While there are a number of features of this account that she highlights, a key element appears in nearly all other pair-bond accounts: the assumption that the function of the female orgasm is to play a role in pair-bonding. She identifies this assumption in the Morris approach.[12] Her identification of the assumption and the role that it plays in Morris's account aids in the analysis of other pair-bond approaches. She takes what she establishes locally and uses it as a guide to identify this element in other research—thus, it serves as a stepping-stone. This strategy for picking out commonalities is combined with an abstracting strategy (ladder up) leading her to one of the primary assumptions that nearly all accounts (not only pair-bond) make: "the function of the female orgasm is to play some role in intercourse" (Lloyd 2005, 75).

This assumption is in turn informed by two key background assumptions that guide most of this research (with the exception of the Symons account): first, the adaptationist assumption that "natural selection, rather than other evolutionary forces, directly shaped the trait into its present form, or that natural selection is currently maintaining the trait in the population" (Lloyd 2005, 230); and second, "the androcentric assumption that males are taken to be the normal type or the exemplar, while to the extent that they differ from the male type, females are invisible" (233).[13] It is these assumptions that she claims are fundamentally responsible for blocking proper consideration of the evidence. Human females do not consistently achieve orgasm with intercourse, and they frequently have orgasm through other means than intercourse. This evidence would seem to count against the importance of the role of orgasm for reproductive success, and any account assuming that importance without explaining these anomalies is problematic.

Although it also has problems, Lloyd prefers Symons's account, because its underlying assumption differs from the other twenty accounts in ways relevant to what counts as evidence. Symons's assumption is that female orgasm is a result of evolutionary forces, but not necessarily a direct result. He argues that it is a byproduct of evolution—a potential in all female mammals but only activated in some (among them, humans). While orgasm in males is necessary for reproduction, it is not in females, but the biological development of males and females is parallel in such a way that the features that lead to orgasm in males (nerves, erectile tissues, etc.) are also present in females. Female orgasm is thus a byproduct of human evolution in much the same way that male nipples are a byproduct. Symons employs an evolutionary assumption that is open to a broader range of evidence that allows for the possibility that female orgasm does not play a role in reproductive success. Lloyd argues that this account is more compatible with all the available evidence than the others.

Lloyd closes her extended case study with a discussion of what can be learned from it using philosophical accounts that have been proposed for the analysis of the role of values in science. There are two main issues that she is concerned with here. The first is how to think of values. She opts to treat them as background assumptions, using Helen Longino's contextual empiricism (1999, 2001). According to Longino, observations only become evidence in relation to background beliefs, assumptions, and values in particular contexts. As a result, theories (or hypotheses) are underdetermined by evidence. As Lloyd (2005, 242) puts it, "Thus, technically, we only have 'data' until background assumptions make it 'evidence' for or against a particular hypothesis." Thus, values, including feminist values, play a role in science by indicating the salience of data and thus its evidential role, filling the gap between the evidence and the theory.

Among the assumptions shaping what counts as evidence are assumptions about the nature of the objects of inquiry. In considering the assumptions underlying research on the female orgasm, Lloyd (2005, 241) notes that assumptions about the nature of the object of inquiry frame the questions (and thus constrain the set of possible answers): "Inquiry into the evolutionary origins of female orgasm requires an evolutionary answer." But other factors such as the interests (and thus values) of researchers constrain the answers, as well, since they further determine which questions are asked.

This analysis brings us to the second issue: the role of values. Once values are recognized as ineliminable from science, we need to be able to determine when they are distorting and when improving scientific knowledge. That is, it is necessary to distinguish between illegitimate (biasing) and legitimate roles for values. To address this issue, Lloyd turns to Anderson's (1995) work on values in science—work that extends Longino's contextual empiricism. Specifically, she refers to Anderson's treatment of values as background assumptions. Such values may be pernicious and potentially distorting of knowledge if they are not themselves responsive to evidence. Lloyd argues that most of the evolutionary accounts of female orgasm do not meet this standard. Symons's account stands out in that its assumptions are responsive to all the available evidence.[14]

Feminist values are relevant here as well, since they inform Lloyd's feminist critique of the androcentric commitments that researchers on female orgasm have held. As previously noted, feminist values include a commitment to considering the relevance of gender. Lloyd argues that the androcentric assumption that male orgasm (and its evolutionary explanation) should serve as an exemplar for the explanation of female orgasm blocks the proper consideration of evidence. That assumption (together with adaptationist assumptions) informs an understanding of what counts as evidence. Based on the androcentric assumptions of the majority of the accounts, the infrequency of female orgasm during intercourse and its presence in other circumstances is less relevant than that such female orgasm occurs at all. Since these androcentric assumptions are shared by the community of researchers, it is difficult to identify them as problematic from within the community. Feminist critique provides the wedge for doing so through its commitment to interrogating gender. The androcentric background assumption should answer to all the available evidence, as should all background assumptions if they are to avoid pernicious—that is to say, knowledge-distorting—bias. In other words, assumptions shaped by values, like androcentrism, should not be held dogmatically.

Lloyd also argues that the success she has in thinking about the biases in this case study as background assumptions in Longino's sense provides support for contextual empiricism. Her argument thus reveals the sort of epistemic iteration that Chang claims is a feature of case studies in the history and philosophy of science. Lloyd takes the philosophical framework provided by Longino and applies it to her investigation (demonstrating applicability). The analysis of the case using that framework is cogent—it is coherent and provides a fuller understanding of what has gone awry than other frameworks that she considers (such as those of Philip Kitcher [1993] and Miriam Solomon [1994]).

In the previous section, I claimed that one way in which we learn from case studies is that they aid in identifying relevant similarities between and among cases. If we use the eight stages of research that Anderson (2005) describes in her discussion of divorce research, we can look for a similarity in the way that values shape the understanding of the object of inquiry in research on female orgasm. As we have seen, Lloyd looks specifically at adaptationist and androcentric assumptions and identifies several that are relevant. For example, she identifies the assumption that female orgasm should be examined only as it appears with intercourse as carrying with it an understanding of female sexuality that treats it as equivalent to reproductive (procreative) sexuality. It is consequently an assumption that limits the evidence considered in a way that Lloyd finds problematic: assuming that the female orgasm must play a role in reproduction and so discounting evidence that suggests it does not.

Thus, both Anderson and Lloyd have identified ways that values can affect the consideration of evidence. Feminist values provide a conception of divorce that allows for the consideration of a broader range of evidence. Sexist values block a consideration of relevant evidence in research on female orgasm—and we should remember also that Symons's research is not value free in contrast but rather is consistent with feminist values in that allows for the inclusion of evidence that comes more directly from women's experience.

Conclusion

Although Lloyd only claims that her case study shows that sexist bias can distort science, in fact, the case study shows far more. Lloyd herself uses it to support contextual empiricism, and she uses Anderson's idea that background assumptions as well as theory must be accountable to the evidence. Similarly, Anderson's examination of Stewart et al.'s work on divorce supports the philosophical account of (at least some) values as responsive to evidence. I have argued that this support is best understood as arguing for the cogency and applicability of these accounts rather than as inductive support.

Anderson's and Lloyd's arguments are structured somewhat differently, although both are iterative in the ways that Chang's analysis clarifies. Anderson supports her conclusion iteratively, starting with a philosophical account that she uses to frame her analysis of the two research programs she examines. The cogency of the analysis serves in turn as support for the viability of the philosophical account. Lloyd abstracts from the research programs investigated and then understands the role of the abstracted background assumptions through applicability of philosophical accounts the philosophical accounts offered by Longino and Anderson.

While Chang's insights guide us in the viability and use of these abstractions, how they fit into a philosophically cogent analysis and are in turn applicable to both the cases examined and potentially (because of their abstract nature) others as well, Morgan's strategies provide a way of understanding how reasoning from cases informs abstraction. Moving from research to abstraction, as Lloyd does, can be interpreted as following what Morgan calls a ladder strategy. Lloyd's (2005, 229) analysis examines various research programs through which she identifies a variety of assumptions that she abstracts to four main background assumptions: adaptationism, androcentrism, procreative focus, and human uniqueness. Of these, she looks most closely at adaptationism, androcentrism, and procreative focus.[15]

Morgan's stepping-stone strategy is also apparent as Lloyd moves from one concrete example of a research program to another. Lloyd first offers an analysis of pair-bond accounts and then finds similar assumptions of adaptationism and androcentrism (and coincident exclusions of evidence) in the other accounts that she considers. The pair-bond account is examined in more detail than the subsequent research programs, suggesting that it serves as the starting point—the first stepping-stone—through which the key features found there can be identified and applied to other accounts.

The philosophical core of both Anderson's and Lloyd's case studies is Longino's contextual empiricism. Interestingly, Longino (2013) herself makes use of the resources of her own account in her recent work exploring research on aggression and sexuality. The analysis of reasoning from case studies that I have outlined here is one in which reasoning from case studies involves abstraction, philosophical argument, and application, which in turn leads to more refined and targeted abstraction, more nuanced philosophical argument, and further application—the pattern of epistemic iteration. In this way, case studies extend our understanding of how values (including feminist values) can operate productively in science.

The analysis of cases in feminist science studies has the potential to reveal more about how we learn from cases. Taking my analysis of Anderson and Lloyd as case studies, I have used the resources offered by Chang and Morgan. I have used Morgan's strategies (both ladder and stepping-stone) to better understand how the case studies operate, and my analysis has been iterative. I consider the accounts that Chang and

Morgan give of reasoning from cases, assess their value for understanding what Anderson and Lloyd are doing, and extend the analysis of the epistemic contributions of case-study work through the analysis of these case studies. I argue that through using the abstract philosophical analysis this work offers, we have a better understanding of the role of case studies in feminist science studies. I have also suggested that a closer examination of how we use case studies can indicate the limits of abstraction from particulars and the circumstances under which we can successfully transport our abstractions to new concrete situations. In effect, I have been reasoning from these cases in much the way that I argue that Anderson and Lloyd reason from theirs.

I close by offering one further reason to value case studies in feminist research. Such work requires close attention to science as it is practiced and so aims at returning philosophical investigation to concrete applications. Since feminist philosophy is a philosophy of action—engaged philosophy—seeking the connection between our philosophical abstractions and the practices of science seems an appropriate pursuit for feminists.

Notes

1. For instance, political science, which had been a heavily case-based discipline, has had methodological debates about the value and appropriate use of case studies during the last two decades. See particularly King, Keohane, and Verba (1994); Goertz and Mahoney (2012).

2. Some examples are Bennett and Checkel (2014); Chang (2012a); Crasnow (2011, 2012); Morgan (2014, 2012); Pitt (2001).

3. The sorts of challenges to feminist critique that characterize it as anti-science argue that by politicizing science, feminists undermine it. Such critiques rely heavily on the traditional view of science as value free and so see attempts to examine underlying assumptions as insertions of ideology where there had been none (except in examples of bad science). Gross and Levitt (1998) are among the best-known proponents of this negative view of feminist philosophy of science. They explicitly accuse Sandra Harding and to a lesser extent Evelyn Fox Keller and Helen Longino of trying to shape science through feminist ideology.

4. This worry follows from the Duhem-Quine thesis, the thesis that a hypothesis is never tested in isolation because in order to perform a test we use background beliefs and auxiliary hypotheses. Suppose, for example, we were to test the hypothesis that water boils at 100 degrees Celsius. In carrying out the

test, we will assume that the test is at sea level, that the water is relatively pure (not mineral laden), that the thermometer used works, etc. Because we are in effect testing the conjunction of all these beliefs together with the hypothesis, if the test result is negative, we do not know *from the test alone* which of the conjuncts should be rejected.

5. Such claims were made in much of the antipostmodernist literature during the late-1990s science wars. For example, Paul Gross (1998) argues that feminist philosophers of science have cherry-picked particular examples of the use of metaphor in the history of research on human reproduction to argue that this research treats the egg as passive and the sperm as active, thus reflecting stereotypical ideas about the passive female and active male. He claims that in doing so they ignore examples of research in which the egg plays an active role. They analyze the research so that it fits their model.

6. Chang (2012a, 110–11) suggests that, rather than referring to these as case studies, we talk about them as "episodes." The analogy that he makes is to episodes of a television series, where we would not think of a particular episode as an instance of the series, the particular to some general that the series represents; rather, the episode is one version of the working out of the abstract ideas of who the characters are and what situation they find themselves in.

7. Anderson calls these "stylized" versions of the research process (Anderson 2004, 11). I take it that they are stylized in that they typically do not occur either distinctly or sequentially.

8. To further explore the question of dogmatism, Anderson looks at other stages of research by Stewart's team to see that they are open to the consideration of evidence that counts against their value-formed understanding of the object of inquiry. She argues that the team actively sought evidence that would count against their preliminary findings.

9. My discussion is an interpretation of what Lloyd does rather than a claim that she follows Anderson's lead. Lloyd's book was published in 2005, and Anderson's divorce article first appeared in 2004, so Lloyd may not have been aware of Anderson's framework at the time that she was writing the book.

10. The question of which factors are relevant and therefore determine what the case is a case of is a thorny issue. Case studies typically pay attention to detail; however, any account will involve making choices about which details are relevant. One element to consider in making this determination is the purpose for which the case is studied—the research question addressed. This is clearly another area in which values play a role.

11. This is a particularly important point that deserves far more attention than I am able to give it in this chapter. The extent to which abstractions are useful for understanding the concrete—where, when, and how they can be useful—is in need of further exploration. But if one were to follow something like

the strategies outlined here for a variety of cases, perhaps some relevant features could be identified.

12. I am reconstructing her argument here, not her reasoning process.

13. There are four assumptions that Lloyd highlights in the accounts. In addition to the adaptationist and androcentric assumptions, she also identifies a procreative-process assumption, that all evolutionarily significant sex is reproductive, and an assumption that female orgasm is unique in humans.

14. Lloyd notes that while the quality of evidence on female sexuality is questionable on a variety of grounds (lack of diversity, much of it not very recent), she is arguing that most of the accounts she considers should still and do not conform to that evidence.

15. Arguably, procreative focus is really a result of androcentrism combined with heterosexism in that it takes the male procreative role of orgasm in heterosexual intercourse as the norm.

References

Anderson, Elizabeth. 1995. "Knowledge, Human Interests, and Objectivity in Feminist Epistemology." *Philosophical Topics* 23 (2): 27–58.

———. 2004. "Uses of Values Judgments in Science: A General Argument, with Lessons from a Case Study of Feminist Research on Divorce." *Hypatia* 19: 1–24.

Bennett, Andrew, and Jeffrey Checkel, eds. 2014. *Process Tracing: From Metaphor to Analytic Tool*. Cambridge: Cambridge University Press.

Chang, Hasok. 2004. *Inventing Temperature: Measurement and Scientific Progress*. New York: Oxford University Press.

———. 2012a. "Beyond Case-Studies: History as Philosophy." In *Integrating History and Philosophy of Science: Problems and Prospects*, edited by Seymour Mauskopf and Tad Schmaltz, 109–24. Boston Studies in the Philosophy of Science 263. Dordrecht, Netherlands: Springer.

———. 2012b. *Is Water H₂O? Evidence, Realism and Pluralism*. Dordrecht, Netherlands: Springer.

Crasnow, Sharon. 2011. "Evidence for Use: Causal Pluralism and the Role of Case Studies in Political Science Research." *Philosophy of the Social Sciences* 41 (1): 26–49.

———. 2012. "The Role of Case Study Research in Political Science: Evidence for Causal Claims." *Philosophy of Science* 79 (5): 655–66.

Goertz, Gary, and James Mahoney. 2012. *A Tale of Two Cultures: Qualitative and Quantitative Research in the Social Sciences*. Princeton, NJ: Princeton University Press.

Gross, Paul R. 1998. "Bashful Eggs, Macho Sperm, and Tonypandy." In *A House Built on Sand: Exposing Postmodernist Myths about Science*, edited by Noretta Koertge, 59–70. New York: Oxford University Press.

Gross, Paul R., and Norman Levitt. 1998. *Higher Superstition: The Academic Left and Its Quarrels with Science*. Baltimore, MD: Johns Hopkins University Press.

King, Gary, Robert Keohane, and Sidney Verba. 1994. *Designing Social Inquiry: Scientific Inference in Qualitative Research*. Princeton, NJ: Princeton University Press.

Kitcher, Philip. 1993. *The Advancement of Science: Science without Legend, Objectivity without Illusions*. New York: Oxford University Press.

Lacey, Hugh. 1999. *Is Science Value Free? Values and Scientific Understanding*. New York: Routledge.

Leonelli, Sabina. 2009. "On the Locality of Data and Claims about Phenomena." *Philosophy of Science* 76 (5): 737–49.

———. 2011. "Packaging Small Facts for Re-Use: Databases in Model Organism Biology." In *How Well Do Facts Travel?*, edited by Peter Howlett and Mary S. Morgan, 325–48. Cambridge: Cambridge University Press.

Lloyd, Elisabeth A. 2005. *The Case of the Female Orgasm: Bias in the Science of Evolution*. Cambridge, MA: Harvard University Press.

Longino, Helen E. 1990. *Science as Social Knowledge*. Princeton, NJ: Princeton University Press.

———. 2001. *The Fate of Knowledge*. Princeton, NJ: Princeton University Press.

———. 2013. *Studying Human Behavior: How Scientists Investigate Aggression and Sexuality*. Chicago: University of Chicago Press.

Morgan, Mary S. 2012. "Case Studies: One Observation or Many? Justification or Discovery?" *Philosophy of Science* 79 (5): 667–77.

———. 2014. "Resituating Knowledge: Generic Strategies and Case Studies." *Philosophy of Science* 81 (5): 1012–24.

Morris, Desmond. 1967. *The Naked Ape: A Zoologist's Study of the Human Animal*. New York: McGraw-Hill.

Pitt, Joseph C. 2001. "The Dilemma of Case Studies: Toward a Heraclitian Philosophy of Science." *Perspectives on Science* 9 (4): 373–82.

Richardson, Sarah S. 2010. "Feminist Philosophy of Science: History, Contributions, and Challenges." *Synthese* 177: 337–62.

———. 2013. *Sex Itself: The Search for the Male and Female in the Human Genome*. Chicago: University of Chicago Press.

Solomon, Miriam. 1994. "Multivariate Models of Scientific Change." *Proceedings of the Biennial Meeting of the Philosophy of Science Association* 1994 (2): 287–97.

Stewart, Abigail J., Anne P. Copeland, Nila Lane Chester, Janet E. Malley, and Nicole B. Barenbaum. 1997. *Separating Together: How Divorce Transforms Families*. New York: Guilford Press.

Symons, Donald. 1979. *The Evolution of Human Sexuality*. New York: Oxford University Press.

Wallerstein, Judith S., and Joan B. Kelly. 1980. *Surviving the Breakup: How Children and Parents Cope with Divorce*. New York: Basic Books.

Wallerstein, Judith, Julia Lewis, and Sandra Blakeslee. 2000. *The Unexpected Legacy of Divorce*. New York: Hyperion.

PART 2

CRITIQUING THE PRACTICE:
THE CASE OF PHILOSOPHY

Chapter 4

The Power and Perils of Example
"Literizing Is Not Theorizing"

LORRAINE CODE

I

The comment cited in the title of this chapter—"literizing is not theorizing"—comes from an anonymous, relentlessly negative review of the manuscript for *Epistemic Responsibility* (Code 1987). This review contributed
to the proposal's rejection from publication by the press to which it was
first submitted. The reviewer was condemning the manuscript, in no small
part, for its appeals to extended examples from literature—from fiction
and/or literary biographies, explicitly populated narratives that draw from
the lives and situations of specific people, be they fictitious or real. These
appeals, written to amplify the book's philosophical position, might not elicit
analogous criticisms in the second decade of the twenty-first century, but
at that time appeals to literature, whether to fiction or narrative biography,
were starkly unorthodox. *S*-knows-that-*p* articulations of necessary and
sufficient conditions for making and evaluating knowledge claims purportedly demonstrated the clearest route toward objectivity and universality,
unsullied by the putatively eccentric particularities that are the stuff of
which literature is made. The legacy of logical positivism was tenacious in
this reader's response: narrated examples carried an unacceptable level of
experiential specificity, which hampered the work's achievements. Prior to
the development of social epistemology and the softening of a rigid divide

between continental and orthodox Anglo-American epistemology, it was not easy to claim space or to anticipate uptake for thoughts such as the manuscript proposed. Unusually and defiantly for state-of-the-art 1980s Anglo-American philosophy, *Epistemic Responsibility* explicitly situates itself within epistemology. Yet, still verging on the unorthodox, it works with ethical questions and elaborated, narrated case examples[1]—several drawn from literature, broadly conceived—to expose and explore the lived ethical-epistemological responsibilities with which would-be knowers seeking, creating, and promulgating certain kinds of knowledge have to engage. The critic cited is reading the larger purposes of this approach as irrelevant and naïve by late-1980s epistemic standards perhaps because, in the manuscript, the "storied" approach is neither announced nor framed as defying philosophical-epistemological orthodoxy. The book's intention is to amplify, to supply some missing pieces to state-of-the-art epistemology: asking, incredulously, what *could* follow—or not—for human lives from knowing, with reasonable certainty, the bare and simplistic fact of a cat's being on the mat, a frequently invoked example in 1980s Anglo-American epistemology, and responding, "Nothing of great import."

This counterproposal in *Epistemic Responsibility* to received epistemological practice amounts to a contention that commitments to establishing guidelines or formulating principles for knowing well, in ordinary human lives, could not responsibly achieve their purpose without fleshed-out, situated-populated examples conveying a sense of the lived implications of the questions and circumstances that generated them. Here, pending elaboration, knowing responsibly requires practices of taking care to know well, of commitments to attending to the would-be "known" in its situatedness, multiple modalities, diverse implications—if rarely all at once or in their totality. It bypasses an overarching epistemological mandate of determining necessary and sufficient conditions for empirical knowledge *tout court*. Nor does it imply that knowing without "literizing" is unworthy of its status. Hence, the "literizing is not theorizing" charge is incongruous when it is directed to this manuscript whose title announces its intention to contest rigidly defended boundaries separating epistemology and ethics/politics, which characterized Anglo-American philosophy in the 1980s before the advent of social epistemology. The proposal announced no intention to discredit empiricist epistemology per se, but it proposed to show how it could be enhanced, humanized, redirected by taking a significantly different—if contiguous—path, where epistemic appropriateness could entail taking subjectivities into account.

To anticipate, recall the starkness of a different, related division: the antipathy between Anglo-American and continental philosophy, which exerted as powerful a force in the 1980s as it still does, if less starkly, in the early twenty-first century. For many anglophone epistemologists, then, a rapprochement between these schools was inconceivable: the boundaries were closely monitored. So, in declaring "literizing is not theorizing," the reviewer is contending that no exact, unambiguous knowledge claims could be offered for verification or falsification from references to novels or other literary forms. These were neither worthy sources of knowledge nor contributions to viable epistemic practice: the approach violated canonical theories and practices of Anglo-American knowledge making *tout court*. The manuscript was rejected by that press, if perhaps not for these reasons alone.

Among targets of the "literizing" criticism were two extended case analyses in the manuscript: of Edmund Gosse's *Father and Son* and William Styron's *Sophie's Choice*. Gosse (1907) tells a semiautobiographical story of the intransigence late-nineteenth-century British naturalists encountered—his father, Philip Gosse, eminent among them—in endeavoring to realize/to know, and to convince a lay community, that certain seashells collected along England's south coast confirmed the validity of then-current attempts to discern visual evidence of evolutionary processes at work: no longer to attribute visible and palpable geological change to creationism, to ongoing interventions of the hand of God. I read the book as a novel because of its narrative presentation, despite its being more factually focused than self-declared literary works often are. Drawing on the epistemic projects and conflicts of specific scientists, researchers, and, by extension, ordinary people faced with fundamental challenges to their ontological-epistemological convictions—to an established, sanctioned world view—it captures the complexity of revolutionary cognitive practices attempting to destabilize an entrenched belief system whose "truth" is pivotal to a settled (instituted) epistemic imaginary, and reasonably so.[2] It shows how specifically situated inquirers, separately or together, face profound, drawn-out struggles to know well, where such against-the-grain knowing can rarely be instantaneous, achieved from an idiosyncratic counterexample, or accomplished in solitary isolation.

Differently in Styron's (1979) novel, readers are required to live, to understand—to experience secondhand[3]—the searing anguish of the choice a young mother, Sophie, is coldly, brutally required by Nazi officials to make. Following a cruelly unbearable train journey, concentration-camp guards force her to choose which of her two children is to accompany her into the camp and which one is to go into the gas chamber. This is no sanitized example of stripped-down either/or moments addressing the conundrum of making hard choices. It calls to onlookers and readers after the fact for existential understanding and compassion. It makes an affect-laden appeal of a poignancy commonly ruled out of order in the sanitized epistemic-ethical practices of the 1980s. Trite though this thought may be, such works show something—borrowing from Clare Hemmings (2011)—of "why stories matter" for knowing and understanding responsibly: they show how, despite its equivocal epistemic standing, affect can contribute to such knowing. This explicit epistemic-ethical connection between knowing and affect counts among the reasons why "literizing" contributes richly, if diversely, to theorizing.

Epistemic Responsibility's larger purpose is to expose the minimal resources available to practitioners of postpositivist empiricist orthodoxy, both as theory and in practice, for coming to know: for understanding, addressing, and acting with/upon the detailed, complex human experiences, emotions, and situations such works of fiction—such "literizing"—make palpable. It aims to show by example how inquiry can be enriched and knowing can be enhanced through enlarged examples of knowing/understanding/being: how philosophical engagement with thought and action can require such resources. The passages I cite from *Epistemic Responsibility* are narrations, tellings. Rather than presenting them in the sanitized *S-knows-that-p* form of then-mainstream epistemological orthodoxy, I narrate them with some of the disorder of things retained (*pace* Michel Foucault), the messiness of their detail intact. They focus on particularities, specificities, motivations, and constraints in exposing lived challenges people face in complex, affectively fraught (or affectively rich) situations, in trying to know the circumstances well enough to confer credence, generate understanding, invite incredulity, or prompt action, or not. These tellings need neither begin nor end with particularities: they endeavor to display, in media res, some lived effects for human lives of specific knowings/believings, to invite readers to think and debate with them across analogous and disanalogous situations. Nor need they eschew epistemological orthodoxy: analogies, too, require evaluation for their credibility, pertinence, and explanatory power. They situate/resituate knowing in the world of lived experiences, not naïvely but, at their best, with enhanced prospects of understanding, of informing thoughtful action. Such examples are open to interpretation, contestation, and debate.

A contrast, then, is with the poverty of traditional one-liners, such as "the cat is on the mat," to offer sufficient complexity for the intricacies of putative knowing to be knowledgeably evaluated, and lived, a thought that contests the exemplary status postpositivist epistemology has accorded to such flat-footed empirical claims as "the cat is on the mat" and "the cup is on the table," proffered as exemplars of verifiable foundational knowledge and touchstones for a quasi-Wittgensteinian affirmation, "Now I can go on" (Wittgenstein 1968, 178–79). Setting such one-liners aside need not reduce to cursory affirmations appeals to "situated knowledges," which, in spaces Donna Haraway (1991) has opened, play a vital part in feminist and other postempiricist inquiry, especially in social knowledge. Explicitly situated knowledges contribute as significantly to *understanding* as to merely knowing "the furniture of the world," to repeat an old empiricist adage. Haraway's essay shows how working from assumptions that knowledge making and its subject matter are explicitly situated—and that features of the relevant situation can contribute to its success or failure—may be truer to the facts of the matter than nonspecific, dislocated empirical claims frequently are, without descending into relativism.

In "Wrongful Requests and Strategic Refusals to Understand," Gaile Pohlhaus (2011) engages such issues by drawing on Patricia Williams's (1992) story of the poverty of explanation and understanding that would commonly be available from a standard one-liner report to the effect that a woman is refused entry to a Benetton store because she is black. By contrast, in her interpretive-narrative construction of the example, Williams exposes the damaging "socially established patterns from which we interact in and with the world" (Pohlhaus 2011, 225): she recreates the episode's affective tone. She tells of a routine episode of preparing to enter the store, early one evening when the lights were on and people inside were shopping. But a young man inside mouthed the words "we're closed" and would not open the door. In highlighting how such minute details of the scene contributed to what she had learned to recognize as racially odious practices of humiliation and denial, Williams reaffirms the power of narrated examples to tell much more than simplified one-liners can achieve: to convey the "taste," the lived *affect* of an experience. The epistemological point is less that the example offers definitive proof of white-black racism than it is to demonstrate the hermeneutic openings such pertinent narrations can create in ongoing public discourse.

With narrated examples, the challenge is to avoid offering merely anecdotal evidence, with the minimal epistemic respect such evidence garners. Instead, the goals are to convey some sense of the lived knowledge/ignorance/belief situations that produce these epistemic puzzles and to recognize the epistemic anguish invoked in such "situated knowledges" (Haraway 1991). The point is less to condemn anecdotal evidence as such than to expose the slenderness of the challenge it can pose, as a one-time utterance. Anecdotes may catch a hearer's or reader's fancy, prompt investigation, animate thinking and acting; they are not, by definition, insignificant. Yet epistemic puzzles can also generate the interpretive openness that figures in deliberating, interpreting, and evaluating such complexly narrated examples as Pohlhaus engages, which may not wear their epistemic credentials on their sleeves. Multiple readings of the import of such events are possible, often necessary, for knowing "well enough." Teasing out their implications can terminate in a puzzle, generate conflict, and challenge inquirers convinced that seeing is believing. They resist closure. Nor can putative knowers always discern what they are seeing: is it an act of kindness or aggression, a crossing of sexual boundaries, a careless gesture, a policy that benefits or harms them? Narrated events and knowledge claims require time for puzzling over them: a hermeneutic approach. Such are their complexities.

In the working philosophical self-understanding that fuels skepticism about examples, knowledge reduces to information, and a wariness of generalizing from particulars haunts inquiry. For Williams, if such wariness claims regulative status, then particularity/singularity/specificity can claim no space in deliberations committed to entrenched standards of epistemic legitimacy. Analogous issues figure in José Medina's (2013) readings of judicial hearings, in *The Epistemology of Resistance*, where he notes that the "lack of legal justice" in the courtroom may attest to a "lack of hermeneutical justice" in the larger society. Referring to domestic abuse, Medina observes that knowledge may appear to reduce to information, but only a current informant's version or like-minded participants' readings claim a hearing: where no interpretive pushback finds space, and first-person tellings can meet with minimal to no hermeneutical uptake (82–84). In consequence, entire areas of action-informing knowing and not-knowing are cast aside as unworthy, as irrelevant to epistemic inquiry. In a courtroom, such failures are writ large: they are centrally alike to Williams's narrative and to Pohlhaus's reading of Williams.

For twentieth-century philosophers, skepticism about the epistemic value of narrated/situated examples had the effect of widening a schism between analytic and continental philosophy. This claim is not intended to declare a stark opposition between these schools but to conjecture that a wariness of narrated examples (of "literizing") derives from an antipathy toward *hermeneutic* engagement, akin to the antipathy that infused positivist and postpositivist epistemology in twentieth-century anglophone philosophy. The resistance derives from convictions (not unwarranted) about the looseness of interpretation, however careful: its failure to distance itself from the messiness of the everyday world and its frequent—if laudable—resistance to closure muddy the putative clarity of decontextualized analyses of empirical examples drawn from the ordinary dailiness (*allgemeine Alltäglichkeit*) of lives lived in putatively typical situations. The worry is real: its universalization is implausible.

In short, while examples may affirm assumptions of typicality, they also work to unsettle and challenge the exemplary status, the rigidity, of presuppositions and prejudices. Feminist philosophy, in its difficult journey over several decades, affirms such a claim. A consequence may be that exactitude and definitiveness are compromised—the exactitude that sustains the putative epistemic power of standard empirical claims, where no value-laden items, no (allegedly) extraneous specificities find a place. A larger philosophical issue comes with the thought that such exactitude has only ever been an impossible dream whose quasi-Platonic standard-setting status has confined western and northern anglophone epistemology to drawing on a narrow range of post-Cartesian and/or positivistic-minimalist "examples"—of what? In light of these thoughts, the overarching desirability of exactitude also demands critical scrutiny.

For Simone de Beauvoir, Albert Camus, and Jean-Paul Sartre, to name only a few, novels and stories were integral to philosophical practice, yet their "literizing," too, sat uneasily with unreceptive critics, for reasons distantly akin to those proffered by the anonymous reader of *Epistemic Responsibility*. They did not offer the monological, self-announcing empirical "evidence" integral to *real* knowledge, with its established criteria of verification or falsification. Still in twenty-first-century analytic philosophy, long after the emergence of social epistemology, engaging with narrated—"storied"—examples and case studies, with their enlarged thinking about meaning, affect, ontology, and specificity, sits uneasily. For the naysayers, it crosses disciplinary boundaries separating real philosophy from softer, less exact inquiry. But, again, well-narrated examples, case studies, and stories can be sufficiently textured, horizontally and vertically, to nourish deliberation, discussion, and interpretation across diverse populations, both academic and "secular," to draw attention to erroneous yet fixed assumptions. Gosse's work is pertinent here. Teachers elaborating specific real-life effects of war require examples, as do feminist philosophers showing what it has meant for women to live under certain sociopolitical rigidities and African American philosophers and teachers drawing readers into the grinding everydayness of slavery and newer forms of racism. Literary examples need be read neither as infallibly truth-telling nor as fabrications: they open doors to discussion (Was/is it really like that?), dwell in plausibility, and prompt and animate thinking well about the complexity of circumstances to which philosophers and others appeal in elaborating epistemic standards—in ways deeper than responses to the question, What is it like to be a bat? These are *tellings*, not fanciful conjectures (Medina 2013, 43). They inform thinking about how it is to live, think, and act in sociopolitically "thicker" ways than one-liners allow: they situate knowing and acknowledge its affinities with affect. Without pretending merely to displace a false story with a true one, they can generate new knowledges, new ways of thinking about and imagining certain situations and/or their analogues (Pohlhaus 2011).

Examples, stories, and case studies integrated into epistemic practice enable understandings of a depth and sensitivity commonly absent from the affirmations of S's knowing that p found in mainstream epistemology. Such is the purpose of the *Epistemic Responsibility* examples: to prompt understandings that are more than the sum of their empirical parts, to animate forms of engagement not often required for knowing cups on tables—unless these are heirlooms or associated with rituals. Then, there could be a story to be told.

Again, the hermeneutic dimension that narrated examples have introduced into thinking and understanding brings an *affective* significance to inquiry in its textured, interpretive engagements with knowing that is *situated*, not just spatially, but temporally, socially, personally, affectively. (Consider a "secular" reading of hermeneutic practices that figure technically, for such philosophers as Wilhelm Dilthey and Hans-Georg Gadamer, in their derivation from age-old engagements with classical and Biblical texts.) In present-day "secular" philosophy, such examples and counterexamples defy tacit rules that insulate Anglo-American post-positivist epistemology from the idiosyncratic vagaries of everyday life. Yet while some examples may sacrifice exactitude, they open spaces for affect, particularity, power, and the politics of knowing, often reclaiming the epistemic efficacy of analogical thinking as they go. Significantly, they point to the elusiveness of certainty and exactitude. At their best, even in resisting closure, examples affirm the power of "literizing" to enrich "theorizing": to enhance its effects for epistemic-ethical practices—perhaps making it less exact, less verifiable, yet enhancing understanding.

Examples sensitive to situational specificities bring to social epistemology an epistemic humility: they promote reserving judgment and resisting hasty generalization or aggregation; pausing before superimposing simplistic readings onto complex situations; and introducing possibilities with a "consider this" approach rather than presenting definitive readings, invoking stereotypes, or claiming premature closure. To repeat this thought in a positive register: in affirming the epistemic value of humility, examples contribute to the sociality of social epistemology, to understandings not merely of individual implications of ways of knowing but of their social—and political—pertinence and effects.

Thus, for example, Rachel Carson "lived" humility in ways that illustrate its multiply laudable effects and the wisdom it can foster. Doing so did not diminish her. Avoiding any rush to judgment in the face of anomalies in the natural world, yet qualified to pass judgment when she must, Carson was committed to "waiting an extra season or two" before acting. Her judgments are careful and humble, opening space for events, plants, and animals to "speak for themselves"; they are admirable, in consequence. That these judgments are stunningly well informed is evident in her presenting them publicly to demand action even from fiercely skeptical, officially accredited, mostly male/masculine scientists and politicians. Epistemologically, she achieves recognition, if tacitly, for the *affective* tonalities of her rigorous, if again unorthodox, research and writing, presenting examples with the care that invites her readers—professional scientists and "people"—to recognize their import, to care in their turn. It would trivialize the integrity of her way of being to represent her as an epistemic role model: she was so much more.

In the anglophone literary (and real) world, humility is often cast as a negative, downtrodden virtue, if it counts as a virtue at all. Its exemplification in the actions of Uriah Heep, in Charles Dickens's *David Copperfield*, conjures a groveling, hand-wringing, insinuating man repeatedly announcing how "umble" he is, despite actions that attest otherwise. Uriah Heep is not the sole source of disdain for *humility* in English-language parlance, but he counts among them, contributing to its negative, self-abdicating associations. Humility is more and other than this disdain suggests. For José Medina (2013), it manifests in declarations of one's cognitive limitations, honoring distance between self and others—other beings in the world, other things. In good listening it finds a place: stopping to hear, resisting such intrusive pronouncements as "I know just how you feel" in their colonizing aspects. It need by no means be construed as a negative attribute.

For epistemologists, such examples can be problematic. They neither lend themselves to analysis within an S-knows-that-*p* rubric nor admit of one-off, true-or-false assessment. Examples can be messy, ambiguous, neither straightforwardly true nor false; they require interpretation, interrogation, and/or contradiction in themselves and their situated import. Such is true of *Sophie's Choice* and of *Father and Son*. But ambiguity often enriches inquiry, prompts multiple readings, generates debate, and blocks hasty generalization. Beauvoir endorses such a thought, even in the title of *The Ethics of Ambiguity*. Apt examples animate deliberation about incorporating and/or containing and amplifying narrative so that it neither overwhelms analysis nor allows particular detail to displace larger theoretical concerns about why it matters to invoke them, why formal analysis is not enough.

A more delicate aspect of the power of narrated examples is in the way they challenge epistemic individualism, the odd idea that epistemic agency is primarily individualistic and monologic, all the way down. This thought is difficult to explain or to defend, but, simply, in their very existence stories and narratives presuppose and/or require interlocutors: hearers, listeners, readers—uptake. These are no utterances into a void nor straightforward conveyances of information, of prearticulated truths. Even told starkly, in the first person, as in Albert Camus's *The Stranger*, a story's addressive claim is to other people. It shows, recreates, the stark existential singularity, the aloneness of its protagonist, shocking its readers into recognizing the affective complexities he lives. It speaks to others, in spite of itself. Thus Beauvoir's exposure, in collaboration with Gisèle Halimi, of the horrors to which Djamila Boupacha was subjected during the Franco-Algerian war presents an urgent, insistent example to French officialdom (Beauvoir and Halimi 1962): the power of their presentation is manifested in the political consequences it generated. An Algerian woman, Boupacha had been taken captive by the French forces during the France-Algeria conflict and was brutally detained, raped, and publicly tortured in France. Beauvoir and Halimi campaigned vigorously—and ultimately successfully—for her release. Rarely do such tellings generalize without remainder from one situation or circumstance to another, but even when they go part of the way in their singularity, they highlight affinities and dissonances in/across diverse ways of being; they can prompt action.

So, while "literizing" may not be "theorizing" (recalling my erstwhile critic), narratives convey an existential sense of lived experiences, horrors, and vivid emotions not readily understood from punctiform assertions. Rather than enumerating details of a story or singular event(s), they engage with it to expose its implications, provocatively, perhaps to a smug, self-contented readership, perhaps to attuned, receptive readers. They spark recognitions. Rarely do they insulate the affective dimensions from the facts of the matter: they present them, recreate them, expose the challenges they convey. Hence, they can generate enlarged understandings and open doors toward renewed hermeneutic engagement. Often such a narrative becomes a touchstone through subsequent inquiries, as thinkers and writers invoke it to understand the cogency—or otherwise—of certain theories or practices. Thus Uriah Heep has become a point-of-reference figure. In the spaces these examples open for innovative idioms and practices, in their newfound emblematic statuses, such situations recall Ludwig Wittgenstein's (1968) pertinent exclamation, "Now I can go on!" (178–79), thinking about the otherwise-perhaps-opaque implications of everyday events. Fortuitously or otherwise, an apt example can break through an aporia in discursive interactions and prompt thinking in new directions.

II

In consequence of shifts in epistemological practice and a closing of divides between ethics and epistemology since 1987, the place of narrated examples and case studies is no longer as contested as it was for *Epistemic Responsibility*'s critics. Two such developments are germane: the birth and growth of social epistemology, including feminist and critical race epistemology, and the softening of a barrier between continental and analytic philosophy. Such shifts, which gained visibility only after the fact, are variously dated. I connect the entry of social epistemology into Anglo-American philosophy with feminist epistemology's and critical race theory's increasing pertinence in the 1980s and with Edward Craig's shift in *Knowledge and the State of Nature*, which moves from the language of knowledge claims uttered into a void to the language of speakers and hearers. Such works have opened conceptual spaces for social epistemology to claim a hearing.

Although, in the twenty-first century, the accusation "literizing is not theorizing" may have lost its sting, a wariness of reliance on examples persists. One explanation manifests in a continued resistance to singularity, particularity, and specificity that persistently troubles Anglo-American epistemologists, attesting to a worry that individuated examples encourage readers to generalize from one particular and to an assumption that one counterexample can destroy an entire philosophical edifice. Few present-day feminists and/or other Others would work from such assumptions. While practices of generalizing from particulars need to be endorsed with caution, in hermeneutically oriented feminist and postcolonial philosophy, the dichotomy is neither so stark nor so intransigent as such examples imply. It is unclear how or why such a shift will have occurred, but it seems to connect to a willingness among social epistemologists to take into account the poverty of explanation and understanding available from epistemic practices inimical to taking narrated examples seriously: to accord them *epistemological* (as contrasted with anecdotal) significance.

Ongoing wariness may derive from challenges invoked in affirming relevance where no rules obtain, as the "singularity" of some examples suggests. Such processes require explanation and interpretation, and standards of accuracy and pertinence are elusive. But neither are these requirements outrageous. Examples require turning aside from the putatively replicable placeholder status of knowers who could be anyone or everyone and from the placeholder status of medium-sized material objects, both of which heralded a route to certainty in their presumed replicability from place to place, example to example, knower to knower. Well-told examples avoid such accusations: they provide sufficient situational-demographic detail to allow their specificity to claim interpretive/hermeneutic acknowledgment (in Wittgenstein's [1969, 96] sense: "knowledge is in the end based on acknowledgement"). Nor need they threaten a descent into relativism. There is no inevitable connection between examples—even singular examples—and contentions that there is no Truth, only your, my, or our truths. For postpositivists, variations on this putative danger assume monumental status, yet warnings of such a descent amount to empty threats: life shows otherwise! While simple one-liners may demonstrate the bare-bones verifiability of claims to know medium-sized material objects in materially replete circumstances, they do not serve as models for knowledge in general or for knowing everyday objects and events.

The conundrum evidently derives from questions about how knowledge of and about specific things, people, and circumstances travels across racial, gendered, conceptual, geographical, and historical distances while retaining its epistemic legitimacy. Time-worn references to cups on tables or cats on mats make poor examples: even they may fail to travel beyond the moment of their utterance. If or when they do, they remain self-contained, so that knowing that a cup is on the table admits of no easy and/or productive elaboration beyond that social world, that cup, that table and their close semblables—despite epistemological resistance to dealing with particulars. Such knowledge cannot, without further ado, claim universal assent: in some situations and cultures there are neither cats, mats, cups, nor tables. Their paradigmatic status is constrained. The dream of achieving certainty even in simple empirical knowing should be recognized as just that: a dream. In its positivist-empiricist articulations, it truncates possibilities of knowing well that fall short of achieving a yearned-for (neo-Cartesian) certainty. Nonetheless, even within such seemingly intransigent requirements, well-narrated examples—not self-contained one-liners—can loosen the exemplary strictures of instantaneous knowledge claims, yielding space to interpretive, hermeneutic practices integral to knowing well across diverse situations and populations. Such knowing requires time: at its best, it is sociocommunally deliberative. Its results may not be definitive, but thinking with them can move toward an epistemology of understanding (*Verstehen*) infused with respect, humility, and affect, where boundaries separating ethics, politics, and epistemology cease to be hard edged.

Odd though it may be to cite yet another example in claiming the power and perils of example, my purpose now is to engage with the evolving power of examples in twenty-first-century epistemology, thirty years after *Epistemic Responsibility* and in consequence of the increasing resources in social epistemology. Consider this: Reviewing David Eltis and David Richardson's *Atlas of the Transatlantic Slave Trade*, Robin L. Einhorn (2011, 36) asks, "What do you know when you know the home ports of the ships that carried the 2.8 million captives who left Luanda and the American destinations of the 2.4 million who survived the trip?" Again, this sense of knowing departs from the knowing of empiricist *S-knows-that-p* epistemology, where the numbers speak for themselves. Here, they are statistically pertinent, but flat, and extraneous or preliminary to the fuller understandings many social epistemologists seek. Animating Einhorn's question is an expectation that knowing in the sense the atlas engages could bring readers to "realize for the first time . . . what that means" (recalling William James; Einhorn 2011, 36): initiating reconfigurations of thought and action about the naturalness, the rightness of slavery. From knowing the home ports and destinations, one knows significant facts; this is no small achievement. But without fleshed-out examples, one knows virtually nothing of how it must have been to experience the everydayness of those facts: of their lived effects for people comprising those millions, the relentless dailiness and cruelty of life—and death—aboard those ships, and after. Nor is it surprising that many Americans responded with incredulity to the fictionalized accounts of slavery in Harriet Beecher Stowe's *Uncle Tom's Cabin*. These non-black Americans lived and prospered within an intransigent social imaginary infused with undifferentiated conceptions of black slaves as naturally childlike and subhuman and with equivalently intransigent convictions about white Christians' entitlement to own, discipline, and "look after" them, to save their souls. How could Stowe convince "southern critics who attacked *Uncle Tom's Cabin* as an uninformed irresponsible dramatization of the conditions of American slaves" (Code 2017, 267)? It would have been a daunting prospect.

Stowe does not offer an unchallenged, factual account of slavery. The book tells a story; she does not claim otherwise. But she rehearses its empirical grounding in *The Key to 'Uncle Tom's Cabin,'* affirming that "her novel is grounded in fact" (Stowe 1998, 462). She was prepared to counter criticisms attacking it as an uninformed dramatization of slavery (although, as Angela Davis [1981] insists, it is as interpretive as it is). Owing to the power of Stowe's examples, the novel is widely praised as a contribution to animating the abolition movement: it generates controversy in a hitherto-uncontested form of life. It prompts readers to reimagine the preconceptions of race, slavery, entitlement, and subjectivity that had infused an instituted social imaginary. Had he known Stowe's book, James might have included it among novels "of the deeper sort" that interrogate and unsettle entrenched habits underpinning human "knowledge." Its affinities with the Gosse and Styron examples are apparent, but affinities are not demonstrations, even when they prompt unsettling questions. Nonetheless, the implicitly antiracist substance of Stowe's analysis elicits stern criticism from Angela Davis (1981), who charges Stowe with producing "an utter distortion of slave life," reading her "central female figure" as "a travesty of the Black woman, a naïve transposition of the mother-figure, praised by the cultural propaganda of the period, from white society to the slave community" (27). The objection does not erase Stowe's (fictitious) picture of slave lives: it animates controversy and urges cautionary readings of the power and limitations of examples.

Beyond the contradictions Davis (1981, 31) finds in Stowe's picture of female slavery is her thought that integral to *Uncle Tom's Cabin*'s appeal is its depiction of the "contradictory nature of women's status in the nineteenth century." Whether this proposal vindicates reading the novel as emancipatory after all remains an open question, but the debates it has generated create spaces for affirming the epistemic value of such "factually derived" narrations and examples for their heuristic potential, whether they affirm truths in the making or provoke debate and contestation. Incredulity is not all bad: it is a force for rethinking, opening spaces for action-animating responses.

III

Having sketched certain laudatory claims for the power of example, I now revisit a situation where enlisting an extended example has prompted a critical yet productive exchange. The criticisms are apt; they open a way into ongoing deliberation. Here, the issue is less about "literizing" than about the power of examples to inform and/or challenge settled under-standings and practices across social-cultural-geographical differences.

At the 2007 Spindel Conference at the University of Memphis, I attempted to explore how far medical/health-care knowledge and practice can travel across cultural-social distances while maintaining credibility and efficacy. Entitled "Advocacy, Negotiation, and the Politics of Unknowing," the paper discusses a 1990s Canadian IDRC (International Development Research Centre) project in Tanzania to "consider certain epistemic demands integral to knowing well across differences from tacitly assumed or explicitly instantiated social norms: differences of gender, race, class, place, circum-stance, demography, culture, inextricably intertwined and reciprocally constitutive" (Code 2008, 32). It asks how an entrenched social-epistemic imaginary can be hospitable to, or erect obstacles against, innovative endeavors to know well across social-political-cultural differences: *radical* differences. The IDRC's aim was to turn "an entire health system around, moving it from ossified methods of gathering, evaluating, and circulating knowledge, and tired old administrative practices and distributions of epistemic power and authority, toward a responsive, responsible, demo-cratic complex of social-natural epistemic interactions" (Code 2008, 35). It required a collaborative interpretive-epistemic approach, attentive to empir-ical factuality in its multiple modalities and to specificities—demographic, local, affective—which are neither clear nor self-evident to social-cultural "outsiders." In such situations, empirical findings may not, perhaps cannot, speak for themselves; they require engaged interpretation. Yet well-crafted examples contribute significantly to seeing such projects through. Knowing/understanding across radical differences requires more than a capacity to move around in the language of "the Other," an approach akin to María Lugones's (1987) "world-travelling," far removed from eleven-countries-in-eleven days tourism: a traveling prepared to spend the time, to practice the humility integral to eschewing sedimented perceptual/interpretive habits and prejudices, to relinquish (following Wittgenstein [1968, 45]) the "pair of glasses on our nose through which we see whatever we look at. It never occurs to us to take them off." Vital to performing this function well—as for the IDRC—is humility, again cast as an epistemic virtue, yet not in a groveling, Uriah Heep sense. It marks a courageous engagement, respectfully pausing to consider and to deliberate. Joni Seager (2003, 145) finds this virtue in Carson's understandings of nature, proposing that "'humility' often has religious overtones, but Carson . . . is speaking to the rash overconfidence of humans who act as though they can remove themselves from the inescapable truth that humans are part of nature." Overconfidence more widely conceived prompts superimposing understandings of social-political circumstances and diagnostic practices onto events that are opaque to practitioners in/from radically diverse situations. The point here, as in the Tanzanian example, is not that symptoms of disease could differ radically across geographical-cultural-social circumstances but that *living* them could be culturally incommensurate across situational/ontological differences. Recognizing a lack of fit can be literally impossible from superficial observations, cursory pronouncements, or diagnoses which invoke conceptions of abnormality. Humility, here, is manifested in a readiness to enter situations where it is an egregious error—a failure of responsible practice—to presuppose that situations will be self-explanatory or knowable owing to the putatively generic expertise of investigators.

Good interpretive practices take time: this is as strong an epistemic requirement as it is a budgetary matter! It should not be allocated from one-size-fits-all presuppositions. In *Ecological Thinking* I discuss Karen Messing's diagnostic practices in studying examples from workplace health, where she shows how diagnoses that are insufficiently specific can fail to uncover symptoms that require time-consuming local interventions. Thus, as I have noted, Messing studies how "work stations, tools, and equipment designed for the 'average man' place many women and some men at a disadvantage, whose effects in pain, stress and discomfort are rarely discernible except in the language of failing to meet an abstract, one-size-fits-all criterion of fitness" (Code 2006, 54). Good treatment requires openness to particular yet contrary-to-the-norm events: pausing before dismissing them as transient anomalies, mere aberrations.

In the Spindel paper on the IDRC's work in Tanzania, I applaud the investigators' departure from a top-down epistemology of mastery to move toward responsive, responsible, democratic practices of local, social-natural epistemic interaction. These were marked by sensitivity to habitus and ethos as well as gradual redistributions of epistemic authority across populations and places. Where distributions of funds and services previously deemed appropriate had drawn on one-size-fits-all assumptions, investigators discerned that this practice had in fact involved dispatching equal sums of money and identical packages of drugs to each district. Often, the fit was not good enough, yet it required *time* to discern why measures effective elsewhere were less so here. It called for careful hermeneutic hesitation—integral to humility—for investigators to discover particularities that were occluded in the too-hasty generalizations informing policy and practice. Here, locally evaluated examples were required, to allow investigators and others to see past the sedimented practices blocking the way to sensitive action; this was the project's purpose. In such circumstances, time and money are urgent: the power of the most carefully crafted examples may stop there.

Retelling this story neither affirms the power of example as effectively change precipitating nor shows that appeals to example consistently generate worthy epistemic outcomes. Sometimes they do. Equally, such readings may fail to produce mind-changing effects, despite the power of an apt example to indicate viable ways of going on. They may be too exotic, too strange to claim a hearing. However, with appropriate examples, hermeneutic engagement can enhance the powers of epistemic challenge to interrupt and inform thought and action. Still, cautionary comments are in order: Incorporating analogical thinking and reasoning into this mix offers a potentially fertile, complex resource. But, like examples *tout court*, analogies are constructed and crafted to function as points of entry into understanding or interpreting events, biases, and situations. Like many good examples, their signature strength dwells in their hermeneutic openness, in the places they open for humility as a contributor to ongoing understanding, negotiating, and rethinking.

The IDRC's mandate was to investigate causes of deaths in rural Tanzanian populations: to know "thickly," not in formulaic (check-the-relevant-boxes) detail, how deaths from malaria occurred across diverse parts of the country and population. To cite my Spindel paper, "one of the most intransigent obstacles in the power/knowledge complex these reversals and consequent 'successes' have encountered has been an entrenched reliance on stereotypes embedded in the instituted social imaginary . . . notoriously resistant to counterevidence . . . through which administrators and other outsiders purport to know local populations" (Code 2008, 40).

This claim connects with thoughts about a failure of humility, a too-readily assigned label or interpretation, a failure to pause and assess the aptness of the fit—a practice essential to learning from an example. It is difficult to enact such a practice in corporate cultures where speed and time are of the essence, blurring the hermeneutic power of exchanges that require a larger hearing if they are to contribute to understanding difference and sameness. Troubling, also, is the practice of taking simplified empirical claims as paradigmatic for knowledge in general. Instead, such claims represent a *kind* of knowledge whose reach is truncated in consequence of *their* limited reach, of the minimal ways of going on they enable.

"Knowing populations"—knowing people and events within population-specific, situational-cultural locations—is not a one-off event; it takes time, deliberation. Yet thoughtfully enacted knowing processes benefit from judicious—humble—appeals to example. The contrast is with generalizing from too few factual or fictional particulars: making the strange familiar, reading newly encountered people, ideas, and situations as fitting too easily into preformed categories and ready-at-hand stereotypes—of women, men, nonwhite people, old folks, the "foreign," the "lesser" class or race—and truncating inquiry and understanding in so doing. Knowing from narrated examples and counterexamples can shake the rigidity of stereotype-sustained typologies and categories, with commendable consequences.

Kristie Dotson's (2008) critical analysis of my Spindel paper, in the *Southern Journal of Philosophy*, offers powerful evidence of the strength and limitations of narrated examples and counterexamples to generate response and critique, advancing understanding across differences without superimposing examples onto events where the fit is less than clear. Published together, our papers enact a critical-constructive debate that draws readers into a sense of what Harvey Cormier, citing William James, calls "ever not quite," which James says "has to be said of the attempts made anywhere in the universe at attaining all-inclusiveness" (quoted in Cormier 2007, 71).

In her critical analysis, Dotson (2008, 52) contends that "effective epistemic practices in the Tanzanian health care example do not necessarily indicate the kinds of just epistemic practices needed to remove epistemic injustice." She notes the absence of Tanzanian voices in my article, which I had failed to notice before she brought it into focus. It attests to a failure of epistemic responsibility on my part, and not a minor failure. These investigations were deliberative, situated, negotiative practices—features I applaud. But these same features had a blinkering effect, prompting my failure to notice, and name, the diverse modalities of voice and interaction such situated inquiry demands. Again, the power of example—Dotson's example—is noteworthy. She reads creatively against the grain of the narrative analyses and examples I invoke, exposing a deeper layer of assumptions that are germane to knowing responsibly across differences, especially when the subjects of inquiry, so to speak, are alive and cognizant of the investigation's purposes. Failure to enlist their voices is an egregious omission; Dotson's charges are apt. Her reading captures a sense of the (intertwined) positive and negative powers of examples, especially where time and listening are available to enable the very hermeneutical readings I advocate. Such readings are rare in Anglo-American philosophy: Dotson enacts something akin to a thesis–antithesis–(possible)-synthesis process, where each step contributes to recognizing and acknowledging the epistemic friction (in Medina's [2013] sense) produced and reproduced in hermeneutic engagement with extended examples and case studies, where the writer does not know well enough whereof she speaks. Read literally, such friction rubs the wrong way, interrupts the potentially smooth to-and-fro passage of analysis. Yet while Medina does not always do so, I am reading such friction as positive, especially in relation to Dotson's reading of my reading of the Tanzanian project. She shows how epistemic friction can spark radical rethinking and action without denying that it can also disrupt and destroy them: the processes are ongoing.

Dotson (2008, 61) maintains, provocatively and convincingly, that "trained interviewers are a manufactured 'third class' of individuals who are authorized by their ability to take up the 'necessary' training to become merely useful sources of information within the structure of evidence-collection procedures that require such sources." *Third*, in this locution, is not merely numerical but descriptive and normative in a negative sense, akin to *third-class citizens*: they do not count as primary or even secondary sources of competence or of knowing and understanding. She deplores the instrumentality of reliance on such "individuals" as epistemic informants, where there is scant evidence of the "epistemic cooperation," the to-and-fro that would attest to these informants being respected and valued as knowers—*as who they are*, not as mere information gatherers, placeholders in a larger project. Again, as she shows, bringing such heuristic interpretations into conversation is facilitated through narrated counterexamples sufficiently powerful to open the way toward understanding differently, displacing an inadequately informed contention: recognizing its lived significance. No outright challenge to the researchers' epistemic authority occurs in my Spindel essay, Dotson rightly notes. It fails to counter the epistemic injustices she perceives, even in the shifting epistemic positionings of Tanzanian interlocutors. The voices of those studied are nowhere audible. Yet despite these omissions, I believe, the examples and counterexamples expose the complexity of local examples at work: their successes and failures, inviting respectful contestation—epistemic friction—in knowing and working to understand complex situations through interpretive-hermeneutic frameworks that are specific yet open ended. They point toward diverse ways of understanding or contesting events, situations, and human interactions, toward enacting engaged, repeatable practices, mutatis mutandis, in situations sufficiently analogous to find epistemic resources in the knowings they detail and sufficiently detailed to highlight their failings. They caution against too-hasty assumptions of sameness and difference; they take time, and a large measure of humility.

IV

In presenting these examples from diverse investigations since the late 1980s, my purpose is neither to illustrate their powers and limitations across randomly selected circumstances nor to recommend generalizing from a small set of particulars. It is to show by example how would-be knowers might read examples, variously, for their epistemic potential as contributors to interpretive understandings and thoughtful actions across a range of knowings, in late-twentieth- and early-twenty-first-century inquiry. Here, I am guided by the apt title of Stephen L. Esquith's (2010) *The Political Responsibilities of Everyday Bystanders*, reading it with Clare Hemmings's (2012) "Affective Solidarity: Feminist Reflexivity and Political Transformation." These works point clearly toward ways of working to understand the power of examples considering their capacity to initiate, contribute to, challenge, or discredit settled modes of sociopolitical thinking.

Esquith's (2010, 1) concern is with bringing everyday bystanders— folk like "us"—to "recognize and meet their shared and institutional political responsibilities for severe violence." My interest is analogous, if less centered. It derives from attempts to articulate and understand such epistemic responsibilities as pervade everyday human lives in the western and northern world, to initiate renewed realizations of responsibilities often unacknowledged yet imperceptibly powerful. Thus, when soon-to-graduate philosophy students in 2016, in an urban Canadian university, know virtually nothing of climate change, of the sociopolitical implications of World War II, of thalidomide, of the politics, racism, and sexism that pervade their society, one asks how they will engage, as participants or as "everyday bystanders," with responsibilities in/to the societies where they live or to other societies where equivalently urgent issues arise, societies made by these and other events. As points of entry into discussion, examples—well-narrated and deliberated examples, again, not just one-liners—can contribute, gradually, to closing such gaps. "Bystanders" must also learn how to read, listen, and deliberate—in other words, to look critically, hermeneutically, beyond the given, where examples can be read as self-contained within the time and place of their making and thus irrelevant to "us." Pedagogically, it is challenging to determine how to start from where students are. The power of intelligently crafted examples can be an invaluable resource. Hemmings (2012, 148) contributes a salient piece to such thoughts, arguing for the epistemic significance of the "affective dissonance that feminist politics *necessarily begins from*" and of the power that infuses/immobilizes such dissonance. The frictions such dissonances generate can unsettle presuppositions and cognitive habits and prompt rethinking and reconsidering. Equally, they can prompt retreat to the status quo. Hemmings's commitment to drawing on the "affective" joins with other current endeavors in western/northern feminist philosophy to restore the legitimacy of care and concern to epistemic practices, moving toward reclaiming respectability for discussions of why and how people care or *should care* about knowing well and recalling Vrinda Dalmiya's (2002) apt question, "why should a knower care?" If the question pertains only to such contrived exercises as follow upon asking "What is it like to be a bat?," there might be no reason whatsoever to care. But engaging with complex modalities of thinking, feeling, and being, together with recognizing the epistemic value of empathy that is common, with variations, to Esquith's and Hemmings's writings, offers a route toward richer responses.

Analogous claims pertain to such works as Sartre's *Nausea*, Camus's *The Stranger*, Beauvoir's *She Came to Stay*, and their twenty-first-century counterparts: novels that draw readers into thinking phenomenologically and experientially *with* people and with their explicitly situated circumstances. They contribute to understanding not just intellectually but affectively. They are integral to the philosophical projects of the existentialist philosophy of their time—and, still, of ours. *Sophie's Choice* finds echoes in these works, as does Anthony Doerr's *All the Light We Cannot See*. Such experiences cannot be understood well enough in distanced analyses. They require engagement—thinking and feeling through and with the protagonists and situations—which formal analyses rarely achieve. They show something of the power and promise of hermeneutic engagement. Clearly, such examples will not enable the yearned-for certainty programmatically characteristic of twentieth-century and some early-twenty-first-century mainstream epistemology, but they prompt reconsidering fixed epistemic assumptions, and they bring the complexities of lives and circumstances into critical ontological thinking. In societies of sound bites, such informed, considered, and thought-requiring matters often fail to claim a hearing. These laudatory thoughts notwithstanding, examples, counterexamples, friction, and disruption are not, as a matter of course, benign or epistemically laudable. Theirs is also the power to offend, disgust, insult, or jar. They reinforce dismal stereotypes as readily as they challenge them. But the point is not to claim a benign, heartwarming function for examples as such. Like all knowledge claims, they require evaluation, argument, thoughtfulness, and hermeneutic engagement.

Because examples are temporally located, evaluating them well can require time, in order to evade damaging evaluations in their turn. "Isn't that just like a woman?" "What else could you expect of a savage?" In each case, events or actions will have prompted such a retort and will show how malign, damaging thoughts and actions equally draw on the power of example. Feminists, people of color, antiracists, and other Others from a going social-political-intellectual mainstream are well aware of such negative effects, beyond philosophical deliberation—in films, blogs, journalism, fiction, advertising. Evaluative practices are rarely linear. Hermeneutic-interpretive engagement and counterengagement are ongoing practices, never quiet, never still. Yet examples and counterexamples commonly, perhaps invisibly, open spaces for rethinking and contesting individual and collective acquiescence in taken-for-granted (instituted) social imaginaries whose enabling and constraining functions call for critical engagement. Racism and sexism are obvious modalities of the thinking-being at issue here, but there are many such, woven so invisibly into a social fabric—a social imaginary—that "everyday bystanders" have to learn to see them. The process is long; it requires thoughtful engagement.

In consequence, examples specific in their discursive positioning with reference to place (as is integral to many good novels) perform the function of contesting epistemic commitments to a "view from nowhere." Literally and phenomenologically, a view from somewhere is germane to endeavors to know people, situations, and experiences responsibly and well. Donna Haraway makes this point clearly in "Situated Knowledges." Most novels rely on details of place, time, and circumstance to render people and situations plausible and imaginable. If "literizing is not theorizing," then a prohibition against drawing on literary, phenomenological, cine-matic, and internet examples becomes a rule of practice, closing off rich sources of inquiry and understanding. Here, epistemic responsibility, be it of readers and viewers or of writers, is no mere generic requirement or virtue but a practice, a way of being and potentially understanding, if variously, within situational/circumstantial diversity. It infuses commit-ments to knowing carefully and well. Nor is responsibility merely generic. It can be specific, and differently specific, within situational/circumstan-tial diversity: requiring multiple layers and sources of understanding. Often, a well-told example engages with everyday specificities to prompt rethinking, animate new understandings, or unsettle sedimented patterns of knowing and thinking, if not instantaneously. Such claims have to be evaluated—hermeneutically—case by case, but case-by-case epistemology is not a new epistemic practice, and well-crafted examples are integral to its successful functioning. These thoughts notwithstanding, it must be noted that examples and counterexamples can truncate pursuits of inquiry, for better or for worse, when they are presented as though they speak for themselves to the extent that no further investigation is required. Rarely can they claim to have the last word.

Notes

1. Case studies are multiple and diverse, according to the specific events and issues of this particular telling. Briefly, they qualify or amplify the matter under discussion, specify its features as a way of differentiating it from similar events in the text, or, in seemingly analogous situations, they narrow or broaden

its purview, working to show why this issue in particular is the one that matters and not that one.

2. Tacit reference to Thomas Kuhn's *The Structure of Scientific Revolutions* (1970).

3. In *Epistemic Responsibility* (2006), I refer to "knowledge by second-hand acquaintance."

References

Beauvoir, Simone de. 1949. *The Ethics of Ambiguity*. Translated by Bernard Frechtman. New York: Citadel Press.

Beauvoir, Simone de, and Gisèle Halimi. 1962. *Djamila Boupacha: The Story of the Torture of a Young Algerian Girl Which Shocked Liberal French Opinion*. London: André Deutsch, Weidenfeld, and Nicolson.

Carson, Rachel. 1962. *Silent Spring*. Boston: Houghton Mifflin.

Code, Lorraine. 1987. *Epistemic Responsibility*. Hanover, NH: University Press of New England.

———. 2006. *Ecological Thinking: The Politics of Epistemic Location*. New York: Oxford University Press.

———. 2008. "Advocacy, Negotiation, and the Politics of Unknowing." *Southern Journal of Philosophy* 46: 32–51.

———. 2017. "Incredulity and Advocacy: Thinking after William James." In *Feminist Interpretations of William James*, edited by Erin Tarver and Shannon Sullivan, 261–80. University Park: Pennsylvania State University Press.

Cormier, Harvey. 2007. "Ever Not Quite: Unfinished Theories, Unfinished Societies, and Pragmatism." In *Race and Epistemologies of Ignorance*, edited by Shannon Sullivan and Nancy Tuana, 59–76. Albany: State University of New York Press.

Craig, Edward. 1999. *Knowledge and the State of Nature: An Essay in Conceptual Synthesis*. Oxford: Oxford University Press.

Dalmiya, Vrinda. 2002. "Why Should a Knower Care?" *Hypatia* 17 (1): 34–52.

Davis, Angela Y. 1981. *Women, Race and Class*. New York: Random House.

Dickens, Charles. 1850. *David Copperfield*. London: Bradbury & Evans.

Doerr, Anthony. 2014. *All the Light We Cannot See*. New York: Scribner.

Dotson, Kristie. 2008. "In Search of Tanzania: Are Effective Epistemic Practices Sufficient for Just Epistemic Practices?" *Southern Journal of Philosophy* 46: 52–64.

Einhorn, Robin. 2011. "An Atlas of Reckonings." *The Nation*, Jan. 19, 2011. https://www.thenation.com/article/archive/atlas-reckonings/.

Esquith, Stephen L. 2010. *The Political Responsibilities of Everyday Bystanders*. University Park: Pennsylvania State University Press.

Gosse, Edmund. 1907. *Father and Son: A Study of Two Temperaments*. London: William Heinemann.

Haraway, Donna J. 1991. "Situated Knowledges: The Science Question in Feminism and the Privilege of Partial Perspectives." In *Simians, Cyborgs, and Women: The Reinvention of Nature*. New York: Routledge.

Hemmings, Clare. 2011. *Why Stories Matter: The Political Grammar of Feminist Theory*. Next Wave: New Directions in Women's Studies. Durham, NC: Duke University Press.

———. 2012. "Affective Solidarity: Feminist Reflexivity and Political Transformation." *Feminist Theory* 13 (2): 147–61.

Kuhn, Thomas. 1970. The Structure of Scientific Revolutions. 2nd ed. Chicago: Chicago University Press.

Lugones, María. 1987. "Playfulness, 'World'-Travelling, and Loving Perception." *Hypatia* 2 (2): 3–19.

Medina, José. 2013. *The Epistemology of Resistance: Gender and Racial Oppression, Epistemic Injustice, and Resistant Imaginations*. New York: Oxford University Press.

Pohlhaus Jr., Gaile. 2011. "Wrongful Requests and Strategic Refusals to Understand." In *Feminist Epistemology and Philosophy of Science: Power in Knowledge*, edited by Heidi E. Grasswick. Dordrecht, Netherlands: Springer.

Seager, Joni. 2003. "Rachel Carson Died of Breast Cancer: The Coming of Age of Feminist Environmentalism." *Signs* 28 (3): 945–72.

Stowe, Harriet Beecher. 1998. *Uncle Tom's Cabin*. Oxford: Oxford University Press.

Styron, William. 1979. *Sophie's Choice*. New York: Vintage Press.

Williams, Patricia. 1992. *The Alchemy of Race and Rights*. Cambridge, MA: Harvard University Press.

Wittgenstein, Ludwig. 1968. *Philosophical Investigations*. Translated by G. E. M. Anscombe. Oxford: Basil Blackwell.

———. 1969. *On Certainty*. Translated by Denis Paul and G. E. M. Anscombe. Oxford: Basil Blackwell.

Chapter 5

What Philosophy Does (Not) Know

GAILE POHLHAUS JR.

I have a keen interest in thinking about what philosophy does and does not know—about what philosophical knowing is and why it is valuable, but also about certain things professional philosophers in particular appear to have trouble knowing and whether there is something about philosophical activity that lends itself to this trouble. I arrive at the first interest, that of describing what philosophy does know, because the humanities in general are, it seems to me, becoming less valued, or, at the very least, administrators, our students, and state and national legislatures want to know why we ought to value the kind of thinking practiced in the humanities. Moreover, public discourse sometimes appeals to the empirical sciences as though they were straightforward and the only truly democratic way of knowing the world (Krauss et al. 2010; Tyson 2014; Nye 2016). This is worrisome given that such appeals disregard how the sciences are shaped by values and obscure from consideration a whole host of epistemic activities that can be utilized to think about values. Importantly, knowers widen, focus, and shift attention to various parts of the world through a variety of epistemic activities that can operate independently of (but also in important conjunction with) the sciences. Nonempirical philosophy[1] is one of the places where knowers engage these sorts of activities. However, it is not always clear to other academics (let alone the nonacademic public) what it is that philosophers are doing when we are engaging in philosophy. This has me thinking about the sorts of epistemic activities philosophers practice, how I might describe those activities well, and how I might help others to understand what exactly I find so valuable about them.

I also find myself wondering about what philosophy does *not* know, because it seems that the blogosphere is a never-ending source of examples of philosophers not knowing what seem to be fairly important things. For example, why is it that some philosophers can remain oblivious to the fact that a good many graduate programs in the discipline contain (and protect) men who are known to serially sexually harass (Schliesser 2014)? How is it that those who work in epistemology can remain oblivious to the last forty years of scholarship (produced mostly, though not only, by women) in feminist epistemology (Pohlhaus 2014b; Rooney 2012)? Or that most training in philosophy in the US is able to ignore the philosophical traditions of the majority of the world, including some US-based traditions (Garfield and Van Norden 2014; Alcoff 2017)?

In addition to these sorts of questions, I am interested, concerned, and even at times just downright curious about what Linda Martín Alcoff (2013), in her presidential address to the Eastern Division of the American Philosophical Association, referred to as philosophy's "demographic challenges"—namely, the low percentages of women and people of color within the discipline, particularly in comparison to other disciplines in the humanities, but also in comparison to many of the sciences. While philosophers have begun to discuss and think about our demographics (which is to say, we are beginning to reflect on who we are and who we might become as a community of knowers), sometimes these conversations have been frustrating. Particularly frustrating are conversations that frame philosophy's homogeneity as either a random coincidence or a result of nondominantly situated persons' dislike of something about philosophical practice. Both routes seem unsatisfactory to me. If philosophy's demographics are random, this is a peculiarly persistent sort of randomness. And the view that philosophical practice is off-putting or uninteresting to nondominantly situated persons occludes my experiences of philosophy as a particularly compelling way of thinking through and grappling with those aspects of my social positioning that marginalize me in relation to others.[2] Instead, I tend to think that philosophy's demographic problems will only be solved if philosophers become more, not less, philosophical—which is to say more self-reflective about who we are, what we know, what we do not know, and why. For example, we might ask whether there is something about the habits of mind cultivated by philosophers that can shield persons who are dominantly situated from having to acknowledge philosophy's demographic problem as a problem to begin with. Furthermore, we might ask, Is there something about the embodied habits of mind cultivated by philosophers that might prevent them from noticing certain things that matter with regard to our demographics and thus lead them to think about those things in unproductive ways and/or to regard them as unimportant?

What I am particularly interested in here is the seeming capacity of dominantly situated philosophers to not know things that nondominantly situated philosophers know by way of doing philosophy. In other words, how might the very same epistemic activities that I find valuable for collective social movement in resistance to dominance and oppression also be activities that insulate and protect social hierarchies within the discipline? In asking this question, I hope not only to think through a perplexity I experience as a philosopher who is, in part, nondominantly situated but also to remain mindful of and vigilant concerning aspects of my own philosophical practice that might maintain relations of dominance and oppression, particularly insofar as I am also, in part, dominantly situated. To be clear, in asking and reflecting on these questions I am not attempting to offer a definitive causal explanation for philosophy's dismal demographic diversity. Instead, I am interested in squaring the liberatory potential I think philosophy has for confronting axes of dominance and oppression with some of the gatekeeping maneuvers[3] I have witnessed in commonplace disciplinary practices among philosophers. Both Kristie Dotson and Linda Martín Alcoff have called attention to how a culture of justification (Dotson 2012) and policing what counts as philosophy (Alcoff 2013, 2017) serve to maintain the whiteness and maleness of philosophy. I hope to add to this literature a discussion of some additional occupational hazards of the discipline that do the same. However, I am also interested in how these hazards might be produced through the use of epistemic tools that are nonetheless vital to resisting dominance and oppression. If this is the case, then this provides one more pressing reason to work on diversifying the discipline while being cognizant of how we might be undermining this task.[4]

Not all ways of describing what it means to know are particularly helpful for thinking through the queries I have about the epistemic activities of philosophers *as* philosophers, but one way of describing knowing that may be helpful here is to think about knowing in terms of epistemic movement.[5] In other words, one way of asking what it means to know or not know is to ask the following: What kind of movement is the epistemic agent engaged in when they engage in acts of knowing or in acts that deflect knowing? What does it mean for the world to move knowers, epistemically speaking? How is it possible for an epistemic agent to become immobilized? Under what conditions would we call a knower epistemically stuck, and what constitutes proper resources for gaining traction in such cases? Moreover, how might an epistemic agent move other epistemic agents who seem fixated in ways that continuously direct epistemic attention away from things that matter to this agent? Finally, what might it mean to move well through and with the world, epistemically speaking? These questions not only shift philosophical attention from epistemic states to epistemic activities but also frame knowing as a kind of coordinating with the world such that epistemic agents are appropriately moved by and responsive to the world and one another. Framing my questions about philosophy's epistemic activities in terms of movement in this manner will, I hope, shed light on how exclusions and ignorances might be maintained within the discipline through unacknowledged epistemic coordinating practices. In addition, I aim to move toward possible remedies for better and wider epistemic coordination.

Case One: Two Philosophers Who Seem to Come at Things from "Out of Nowhere"

Some time ago, I spent a year thinking with an interdisciplinary group of scholars at my university about the human/nonhuman distinction.[6] Over the year of our work together, it struck me that the two philosophers in the group often appeared to say things and ask questions that seemed strange or out of place to the rest of the group—as one member put it on one occasion, "It's like I don't even know where you two are coming from!"[7] In light of these difficulties, I began to wonder why the questions it seemed normal for the philosophers to ask and the thoughts we thought it important to consider seemed strange or pointless to others in the group, even though we were all clearly concerned with thinking carefully about the human/nonhuman distinction. Significantly, I felt that my colleague in philosophy and I were often trying to convey something fairly important precisely at moments when we had the most difficulty getting the rest of the group to understand what we were saying.

This sort of difficulty is, of course, likely to occur within any interdisciplinary group of scholars insofar as members of the group will be trained in different disciplines and so approach the world guided by different assumptions and methodologies. Nonetheless, there was a certain irony in hearing my colleagues outside of philosophy suggest that my own queries seemed to come from "out of nowhere" given that as a feminist epistemologist I am committed to the idea of the situated knower. Moreover, I am wary of the notion that knowing can take place from "nowhere." And yet here I was, appearing to approach the group's collective epistemic project in exactly this way. It gave me pause. Perhaps holding the view that all knowledge is situated is not the same as actually practicing it.[8] Perhaps committing oneself to this sort of claim requires moving through and being moved by the world, epistemically speaking, in a way that I was not trained to move and be moved as a philosopher.

While there were certainly times when other members of the group were misunderstood or had difficulties communicating, this expression "coming from out of nowhere," as well as the expression "having no idea where you are coming from," seemed to emerge in response to the philosophers in particular. Rather than providing a common ground or neutral starting place that might facilitate inquiry (as the "nowhere" of which I am critical is often said to provide), this "nowhere" posed problems for our thinking together. Not knowing the "where" from which the philosophers were coming left our colleagues with no basis for getting in sync with the direction of our thinking. And by this I don't mean that we couldn't identify the premises from which we were starting, but something different.

For example, when discussing work being done to establish legal rights within the judicial system for nonhuman primates,[9] I worried that arguments to extend rights to nonhuman animals might further entrench human animals as the standard by which all others are evaluated, thereby perpetuating hierarchies between the human and nonhuman. What my colleagues outside of philosophy seemed to hear when I expressed these concerns was that I did not think we should extend rights to nonhuman primates. And, in a sense, they were correct. But, in another sense, they seemed to miss my point entirely. Frustratingly, they seemed to be taking the claim I was offering for consideration in a direction that was completely counter to how I meant it. Describing the problem as one that could be resolved by identifying and stating a set of starting premises seems to miss something crucial in our interaction—it makes the problem seem too simple or more straightforward than I (and, I think, they) experienced it to be.

The problem in this particular case might be described as not considering a claim in the proper light. While this description is closer, it nonetheless fails to capture some of the dynamics of our interaction worth highlighting. Instead, I would describe our interaction as a kind of epistemic discoordination. To be clear, by epistemic discoordination I do not mean that we were in disagreement, but rather our discoordination rendered the claim I wanted the group to consider outside the scope of intelligible consideration. In other words, the claim that we might not want to utilize a rights framework to value nonhuman primates could only be understood as "we might not want to value nonhuman primates." As such, our epistemic discoordination did not allow for (mutual) consideration of a particular claim concerning which we might agree or disagree—whether the rights framework was the best or only framework for valuing others.

This sort of difficulty is akin to a problem to which Lorraine Code (1995) draws attention with her use of the term "rhetorical space."[10] In using this term, Code is concerned with the issue of uptake, or whether a claim is duly considered. In particular, she notes that propositions are not self-contained but rather located within a discursive and material context within which they make sense, so that claims that refer to material impossibilities (such as those concerning airports made in the year 1600) or that refer to discursive impossibilities (such as those about gay marriage made within the context of Roman Catholicism) are neither true nor false but rather fail to "go through," or make sense (Code 1995, x). It is not just that people refuse to give uptake to the claims in these instances, but rather the conditions that would facilitate uptake (either positive or negative) are missing. These conditions, the discursive and material contexts that facilitate uptake, she calls "rhetorical space."

While the term *rhetorical space* suggests a context within which knowers move, adding two more concepts can help clarify what I mean by epistemic discoordination. The first concept is the social model of disability developed within disability studies, which, among other things, highlights how movement is enabled and disabled by environments (Wendell 1996; Siebers 2008). For example, a space with ceilings that are three feet high will accommodate people under three feet tall while disabling those who are much taller than three feet. Likewise, the rhetorical space inhabited by knowers can enable and disable the consideration of particular claims.[11] For example, Uma Narayan (1997, 83–117) notes that sometimes claims made about women in India take on a very different sort of meaning when they travel across national contexts to the United States due, in part, to differences in what different contexts make salient. In a similar fashion, Patricia Hill Collins (2017) warns that concepts developed within the context of activism can become depoliticized and distorted when they travel within the context of the academy. Both examples highlight the variability of material and discursive possibilities across constituencies.[12] In both cases, claims that can be made and understood well within one context become extraordinarily difficult, sometimes even impossible, to make understandable in another.[13] Thinking about rhetorical space in terms of the social model of disability helps to keep in mind that the shape of rhetorical space can both facilitate and limit epistemic movement.

The second concept I'd like to bring to Code's notion of "rhetorical space" is Sara Ahmed's (2006) notions of "orientation" and "orientating," which she uses to describe, among other things, our directed attention toward the world and how directed attention can be impacted by the directed attention of others in proximity. Bodies that are similarly orientated or aligned find it easier to move in unison, whereas bodies that are not aligned find it more difficult, as when one walks with or against the flow of pedestrian traffic. Ahmed's notions of orientating and orientation add to the social model of disability an explicit reminder that the shape of a given space is, in part, constituted by those who occupy it and how they move through it. Moreover, the coordinated movement of others can be disorienting to someone who is not "in step" with the group. There are a number of ways in which a knower's epistemic movement can be halted or redirected by the epistemic movement of others. Not all of these instances are epistemically unproductive, let alone epistemically harmful.[14] In addition, disorientation can, at times, be epistemically productive. However, it is not always apparent what sort of hindrance or disorientation one is confronting. Rather than sort through the various ways in which the epistemic movement of some knowers can help or hinder individual epistemic agency,[15] I am going to return to the example with which I began in order to highlight two things: (1) the difficulties involved in making judgments about what sort of epistemic block one is experiencing and (2) how to characterize some aspects of philosophical epistemic movement.

Returning to the difficulties I encountered in the interdisciplinary research group, we might say that, at least in some instances, difficulties arose when members of the group were differently orientated, or guided by different habits of attention, and this affected the rhetorical space shared by the group so that it became difficult at times to make claims understandable to one another. In other words, the rhetorical space within which we thought together was affected by how members were accustomed to moving and being moved, epistemically speaking. Since there was divergence in customary epistemic habits, this made it difficult at times to think together. Again, by this I do not mean that we were unable to agree or that we had difficult disagreements. Instead, we had difficulty inhabiting a mutually shared space within which agreement and disagreement could take place. As such, no party was served, epistemically speaking, either by the sort of external affirmation that steadies a warranted belief, allowing one to move further in that direction, or by disagreement that loosens an unwarranted belief or helps clarify better warrant for maintaining it, allowing one to move in a slightly different direction.[16]

In addition, however, this particular example sheds an interesting light on Code's notion of "rhetorical space," for in this case my claim was not only unrecognized but also *mis*recognized in a manner that was directly counter to my aim. So we can add that the shape of rhetorical space can render a claim at odds with the intended epistemic movement of the agent who is making that claim. This is particularly troubling given that productive disagreement can be an important epistemic resource for a variety of reasons. In contrast, the appearance of productive disagreement in cases where there is epistemic discoordination can be characterized, at the very least, as a failure to consider a claim. At worst, it may lead to a loss of warranted belief insofar as the appearance of genuine disagreement in combination with the disorientation that can result from epistemic discoordination may be taken as counterwarrant to a given belief.

While this helps to develop the language of epistemic movement and epistemic (dis)coordination further, it does not yet help to clarify what might be peculiar about the epistemic movement of philosophers *as such* since, as noted earlier, any interdisciplinary group is likely to run into difficulties coordinating habits of attention. I suspect part of the difficulty the philosophers encountered was due to a (particularly unhelpful) habit of proceeding as though that toward which we were oriented were self-evident, such that we were not in the habit of orienting our interlocutors within the rhetorical space from which we were making our claims. In addition, though, this difficulty may have been compounded by the fact that, as philosophers, we were often oriented toward the very rhetorical space within which our interlocutors were making particular claims.

For example, in the instance of my worries about using a rights framework to value nonhuman primates, given that I was attempting to challenge a picture that was orientating the attention of several members of the group, it makes sense that the challenge could seem to "come out of nowhere"—I was not only orientated differently but also orientated toward the rhetorical space that was orientating the group. My thoughts were not directed within (and so not coordinated with) the rhetorical space within which several members of the group were thinking. In attempting to bring the background conventions governing rights discourses to the foreground, I was not, however, operating without convention. Said differently, in not inhabiting the conventions I was foregrounding, my thoughts were not coming from nowhere. For example, my concern about the language of rights was informed by discussions concerning the ways in which certain bodies are often assumed as the standard to which other bodies must approximate in order to be considered of value where difference from the assumed standard is a liability (as when workers' rights are conceived in terms of bodies that cannot become pregnant and give birth). This sort of assumption can have the effect of establishing certain bodies as universal standards and others as inadequate particulars. During the conversation in our research group, the move to consider how an unmarked body might be functioning as a standard that would render other bodies less valuable appeared obvious to me. It was a move I was fairly used to making, but one that did not immediately bring to mind all of the previous discussions that enabled me to make it. My previous epistemic interactions with countless others enabled me in this case to shift my attention toward some of the discursive conventions that governed the particular rhetorical space facilitating the sense of the group's claims concerning granting and extending rights. Moreover, as a philosopher, I was concerned about whether these implicit conventions might be in conflict with the group's expressed values.[17]

Here, then, is a distinct benefit of one form of epistemic movement practiced in philosophy that may come with a distinct occupational hazard. Insofar as philosophers direct attention and move toward considering the conceptual conditions[18] that enable epistemic activity, engaging in philosophy provides an opportunity for reflecting on whether the conventions governing our epistemic movement are in line with our avowed commitments. In other words, one sort of epistemic movement practiced in philosophy is to direct attention to the rhetorical space within which our concepts reside and to attempt to understand how those spaces work. The sort of epistemic movement that draws attention to these contours can be critically important to nondominantly situated persons. For example, sometimes we find that the contours of particular rhetorical spaces make thinking about our lives and what is important to us difficult, perplexing, or impossible.[19] In other words, analyzing how rhetorical spaces direct epistemic movement may be critical to identifying when it uniformly curtails the epistemic agency of some, making it difficult to make sense of and call attention to the way the world presses upon particular persons.

Along with this benefit, however, comes a distinct hazard: that in reflecting on the contours of some rhetorical spaces, one may forget that this activity itself is grounded within a rhetorical space that makes such questions and observations themselves intelligible. That philosophers are in the habit of this sort of forgetting is evidenced by the degree to which we resort to insisting that some claim or other is "obvious."[20] In addition, however, when philosophers mutually inhabit a shared but *unacknowledged* rhetorical space, they may appear to themselves (and perhaps to others) as though they actually are making sense from a disembodied, acontextual "nowhere." Collective disavowal of the context(s) within which one is operating epistemically can function as (in Sara Ahmed's [2006] terminology) a "straightening device," forcibly requiring others to inhabit and animate rhetorical spaces that facilitate some epistemic movement at the expense of disabling others. In other words, the habit of regarding and questioning the conditions of possibility for particular claims and concepts may give the semblance that one's own thinking is unconditional. Proceeding as if one's claims are unconditional can be a way of insisting that others follow the conventions of the rhetorical space that gives sense to one's claims. Ironically, one sort of epistemic movement that philosophical thinking engages, the sort that directs epistemic attention to rhetorical space, may be engaged in a way that prevents directing epistemic attention to its own rhetorical space. In other words, a critically important way of moving in philosophy may lead some philosophers to be forgetful about their own conditions. This sort of forgetfulness can be a way of refusing to allow oneself to be moved to consider what the directedness of one's own thinking does, which avenues of thinking it makes salient, and which it makes obscure. To bring attention to the sort of problems I have in mind, I turn to another example.

Case Two: Not Acknowledging Resonance at Traditional Conferences

Consider the following case. On the philosophy blog *Daily Nous*, Justin Weinberg (2016) proposed making a distinction between what he calls "resonance" conferences and traditional philosophy conferences. The difference between the two, Weinberg suggests, is that at the former one can expect agreement with "some set of substantive claims," whereas at the latter "one goes in expecting disagreement from top to bottom." I focus on this case because I think Weinberg has vocalized fairly accurately a self-conception of traditional philosophy that is problematic, since it fails to recognize the degree to which philosophical practice relies on substantial agreement. If there were no significant areas of agreement at traditional philosophy conferences, it would make epistemic movement impossible, as in a comic sketch from *Monty Python's Flying Circus* (1972), "The Argument Clinic," in which patrons pay to have an argument but then find they have purchased an interaction with someone who insists on arguing about whether they are in fact having an argument. For epistemic movement to be possible, there must be some degree of epistemic coordination or agreement within which matters of disagreement and careful analysis of disagreement can take place. Yet where agreement lies and how it facilitates epistemic movement can be difficult, at times, to detect.

Here, one might wish to say that at traditional philosophy conferences agreement lies precisely in agreeing to submit all claims to scrutiny, to hold no viewpoint as sacred or beyond reproach, whereas at so-called resonance conferences there is agreement in certain assumptions that are held to be beyond reproach. However, the kind of agreement that facilitates epistemic movement is not aptly characterized simply as "a set of claims that we all hold," since the norms that govern epistemic movement include things like what it is warranted to ask, how one attends to claims, and the range of responses to an argument that register as "making sense" and those that do not. Moreover, these norms are not something one "holds" but rather are ways of moving. When one does not follow or move in accordance with them, one is not necessarily explicitly subjecting claims to scrutiny or reproach but rather moving epistemically in a way that is not coordinated with particular norms, making epistemic movement difficult.

Returning to Weinberg's distinction between traditional and resonance conferences, I think it is more accurate to say that the difference between the two is that at the latter (at least part of) what coordinates epistemic agents, facilitating epistemic movement (the so-called resonance), is more fully identified and stated (for example, "this conference is *feminist*"). At such conferences, participants acknowledge the rhetorical space within which we are working—and perhaps also make an open (as opposed to unacknowledged or implicit) commitment to inhabiting and sustaining a particular rhetorical space, such as one from which we can question and analyze such things as how dominantly held claims might "make sense" owing to antifeminist commitments.[21] Within such a space, for example, one can sensibly ask whether a paper is oriented in a manner that upholds antifeminist assumptions or habits of mind that silence and disregard particular groups of women.

In contrast, at standard philosophy conferences, orientations are unacknowledged and implicit. In other words, when attention is not drawn to the rhetorical space that governs a conference (as in traditional philosophy conferences) and no substantive norms are explicitly stated, the norms that enable epistemic movement will be determined by the epistemic habits of those who have historically inhabited those spaces together and whose collective epistemic movement has historically shaped the rhetorical space. Without any stated commitments, those who are already aligned with the majority of knowers will be enabled to think together (to move, be moved, and move others, epistemically speaking), even when disagreeing with one another. Those who are not similarly aligned, but guided by other concerns and commitments, will find themselves outside of the rhetorical space within which agreement and disagreement is taking place, making it difficult to move, epistemically speaking, in such spaces. Moreover, the conventions of such a space may be forcibly unacknowledged owing to the illusion that it is possible to move and be moved, epistemically speaking, without occupying any space at all.

This lack of acknowledgment does not mean that there is not agreement in orientations, facilitating epistemic movement in some directions while disabling it in others, at traditional philosophy conferences. For example, currently at most traditional philosophy conferences, the question as to why a paper fails to engage philosophical work outside the small subset of European and Euro-American philosophers is generally not considered a question that must be considered and carefully engaged if asked. Neither is the question of why a paper fails to cite and engage with philosophical work by women. Such a question will appear to "come out of nowhere" at traditional philosophy conferences and will very likely fail to be received, let alone seriously engaged or grappled with. Of course, such a question is rarely (if ever) asked at traditional philosophy conferences given the degree to which philosophers at such conferences resonate so closely together.

Ironically, Weinberg fails to notice this very convention operating in one of the cases that prompted him to make his distinction in the first place. One of the two controversies that was catalyst for his thinking that some philosophical conferences (i.e., those where he notices resonance) ought to be distinguished from traditional philosophy conferences (i.e., those where he does not notice resonance) was over the frustration some attendees experienced when a keynote speaker at a feminist philosophy conference failed precisely to consider seriously a question about his use of Black women as objects of knowledge without engaging philosophical work by Black women as subjects of knowledge. In other words, at what Weinberg identifies as a "resonance" conference, a keynote speaker, following the conventions of a traditional philosophy conference, refused (or was unable) to engage seriously with a matter of potential disagreement. The question did not register as properly philosophical to the speaker. Within traditional philosophy conferences, collective epistemic movement provides no space for such a question to be sensibly and seriously asked. Given the position in which traditional philosophy conferences stand in relation to feminist philosophy conferences (which is to say, given the legitimacy accorded to traditional conferences in relation to the legitimacy often withheld from feminist philosophy conferences), the speaker was able to rely upon typical conventions of traditional philosophy conferences that *preclude* certain sorts of disagreement, thereby disrupting the rhetorical space within which it makes sense to expect precisely this sort of disagreement. On Weinberg's account, what caused a stir at the conference was the keynote's failure to be in the sort of "substantive" agreement Weinberg assumes is present only at a "resonance" conference. However, the controversy could very well be understood as being caused by the keynote speaker's failure to expect "disagreement from top to bottom," including disagreement with regard to the sources he failed to engage. In other words, the keynote speaker might be characterized as relying upon one aspect of the substantive agreement present at traditional philosophy conferences that precludes certain types of disagreement.

If philosophers truly do find and expect ourselves to be in disagreement "from top to bottom," we do it from within a rhetorical space that itself delineates what counts as the range "from top to bottom." Not recognizing how rhetorical space guides and contains philosophical epistemic movement can be a way of *not* questioning certain things. For example, at traditional philosophy conferences, the question of whose interests are served in asking and not asking particular questions may be treated as an unfair question. Treating such a question as unfair (or even uninteresting) can be a way of protecting certain rhetorical spaces from philosophical scrutiny. Such policing at standard philosophy conferences can take place without acknowledgment and without people even realizing that they are policing, so long as they (and those they are surrounded by) are habituated toward asking and not asking certain things. When a discipline is deeply homogenized, as is the case in philosophy, this habituation can create a tightly sealed rhetorical space within which only certain assumptions may be questioned and disagreed upon, where collective epistemic movement makes some questions and disagreements appear obvious and others not at all.

Because feminist philosophers have begun to inhabit our own collective philosophical spaces, we have a "where" from which to identify some tendencies of (nonfeminist) traditional philosophy's close resonances as well as the thought-stifling effects of those tendencies. Still, a good deal of philosophy remains unaffected by this enormously useful space from which to think about and consider how traditional philosophy does and does not direct philosophical attention. This phenomenon is curious given that thinking about thinking is something typically conceived as essential to the discipline of philosophy.

It is less curious if we consider the costs and gains of leaving particular rhetorical spaces in order to examine them from others. For example, one way of avoiding particular disagreements is to fail (or refuse) to inhabit the rhetorical space that provides sense for the disagreement. Failure or refusal to inhabit particular rhetorical spaces may render claims unintelligible, misplaced, or irrelevant. Such failures or refusals can be ways of insulating oneself from the possibility of being epistemically moved by another's claims or line of thought.

However, what at first appears unintelligible, misplaced, or irrelevant can become intelligible, well placed, and relevant when one reorients oneself and becomes accustomed to a particular way of thinking. We can describe this sort of transformation as moving from one rhetorical space to another. Epistemic movement in philosophy is sometimes like this; innovative moves, particularly those that disrupt and displace long-held philosophical conventions, can be disorienting at first and may require a careful recalibrating of attention, but they can shift the manner in which philosophers move, epistemically speaking, in productive ways.

What holds interlocutors together so that they can begin to inhabit new rhetorical spaces effectively? Here, I think something like trust in the other as making a point worth trying to understand might be necessary, as when one gives one's interlocutor the benefit of the doubt. In the case of my interdisciplinary research group, all parties were genuinely perplexed by the degree to which we were talking past one another but persisted under an assumption that we could learn something important from one another. Without this trust, it would have been easy for each party to dismiss the other without really understanding the significance of the claims each was making. The need to rely on this sort of trust, however, may put those who are nondominantly situated at a distinct disadvantage when engaging with philosophers insofar as those who are afforded the benefit of credibility are more than likely to be those who are dominantly situated (Hutchison 2013; Cherry and Schwitzgebel 2016). This disadvantage may insulate philosophers from being epistemically moved by philosophers from traditionally underrepresented groups. In addition, the need for epistemic trust when attempting to coordinate epistemic movement coupled with disparities in social power can work to entrench what José Medina (2013, 43) calls "areas of an intense but negative cognitive attention, areas of epistemic hiding." In other words, epistemic discoordination can be the result of a vested interested of some not to scrutinize certain aspects of reality in a philosophical manner. For this reason, it may be wise to make a habit of considering when, how, and why one is moved or remains unmoved, epistemically speaking.

Case One Revisited

Given that it may be important to inhabit particular rhetorical spaces in order to attend to particular aspects of the world with greater care, we might understand case one, where my calling attention to features of the rhetorical space within which a claim is made was met with frustration, differently.[22] My assumption was (and the way in which I presented the case earlier suggests) that the other thinkers with whom I occasionally had trouble communicating were simply unfamiliar with and so unable to engage a particular sort of epistemic movement, namely, the sort that attends to the contours of a particular rhetorical space, including the manner in which rhetorical spaces facilitate and direct epistemic movement. There is another way of understanding the difficulty, however, if we pay attention not only to what I was attempting to do in this interaction but also to the possible effects of my own epistemic movement in this instance.

As noted already, calling attention to and questioning the contours of the rhetorical space within which a group is thinking together may appear to "come out of nowhere" despite one's coming from a "somewhere" in doing so. Since the "where" from which one attends to the contours of a particular rhetorical space is not necessarily within that space itself, it is likely to follow different conventions than the spaces it examines. Consequently, asking others to attend to some of the contours of a rhetorical space within which they are moving, temporally at least, asks them to shift from one rhetorical space to another. Specifically, it attempts to remove one's interlocutor from the rhetorical space within which they are making and considering claims. Moreover, it attempts to move one's interlocutor to a different rhetorical space, one that directs attention to the conventions that govern epistemic movement in the rhetorical space in which they are currently moving. Calling into question a rhetorical space can be a way of suggesting that it ought to be abandoned altogether (which in this particular instance was a real question for me). I originally assumed that my interlocutors were unable to move differently, that is, were unable to move outside of the rhetorical space guiding their investigation. Perhaps, instead, they were able to do so but refused to abandon the only currently available space that facilitated epistemic attention and movement toward matters of grave importance to them. Considering the case from this direction, my interlocutors may have been resisting my disruption of their own epistemic movement because it was pushing them away from parts of the world that were epistemically *pressing* upon (and for) them. In effect, they may have been implicitly saying to me, "The matter under consideration within this rhetorical space is urgent, and your calling attention to the space itself is directing attention away from that which requires attention."

For example, the colleague who most strenuously resisted me in this case was a field primatologist with a good deal of experience with non-human primates and also a greater understanding of the degree to which human beings subject them to unnecessary harm, suffering, and cruelty. Given her epistemic relationship to the category *nonhuman primates* and to the actual world of nonhuman primates as epistemically pressing (or placing epistemic pressure) on her, my questioning the very framework within which she was calling attention to their plight might have been stymieing her ability to be epistemically responsive to that part of the world that puts epistemic pressure upon her. My stake in this particular debate, for the most part, was oriented toward nonhuman primates as I imagine them in general,[23] whereas hers was oriented toward particular beings that have shaped her as an epistemic agent, making the matter she was bringing under consideration more pressing, including much more *epistemically* pressing, for her. Given her lived experience of nonhuman primates, they are a part of the world she knows more thoroughly and directly than I do. Typically, having something at stake and being pressed toward something are framed as liabilities when it comes to epistemic matters. However, considering this case with the language of epistemic movement reveals the opposite. In this instance, having something at stake means that her knowing nonhuman primates, as a scientist with a great deal of experience of them, has shaped her as an epistemic agent. As such, nonhuman primates are part of the world that moves her epistemically in a way that my lack of experience leaves me unmoved, and so less reliable in terms of epistemic responsiveness to this part of the world.[24]

To question the rhetorical space within which my colleague was calling attention to the plight of nonhuman primates, to abandon this particular way of moving together, epistemically speaking, had the real possibility of making more obscure her direct witnessing of their suffering. Under such conditions, *even if* the rhetorical space within which she was working were less than perfect, and *even if* she might choose in the future to abandon that space for a better one within which to accomplish her epistemic and practical goals,[25] it might not be worth the epistemic costs of presently abandoning this one, which, at least for the time being, provided some possibility for attending to what was epistemically pressing on (and for) her.[26]

Situations like this sometimes occur when philosophers who are differently socially situated talk about matters that place unequal pressures upon those who are in conversation. In other words, philosophers' capacity to halt epistemic movement, through skepticism, making a rhetorical space an object of scrutiny, and questioning the conditions that give sense to claims, can be used (consciously or unconsciously) to preempt philosophical thinking and inquiry that disrupts or philosophically scrutinizes social hierarchies.[27] This is why the question "How is this philosophy?" can be both useful in some contexts and dismissively antiphilosophical in other contexts.[28] In the latter sort of case, philosophers may rely on the defense "But I was just attempting to pursue philosophical inquiry!" when, in fact, the epistemic effects of their movement may be closing philosophical inquiry down. For example, the guise of philosophical inquiry in this sort of case can be utilized to forcibly remove an epistemic agent from a particular rhetorical space, relegating them to the painstaking and infinite task of justifying the conditions that give sense to their own philosophical inquiry. Nora Berenstain (2016) has identified this sort of maneuver as a form of epistemic exploitation. Epistemic exploitation, in philosophy and elsewhere, can have the real effect of stalling epistemic movement and directing it away from what is significant and epistemically pressing to nondominantly situated knowers. When other knowers systematically foreclose lines of inquiry that pertain to aspects of the world that *press upon* an epistemic agent, this can be epistemically arresting. Moreover, the demand that one continue to engage from within such a space until one can complete the infinite task of justifying a move elsewhere is, at best, insulting.

In light of the dynamics among epistemic pressure, epistemic movement, and rhetorical space, we might rethink the insult "I don't find that (sort of) work terribly impressive" (which is routinely leveled at work that expands philosophical attention to matters concerning dominance and oppression). Impressions such as these may say more about how the world presses on some epistemic agents and not on others. Moreover, when philosophers are pressed and impressed in ways that move them in different directions, we might begin to ask and wonder, Which aspects of the world are pressing this particular claim into focus and which are not? How does understanding a claim in a particular way narrow, widen, or shift the range of sensible responses to that claim? And, finally, what would need to be in place in order for this claim to press upon a given set of epistemic agents differently?[29]

Notes

1. By this, I do not mean that philosophers who engage the empirical disciplines more directly are not philosophers. I only mean to call attention to an aspect of philosophy that is irreducible to empirical science, just as there are aspects of the empirical sciences that are irreducible to philosophy. For this very reason, exchange between the two is critical. Philosophy ought to be tempered by the sciences, just as the sciences ought to be tempered by philosophy, among other disciplines.

2. Moreover, I am not alone in experiencing philosophy in this manner. See, for example, Bettcher and Goulimari (2017); Bettcher (2015) and other interviews on Krishnamurthy's *Philosopher* blog; interviews in Tremain's "Dialogues on Disability" series; hooks (1994); and Ginzberg (1991).

3. By *gatekeeping maneuvers* I mean any sort of activity (intentional or unintentional) that serves to indicate to members of underrepresented groups that they do not belong in the discipline and/or that seriously reflecting upon matters that concern them is unwelcome in the discipline.

4. To be clear, I do not think nondominantly situated people need professional philosophy. In fact, there is a good deal of philosophical thought within

various traditions outside the recognized Western philosophical canon and a good deal of philosophical thinking that thrives outside of philosophy departments. If anything, those within the discipline ought to feel the absence of these traditions and voices as undermining the discipline's own ability to think well. This chapter is, in part, an attempt to exert the kind of epistemic pressure that would allow more members of the discipline to feel this absence more pressingly.

5. While knowing is often described by philosophers in terms of epistemic states, there is no reason to do so exclusively. Moreover, thinking about epistemic movement would highlight two aspects of philosophical knowing that pertain to my interest in thinking about what philosophers do (not) know. On the one hand, emphasizing the activity of knowing (rather than its product) can help keep focus on the value of *practicing* philosophy. On the other hand, it can also help us attend to what this sort of practice *does* that might lead to a failure to notice matters that pertain to our lack of demographic diversity.

6. While our discussions encompassed a wide range of topics, including human relations to nonhuman entities (e.g., the environment), the posthuman, and treatment of some humans as less than human, the conversation recounted here, concerning rights for nonhuman primates, sticks out as an instance in which the sort of difficulty with which I am concerned was particularly salient.

7. Curiously also, the other philosopher and I were trained in very different sorts of graduate programs, she in a well-known analytic program and I in a predominantly continental one, yet we had no trouble making sense to one another, just (at times) to the rest of the group.

8. Here, I am reminded of María Lugones's (2003, 5) maxim, "I won't think what I won't practice."

9. This was just one among many topics we discussed over the year. See note 6 for further detail.

10. Olúfẹ́mi Táíwò (2017) utilizes C. G. Woodson's notion of "systems of mis-education" to demonstrate how coordinating knowers in line with axes of dominance and oppression can have the effect of turning particular truths into pernicious pieces of propaganda that he calls "Trojan horses." His argument develops a different language for identifying some of the issues I am attempting to identify with the language of epistemic movement. In addition, the essay is a nice example of precisely the sort of engagement with philosophical epistemic movement that I think is routinely engaged by nondominantly situated knowers insofar as the essay identifies within the US Black intellectual tradition careful analysis of epistemic systems and moves toward further development of that epistemological work.

11. Shannon Sullivan (2007) makes a similar point within the context of the literature on epistemologies of ignorance. Sullivan uses the term "knowledge/ignorance" to identify the ways in which knowing some things about the world may simultaneously prevent one from knowing others.

12. While it might seem that knowledge of material possibilities would be the same across different constituencies, one's material realities inform habits of attention within which claims are understood and objects of knowledge are considered. For example, Narayan (1997, 43–80) notes that the way kitchens are typically designed in India, with kerosene stoves, makes claims about kitchen fires resonate very differently to people who have no lived experience with these sorts of kitchens than to those who do, just as claims about gun deaths might resonate very differently to those who live in the US as opposed to other countries where gun ownership is highly irregular.

13. Perhaps with infinite time they could be made understandable in all (or most) contexts. However, epistemic agents are not the sorts of creatures that engage in knowing under no temporal constraints, so it strikes me that thinking about knowing in this way is a distraction from what is important and pressing upon me as a nondominantly situated philosopher who is concerned about what philosophers continue not to know.

14. For example, Medina (2013) argues that friction between knowers is a necessary component to knowing well. Nonetheless, he is also concerned with how epistemic movement can be halted or remain stuck. The former provides impetus for movement, whereas the latter prevents movement.

15. I have detailed elsewhere some of the ways in which the epistemic movement of some knowers can unjustly impinge upon the epistemic agency of others. See Pohlhaus (2017a, 2017b, 2014a, 2011). Dotson's (2011) notion of "testimonial smothering" also provides a good example of how epistemic dis-coordination (through testimonial incompetence that follows from pernicious ignorance) can oppressively stymie the epistemic agency of other knowers. In addition, see Ahmed (2006, 157–79) and Berruz (2014).

16. While it might be said that I was in fact epistemically served insofar as this interaction provided motivation and opportunity for me to consider the thoughts I have articulated here, I think it very important to emphasize that the interaction was not epistemically productive in the moment and could have ended there. Moreover, I was led to further consider the interaction not on account of the interaction itself but rather on account of my epistemic esteem for the other members of the group and the degree to which I had reason to trust them, both personally and epistemically. These two factors, concerning mutual respect and trust, are where I would place warrant for thinking further. Consequently, it is these two factors that allowed for epistemic productivity, not the discoordination as such.

17. Jason Stanley (2015) offers an account of how speech can be self-undermining in precisely this way, although the concerns that govern his account are slightly different than those directing my own.

18. Philosophy can also draw attention to the material conditions that enable and disable concepts. For example, I take standpoint epistemology to be engaged (at least in part) in bringing attention to these sorts of conditions.

19. For philosophical work that takes up these sorts of problems explicitly, see, for example, Lugones (2003, 86–90); Butler (2004); Scheman (1996, 1997).

20. To a certain extent, experimental philosophers push back on this sort of insistence in philosophy that some things are obvious by demonstrating that particular thought experiments purported to make certain intuitions obvious in philosophy do not always do so for a significant number of people outside of philosophy. Nonetheless, experimental philosophers also take some things to be obvious by way of relying upon particular rhetorical spaces, which can be brought into question themselves (Pohlhaus 2015).

21. Nonetheless, as intersectional feminists have pointed out, feminist philosophy conferences may rely on implicit, unacknowledged resonances that serve to exclude certain groups of women. One possible benefit of explicitly identifying aspects of the rhetorical space within which a conference takes place is that the question of how the rhetorical space is structured can be raised—for example, structures that serve to position some women in relations of dominance and oppression with regard to other women can be identified on the basis of the feminist commitments avowed at such conferences.

22. That the case can be examined from two different directions does not mean that we must opt for one over the other (although in some cases it might).

23. It could also be said that my stake in this conversation was attempting to be responsive to the epistemic pressures from my own history of experience concerning the effects of normalizing some human bodies in relation to others.

24. This is not to say that I could not endeavor to make these matters more epistemically pressing upon me, but doing so would require more than just thinking about them. It is also not to discount what pressed upon me within this conversation and led to epistemic discoordination.

25. The epistemic and the practical are intertwined here insofar as part of ending the suffering of nonhuman primates at the hands of human primates is to bring greater attention and understanding to this issue.

26. I take something like this to be at play when, in certain contexts, LGBT+ people participate in narratives that in other contexts we would seriously question and criticize. For example, while ultimately I would question the rhetoric that LGBT+ people "are born this way" and "can't help being LGBT+," these sorts of claims can helpfully direct epistemic attention, providing training wheels for others who are not yet in the habit of regarding us justly. Nonetheless, they are training wheels that ought eventually be left behind.

27. Moreover, those outside the discipline can display quite a bit of adept philosophical skepticism and call for conceptual clarity when attempting to avoid seriously considering claims that disrupt social privilege, as routinely happens in my classroom when students who had trouble thinking through Cartesian skepticism have no trouble engaging all sorts of skepticism with regard to matters of race in the US.

28. The extent to which nondominantly situated philosophers do entertain such questions when posed by those who stand in relations of dominance to them evidences either the degree of trust they have established with a particular interlocutor or the degree of power that interlocutor wields over them. It may not be easy to discern the difference from a dominantly situated position.

29. I wish to thank Madelyn Detloff, Heidi Grasswick, and Nancy McHugh for helpful feedback in clarifying this essay. I also wish to thank the Miami University Humanities Center and the Altman Scholars and Fellows in the Human and the Nonhuman program for providing me the opportunity to think with care about philosophical epistemic movement.

References

Ahmed, Sara. 2006. *Queer Phenomenology: Orientations, Objects, Others*. Durham, NC: Duke University Press.

Alcoff, Linda Martín. 2013. "Philosophy's Civil Wars." *Proceedings and Addresses of the American Philosophical Association* 87 (November): 16–43.

———. 2017. "Philosophy and Philosophical Practice: Eurocentrism as an Epistemology of Ignorance." In *The Routledge Handbook of Epistemic Injustice*, edited by Ian James Kidd, José Medina, and Gaile Pohlhaus Jr., 397–408. New York: Routledge.

Berenstain, Nora. 2016. "Epistemic Exploitation." *Ergo* 3 (22): 569–90.

Berruz, Stephanie Rivera. 2014. "Inhabiting Philosophical Space: Reflections from the Reasonably Suspicious." *Hypatia* 20 (1): 182–88.

Bettcher, Talia. 2015. "Other 'Worldly' Philosophy." Featured Philosop-her: Talia Bettcher. *Philosopher* (blog), edited by Meena Krishnamurthy, August 16, 2015. https://www.politicalphilosopher.net/2015/08/16/featured-philosop-her-talia-bettcher/.

Bettcher, Talia, and Pelagia Goulimari. 2017. "Theorizing Closeness: A Trans Feminist Conversation." *Angelaki* 22 (1): 49–60.

Butler, Judith. 2004. "Doing Justice to Someone: Sex Reassignment and Allegories of Transsexuality." In *Undoing Gender*, 57–76. New York: Routledge.

Cherry, Myisha, and Eric Schwitzgebel. 2016. "Like the Oscars, #PhilosophySo White." *Los Angeles Times*, March 4, 2016. https://www.latimes.com/opinion/op-ed/la-oe-0306-schwitzgebel-cherry-philosophy-so-white-20160306-story.html.

Code, Lorraine. 1995. *Rhetorical Spaces: Essays on Gendered Locations*. New York: Routledge.

Collins, Patricia Hill. 2017. "Intersectionality and Epistemic Injustice." In *The Routledge Handbook of Epistemic Injustice*, edited by Ian James Kidd, José Medina, and Gaile Pohlhaus Jr., 115–24. New York: Routledge.

Dotson, Kristie. 2011. "Tracking Epistemic Violence, Tracking Practices of Silencing." *Hypatia* 26 (2): 236–57.

———. 2012. "How Is This Paper Philosophy?" *Comparative Philosophy* 3 (1): 3–29.

Garfield, Jay L., and Brian W. Van Norden. 2016. "If Philosophy Won't Diversify, Let's Call It What It Is." *The Stone*, May 11, 2016. *New York Times*. https://www.nytimes.com/2016/05/11/opinion/if-philosophy-wont-diversify-lets-call-it-what-it-really-is.html?_r=0&pagewanted=all.

Ginzberg, Ruth. 1991. "Philosophy Is Not a Luxury." In *Feminist Ethics*, edited by Claudia Card, 126–45. Lawrence: University Press of Kansas.

hooks, bell. 1994. "Theory as Liberatroy Practice." In *Teaching to Transgress: Education as the Practice of Freedom*, 59–76. New York: Routledge.

Huthcison, Katrina. 2013. "Sages and Cranks: The Difficulty of Identifying First-Rate Philosophers." In *Women in Philosophy: What Needs to Change?*, edited by Katrina Hutchison and Fiona Jenkins, 103–26. New York: Oxford University Press.

Krauss, Lawrence, Simon Blackburn, Sam Harris, and Steven Pinker. 2010. "Can Science Shape Human Values? And Should It?" Hosted by Ira Flatow. *Talk of the Nation*, November 5, 2010. NPR radio episode, 48:07. https://www.npr.org/templates/story/story.php?storyId=131099083.

Lugones, María. 2003. *Pilgrimages/Peregrinajes: Theorizing Coalition against Multiple Oppressions*. Lanham, MD: Rowman & Littlefield.

Medina, José. 2013. *The Epistemology of Resistance: Gender and Racial Oppression, Epistemic Injustice, and Resistant Imaginations*. New York: Oxford University Press.

Monty Python's Flying Circus. 1972. "The Argument Clinic," in season 3, episode 29, "The Money Programme." Written by John Cleese and Graham Chapman. Aired November 2, 1972, on BBC.

Narayan, Uma. 1997. *Dislocating Cultures: Identities, Traditions, and Third-World Feminism*. New York: Routledge.

Nye, Bill. 2016. "Hey Bill Nye, 'Does Science Have All the Answers or Should We Do Philosophy Too?' #TuesdaysWithBill." February 23, 2016. Big Think video, 3:41. https://www.youtube.com/watch?v=ROe28Ma_tYM.

Pohlhaus Jr., Gaile. 2011. "Wrongful Requests and Strategic Refusals to Understand." In *Feminist Epistemology and Philosophy of Science: Power in Knowledge*, edited by Heidi E. Grasswick, 223–40. Dordrecht, Netherlands: Springer.

———. 2014a. "Discerning the Primary Epistemic Harm in Cases of Testimonial Injustice." *Social Epistemology* 28 (2): 99–114.

———. 2014b "Resistance and Epistemology: A Response to José Medina's *The Epistemology of Resistance*." *Social Philosophy Today* 30: 187–95.

———. 2015. "Different Voices, Perfect Storms, and Asking Grandma What She Thinks: Situating Experimental Philosophy in Relation to Feminist Philosophy." *Feminist Philosophical Quarterly* 1 (1): article 3.

————. 2017a. "Knowing without Borders and the Work of Epistemic Gathering." In *Decolonizing Feminism: Transnational Feminism and Globalization*, edited by Margaret A. McLaren, 37–54. London: Rowman & Littlefield.

————. 2017b. "Varieties of Epistemic Injustice." In *The Routledge Handbook of Epistemic Injustice*, edited by Ian James Kidd, José Medina, and Gaile Pohlhaus Jr., 13–26. New York: Routledge.

Rooney, Phyllis. 2012. "What Is Distinctive about Feminist Epistemology at 25?" In *Out from the Shadows: Analytical Feminist Contributions to Traditional Philosophy*, edited by Sharon L. Crasnow and Anita M. Superson, 239–76. New York: Oxford University Press.

Scheman, Naomi. 1996. "Forms of Life: Mapping the Rough Ground." In *The Cambridge Companion to Wittgenstein*, edited by Hans Sluga and David G. Stern, 389–416. New York: Cambridge University Press.

————. 1997. "Queering the Center by Centering the Queer: Reflections on Transsexuals and Secular Jews." In *Feminists Rethink the Self*, edited by Diana Tietjens Meyers, 124–62. Boulder, CO: Westview Press.

Schliesser, Eric. 2014. "Michael Tooley, Sees No Evil, Hears No Evil." *Digressions and Impressions* (blog), March 4, 2014. https://www.digressionsnimpressions.typepad.com/digressionsimpressions/2014/03/michael-tooley-sees-no-evil-hears-no-evil.html.

Siebers, Tobin. 2008. "Disability Experience on Trial." In *Material Feminisms*, edited by Stacy Alaimo and Susan Hekman, 291–307. Bloomington: Indiana University Press.

Stanley, Jason. 2015. *How Propaganda Works*. Princeton, NJ: Princeton University Press.

Sullivan, Shannon. 2007. "White Ignorance and Colonial Oppression: Or, Why I Know So Little about Puerto Rico." In *Race and Epistemologies of Ignorance*, edited by Shannon Sullivan and Nancy Tuana, 153–72. Albany: State University of New York Press.

Táíwò, Olúfẹ́mi. 2017. "Beware of Schools Bearing Gifts: Miseducation and Trojan Horse Propaganda." *Public Affairs Quarterly* 31 (1): 1–18.

Tremain, Shelley, ed. *Discrimination and Disadvantage* (blog). https://philosophy commons.typepad.com/disability_and_disadvanta/.

Tyson, Neil deGrasse. 2014. "Neil deGrasse Tyson Returns Again." Interview by Chris Hardwick. *Nerdist*, episode 489, March 7, 2014. Podcast. http://nerdist.nerdistind.libsynpro.com/neil-degrasse-tyson-returns-again.

Weinberg, Justin. 2016. "A Tale of Two Conferences." *Daily Nous* (blog), September 25, 2016. https://www.dailynous.com/2016/09/25/tale-two-conferences/.

Wendell, Susan. 1996. *The Rejected Body: Feminist Philosophical Reflections on Disability*. New York: Routledge.

Chapter 6

Doing Things with Case Studies

CARLA FEHR

A few years ago, I, and about twenty other philosophers, attended a lecture based on a case study revealing a common flaw in pharmaceutical
research leading to exaggerated conclusions about the positive effects of
some prescription drugs. Thoroughly researched, carefully argued, and
delivered with zeal, the lecture, which culminated with a description of the
distressing public-health implications of this research, was a great success.
However, a deep unease fell over me when during the question-and-answer
period I heard something like the following:

> QUESTIONER: Thank you so much for doing this research. What
> is happening to rectify this situation?

> SPEAKER: I'm just presenting the case study.

> QUESTIONER: Yes, but this is a serious problem. What are you
> doing to make sure that your work can actually contribute
> something to fix this?

> SPEAKER: My job is to discover the problem. It's someone
> else's job to fix it.

> SESSION CHAIRPERSON: Let's move to the next . . .

QUESTIONER: How can this research [get into their hands to] help them do that job?

SESSION CHAIRPERSON: Next question.

With a sinking feeling, I realized that unless the information in this lecture made it out of the room and beyond the boundaries of academic philosophy, the sole benefits arising from this research could be limited to the advancement of a philosopher's career and the awareness of a group of scholars poorly situated to act on this information. The "success" of this talk hinged on the scholar identifying but not actively addressing a situation involving potential and actual harms to patients, the general public, and the institution of pharmaceutical research.

While the philosopher presenting this paper may have gone on to engage policy makers or publish their findings in highly accessible venues, they gave no indication of any plan to do so. Furthermore, the request for a discussion of a plan was met with incredulity by the speaker, and the audience of philosophers, many of whom also conducted research with the potential to affect public welfare, appeared uninterested and unfazed by the lack of such a plan. This example provides insight into how this individual speaker understood the limits of their professional practices and responsibilities as well as insight into the disciplinary norms shared by the other philosophers in the room.

The philosopher studying pharmaceutical research methods was conducting what I call a socially significant case study (SSCS). In this chapter, I (1) develop the concept of an SSCS, (2) provide ethical and epistemic reasons why philosophers conducting SSCSs should do something with their work that addresses the situation their SSCS documents, and (3) offer suggestions about the kinds of things that philosophers, as well as the discipline of philosophy, can do. By showing that there are better and worse ways of conducting SSCSs, I offer the beginning of a normative approach to case studies as a methodology in philosophy.

Doing Things with Socially Significant Case Studies

This chapter advances research conducted by Kathryn Plaisance and me on socially relevant philosophy of science (SRPOS) (Fehr and Plaisance 2010; Plaisance and Fehr 2010). We identify SRPOS as a pluralistic endeavor that includes any of the following three sorts of philosophical activities. First, SRPOS can involve "philosophical analyses of scientific research topics and practices that are directly relevant to public welfare" such as biomedical or climate research (Fehr and Plaisance 2010, 302). Second, it includes philosophy of science that focuses on or engages with stakeholder groups including scientists and policy makers as well as people and groups involved with and affected by the scientific research in question. And finally, SRPOS embraces knowledge production and dissemination practices that philosophers can use to "maximize the social impact" of philosophical investigations of scientific research (Fehr and Plaisance 2010, 303). In this chapter, I argue that there are both ethical and epistemic reasons why people conducting SRPOS research that employs some types of case studies should focus on engaging a wider range of stakeholders and maximizing the social impact of their work. Although this chapter is primarily located within SRPOS because SSCSs are common and important within SRPOS, as will become apparent later in this section (see "What Is a Socially Significant Case Study?"), SSCSs can also be found in a wide range of philosophical subfields. Because the arguments I advance are associated with the *social significance* of the case study, these arguments will be applicable to philosophical investigations beyond SRPOS if those investigations are of socially significant case studies. I will characterize a socially significant case study shortly.[1]

SRPOS relies heavily on case studies. Many disciplines across the social sciences and humanities have developed taxonomies of kinds of case studies as well as a range of methods for conducting case studies and are constrained by ethical guidelines regarding case-study research. However, philosophers tend to use the term *case study* in a variety of ways; they seldom explicitly discuss methodology at all, let alone case-study methodology; and philosophical research (unlike social-science research) is generally not accountable to external ethics review. As I argue in the next section, this lack of attention to methodology can have unfortunate ethical and epistemic consequences.

In this section I develop the notion of a philosophical case study as a detailed real-world example; characterize socially significant case studies (SSCSs), which are a particular kind of philosophical case study exemplified by the philosophical research presented in the pharmaceutical research methods example that I opened with; and provide an initial overview of how philosophers using SSCSs can do things to maximize the positive social impact of their research.

What Is a Case Study?

In this chapter, by *case study* I mean a detailed description or analysis of a real-world example. Philosophers use detailed descriptions of real-world examples in a range of ways. Some philosophers use case studies to explore and develop philosophical positions. For example, Lorraine Code (2006, 25–51) fleshes out her notion of ecological thinking through a detailed account of Rachel Carson's scientific practices. Code's apparatus of ecological thinking respects the interdependence of knowers and positions epistemology as a means of knowing responsibly in order to live well together in environments that are partially shared. She is sensitive to the notion that people who are differently situated have different kinds of access to and are differently served by orthodox knowledge-production practices. According to Code, creating knowledge for living well together will involve working within orthodox practices and cultures while negotiating particular experiences in actual contexts. Ecological thinking is complex and nuanced. Code makes ecological thinking more understandable by developing a case study about Rachel Carson's scientific practice. Code shows that Carson functioned within the scientific orthodoxy—Carson was a working scientist who gathered and deployed empirical evidence to support her claims. However, there were also elements of Carson's practice that were in tension with the scientific orthodoxy—Carson had a deep respect for testimonial evidence, wrote for a broad and not only an academic audience, and was sensitive to relationships among different kinds of evidence as well as the context in which evidence was gathered, interpreted, and used. Code makes her abstract apparatus of ecological thinking an understandable and plausible model of knowledge production through her use of Carson as a philosophical case study.

In addition to using case studies to explore and develop their views, philosophers use case studies as evidence supporting a philosophical position (Crasnow, this volume). There is overlap between using a case study to develop and explore a philosophical position and using a case study as evidence supporting a philosophical position. For example, when one uses a case study to explain a philosophical position, it seems to both provide evidence and help to explore and develop that position.

Finally, sometimes philosophers develop case studies for their own sake. By this, I mean that the description and analysis of a situation can be philosophically interesting on its own merits, even if it is not connected to or used to advance a more general philosophical position. For example, it can be useful to develop an understanding of argumentative structure or social context of a particular scientific or medical practice even if that understanding is not linked to any overarching ethical or epistemic theories. The lessons learned from a case study need not apply across different contexts. I don't intend this list of ways that philosophers use case studies to be comprehensive; the point is that philosophers use case studies in a variety of ways.

Philosophical case studies can focus on a wide range of phenomena, such as a person, group, or institution or an experiment, area of research, or discipline. Examples include Sarah Richardson's (2013) detailed analyses of the influence of gender values on our understanding of the structure and function of sex chromosomes and Emily Martin's (1991) demonstration of how gender stereotypes twisted scientific and medical accounts of mammalian fertilization. Case studies can also focus on historical periods or geographic areas. For example, one might choose to explore the study of biological evolution in Victorian England (Hubbard 1990, 87–107) or the health effects of pollution on a particular community over a short period of time (Shrader-Frechette 2010). In addition to case studies having a variety of uses, case studies can be about parts of the world that are delineated using different sorts of criteria. In this chapter, irrespective of how an example is used (evidential, illustrative, or for its own sake), the kind of thing it is about (people, processes, communities, or institutions), or how it is bounded in time and space, as long as it is a detailed account documenting something that actually happened, or actually exists, it is a case study.[2]

WHAT IS A SOCIALLY SIGNIFICANT CASE STUDY?

Case studies vary in terms of their ethical or political valence. Some case studies reveal or in some way trade on injustices or harms faced by individuals or groups of people in fairly direct ways. For example, Sara Weaver (2017a, 2017b) provides a detailed analysis of the emerging field of feminist evolutionary psychology. Weaver's studies of feminist evolutionary psychology reveal that there are unaddressed biases and harmful gender values along with other methodological weaknesses woven throughout this research program. Feminist evolutionary-psychology research, because it tends to reinforce gender stereotypes and is consistent with patriarchal norms about men and women and the gendered distribution of labor while also bearing the label *feminist*, is harmful to women. Weaver's work on feminist evolutionary psychology is not only a case study, it is a socially significant case study. Weaver's case study is socially significant because the situation under study relates to harms, even though it often doesn't directly focus on the people who are harmed. Philosophy research that draws in a significant way on a case study that focuses on, reveals, or in some way trades on injustice or other harms to people or groups of people constitutes what I call a socially significant case study (SSCS). Some readers might be tempted to ask how significant a role the case needs to play in the philosophy research or how much injustice needs to be involved for the work to count as a SSCS. However, given that there is much SRPOS research that clearly focuses on detailed examples in which injustice and harm play a role, at this point, I am more interested in exploring these clear instances rather than demarcating how significant an example has to be in a research program or the degree of harm and the relevance of that harm that must be documented in a case for it to count as a SSCS. For the time being, there is a host of clear examples that beg analysis.

In the pharmaceutical research methods (PRM) example, the philosopher clearly presented a SSCS. The case studied was a detailed description and analysis of a real-world example of flawed research practices that result in overestimates of the effectiveness of prescription drugs—a state of affairs that has the potential to hurt patients and the general public and to contribute to cynicism about and distrust of the pharmaceutical industry. This flawed interpretation of experimental results is not just an epistemic failing. It is also an ethical failing, because those interpretive flaws can hurt people.

An important feature of the PRM example is that the potential harms it entails provide significant motivation for conducting the philosophical analysis in the first place and contribute to the audience of philosophers' assessment of the importance of the topic. An example of scientific research that exemplified the same interpretive errors but had much less potential to cause harm would likely be less interesting and important. The harms inherent in the PRM case study gave the philosophy lecture immediate significance, contributing to its philosophical importance and the corresponding success of the work and the author.

Doing Things

In this chapter, I argue that philosophers working on SSCSs should *do* something to address the harm or injustice represented in the case. When

I argue that philosophers should do things with their SSCSs, I mean that they should take direct action (such as lobbying policy makers or directly engaging those affected by the case study) or put their research in the hands of other people who are in positions to take direct action to address the situation described in the case study. The difficulty with the PRM example is that the author did not consider addressing the problem they discovered to be part of their job and provided no evidence that they had done anything to put their research into the hands of anyone who could address the problem. While the exchange I paraphrased at the beginning of this paper is rare in terms of being stark and explicit, it provides an enlightening glimpse of a common attitude toward philosophical work that is present even when that work goes beyond abstract philosophizing and involves concrete case studies.[3] My concern is that philosophers are rarely trained or expected to think about doing things with the knowledge they create that will facilitate that knowledge being used to make the world a better place. In the third section of this chapter, I explore some of the specific things that philosophers can do to maximize the positive social impact of their SSCSs. These things include a wide range of possible advocacy, dissemination, collaboration, and capacity-building activities. But first, it is useful to characterize some of the ethical and epistemic reasons why philosophers should ensure that their SSCS research contributes to solving the problems they represent.

Why Should Philosophers Do Things with Case Studies?

There are both ethical and epistemic reasons why philosophers working on socially significant case studies should take steps to help their research address the harms related to the situation they document.

ETHICAL REASONS: OBJECTIFICATION

The ethical imperatives of philosophical work on SSCSs go beyond narrowly construed issues of academic integrity such as crediting sources and eschewing plagiarism. Some of these ethical matters are exemplified in the work of Kristin Shrader-Frechette, a philosopher who has a long and distinguished track record of SSCS research. Her work focuses on the harms of environmental contamination, on the inequitable and unjust distribution of the risks of these harms, and on flawed science that masks these risks and harms. The environmental problems she investigates range from the effects of nuclear waste and pesticides to the impact of diesel exhaust fumes on the health of children in East Los Angeles (Shrader-Frechette 1991; Shrader-Frechette and McQuestion 2016; Shrader-Frechette and ChoGlueck 2017). Shrader-Frechette does more than publish this research in philosophical or even academic journals. She engages in many activities to improve the situations she studies. For example, she "has been invited to join important science-advisory/policy groups, e.g., boards/committees of the US National Academy of Sciences; regulatory committees of the US Department of Energy, the US National Commission on Radiological Protection and Measurement, etc.; international radiation-standard-setting committees (as the US delegate) of the International Commission on Radiological Protection; and various science-advisory committees, e.g., the US Environmental Protection Agency Science Advisory Board" (Shrader-Frechette 2010, 465).

Kristin Shrader-Frechette not only researches SSCSs, she *does things* with her research and uses her expertise to address the problems she investigates. She also advances the view that, like scientists and engineers, philosophers of science have a professional duty to protect the public. In Shrader-Frechette's (2010) work, this means helping to correct the flawed science used to justify unfair distributions of risks in environmental assessments.

Shrader-Frechette works on SSCSs, does things to address the harms that her SSCSs explore, and explicitly argues that philosophers have professional responsibilities to address the risks and harms their work reveals. In addition to these sorts of arguments regarding professional duties, I argue that individual philosophers should be wary of objectifying the people harmed by the SSCSs that those philosophers deploy.

The PRM example is striking because, presumably unintended and unnoticed by the speaker, chair, and most of the audience, the people put at risk by the flawed science were being used as a means for the career advancement of the scholar and the engagement of the audience. However, the people put at risk received no benefit from the SSCS research or the lecture. It was the risk to patients and the harm to the general public that made the case study urgent and significant. The speaker was aware of and benefited from the existence of the harms but seemed to shirk any responsibility to act against these harms, even the minimal action of disseminating their research to someone in a position to act against these harms.[4] This is a case of problematically objectifying the people affected by the science under consideration.

Although there are multiple philosophical accounts of objectification (Papadaki 2018), in this chapter, by *objectification* I mean treating people as objects in the sense of using them as instruments to advance one's goals and interests. Although this sort of objectification research need not be ethically problematic per se, it *is* problematic when coupled with a lack of respect for and care about the well-being of the people in question.[5] In SSCSs, the people involved in or affected by the science in question are at least instruments for the advancement of a philosopher and of philosophy itself insofar as the risks or harms or injustices they face (1) are described in the case study, (2) contribute to the motivation for conducting the case study in the first place, or (3) are a factor in the positive uptake of the case study by the philosophy community. If the author of the SSCS and the discipline itself take no meaningful action to address the risks, harms, or injustices faced by the people or communities involved in the case study, then the researcher and the field are demonstrating a lack of care and respect for those people. This lack of care and respect makes the objectification morally wrong. For SSCSs about science that does harm, such as the Tuskegee syphilis study, an infamous investigation of the progression of syphilis in which Black men with the infection were neither told they were infected nor provided treatment, a lack of care and respect would manifest itself as not doing anything to stop the experiment, help the infected people, or support the development of policy or law to stop such experiments and protect people. For SSCSs about science that reveals or leads to harm, such as the PRM case study, a lack of care and respect can manifest itself as doing nothing to stop the science that is causing harm or to alert people to the harms they face. Worries about the specific harms of problematic objectification apply most clearly in cases where the author of the case study, or a relevant group of which the author is a member, is not subject to the harms and risks under investigation. After all, it can be confusing to consider whether one can objectify one's self. However, I suspect that in many instances where the author has the potential to be harmed, they may, perhaps even unconsciously, use their individual knowledge of the case to ameliorate risks they might face. For example, a philosopher who gained in-depth knowledge of pharmaceutical research practices from their case-study research may change their behavior. They may ask more questions of prescribing physicians, exhibit a more conservative approach to medication, or avoid some over-the-counter drugs altogether.

One might object that even if SSCS research does not address the harms it documents, it does provide a vital social benefit just because it produces new knowledge and knowledge is inherently valuable. However, as long as this knowledge is produced in a way that makes use of another person or group without affording them respect and caring about their well-being, it is still a case of problematic objectification. Even if we decide that knowledge production does trump concerns about objectification, what we end up saying is that we are willing to accept problematic objectification because there are overriding benefits, not that objectification is absent. However, as Heather Douglas (2003) argues, knowledge production does not trump all other values—we put ethical constraints on scientific knowledge production all the time. So, this objection becomes a call to weigh the value of knowledge production against the harms of objectification that might ensue when nothing is done with the case study. This weighing is difficult to do in the abstract, and so to develop this objection, it is necessary to look not at the abstract value of knowledge but rather at the value of the particular knowledge under consideration—the knowledge produced in a particular case study.

In the PRM example, the philosopher develops an SSCS involving a description and analysis of flawed science. They are not just creating any new knowledge; they are creating knowledge of flaws in the pharmaceutical research. Moreover, they are raising awareness of these flaws by giving a lecture on the topic. When the objection is framed in terms of the production of particular knowledge, the objection no longer focuses on the value of knowledge as an abstract good but points out that this particular knowledge is valuable *because* it is about and has the potential to address the case under consideration. In this way, the person raising the objection could be arguing that the objectification in this example is not problematic. It is still an example of objectification because the SSCS is advancing the philosopher's career, but the philosopher is exercising care and respect by creating this particular knowledge, so it is not an example of problematic objectification.

However, this is not demonstrating sufficient care and respect (if it is demonstrating any at all), because there is a difference between creating knowledge that *can* be used and creating knowledge that is *likely* to be used. If immediately after creating this knowledge the philosopher removed themselves from all human contact, then even if this knowledge of the flawed pharmaceutical research could be used to address problems associated with the case, it wouldn't actually do so. This silly hermit example is meant to emphasize the idea that knowledge has to live somewhere. Once it is created, it is not telepathically disseminated across the cosmos, or even across the street. One cannot assume that the presence of an SSCS in a philosophy journal or at a philosophy conference will reach anyone outside of the discipline unless one takes active steps to create and communicate that knowledge in a way that is accessible and useful to those who are in positions to act on it. The practices of knowledge creation and dissemination, as well as the social locations and relationships among philosophers, stakeholders, and policy makers, can influence whether or not SSCSs have a genuine potential to address the situations they describe.

The objection that the philosopher in the PRM example was producing knowledge that could be used to address the example and so was not problematically objectifying the people affected by the case boils down to whether the philosopher's research had or was likely to have positive consequences for the people affected by the SSCS. Was creating this knowledge and raising awareness in this way enough? The philosopher said that it was their job to discover and present the problem but that it was someone else's job to fix it. The objection I've been considering says that it is the philosopher's job to be part of the solution to the problem, but that by conducting the research and giving a talk to other philosophers, the philosopher did that job, or at least accomplished enough of it. Unfortunately, the social impact of philosophical research is rarely measured, philosophers are rarely taught how to use their research to do good, and it is easy to overestimate the good this research does. Assessments of philosophical research tend to use measures of professional publications and talks; they do not, or they rarely, measure social impact.

One of the fundamental questions that feminist epistemology poses is, "Whose knowledge?" (Harding 1991). Knowledge is not just floating free out there in the ether, good for everyone and available to all. It lives in particular people and communities and documents and servers. In practice, philosophical research tends to be highly inaccessible, lodged behind paywalls and laden with jargon. If knowledge is to be a good thing in a more general way, it needs to be available to more people—in particular, the people who are in a position to have some impact on the situation under consideration.

One could further object that research on SSCSs published in professional philosophy journals can provide resources to other scholars and activists, who could work to address the harms. Though this is possible, knowledge does not mobilize itself, and philosophers need to take steps to make communication across these groups likely if they are to discharge their responsibilities for the amelioration of the harms they exploit.

Finally, it is useful to attend to both individual-level ethical concerns and the disciplinary norms that inform philosophical practice. The PRM example reveals the individual speaker's understanding of their professional responsibilities as well as the norms of the community of philosophers listening to that lecture. In general, if one focuses on the individual, it may be that the responsibility to do something to address the case study under consideration varies with the extent of the harm or injustice associated with that particular case. However, even if an individual philosopher decides not to act, or to do very little to address the case because the harms or injustices associated with a that case are minimal, if this decision contributes to or strengthens a professional norm of inaction, then there may still be ethical costs associated with this relatively benign individual choice.

In this section, I argue that to avoid problematically objectifying those people harmed or put at risk by the SSCSs that philosophers study, philosophers should take steps to address the harms and risks on which their work relies. Taking steps to address these harms and risks demonstrates care and respect for those people who are part of the case study that advances the scholar's career and contributes to the discipline of philosophy. I will discuss those steps in the next section of this chapter. But first I will address how focusing on the social impact of SSCSs in addition to addressing ethical concerns can also protect philosophical research against potential epistemic weaknesses.

Epistemic Benefits

Maximizing the social impact of SSCSs provides opportunities to improve the rigor and usefulness of philosophical research. Doing so requires engaging in research- and knowledge-mobilization practices that expand the epistemic community to which SSCSs are exposed. This expanded epistemic community should include people who are affected by or who have the capacity to address the situation described in the case study.

Improved Rigor

Mobilizing research on SSCSs beyond the disciplinary boundaries of philosophy and hence expanding the epistemic community to which the case is exposed can improve the rigor of the case by subjecting this research to critical scrutiny from new perspectives. By deliberately disseminating research to knowers outside of their immediate epistemic communities, philosophers have the potential to reap the benefits of critical scrutiny of their work from a broader range of perspectives. This is particularly important when case studies are evidential or illustrative.

Helen Longino (1990) argues that the objectivity of scientific knowledge increases when knowledge is subject to critical scrutiny from multiple points of view. Longino points out that there is an inferential gap between the hypothesis under consideration and the evidence that is supposed to have bearing on that hypothesis, and that the researcher's assumptions play a role in bridging this gap. The assumptions involved in research are often implicit and go unnoticed by researchers unless they engage in practices to actively seek them out and evaluate them. A good way to notice one's assumptions is to engage in constructive critical dialogue with those who hold different assumptions, which can be accomplished by subjecting scientific-knowledge claims to the critical scrutiny of a community of people with a range of points of view. This social practice increases the objectivity of scientific knowledge because it makes assumptions explicit and hence subject to critical evaluation.

Longino (2002) has expanded her view of the objectivity of scientific knowledge to encompass the justification of knowledge claims in general. She has come to call this view *critical contextual empiricism*. If critical contextual empiricism applies to knowledge claims in general, then surely it applies to knowledge claims made by philosophers in the course of their research. If Longino's view is applied to the production of SSCSs, it follows that exposing those SSCSs to a broader and more diverse community, particularly a community that includes nonphilosopher experts on the case study, can help philosophers improve the rigor—the objectivity or justification—of their knowledge claims.

When philosophers use case studies as illustrations or evidence, it makes sense to attend to the gap between the evidence and the conclusions drawn. By ensuring that the outputs of philosophical case studies are accessible to people outside of philosophy, particularly people who are affected by or in positions to use this knowledge, philosophers can subject their work to critical scrutiny from a wide range of perspectives. This has the potential to reveal assumptions in how philosophers define terms and concepts and can help philosophers understand and use concepts in ways that are consistent with the culture, community, and history relevant to the case study. In this way, philosophical analyses that involve evidence can be evaluated from a wide range of perspectives, which improves the rigor of these analyses. Doing so with the goal of addressing the harms and risks revealed in SSCSs has the potential to be very effective because it will generally involve ensuring that this range of perspectives includes those who are well informed about the case at hand.

USEFULNESS

In addition to improving the rigor of SSCSs, strategically mobilizing SSCS research beyond philosophy and reaching people particularly connected in some way to the case study helps philosophers come to know if the knowledge they produce is useful for improving the situation described in the case study. Iterative interactions with this extended epistemic community provide opportunities for philosophers to produce increasingly useful knowledge. Many philosophers who work on SSCSs do so because they are distressed by, and hence want to address, the harms and risks inherent in or caused by the case. Engaging with relevant stakeholders and people affected by the case can help philosophers understand whether their work meets this goal or how it might better meet this goal.

If philosophers are engaging and exploring a case study because they are distressed by the injustice and harms they see, it is essential to know if they are producing knowledge that is useful or has the potential to be useful in meeting this goal. While philosophers can test whether they can use that knowledge through direct advocacy work, they can also put their SSCS in the hands of the people it concerns, scientists, or policy makers and ask those people if the results of the case study can be used to improve the situation the case study documents. For example, if a philosopher is exploring harmful assumptions within a scientific research program, scientists could provide useful information about whether the philosopher's work is focusing on the most pertinent science, whether the philosopher's discussion of values is presented in a way that is likely to get uptake, or whether the philosopher's analysis conflicts with other aspects of the science of which the philosopher is unaware.

It is common to develop an SSCS over an extended period and to hone the case study over the course of many talks and several publications. When we consider this extended process of developing an SSCS, the notion of strategically mobilizing philosophical research to an expanded epistemic community starts to look more like collaborating with, rather than disseminating to, stakeholders or policy makers. This involves a shift toward considering philosophical research as a social practice that includes people who are not themselves professional philosophers. I will develop this thought in more detail in the next section.

There are both ethical and epistemic reasons for philosophers developing SSCSs to ensure that their research can in some way address the situation that they are studying. Ethical reasons include personal and professional duties to protect the public as well as demonstrating care and respect for those affected by the case study. Epistemic reasons include improving the rigor of the SSCS and coming to know whether the SSCS is helpful and how it could be made more helpful in addressing the situation the case describes. However, the dividing line between ethical and epistemic reasons is not as sharp as one might think. For example, avoiding objectification involves effectively addressing the situation described by the SSCS, and philosophers can more effectively address the situation if they take advantage of the epistemic opportunities that arise from disseminating their work to an extended epistemic community. In other words, philosophers can better address the situation described by the case study if the knowledge they produce is as accurate as possible and practically useful.

What Should Philosophers Do with Their SSCSs?

When I talk about doing things with case studies, I mean taking steps to make it possible and hopefully likely that philosophical research on an SSCS can be used to address the risks, or harms, or injustices associated with that case. While in some situations the production of a philosophical paper or lecture can be an essential step toward addressing the issues inherent in an SSCS, these philosophical research products are rarely, if ever, sufficient to do so. In this section, I discuss how philosophers can deploy strategic dissemination practices, engage in collaboration, and support structural/institutional changes to make SSCSs more influential and better able to address the problems they describe.[6]

Strategically Disseminate Philosophical Work to Appropriate Publics

Strategic dissemination involves making philosophical research available and accessible to nonphilosophers. It means taking steps to ensure that philosophical research escapes not only the disciplinary borders of philosophy but also the academy itself and makes it into the parts of the world it describes. The two most common means of disseminating philosophical research are by way of academic articles and conference presentations. More often than not, these articles end up cloistered behind paywalls and presented at conferences that are neither open to nor easy for nonphilosophers to attend. One way that philosophers can make their research more available to people outside of philosophy and outside of the academy is by submitting their work to open-access journals and by giving talks in venues that are open to nonphilosophers—to scholars in other disciplines and in spaces open and inviting to the communities the philosopher hopes to engage.

Much philosophical research is written in ways that are inaccessible to nonphilosophers. It is produced for professional-philosophy audiences, it is framed to advance professional-philosophical debates and positions, and it is often explained with obscure technical language. These practices are not in themselves wrong. Philosophy, like other disciplines, has its professional discourse that it is the job of philosophers to engage. However, when the communication of philosophical research is limited to these professional and technical genres, it will likely remain within the discipline. This can limit the epistemic community that will engage this work, which I have shown can have negative ethical and epistemic consequences, particularly for SSCSs.

Expanding philosophy's epistemic community can be facilitated by writing in a wider range of genres for a wider array of venues. This can include public philosophy practices such as writing op-eds, blog posts, and white papers or talking with policy makers. The goal is to take philosophy out of the university or the professional philosophy conference and to people who are affected by that philosophical work and who can use that work, as opposed to waiting for those people to come to the philosophy journal article or conference presentation. Some philosophers already engage in these broader dissemination activities.[7] However, the ethical and epistemic benefits that I have described suggest that philosophical work would improve should philosophers do more of this, and, in order for philosophers to do more, such work has to become more highly valued by philosophy departments and the discipline itself.

The public affected by or in a position to act on some SSCS research often includes social and natural scientists and engineers who work in the academy, government, or industry. In socially relevant philosophy of science, philosophers often explore ways to improve scientific practice as well as influence policy. For example, Nancy Tuana's (2010, 2013) philosophical research on climate science has revealed values within some climate-modeling methods that may put poor nations at more risk than wealthier nations. Tuana has developed research partnerships with climate scientists to explore these issues in collaboration with them and has coauthored papers published in a wide range of venues about these topics (for example, Goes, Tuana, and Keller 2011). Philosophers writing articles for academic journals in other disciplines and giving talks at other disciplinary conferences can be a way for philosophical research to have a positive, practical impact (Fehr and Plaisance 2010).

The tone as well as the theoretical perspective and language with which philosophers present their research can bear on the uptake of philosophical work by scientist colleagues (as well as by members of other groups). For example, philosophers have written reams of research critical of arguments and biases in evolutionary psychology. Despite ample philosophical criticism of evolutionary psychology, harmful sexist and androcentric values remain entrenched in that science. There are rude and mean (even though correct) philosophical critiques of this research. The relative absence of constructive scholarship is one barrier to effective communication with and reform of evolutionary psychology (Fehr 2012). The culture of philosophy has been described as a "blood sport" (Swartz 1994), and the tone of philosophy talks and conferences is often much more confrontational than talks and conferences of other disciplines that I have attended. The goal of strategic dissemination is to make SSCS research useful in the world. This goal is supported not only by dissemination practices that take philosophical research to the people who can use it and expressing the research using accessible language but also by expressing it in a way that invites uptake from nonphilosophical audiences.

So far, I have discussed strategic dissemination under the assumption of a one-way information flow in which philosophers create knowledge and then share it with appropriate audiences. This dissemination model has the potential to address some of the ethical concerns that arise with SSCS research but does not maximize the epistemic benefits of improving the rigor and usefulness of philosophical research, because those benefits arise from interactions among philosophers and members of nonphilosophical communities. An alternative and additional strategy is to partner with relevant nonphilosopher experts in the production of philosophical knowledge.

COLLABORATE

It might be tempting to think of philosophical-research practices as being separate from knowledge-transfer practices. But one way to ensure that SSCSs make it beyond the boundaries of philosophy and hence have the potential to address the harms documented is to engage in collaborative research with stakeholders, policy makers, and others who are in positions to do things with case studies. By engaging in collaboration during the genesis, planning, and conduct of research, philosophers embed know-ledge transfer in the knowledge-production process itself. Collaboration throughout the research process can be an effective way to garner the epistemic benefits I discussed earlier in this chapter.

Noncollaborative research is produced and then brought to nonphil-osophers with the hope that they will evaluate the research for things like hidden assumptions, conceptual accuracy, appropriate contextualization, and relevance. Giving this research to nonphilosophers and asking them to assess the usefulness of the finished product can be valuable, even if it doesn't go as far as collaborative research does in ensuring full engagement with the communities.

While sharing the finished product with nonphilosophers makes it possible for those people to engage SSCSs, philosophers should also con-sider the extent to which their practices make this sort of engagement with nonphilosophers likely and effective. There is a difference between provid-ing an invitation and being inviting. Engaging in collaborative practices throughout the research process creates a diverse epistemic community; it allows nonphilosopher collaborators to ensure that the research progresses in a way that meets their needs, which in turn can motivate the sorts of epistemic engagement that strengthens the research itself.

There are philosophers working in socially relevant philosophy of science who engage in cross-sector and cross-disciplinary collaboration. For example, Nancy Tuana (2010, 2013) collaborates with climate scien-tists to reveal and assess values inherent in their research practices, and Kristin Shrader-Frechette (2010) has a long history of working with sci-entific advisory and policy groups on topics such as pesticide threats and nuclear-energy risks. By asking philosophers to collaborate beyond their discipline to improve public welfare, I am not asking for a novel practice. I am emphasizing that, like strategic dissemination, this practice provides significant epistemic and ethical benefits to philosophers working on

SSCSs, and so I am arguing that it is important to support philosophers engaging in collaborative research.

REMOVE BARRIERS AND CREATE INSTITUTIONAL SUPPORT

Ideally, philosophers working on SSCSs would enjoy genuine disciplinary and institutional support for strategic dissemination and collaboration because these practices contribute to ethically and epistemically good philosophy. However, a wide range of barriers can block philosophers conducting SSCSs, as well as other kinds of research, from doing things with their work to address that cases they describe. Addressing these barriers is something that the profession of philosophy can do to support philosophers working on SSCSs and help them to do ethically and epistemically good work. Plaisance and I point out that philosophers can face disincentives to disseminating their work in venues that are accessible to nonphilosophers (Fehr and Plaisance 2010). For example, many philosophers perceive there to be scant professional rewards for writing op-eds or blogs for a general audience. Indeed, calling philosophical work "journalistic" is a way of disparaging work that is considered lightweight or unimportant. Similarly, in some philosophical communities, academic papers written for other disciplines count less toward a scholar's professional advancement than papers written for strictly philosophical audiences.

Philosophers working on SSCSs can also face barriers to engaging in practices that directly address the cases under consideration, such as testifying at public hearings or advising policy makers or political action groups. Given the finitude of time and pressures to publish, philosophers can come to believe that working to address the situation their SSCSs describe can block career advancement or the attainment of job security. The way a philosophy department writes up its tenure expectations as well as the function of a department's unwritten expectations and norms can have a significant impact on a faculty member's decisions about whether to engage in these sorts of advocacy and dissemination activities.

There is a need for empirical evidence about the extent of these barriers. It is not clear how significant an effect they actually have on a scholar's career development. However, the mere perception of these barriers, by the scholars themselves or by senior mentors in the field, can be enough to inhibit scholars from engaging in strategic dissemination, collaborative research, or advocacy. So, even if one does not feel that these barriers are significant, publicly supporting these dissemination and collaboration practices can be influential.

So far, my discussions in this paper have presupposed that the philosopher conducting SSCSs is outside of the community affected by the case. This is often not true. Particularly when cases involve members of marginalized groups, it is not uncommon for philosophers who are members of those groups to investigate these cases. While there is no systematic data demonstrating this point, it is evident that many feminist philosophers are people who identify as women, many philosophers of race are people who are members of racialized groups, and so on. Insofar as SSCSs are more likely to be conducted by members of marginalized groups, disciplinary and institutional practices that block strategic dissemination and collaboration practices not only undermine the production of ethically and epistemically good philosophy but, in doing so, also disproportionately penalize scholars who are members of marginalized groups.

Consideration of the barriers that philosophers may face when doing ethically and epistemically good work on SSCSs makes it apparent that strong SSCS research benefits from support from the discipline and the academy. There are many ways in which all philosophers can provide structural and institutional help for their colleagues who wish to improve the social relevance of their SSCS research. For example, philosophers can bolster open-access publishing venues, create mechanisms for evaluating nontraditional research publications and different kinds of collaborative research, and develop professional organizations and networks to improve the philosophical stature of strategic dissemination and collaboration.

BOLSTER OPEN-ACCESS PUBLISHING

Strategic dissemination requires at the very least that SSCSs be available to people who can use that research to address the problems described in the case. Philosophers working on an SSCS can increase the availability of their work by publishing it in online open-access journals. These venues are open to people who are not affiliated with a university, and their content is not blockaded behind paywalls. The trouble is that many open-access journals are relatively new and have not had time to develop the institutional prestige needed to support a junior scholar's career advancement. Nurturing open-access journals is one way that the discipline can support scholars working on SSCSs. When senior scholars take time to work for, lend their names to the editorial boards of, and submit their research for publication in these venues, they contribute to the prestige and reputation of the journal. Building open-access publishing can improve the availability of all scholarship, and, in doing so, it supports ethically and epistemically good SSCS research as well as the philosophers doing this work.

CREATE MECHANISMS FOR EVALUATING NONTRADITIONAL RESEARCH PUBLICATIONS AND DIFFERENT KINDS OF COLLABORATIVE RESEARCH

Philosophy departments can develop policies and practices to support philosophers who strategically disseminate their work and engage in collaborative research by creating mechanisms for evaluating strategic dissemination and collaborative research practices. The process of peer review and common understandings of the prestige of academic journals provide commonly accepted ways of assessing the value of traditional research papers. While blog posts, op-eds, and white papers are not typically peer reviewed, departments can develop ways of assessing the quality of these different genres of knowledge mobilization. It may remain prudent for philosophers to develop a body of work that includes traditional peer-reviewed academic papers. But if writing in these alternative genres improves the rigor and usefulness of the philosophy and contributes to philosophers' capacity to produce ethically responsible research that avoids objectifying those affected by that research, then these alternative genres and venues are part of good philosophical practice, and excellence at this practice ought to contribute to a scholar's professional advancement.

Departments can support scholars working on SSCSs by valuing research published in online open-access journals. Although these journals do not have the same level of prestige as journals with a long history, there are other ways of evaluating the merit of these venues. For example, some open-access journals have very stringent, triple-anonymous review processes and are very transparent about those review practices. Even though new venues may lack the cachet of long-running journals, they may have review practices that are more rigorous and transparent than older publication venues. This is the kind of thing that a department can decide to value when it comes to the career advancement of its members.[8]

Departments can also develop transparent evaluative measures for a wider range of collaborative research practices. In many disciplines, coauthored papers are the norm, but in philosophy this is a fairly rare practice. It would be useful for departments and the discipline to develop standards for assessing research papers with multiple authors and to consider that collaborations across disciplines or sectors can be extremely time and labor intensive.

Departments also can be proactive in supporting scholars doing things with SSCSs by developing frameworks for valuing and evaluating collaborative talks and publications; by valuing publications in venues that are not blocked by paywalls; by valuing a wide range of research products including public outreach, white papers, and other sorts of public philosophy; and by creating measures to evaluate the social impact of research on SSCSs.

Develop Professional Organizations and Networks

Professional organizations whose mission includes a focus on strategic dissemination and collaboration can play a significant role in helping scholars working on SSCSs produce ethically and epistemically good research. In addition to being spaces where philosophers can develop and share strategies for doing things with case studies, these organizations can also play a role in developing criteria for assessing strategic dissemination practices and collaborative research. These criteria can be an important resource that departments can use to create evaluative frameworks for the nontraditional dissemination and research practices of their members. Finally, the existence of professional organizations that include well-recognized scholars can demonstrate the significance of strategic dissemination and collaboration activities. This can provide departments with information they can use to support philosophers doing ethically and epistemically good work with SSCSs. The Consortium for Socially Relevant Philosophy of/in Science and Engineering is a good example of this sort of institution.[9] The following is an excerpt from its mission statement: "This consortium supports, advances, and conducts philosophical work that is related to science and engineering and that contributes to public welfare and collective wellbeing. We aim to improve the capacity of philosophers of all specializations to collaborate and engage with scientists, engineers, policy-makers, and a wide range of publics to foster epistemically and ethically responsible scientific and technological research" (SRPoiSE, n.d.).

There is a wide range of things that philosophers can do to help their SSCS research address the situations on which it relies. In addition to direct advocacy, such as the work performed by Kristin Shrader-Frechette, philosophers can take steps to strategically disseminate their research, making it available and accessible to a wide range of audiences by writing in a variety of genres and venues. Strategic dissemination activity puts philosophical research in the hands of people who are affected by the case and people who have the capacity to address the situation described in the case study. Philosophers can also perform collaborative research, working with those affected by or in positions to address the case.

All three of these activities—advocacy, strategic dissemination, and collaboration—are not the primary activities of mainstream philosophy. As a result, it is useful to include an institutional as well as an individual perspective on these practices. Philosophers can be encouraged to reap the ethical and epistemic benefits arising from advocacy, strategic dissemination, and collaboration by the active support of their departments and the discipline.

Conclusion

In this chapter, I characterize a philosophical case study as a rich description or analysis of something that has actually happened or is actually happening. A socially significant case study (SSCS) draws on, reveals, or in some way trades on injustice or other harms to people or groups of people. I argue that philosophers conducting SSCS research should do things with their work to address, or to help other people address, that situation described in the case.

There are ethical reasons why they should do so. I argue that if philosophers don't take steps to protect people from the harms that their philosophical research reveals or in some way trades on, they risk problematically objectifying the people affected by the case. The objectification is problematic because it involves treating people as a means for advancing one's research without demonstrating care or respect for the people in question. To demonstrate care or respect, philosophers should take steps, actual steps, to address the harms inherent in the case or to enable others to do so. Making SSCS research available to those impacted by the case or those who can address the problem inherent in the case also has epistemic benefits. These benefits arise because making philosophical research genuinely available to a wider range of publics expands the epistemic community that can assess the research and opens the research up to constructive criticism from a wide range of perspectives. These ethical and epistemic benefits are closely intertwined—presumably, improving the quality and usefulness of SSCSs can improve their positive social impact, and the same sorts of activities can provide both ethical and epistemic benefits.

There are many things that philosophers can do to enable their SSCSs to make the world a better place. These things include strategically disseminating philosophical research and engaging in cross-disciplinary and cross-sector research collaborations. These practices, though, require systematic and deliberate institutional support. It would be a shame if arguments about objectification and corresponding fears about the harms of objectification discouraged individual philosophers from engaging in socially significant research. However, the answer to this is not to lower the ethical or epistemic standards for this sort of work. Rather, the institutions in which philosophy is practiced and the discipline itself ought to develop a culture of professional support and accolades for philosophers who conduct epistemically and ethically good philosophical research. Socially significant case studies need to be used to make the world a better place.[10]

Notes

1. I am exploring maximizing the social impact of philosophical research on a particular sort of case study. However, I expect that many of my points can be applied to a wider range of philosophical methods and approaches.

2. Distinguishing case studies from other sources of insight such as thought experiments or literary examples is methodologically significant because ethical and epistemic demands arise from the involvement of real people.

3. Thanks to Heidi Grasswick for helping me clarify this point.

4. See McHugh (2015), who points out that while scholars benefit from publishing research, those benefits tend not to support the subjects of the research.

5. This is intentionally parallel to Martha Nussbaum's discussion of sexual objectification. Nussbaum (1995, 257) lists seven features of objectification, one of which is instrumentality, which means using a person as a tool to advance one's goals. She also argues that treating someone as an object, even a lover, need not be problematic unless it involves the absence of equality, respect, and consent (265).

6. The Public Philosophy Network (https://www.publicphilosophynetwork. net/) and the Society of Philosophers in America (https://www.philosophersin america.com) provide excellent resources for effectively doing things with case studies (Meagher and Feder 2010; Meagher 2013).

7. In addition to the Consortium for Socially Relevant Philosophy of/in Science and Engineering (SRPoiSE, http://www.srpoise.org), which focuses on

philosophy of science, I also refer the reader to the Public Philosophy Network and the Society of Philosophers in America for examples of this kind of work already being done. Some of this work specifically uses case studies, though these organizations and the people who comprise them are part of a broader movement to make philosophical work accessible and relevant for lay persons.

8. I want to disclose that I am an editor of *Feminist Philosophy Quarterly*, a young, online, open-access journal with triple-anonymous review practices.

9. In the interest of disclosure, I would like to point out that I am one of the founders of this organization.

10. I am very grateful to Heidi Grasswick, Ness Lamont, Katrien Jacobs, Nancy McHugh, and Kathryn Plaisance for generous conversations about this chapter and thoughtful, constructive comments on various drafts of the chapter.

References

Code, Lorraine. 2006. *Ecological Thinking: The Politics of Epistemic Location*. New York: Oxford University Press.

Douglas, Heather E. 2003. "The Moral Responsibilities of Scientists (Tensions between Autonomy and Responsibility)." *Americal Philosophical Quarterly* 40 (1): 59–68.

Fehr, Carla. 2012. "Feminist Engagement with Evolutionary Psychology." *Hypatia* 27 (1): 52–72.

Fehr, Carla, and Kathryn S. Plaisance. 2010. "Socially Relevant Philosophy of Science: An introduction." *Synthese* 177 (3): 301–16.

Goes, Marlos, Nancy Tuana, and Klaus Keller. 2011. "The Economics (or Lack Thereof) of Aerosol Geoengineering." *Climatic Change* 109 (3): 719–44.

Harding, Sandra. 1991. *Whose Science? Whose Knowledge? Thinking from Women's Lives*. Ithaca, NY: Cornell University Press.

Hubbard, Ruth. 1990. *The Politics of Women's Biology*. New Brunswick, NJ: Rutgers University Press.

Longino, Helen E. 1990. *Science as Social Knowledge: Values and Objectivity in Scientific Inquiry*. Princeton, NJ: Princeton University Press.

———. 2002. *The Fate of Knowledge*. Princeton, NJ: Princeton University Press.

Martin, Emily. 1991. "The Egg and the Sperm: How Science Has Constructed a Romance Based on Stereotypical Male-Female Roles." *Signs* 16 (3): 485–501.

McHugh, Nancy. 2015. *The Limits of Knowledge: Generating Pragmatist Feminist Cases for Situated Knowing*. Albany: State University of New York Press.

Meagher, Sharon M. 2013. *Public Philosophy: Revitalizing Philosophy as a Civic Discipline*. https://www.api.ning.com/files/C*75Xw4bA4cU7vHOHS-zlLRm kdBskXa9IzuVBCJKtjhmSgMrQy8tWTu1s9vqumPuG2gyJfaPzwWJ1Tu4*No JIUVYUXtPpC37/KetteringreportfinalcorrectedFeb2013.pdf.

Meagher, Sharon M., and Ellen K. Feder. 2010. *Practicing Public Philosophy*. https://www.api.ning.com/files/--qSpH8VZdwkMHPvCiExMFpvuAT6MqF7LLfHv0 zW5fcWV6h*NqVobeBlwQP8oYSJd1Fl7J8RXK6dpB1DkEyz40z6HqqIww yV/publicphil_report_draft_June_3finalfinal.pdf.

Nussbaum, Martha C. 1995. "Objectification." *Philosophy and Public Affairs* 24 (4): 249–91.

Papadaki, Evangelia (Lina). 2018. "Feminist Perspectives on Objectification." *Stanford Encyclopedia of Philosophy*, edited by Edward N. Zalta. Summer 2018 ed. https://www.plato.stanford.edu/archives/sum2018/entries/feminism-objectification/.

Plaisance, Kathryn S., and Carla Fehr, eds. 2010. "Making Philosophy of Science More Socially Relevant." Special issue, *Synthese* 177 (3).

Richardson, Sarah S. 2013. *Sex Itself: The Search for Male and Female in the Human Genome*. Chicago: University of Chicago Press.

Shrader-Frechette, Kristin. 1991. "Ethical Dilemmas and Radioactive Waste: A Survey of the Issues." *Environmental Ethics* 13 (4): 327–43.

———. 2010. "Conceptual Analysis and Special-Interest Science: Toxicology and the Case of Edward Calabrese." *Synthese* 177 (3): 449–69.

Shrader-Frechette, Kristin, and Christopher ChoGlueck. 2017. "Pesticides, Neuro-developmental Disagreement, and Bradford Hill's Guidelines." *Accountability in Research* 24 (1): 30–42.

Shrader-Frechette, Kristin, and Catherine McQuestion. 2016. "'Special-Interest Science' Harms Diesel-Polluted Communities Like East Los Angeles." *Journal of Community Medicine and Public Health Care* 3 (16): 1–10.

SRPoiSE (The Consortium for Socially Relevant Philosophy of/in Science and Engineering). n.d. "Home." SRPoiSE. http://www.srpoise.org.

Swartz, Norman. 1994. "Philosophy as a Blood Sport." Simon Fraser University (website). April 9, 1994. https://www.sfu.ca/~swartz/blood_sport.htm.

Tuana, Nancy. 2010. "Leading with Ethics, Aiming for Policy: New Opportunities for Philosophy of Science." *Synthese* 177 (3): 471–92.

———. 2013. "Embedding Philosophers in the Practices of Science: Bringing Humanities to the Sciences." *Synthese* 190 (11): 1955–73.

Weaver, Sara. 2017a. "A Constructive Critical Assessment of Feminist Evolutionary Psychology." PhD diss., University of Waterloo. UWSpace. http://hdl.handle.net/10012/12772.

———. 2017b. "The Harms of Ignoring the Social Nature of Science." *Synthese* 196 (4): 355–75.

PART 3

CASE STUDIES FOR SOCIAL JUSTICE

Chapter 7

Singing the "Blues" for Black Male Bodies

Epistemic Violence, Non-alterity, and Black-Male Killings

SHADAWN BATTLE

And may every nigger like this nigger end like this nigger—face down in the weeds!

—James Baldwin, *Blues for Mister Charlie*

Laquan McDonald was a seventeen-year-old Chicago teen murdered by then-officer Jason Van Dyke in 2014. The video of his murder reveals McDonald walking anxiously across a street with a pocketknife in hand, away from a small brigade of police officers, until he falls prey to the first bullet unleashed by Van Dyke. McDonald twirls in midair, almost theatrically, before his body hits the pavement. This is followed by a barrage of bullets—fifteen more, to be exact. Van Dyke managed to unload sixteen shots in a span of fifteen seconds. As the police report disclosed, Van Dyke feared that a boy with a four-inch pocketknife held in his right, *outside* hand, walking in the *opposite* direction of his pointed gun, would somehow endanger *his* life (Sanchez 2017). One might claim that Van Dyke had misinterpreted McDonald's actions as threatening his life. But this killing should be understood as part of a framework in which young Black males are killed because they are believed to be predators in the minds of racists.

Unfortunately, distorted versions of reality such as Van Dyke's have come to represent "an officially sanctioned reality"[1] in this country, to the detriment of Black and brown bodies. Thus, for young Black males like McDonald in the United States, singing the blues—or, figuratively and quite literally relying on the Black American expressive "impulse to keep the painful details of a brutal experience alive in one's aching consciousness"[2]—would be an apposite response to their predisposition to gratuitous violence at the hands of white racists. This violence often occurs in the most quotidian spaces (e.g., a public street, a park, or an aisle of Walmart). It is usually state sanctioned, incommensurate to the alleged crimes committed, and deadly. The recent killings of Laquan McDonald, Michael Brown Jr., Richard Collins III, Trayvon Martin, Jordan Davis, Tamir Rice, Eric Garner, John Crawford III, Alton Sterling, Freddie Gray Jr., Samuel DuBose, Walter Scott, Terence Crutcher, Philando Castile, and a long list of others, at the hands of a white, repressive power structure, are testaments to the very material consequences of the oppression of Black males in the US. But why are young Black males targeted by racist factions?

Black men and youth are killed because they are said to be that which they are not: animals and menaces to society with no human value. Yet the Black-male "superpredator"[3] is but a pathological construction in a white racist imaginary. It arises from a particular epistemic framework anchored in the white-supremacist project of discursively muting, as it were, marginalized subjects, impeding their abilities to produce knowledge on or about themselves, so as to bury them beneath a quagmire of dehumanizing stereotypes. In "Can the Subaltern Speak?" postcolonial theorist Gayatri Spivak ([1988] 1994) identifies the silencing of marginalized groups and the subsequent misrepresentations of these groups as "epistemic violence." Epistemic violence licenses repressive apparatuses, such as the police or a white-nationalist hate group, to destroy Black bodies, both male and female. But at the heart of this chapter is the destruction of the Black *male* body and the epistemic fabrications (at the level of the overdetermined construction of this body by the white racist imaginary) that underlie the epidemic of Black-male killings.

I rely on James Baldwin's 1964 drama, *Blues for Mister Charlie*, a loosely fictionalized retelling of Emmett Till's 1955 lynching, as well as the 2014 murder in Ferguson, Missouri, of eighteen-year-old Michael Brown, at the hands of a white police officer, to argue that the violence to which young Black men are subjected is symptomatic of the multiple ways in which Black male bodies are relegated to the splintered realm of the nonhuman in a white racist psyche. More specifically, I demonstrate how Baldwin's fictional protagonist, Richard Henry, and the late Michael

Brown are victims of epistemic violence insofar as they are silenced and spoken for by white racist authority as overdetermined variations of the nonhuman—as animals, objects, expendable raw material, and phantoms—to "justify" their murders.

In the first section of this chapter, I discuss the theoretical and philosophical lenses that inform my argument. I revisit the anticolonial theory articulated by Frantz Fanon in *Black Skin, White Masks* ([1952] 2008) regarding the self-other dialectic and the psychical transactions between the Black body and the racist white gaze in a colonial regime. Fanon provides a critical lens through which to examine the shifting variations of the nonhuman, overdetermined construction of Black males in a twenty-first-century US context. This is so given his extrapolation of the Black body severed from its subjectivity by the white colonial gaze. Furthermore, I discuss the role of epistemic violence—particularly practices of silencing marginalized persons—in the destruction of Black male bodies in the US. Silencing practices, such as the dismissal of one's testimony, the preclusion of self-defined, communicative performances of identity, or even political underrepresentation—privilege white-supremacist modes of "knowing" the oppressed "Other." This means that "misinterpretations" are often malicious and, in most instances, extremely consequential.

The second section analyzes Baldwin's *Blues for Mister Charlie*. Baldwin's play vivifies how psychical imprisonment occurs in the dramatization of Richard Henry's murder at the hands of the racist white townsman, Lyle Britten, and his accomplice, the white racist community. The play can be read as depicting how, to justify the gratuitous violence enacted upon Richard's body, white-supremacist discourse does not merely "other" the Black body but also ensures that it is denied any modicum of intelligibility within the racist episteme of the time. I argue that this imprisonment is manifold in nature and exemplified first through Baldwin's unmasking of the construction of his Black male protagonist, Richard Henry, as animal. This is followed by an explication of the need to secure Henry as object and as expendable matter to substantiate white identity. I end this section examining how Henry is reduced to a mere predatory phantasm in the testimony of a racist white subject.[4]

In the third section, I provide a parallel analysis of the murder case of Michael Brown. Like Richard Henry, Brown was relegated to an object for the sake of validating white identity through a scuffle that unfolds between him and his white oppressor. I then highlight Brown's monstrous construction in the fantastical testimony of his murderer, which is eerily analogous to the testimony provided by the wife of the alleged murderer of Richard Henry in *Blues for Mister Charlie* (and analogous to Jason Van Dyke's description of Laquan McDonald). Finally, I elucidate how Brown's murder by then-officer Darren Wilson and the disposal of his body, not unlike Richard Henry's, are suggestive of the disposability of the Black male body to racist repressive agents.

Each of the above nonhuman constitutions of the Black male discussed in the fictionalized case of Richard Henry and the murder of Michael Brown reinforces the psychic formulation of Black maleness consigned to what I will later refer to as *Fanonian non-alterity*, or the state of imprisoning Black bodies as non-Others to disenfranchise them of subjectivity. Their relegation to the realm of non-alterity is aided by epistemic practices of silencing and the mobilization of ignorance employed by the white hegemony. If there is any hope of liberating Black male bodies from the white-supremacist social imaginary of them as non-Others, closely examining the epistemic terms and extent of their imprisonment is a necessary step in the process.

Fanonian Non-alterity and Epistemic Violence

Fanonian Non-alterity

In *Black Skin, White Masks*, Frantz Fanon ([1952] 2008) makes clear that the European colonial gaze consigns the Black body to the realm of "objecthood," with no hope for escape. To illustrate this "object" constitution in his chapter "The Fact of Blackness," Fanon evokes the Sartrean "being-for-others" paradigm,[5] in the context of a Black body encountering a white world. At the sight of a Black body, a French child yells, " 'Dirty Nigger!' or simply 'Look! A Negro'!" (89). Fanon recognizes that the Negro had been "fixed" by the gaze of the white Other as an "object among objects" (89). He maintains, "For not only must the black man be black; he must be black in relation to the white man" (90). Thus, for Fanon, on the one hand, the Negro is a "being-for-others," trapped within a semiotic system of racial difference by a historical white imaginary. On the other hand, as "being-for-others," the Negro is also relegated to the status of perpetual "not-Other" as object. The "being-for-others" paradigm in a colonial context requires a denial of Black subjectivity to validate the white Subject as the locus of personhood. For the white child to recognize himself as the antithesis of a "dirty Nigger," the child can only solidify his subjective identity if the "other Black body" is an object onto which the child exerts his "superior" subjectivity. Thus, within a colonial social order wherein the system of governance is predicated on the maintenance of this dialectic, it is essential that the Negro's access to subjectivity is irrevocably denied.

In "Interior Colonies: Frantz Fanon and the Politics of Identification," theorist and literary critic Diana Fuss (1994, 20–21) interprets Fanon's complex postulation of "racial othering" and "psychological alterity" in *Black Skin, White Masks* as a theory of "(non)alterity."[6] Pivoting from Fanon, Fuss defines "(non)alterity" as the psychical and social confinement of the Black body in a "white racial phantasm," whereby the colonized African was "denied entry into the alterity that underwrites subjectivity" (21). Fuss maintains, "If psychoanalysis is right to claim that 'I is an Other' [Lacan 23], then otherness constitutes the very entry into subjectivity" (21). In other words, if the Negro is an Other, then so, too, is the French child to the Negro. To preserve hegemonic race relations, the Negro is "neither an 'I' nor a 'not-I'" (Fuss 1994, 26). Like animals and objects, he is outside of otherness. His status is one of non-alterity. Fanonian non-alterity manifests itself in the "being-for-others" scenario discussed above insofar as the Black body is reduced to a perpetual object without any potential for subjectivity. It also plays out in the violent struggles that transpire in both *Blues for Mister Charlie* and the Michael Brown murder case, between Richard Henry and his murderer, Lyle Britten, and Michael Brown and his murderer, Darren Wilson. These two Black males are also denied access to otherness via their construction as predators, objects, expendable raw material, and mere phantoms in a racist imaginary.

EPISTEMIC VIOLENCE: SILENCING PRACTICES

The "non-alterity" constitutions of Black males reveal the functionality of what philosopher Charles Mills refers to as the "racial contract." Mills (1997) argues that white supremacy and systems of Western domination have been the result of a "racial contract" that rests upon an "epistemology of ignorance" (18), insofar as the white populace engages is consensual obfuscations of realities (3). The project of perpetually mobilizing mistaken perceptions (e.g., an objectified Negro) has historically abetted and justified hegemonic practices in the West and is how "the modern world came to be" (Mills 1997, 3). But for ignorance to be heard and effectively prevail, it is necessary to silence other competing voices. Hence, the physical violence suffered by Henry and Brown must be conceptualized as part of the practice of denying the non-Western colonial Other the faculty of self-representation, which, according to Spivak ([1988] 1994, 76), is the "clearest available example" of epistemic violence.

In the context of my argument, epistemic violence can be discerned in the manner that white-supremacist agents deny the social group of young Black males the right to define themselves as thinking, autonomous social agents—as musicians, sons, lovers, and young *men*. In *Black Skin, White Masks*, Fanon ([1952] 2008, 92) defines the Negro's initial consciousness of the self as a holistic, *human* entity as first-person consciousness. This primordial self-knowledge has been historically "disqualified from the hierarchy of knowledges and sciences" (Foucault 1980, 82). I understand the silencing of Black-male declarations of selfhood as both a prerequisite for and a consequence of consigning Black male bodies to the region of non-alterity. In place of their silenced performances of self-defined identity, we have historically heard the voices of "master," "colonizer," "Mister Charlie," and the representatives of state power, as well as their constructions of Black male bodies as nonhuman animals.

Kristie Dotson's work on epistemic violence offers a nuanced perspective of this silencing. Dotson (2011) claims that "misinterpretations" of events and "the Other" often harm the silenced person. She terms a harmful cognitive lapse "pernicious ignorance" and insists that it underwrites epistemic violence (238). Pernicious ignorance denotes ignorance that is "reliable" and proves to be harmful to a person or group. Reliable ignorance "follows from a *predictable* epistemic gap in cognitive resources" (238; my emphasis). That is to say that this form of ignorance does not merely manifest itself in isolated cases or by happenstance. Rather, it rears its head as an established pattern of not-knowing. When reliable ignorance causes harm, it constitutes pernicious ignorance. Pernicious ignorance fails, consistently, in the necessary communicative reciprocity between a hearer and the testimonies of a speaker, silencing the speaker in the process (Dotson 2011, 238).

While Dotson identifies one form of suppressing the testimonies of marginalized speakers as the act of "testimonial quieting," likewise, Miranda Fricker (2007) argues that "testimonial injustice" occurs when prejudice prevents a hearer from rendering a speaker's testimony *credible*. Both philosophers insist that privileged hearers consistently fail and refuse to acknowledge oppressed speakers as knowers, owing to discriminatory propositions rooted in reliable ignorance. But Dotson borrows from Patricia Hill Collins's (2000) work on "controlling images" of Black women as a case in point. Following Collins, Dotson insists that because Black women have been consistently confined to disparaging stereotypes, they have been stripped of the faculty of knowing and thereby rendered incompetent and exempt from intellectual traditions (Dotson 2011, 242–43; Collins 2000, 3–8). In this case, reliable ignorance proves harmful for the subjects in question.

However, I am concerned with a much more fatal consequence of testimonial quieting and injustice, to which both Black men *and* women are subjected. Black bodies in general assume an epistemological disadvantage given they are, echoing Fanon ([1952] 2008, 91), "woven" into being. Privileging a mode of knowledge that often constructs Black bodies as threatening animals, for instance (in the face of "cognitive resources" that prove otherwise [Dotson 2011, 238]), is harmful given it warrants the eradication of these "predators" from the social world.[7] Black male bodies that are relegated to the status of non-alterity are, following Helen Fein's (1979) work on genocide, "outside the sanctified universe of obligation— that circle of *people* with reciprocal obligations to protect each other" (4; my emphasis). Epistemic violence and physical violence are inextricably bound, as the pernicious ignorance inherent in the former often institutes the latter. Baldwin's visceral dramatization of the Richard Henry murder and Michael Brown's murder case both depict the workings of the "racial contract," epistemic violence and silencing practices, and, subsequently, the destruction of the Black male.

Richard Henry: Non-alterity Examined in Baldwin's *Blues*

THE "BUCK"

"Mister Charlie" is the white-supremacist patriarch revealed in Baldwin's *Blues*. He commits unspeakable crimes against the Black race and then protects himself from the resulting madness. He is trapped in the fictions of his own "supreme" identity (Baldwin [1964] 1995, xiv). But Baldwin does not merely reveal to his readers the pathetic figure of Mister Charlie. Baldwin's brush strokes yield a portrait of the mythologized American Negro *man* for whom we should also sing the "blues." This is so as he is trapped, in the racist psyche of "Mister Charlie," as the overly embodied, prototypical animal, despite any self-defining proclamations such as "I'm a man" (119). This Negro materializes on Baldwin's easel in the character of Richard Henry—the dejected, former dope-fiend musician and son of Reverend Meridian Henry.

Though Richard declares "I'm a man" to his would-be murderer just before he is killed (119), his self-defined identity is silenced and is never even considered before that moment. In this white-supremacist town that polices the boundaries of racial identity, the only articulation of his identity that attains full audibility is his construction as a predator. Reducing the Black male body to that of predatory animal warranting destruction is one of many methods of consigning it to non-alterity, as an animal can never be an Other. Evidence of Richard Henry's discursive classification as animal can be discerned in his portrayal as a predatory, disposable "buck."

It is not until after the murder of Richard Henry that readers learn of his "buck" construction. Baldwin begins the play with Richard's murder. The ghastly opening lines—"And may every nigger like this nigger end like this nigger—face down in the weeds!" (2)—are uttered by Lyle Britten after he has shot and killed Richard, who has returned from a troubling life in the North as a musician. The events thereafter unfold in a series of flashbacks that recount the details from Richard's return to Plaguetown, USA, to the moment of his murder outside of a juke joint. The flashbacks disclose conversations held between the Black folks in "Blacktown" and their counterparts in "Whitetown" and also provide an opportunity for readers to glean the epistemic violence (in the form of silencing the Black body and constituting the Black body as a non-Other) that permeates throughout Whitetown where "the Negro" is concerned—namely, Richard.

In act 1, through a flashback discussion between Lyle Britten and Parnell James (the white editor of the local newspaper and self-declared "liberal" friend of both the whites and Blacks), readers learn that Lyle is unquestionably a bigot. He declares to Parnell, "I'll be damned if I'll mix with [colored folks]" (114). His rationale: "I don't want no big *buck* nigger lying up next to Josephine [his wife] and that's where all this will lead to and you know it as well as I do!" (14; my emphasis). Lyle Britten's antimiscegenation anxiety is provoked by the return of Richard Henry and, consequently, by the fear of *his* white woman subjected to the mercies of this Black male "buck." The late-nineteenth- and twentieth-century trope of the Black male "buck" depicted the emancipated Black man as a predator of white society after slavery, imbued with the sole desire to violate the mythic pure white woman. It is no wonder, then, that Richard's reappearance in Plaguetown is cause for concern for the white townsfolk.

In act 2, friends of Lyle and Jo Britten gather in their home to expedite Lyle and Jo's anniversary celebration given the forthcoming murder trial. After indulging in bourbon, they all lament the latest shift in racial dynamics in Plaguetown since desegregation. The "niggers," they all agree, have overstepped the "God-intended" structure of racial hierarchies (48). Ellis, a white townsman, informs the group that the Negro's alleged one and only interest is still "below the button" (49). He then assures Jo Britten that being raped by a "nigger" is akin to being "raped by an orang-outang out of the jungle or a *stallion*"—that either "couldn't do [her] no worse than a nigger" (50).

The scene above is revelatory of discursively consigning Richard to the realm of non-alterity via the "buck" construction. It also reveals *how* this ideological imprisonment is established and maintained. In the first place, the false construction of Richard as buck is premised upon pernicious ignorance given the reliability of the ignorance underway and the proven record of harm inflicted upon Richard and others as a response to the recurring trope of the Black male buck. The trope emanates from breeding narratives of slavery. As literary critic Carlyle Van Thompson (2004, 2) writes in *The Tragic Black Buck*, "Linking black males to animals, white society literally considered slaves subhuman, beasts. They were dangerous breeding animals who were never more content than when . . . they were rapists of white women." The trope was solidified in postemancipation discourse thereafter and impregnated the public imagination well into the twentieth century, particularly in D. W. Griffith's 1915 film *The Birth of a Nation*. It is here critiqued in *Blues for Mister Charlie* in the 1960s. Hence, it is a *predictable* form of ignorance—one discursively reproduced in every era in the US since slavery. The deleterious consequences of the "buck" construction is evidenced by the 4,743 cases of lynchings in the US between 1882 and 1968—72 percent of which were of Black men, most of whom were falsely accused of violating a white woman (NAACP 2018). Baldwin appears attentive to the inveterate myth of the Black male buck in the white racist imaginary given its centrality in *Blues*, which is a loose retelling of the lynching of Emmett Till, who had also been falsely accused of accosting a white woman in 1955.

Moreover, the pernicious construction of Richard is maintained via its communal and contractual institution. Reverend Phelps's consoling statement to Lyle, "we're with you and every white person in the town is with you" (Baldwin [1964] 1995, 55), is symptomatic of the formation of an epistemic community—an outcome of the "racial contract." Mills

(1997) argues that members of the white racist polity establish an "idealized consensus about cognitive norms" (17), resulting from a mutual understanding of skewed facts, ideas, and events, or from simply "see[ing] the world wrongly" (18). Mills conceives of this phenomenon as an "epistemology of ignorance" (18). He posits, "There is an understanding about what counts as a correct, objective interpretation of the world, and for agreeing to this *typically distorted* view, one is ('contractually') granted full cognitive standing in the polity, the official epistemic community" (17–18; my emphasis).

It is therefore no wonder that Reverend Phelps, Lillian, Ellis, and George gather in the Brittens' home to celebrate the actions of the chairman of the polity, Lyle Britten. Britten is heralded for fulfilling "his duties, both public and private" by ridding Plaguetown of this sexualized predator (Baldwin [1964] 1995, 48). In fact, the townspeople drink and sing "For He's a Jolly Good Fellow" (48). That all the white townsfolk stand convicted in their support of Lyle indicates a collective concession to the hierarchal social relations of subjection between themselves and the Negroes and the predatory construction of the Black male as "buck," and they agree to the routinized destruction of a predator that threatens the white woman and white male authority. "Whitetown" can therefore be understood as an epistemic community given that it tends toward (and achieves) collective inquiry and *distorted* knowledge goals regarding Black bodies and because of the epistemic dimensions of the community that support specific social structures of power, such as practices of silencing and the refusal of self-definition for the Black folks of Plaguetown.

The problem with Plaugetown's "racial contract" is that the knowledge produced of the subject in question—Richard Henry—is distorted in the face of the actual subject and his first-person consciousness. The process of *collectively* mobilizing pernicious ignorance results in *collectively* suppressing self-defining articulations of identity communicated by the Other. The epistemic community denies Richard Henry the right to conceive of himself as a man and an epistemic agent prior to his murder. Instead, he is secured as not-Other. His denied testimony is facilitated by another strand of epistemic violence known as hermeneutic injustice, which, according to Miranda Fricker (2007, 4 and 148), occurs when disadvantaged subjects have unequal access to the generation of social meanings because of the privileged interpretive prejudices of a dominant group. Here, the dominant hermeneutical framework refuses to render intelligible any construction of Black men incongruent to that which it has "woven into being" from ignorance. The folks of Whitetown are the sole epistemic agents who produce "incontestable Knowledge" on the Black male who is imprisoned in the realm of non-alterity as an overly embodied animal with the foremost desire to sexually violate the white woman—despite opposing testimonies. Below, I provide two examples of this silencing.

Upon his return, Richard attempts to render his humanity legible. In an implicit example, he proves his intentions are *not* to violate the white women of Plaguetown. In act 1, soon after he returns from the North, Richard's grandmother inquires about what kept him away for so long. Richard retorts, "I didn't want to come back here like a whipped dog. One whipped dog running to another whipped dog" (Baldwin [1964] 1995, 20). He is referring to his father's powerlessness against the white mob that had murdered his mother when Richard was a child. Richard resents his father's inertia at the time of his mother's murder: "But I just wish, that day that Mama died, he'd took a pistol and gone through that damn white man's hotel and shot every son of a bitch in the place" (20).

The narrator then discloses that Richard is carrying a "sawed-off pistol" (20). The underlying implication is that he has returned because he is *not* a "whipped dog." Richard is an agential Subject. He is a *man* seeking to *act*—to possibly avenge the murder of his mother rather than violate white women, since his father "couldn't say nothing, he couldn't *do* nothing" (20). Here he discursively and performatively counters Whitetown's dehumanizing construction of him through the conflation of personhood and manliness, for he defines himself in opposition to a "whipped dog," the obverse of humanness and heroic masculinity. This conflation was not uncommon during the mid-twentieth century, given the tenuous boundaries separating manhood and masculinity concerning "the Negro" in the US.[8]

Later, Richard articulates his humanity more explicitly, again through a masculine assertion of identity. Juanita (his former childhood friend and current love interest) tries to convince him of the possibility of fleeing Plaguetown together to begin a life anew elsewhere. Richard, however, divulges that he is no longer going to run—that he "was going to stay and be a man—a man!—right here" (99). Perhaps Richard's exclamatory and iterative articulation of "man" serves as a hubristic counterresponse to the denial of Black masculinity that he and other Black men had experienced in Plaguetown, given it is uttered in the context of standing his ground in the face of white male power. Richard's resolve to remain in Plaguetown (this time) indicates an exigent demand for white-supremacist patriarchal forces to finally recognize his masculine prowess and, by extension, his personhood, but to no avail.

The point is that epistemic agents operating under the epistemologically ignorant dictates of the "racial contract" employ perfidious tactics to secure Black bodies squarely within the realm of non-alterity. Nonhuman constructions of the Black male body, such as that of the "buck," are often consolidated by an epistemic community that denies Black men the right to self-define. The denial of their testimonies yields the emergence of dehumanizing images of "blackness" and Black maleness. This predator, born from reliable ignorance, is routinely destroyed. It is from this framework that one must make sense of a law-enforcement agent who dumps more bullets into a teen than the seconds it takes to do so.

"Being-for-Others"-Object

One other manner to guarantee this imprisonment is by securing the static-object status of the Black body. This plays out during the violent scuffle that unfolds between the two in Lyle's store, and it occurs again outside of Papa D's juke joint, eventuating in Richard's murder. Lyle does not kill Richard solely out of a need to rid Plaguetown of the predatory "buck." Their violent interactions are indicative of Lyle's efforts to instantiate white male dominance and to deny Richard's manhood by securing him as a "being-for-others" and, by extension, an object upon which to validate Lyle as "Supreme Subject." They also reveal Richard's desperate attempts to evade this dialectic, which proves fatal for him, precisely because the myth of white supremacy necessitates a delimited "freedom of movement (psychical and social)" for Black bodies (Fuss 1994, 21). The events that precipitate Richard's murder are disclosed in act 2 during a flashback discussion between Lyle and Parnell, relayed through an omniscient narrative perspective.

Richard and another Negro student, Lorenzo, are walking down a dirt road when Richard decides to buy a Coke out of Lyle's store. Inside the store, Richard insults the Brittens when they do not have enough money in their register to change out his bill. Business is slow, and Lyle Britten lacks viable economic power as a struggling white merchant. In *Black Bodies, White Gazes*, philosopher George Yancy (2008) lends insight into poor whites' tutelary investment in "transcendental whiteness" as the norm in relation to historical signifiers of racial inferiority. He argues that poor whites "dutifully juxtapos[e] themselves to those inferior Black bodies, safeguarding the appellation 'white' as a magical category that names, fixes, and substantiates their ontological superiority and special status within the Great Chain of Being" (3). This is so as the axiological value assigned whiteness in North America allows poor whites the opportunity to transcend their lower-class standing (3–4). However, Richard decenters the markers of *racial* difference, as signified by his very presence, and instead highlights the Brittens' financial woes: "You all got this big, fine store and all—and you ain't got change for *twenty* dollars" (Baldwin [1964] 1995, 72). In doing so, Richard paradoxically exacerbates the racial tension by compromising Lyle Britten's one claim to the "magical category" of "superior" whiteness (Yancy 2008, 3). As Trudier Harris (2009, 35) acknowledges in *The Scary Mason-Dixon Line*, Richard then transposes economic lack into sexual lack: "Stud ain't got nothing—you people been spoofing the public, man" (Baldwin [1964] 1995, 73). Later, Richard even directly signifies Lyle's alleged impotence when he calls Lyle a "ball-less peckerwood" (74). Here, it is Lyle who is overdetermined, somatically understood, and subsequently positioned outside of "otherness" as one who has been reduced to his genitalia.

Additionally, and decidedly more provokingly, because Richard understands that the symbolic constitution of the Black man in American race relations is predicated on recurring, perceptual misjudgments of "blackness," he makes sexualized passes at Jo. He condescendingly "admir[es]" her "daintiness" and how "pretty" she is (72). Richard's flippancy, his performance of sexual deviance (reminiscent of Emmett Till's said whistling at a white woman inside of a grocery store), and his refusal to recognize the "dominance" of Lyle Britten induce physical violence. Lyle raises a hammer to Richard and a struggle ensues. Recalling Hegel (1998, 113–14), their violent interaction is inevitable, as "the relation of the two self-conscious individuals is such that they [must] prove themselves and each other through a life-and-death struggle." That Richard Henry is impelled to struggle for the recognition of his manhood indicates his knowledge of a man reduced to an "object among other objects" (Fanon [1952] 2008, 89). Richard is momentarily victorious, though, since the confrontation ends with Lyle "on his ass" with "his woman watching," as Richard taunts (Baldwin [1964] 1995, 75).

Richard has, in this scene, disrupted the Sartrean "being-for-others" paradigm. The prevailing episteme of this era and within Whitetown, as we have already discovered, relies on the mythic representation of the Black

192 | ShaDawn Battle

male "buck." Hence, if the Black male body is animal, the white man is the ideal Subject / embodiment of man, who presides over the Negro-animal. This animal is thus the object through which the master's identity is affirmed, consistent with Sartre's paradigm. Richard refuses to validate Lyle's self-conscious awareness of self as Master-Subject, though. Instead, he illuminates the fallacy of the white male as the only true incarnation of man when he interpolates the white male subject through his verbal castration of Lyle, and when he yells, "Now, who you think is the better man?" to a defeated Lyle Britten (75). Richard also mocks the idea of the existence of a superior white race, or the said white male prerogative to preside over the "Black animal": "Ha-ha! The master race! You let me in that tired white chick's drawers, she'll know who's the master! Ha-ha-ha!" (75). Not only does Richard reconstruct a social order wherein he is not an animal subjected to the whims of a "master" but he also deposes the authoritative figure and substitutes himself in lieu of the white "master."

Furthermore, Richard refuses his said object constitution again when, just before Lyle shoots him outside of the juke joint, he returns the Sartrean look of affirmation. After Lyle demands an apology from Richard for his behavior inside of his store, Richard informs Lyle, "You a man and I'm a man" (119). But Lyle attempts to reinscribe the racial hierarchy and the "being-for-others" paradigm by defining Richard's refused deference and object constitution as heresy: "Nigger, you was born down here. Ain't you never said sir to a white man?" Richard retorts, "No. The only person I ever said sir to was my Daddy" (119). In other words, Richard deposes Lyle (and other "Mister Charlies"), not as a man, but as superior Subject in the Great Chain of Being and, by Lacanian accounts, as Father/Law who prevents the (Black) "child" from an innate desire, in this case, to self-actualize as his own man. Richard thus establishes a subjective sym-metry where one is not expected to exist but does. This is precisely why it is essential for the Negro to remain "neither 'I' nor 'not-I'" (Fuss 1994, 26), as the reciprocal othering underway suggests that both understand themselves to be subjects unto themselves. Richard understands himself to be a Black man with agency and with a social existence apart from Lyle's. He advises Lyle, "Why don't you go home? And let me go home?" (Baldwin [1964] 1995, 118). Beyond this, he is a son with future aspirations, or "lots of stuff to *do*" (119; my emphasis). Lyle's declaration "I got things to do, too. I'd like to get home, too" (119)—is Baldwin underscoring an intersubjective interaction underway, similitude between two *men*, and, by extension, Richard's escape from the psychosocial domain of non-alterity.

Sadly, though, the preclusion of the "being-for-others" paradigm is a transient moment of triumph. Richard's testimony of personhood falls on deaf ears as Lyle Britten's subsequent actions illuminate "Mister Charlie's" unwavering conviction to maintain the animal-object status of the Negro, since the attainment of his own "exclusively human" and "superior" ontology necessitates doing so. That is, to maintain the social framework, Richard *had* to die, because his objectification is what secures him in the realm of non-alterity.

DISPOSABLE RAW MATERIAL

Like I will later demonstrate for Van Dyke, Michael Brown's murderer, Lyle Britten "had to kill [Richard]" (Baldwin [1964] 1995, 120). Lyle was left no other choice but to destroy and dispose of the expendable "animal" that interrupted the psychodrama wherein white solipsism is dialectically linked to the objectified "other Black body." This is made clear in Lyle's final rant to Parnell: "I had to kill him. I'm a white man! Can't nobody talk that way to *me*! I *had* to go and get my pick-up truck and load him in it—I *had* to carry him on my back—and carry him out to the high weeds. And I dumped him in the weeds, face down" (120; my emphasis on "had"). These lines and Lyle's behavior authenticate what according to postcolonial theorist Achilles Mbembe is a distinctive feature of the "sovereign" colonial order, as theorized in *On the Postcolony*.

Mbembe (2001, 26) defines the organizational structure of francophone colonies in part through the said corporeal nature of "blackness" and the expendability of the "animal" Negro body when it did *or* did not serve an exploitative end. The colonizer would declare that the "prototypically animal" colonized "could in no way be another 'myself'" (26). While Baldwin's narrator calls attention to the physical separation of Blacktown from Whitetown in the opening of the play (Baldwin [1964] 1995, 1), the animalized construction of the Negro thereafter solidifies this unbridgeable distance in Plaguetown. As animal, Mbembe (2001, 27) argues that the colonized "can be destroyed, as one may kill an animal, cut it up, cook it and, if need be, eat it." He maintains, "As for his/her death, it mattered little" (27). This was precisely because the Black body was but disposable "raw material" (21 and 33). This method of disposing of the Black mass of materiality without conscience, "face down in the weeds," as if it were animal, is a normalized reality in Plaguetown given that the white townspeople are bewildered when they hear of a funeral underway in Blacktown. Parnell insists that Black bodies typically receive proper burials when "the dogs leave enough to bury" (Baldwin [1964] 1995, 52).

ANIMALIZED PHANTASM AND EPISTEMIC VIOLENCE

Finally, Richard Henry's non-alterity designation is verified in the legal discourse surrounding his murder. The Black male body is now held captive in the realm of non-alterity insofar as it is reduced to a phantom nonpresence, a consequence of its excessive materiality/predatory "buck" construction. Jo Britten fabricates the events that unfolded in their store by informing the jury that Richard "was just like an animal, I could—smell him" (84). But she does not actually "see" Richard. Conjuring the events with enunciative difficulty, she continues: "I—I give him two Cokes, and he—tried to grab my hands and pull me to him, and—I—I—he pushed himself against me, real close and hard" (84). Of course, since these events are relayed through an omniscient narrator during an earlier flashback, readers know that Richard never physically accosts Jo Britten. Instead, Richard Henry is a predatory phantasmagoric presence in Jo Britten's imaginary.

It would therefore be a myopic reading to infer that the disruptions in Mrs. Britten's speech indicate that she is merely lying. While this is true, the lie owes to her state of cognitive incapacitation, which enables her to "misinterpret" what actually occurred in the store. This individual act, marked by broken speech patterns, is reflective of what Mills (1997) terms as "cognitive dysfunction," which is itself symptomatic of a broader and collective epistemic ignorance. According to Mills, "cognitive dys-function" can be "psychologically and socially functional" in the service of white supremacy's "epistemological ignorance" (18). That is, Jo Britten convinces herself of Richard's predatory behavior in the store since the narrative she conjures during her cognitive recall is consistent with the detrimental, *reliable* misconceptions of "blackness" in Plaguetown and throughout the US in the twentieth century. More specifically, her version of the event substantiates the overly embodied, predatory construction of the Black male body prior to Richard's death, and even his birth. Her version thus situates Richard, even posthumously, outside of "otherness."

But complicating Mrs. Britten's hallucinatory testimony is the credibility it is afforded. Marginalized people suffer what Fricker (2007, 4) calls a "credibility deficit," which means their words are viewed with testimonial suspicion that results from "identity prejudices" marginalized persons suffer. As such, "the State" and the all-white jury—the juridical component of the epistemic community ("Whitetown") that views Negroes as "objects among objects" (Fanon [1952] 2008, 89)—appear to concede the credibility of Mrs. Britten's delusional testimony while offering "a deflated level of credibility" (Fricker 2007, 1) to Richard's pre-death testimonies of manhood, as reiterated by those Black bodies that testify on his behalf: his father, his grandmother, Juanita, and Lorenzo. For instance, during his testimony, Richard's father informs the jury that Richard labored to prove himself a man but that it "undid" him (Baldwin [1964] 1995, 103). Yet the State labored to produce counterevidence of Richard's manhood, thus rendering such testimonies from the Blacks implausible. As a case in point, incredulous at the idea that the Richard-Lyle violent scuffle was the result of a twenty-cent Coke, in a badgering tone, the State suggests to Lorenzo that "there was some other reason" (92). Taking into account Richard's "buck" construction in Plaguetown and the State's later overt reference to Richard as "rapist" (105), it is safe to assume that the State is alluding to Richard's said animalistic behavior/nature as the cause of the scuffle, which authenticates Mrs. Britten's fantastical version of the event and evidences colluding efforts to secure the Black body in the realm of non-alterity.

Consequently, Richard is doubly silenced as a knower of self. He is effectively silenced through murder, and through the fact that those who can speak for him, on behalf of his personhood, are said to lack testimonial credibility to effectively do so if no testimonies emanating from resistive Black bodies have merit in a social order that privileges white narratives regarding Black ontology. Thus, the testimonial quieting that Richard suffers—compounded with Jo Britten's hallucinatory state, which permits her to testify having seen him morph into a predatory animal—means that Lyle Britten was well within his rights to destroy this animal. Thus, "cognitive dysfunction" can be "psychologically and socially functional" (Mills 1997, 18) because it is enabled by silencing practices and produced in an economy of ignorance, which makes possible desirable outcomes for the white hegemony.

In short, "Mister Charlie" murdered Richard eons before Lyle Britten "put two slugs in his belly and dumped his body in the weeds" (Baldwin [1964] 1995, 12). Just after Lyle shoots him the first time, Richard rhetorically asks Lyle, "Why have you spent so much time trying to kill me?" (120). Richard and other Black men alike have died a thousand deaths, as it were, since rendering them animal, disenfranchising them of their subjectivity, and reducing them to overdetermined, predatory phantasms deprives them of life. We must impute responsibility on the racist episteme of the time for imprisoning Richard within the psychic confines of non-alterity by collectively agreeing to an "epistemology of ignorance." It appears as if Lyle Britten's presaging wish for other "niggers" like Richard Henry to share his fate comes to fruition in that many other "niggers" in succeeding decades have been brutally beaten or murdered by white supremacists. Michael Brown is one of them.

Non-Alterity Examined in the Murder Case of Michael Brown

Examining Michael Brown's death through the lens of James Baldwin helps us to understand the killing of Black males across time and geographies on a historical continuum. There exists a conflated Black male body tucked neatly away in the dark American psyche. Though he does not exist, he is repeatedly reborn. Richard Henry is the fictionalized reincarnation of Emmett Till, brutally murdered in 1955, and Michael Brown (and McDonald), shot by police in 2014, personified, in many ways, the character of Richard Henry. Brown was an aspiring musician, and Henry is a blues man. Both were connected to convenience-store interactions that led to violent altercations and their murders shortly after. Both boys are also left face down—one in weeds, the other in the middle of a street. It is thus no wonder that, as reported by Liam Otten (2015), the St. Louis Black Repertory Company, directed by Ron Himes, restaged *Blues for Mister Charlie* in St. Louis in 2015, drawing analogies to the Michael Brown murder case. To make sense of Brown's various non-alterity constitutions, I highlight the parallel epistemic injustices that are replicated fifty years after the publication of *Blues*, in Ferguson, Missouri.

In August 2014, eighteen-year-old Michael Brown was a resident in Ferguson, a predominantly Black, economically impoverished suburb of St. Louis. As a poor, Black, male teen, Brown was classified, to borrow from Sylvia Wynter (1994), as "no humans involved" ("N.H.I.")[9] and so was expendable. At the time of his murder, only months after his high school graduation, Brown was preparing to attend a trade school. Nevertheless, because he was unemployed at the time, Black, young, and male, he was scripted (by white racist society) as deviant, and quite possibly as an unproductive citizen-subject to the nation state—especially to the consumer culture, an integral element of the capitalist infrastructure. Notwithstanding the fact that Brown seemed to affirm his construction as a deviant menace to society, the criminal behaviors of youth of color in urban communities are often the handiwork of structural racism and systematic practices that manufacture impoverished conditions and resulting behaviors. As Wynter (2014, 43) insists, echoing Helen Fein, young Black men are often "made into" and "behaved towards" this criminal disposition. Hence, as I see it, Brown consciously reacted against the concentrated poverty in Ferguson that adversely affected its 95-percent-Black population (and still does).

For instance, it was alleged that, prior to Brown's execution by then-officer Darren Wilson, he was captured via store video camera in the act of a petty theft. After reputedly shoving a resistant store clerk, he ran out of the Ferguson Market convenience store without paying for cigarillos. The authorities were alerted. Though it was not his call and he admitted during his testimony to being unprepared to handle this call, Wilson was the responding officer who appeared and canvassed the nearby area in search for the alleged perpetrators. This was when Wilson happened upon Brown and his companion as they were walking home in the middle of Canfield Drive. Brown's alleged theft, his altercation with Wilson, and the ensuing court testimonies illuminate a real case study of the confinement of Black maleness to non-alterity, exemplified via his construction as a dialectical "object," as a predatory monster-phantasm, and as a disposable mass of flesh.

"Being-for-Others" Object

Like Richard Henry, Michael Brown interrupts the "being-for-others" requisite, which perpetuates the Black body's objectified, non-alterity imprisonment. The "being-for-others" paradigm is here predicated, in part, on a system of racialized indebtedness. To elaborate, the abolition of slavery meant the white imperial body was no longer defined by the property (Black bodies) he owned. But, following Karl Marx, race theorist Saidiya Hartman (1997, 120) reminds readers in *Scenes of Subjection* that modern forms of bondage, such as debt peonage and indebted labor, reinstated the modern, captive, laboring Black body as "a medium of [whites'] power and representation" after slavery. It can be argued that this Sartrean structure persists in today's political economy, especially in Ferguson, Missouri.

To understand the Black body as the " 'sign and surrogate' of the master's body" today (Hartman 1997, 120), a closer evaluation of the uneven distribution of wealth and resources in Brown's environment is warranted. In the Canfield Green neighborhood of Ferguson in which Michael Brown resided and was murdered, inhabitants' median income at this time was less than $27,000, "making it the eighth-poorest census tract in the state" (Casselman 2014). In 2014, the year Brown was murdered, "nationally, 36 percent of African-American adults under age 25 [were] employed, compared to 50 percent of young whites; even fewer [were] working full time." Minimum wage in Missouri, at the time, was $7.50 per hour.[10] I read the racialized economic crisis in Ferguson as a postmodern system of debt peonage. Michael Brown's alleged theft, however, displaces his object constitution, a byproduct of this system. If white autonomy, power, and inviolable subjectivity is consolidated via, in this context, indebtedness to the white-controlled (economic) power structure, the (temporarily) unemployed menace had seemingly refused to enter into a debt-peonage, obligatory-labor-contract dialectic with his captors, which would have solidified, based on the logic of the Sartrean paradigm, his Black body as perpetual object.

But Brown had not only entered into such a relationship of power that merely supplants a vexed history where white subjectivity is constituted through "property in the Black body" (Hartman 1997, 120). Additionally, he manifested himself as a "self-possessed," "willful agent" (Hartman 1997, 120) who secured his own "material basis of . . . existence" (Wynter 49) by appropriating Western techniques of domination: violence and thievery (granting that the store's video indeed reveals Brown as the perpetrator). This is similar to Richard's self-substitution in Lyle's shoes as white patriarch defined by masculine prowess. As an agential subject whose behavior mirrored the imperial white Subject, Brown displaced the "being-for-others" paradigm, which required of him absolute objectivity, and which permitted whites' exclusive claims to humanity and subjectivity.

Furthermore, the Hegelian-Sartrean struggle for identity discussed earlier also plays out in the case of Brown's violent interaction with Officer Wilson, and it further unmasks the imposition of the Black body as stationary object in a perverse dialectic. According to witness reports and the statements provided by Dorian Johnson (who was with Brown when they were accosted by Officer Wilson), Brown and Johnson were traveling in the street when Officer Wilson demanded that they "get the fuck on the sidewalk." Brown declined the officer's hostile directive, explaining that they would exit the street when they reached their nearby destination.

Brown's alleged recalcitrance, as Darren Wilson testified, prompted Wilson to put his police car in reverse, back up to the boys, and call for backup.

Considering the complexity of the psychodrama that unfolded thereafter, Brown refused to acknowledge Wilson's conscious awareness of self as supreme Subject, which stemmed from his authoritarian position as well as from his whiteness. This self-recognition would have been validated by Wilson's ability to regulate the movements and behaviors of those "animals" external to him—in this case, the spaces those "animals" are permitted to occupy. Although Wilson's account drastically differed, according to Johnson, Wilson responded aggressively, for, in Hegelian terms, he *had* to "supercede" Brown's ability to threaten his "Lordship," just like Lyle Britten *had* to destroy Richard Henry following his unsettling of the "being-for-others" dialectic. Like Richard, Brown allegedly squared up with his opponent, purportedly returning what Sartre considers the look of self-affirmation as well as physical blows.[11] In so doing, Brown substantiated his "being-for-itself" identity by way of the "redemptive" blows to Wilson, which had deadly and incommensurate consequences. Brown had to either remain a fungible object in a racist dialectic—or perish. When Richard will not apologize to Lyle for refusing the deferential recognition that enables Lyle to construct himself as supreme Subject, Lyle asks Richard, "Do you want to live?" (Baldwin [1964] 1995, 119). White racists are, therefore, unwilling to relinquish the objectified Black male imago from their racist psyches, for it requires their own suicide. Homicide appears to be the only tenable solution to the Black man who exists for himself before racist white men.

MONSTER-PHANTASM AND EPISTEMIC VIOLENCE

Epistemic violence also underwrites the construction of Michael Brown by the white racist episteme during the trial. The testimonies were marked by the omission or de-emphasis of any characterization of Michael Brown as a son, grandson, brother, recent graduate of Normandy High School with plans to attend trade school, or as a teen with aspirations to be a music artist. Officer Darren Wilson, the defense attorneys, and the media, no different than Whitetown during the trial, were unrelenting in stripping bare Brown's humanity to unveil what one op-ed writer, Dexter Thomas (2014), refers to as the "monster within." Brown was also construed to the grand jury, by Wilson's supporters and Wilson himself, as a thug and a threatening object. Brown's artistry is recast in the context of deviance, and he is spoken for as an overly embodied monster. As Thomas writes, he was tall and big—and, worse, "he made rap songs."

Wilson mentioned during his testimony, "just for the conversation," that he did not bother to learn Michael Brown's and Dorian Johnson's names until "the following day," or so he "think[s]" (Missouri v. Wilson 5 U.S. 207 [2014]).[12] If naming is an ontological act, failing to, at the very least, learn Brown's and Johnson's names upon encountering them underscores the objectification and ontological negation that often occurs when white gazes meet Black bodies. In fact, the very thing that Wilson *did* recognize, by his own admission, was the "size of the individuals"—that one was "really big" (207). Although Wilson at the time stood six foot four, 210 pounds to Brown's six-foot-five, 289-pound frame (Eisler 2014), Wilson embellished the narrative, circumscribing a figure of subhuman proportions in relation to his own normative and infantilized self-perceived constitution. "And when I grabbed him," he recounts, "the only way I can describe it is I felt like a five-year-old holding onto Hulk Hogan." He then repeated himself when asked to clarify his phantasmatic depiction of Brown: "Hulk Hogan, that's just how big he felt and how small I felt" (Missouri v. Wilson 5 U.S. 212 [2014]). There is no mention of Brown's face, the most visible and central signifier of identity. Rather, the very next thing he noticed, after internalizing their size, were Brown's socks "that had green marijuana leaves as a pattern on them" (208).

Wilson embodied the interpolating white gaze, which, according to Fanon ([1952] 2008, 92), amputates the Black body, severing it from its subjectivity. Brown was reduced to an overly embodied, Incredible Hulk–like phantasm and then to a pair of socks bearing an emblem that symbolizes a disreputable social norm typically associated with the ills of Black culture. The latter constitution further negates his ontological existence, given that, as Baldwin laments in "Many Thousands Gone," the Negro is a mere "social problem" and not a human one ([1955] 1998, 19). The presumably weed-smoking Michael Brown had to have been a contributor to the social degeneracy of the current social order, in the same way that Whitetown ruminated on how new-age "niggers" (namely Richard) were nothing like the "peaceful" "niggers of old" (Baldwin [1964] 1995, 48). Accordingly, Wilson was well within his rights to destroy this rapping monster-animal because, as he informed the grand jury in his testimony, "it look[ed] like a demon" (Missouri v. Wilson 5 U.S. 225 [2014]) and it "looked like he was almost bulking up to run through the shots, like it was making him mad that I'm shooting at him" (228).

We can only speculate about what happened in the jury, comprising nine white and three Black members. But if the jury mirrors the rest of US white-supremacist culture, we can conjecture that any of the twelve jurors who may have been taken aback by Wilson's fantastical Incredible Hulk portrayal of Brown and who instead affirmed Brown's personhood were likely to have been one of the three Black jurors. It is also likely that they themselves were probably not afforded epistemic space to offer their honest opinions. Similar to Richard's family and friends who testify on his behalf, the Black jurors (and Brown's family, neighbors, and companions, like Dorian Johnson, who was actually present that day) may have also experienced testimonial injustice and may have been silenced by the largely white jury that rendered Wilson's testimony tenable.

On the other hand, the not-guilty verdict speaks to the credibility afforded Wilson's testimony, which itself reveals the workings of an epistemic framework underwritten by a mutual concession to distorted worldviews among the (white) "polity" in the "official epistemic community" (Mills 1997, 17–18). Even if the white jury members were personally devoid of any prejudices, as Fricker (2007, 5) argues, the racial episteme in which a speaker's credibility is decided "is one in which there are inevitably many stray residual prejudices that threaten to influence our credibility judgments." But why are these "prejudices" so entrenched in the collective racist white consciousness? As Mills (1997, 18) points out, in white-supremacist societies, value judgments and interpretations of events emanating from white bodies are typically deemed to be objective and truth producing but are in fact "divergent from actual reality." This is so since white folks have historically and singlehandedly determined the social meanings in the social worlds in which they exist. Hence, in this case, like Jo Britten (and Laquan McDonald's murderer), Wilson imaginatively recalled the event through a "racially saturated field of visibility" (Butler 1993, 15), and the jury appeared to have gained knowledge of what occurred that day without rehearsing the inferences (Fricker 2007, 62) drawn from Wilson's narrative that revealed Brown to be an overly embodied monster. Likewise, in *Blues*, the State, as the "racial contract" would have it, dogmatically accepts Jo Britten's testimony as an "officially sanctioned reality" (Mills 1997, 18). For, in both cases, how could the white jurors have negated or suppressed the late-nineteenth- and early-twentieth-century discourse that mythologized Black men in the social imaginary as monstrous brutes? The residue of this ignorance persists, proven by Wilson's monstrous depiction of Brown and the credibility afforded his account.

It is, however, probable that Michael Brown had, at one point, advanced toward his assailant. But after realizing that his fists were no match for Darren Wilson's .40-caliber SIG Sauer, which held twelve rounds in the magazine, Michael Brown purportedly froze in place with his hands upraised as a symbolic gesture of surrender. But the credibility of *this* narrative is proven questionable. Rapper Kanye West has used his music to interrogate this aspect of Brown's murder. In "Feedback," a song on West's 2016 album, *The Life of Pablo*, West adds to the emergent discourse surrounding the details of Brown's raised arms in rap culture. "Hands up, hands up like the cops taught us," West raps. "Hands up, hands up, then the cops shot us," he continues. Undoubtedly, West is highlighting a semiotic paradox that exists between repressive forces and Black bodies. He is suggesting that a nonthreatening posture like Brown's raised arms—a nonverbal signal for officers to de-escalate—did not impel the officer to withdraw his weapon and to instead consider preemptive measures that would result in the preservation of life. Richard verbally surrenders and asks to go home but is still destroyed. Here, white social agents have again reassigned social meaning to Black gestures of surrender—in this case, upraised arms. In so doing, they have (re)defined how one interprets bodily signification of passivity, which is reconfigured as aggression—to the detriment of bodies like Brown's.

The false interpretations of Brown's body and intent by Wilson signify epistemic violence and epistemic ignorance. Wilson's murderous resolve in the face of Brown's nonthreatening posture owed to his state of phantasmagoria—a state of cognitive dysfunction that allowed him to misinterpret the unarmed, six-foot-five, 289-pound teen as a monster. Wilson was seeing what he wanted to see even though there was counter-vailing evidence, both immediately present and within the cultural lexicon, to alert him that his interpretation was false and racist. And worse, "the State" and the grand jury corroborate this mistaken perception because the "racial contract" is facilitated by the assembly of a "racial fantasyland" in which the primary operative function is "'consensual hallucination'" (Mills 1997, 18). Moreover, a phantom with superhuman proportions is not an Other, and so members of the racist polity are not obligated to preserve its life. But the Incredible Hulk–like monster was not present on that day; it was a phantom in the racist imagination of Wilson and the broader racist epistemic community.

Not surprisingly, Wilson's dehumanizing testimony is not an isolated case in the modern era. In *Look, a Negro!* political scientist Robert Gooding-Williams recounts the testimonies of the perpetrators in Rodney King's beating in 1991, which mirror Wilson's testimony in light of his fantastical description of Brown in 2014. Wilson declares, "[Brown] turns, and when he looked at me, he made like a grunting, like aggravated sound and he starts, he turns and he's coming back towards me" (Missouri v. Wilson 5 U.S. 227 [2014]), and Gooding-Williams (2006, 10) describes this act of "seeing" King's overdetermined Black body through a similar racist interpretive lens: "The defense attorney elicited testimony from King's assailants that depicted King repeatedly as a bear, and as emitting bear-like groans. In the eyes of the police, and then again in the eyes of the jurors, King's black body became that of a wild 'Hulk-like' and 'wounded 'animal, whose every gesture threatened the existence of civilized society." This recurring paradigm constitutes pernicious ignorance insofar as these testimonies, over twenty years apart, involve reliable manifestations of ignorance (Dotson 2011, 239) since there is a persistent absence of collective cognitive capacities to objectively interpret threatening or non-threatening gestures of Black male bodies during interactions with white male power, proving harmful to these bodies. Ignorance of this kind is inculcated in every era in the US. As Judith Butler (1993, 19) argues in "Endangered/Endangering," which examines the hermeneutic distortions of cases (namely King's) of anti-Black violence in the digital age, charging a feeble white victim "is an action that the black male body is always already performing within that white racist imaginary." Since Brown's and King's assailants convinced themselves of "seeing" Brown and King morph into hulking beasts, no different than Lyle Britten did, they had fulfilled their duties to the epistemic community to which they belonged by dumping six rounds into the flesh of Michael Brown or beating King mercilessly.

DISPOSABLE RAW MATERIAL

Brown's postmortem images, widely circulated in the media immediately and long after his death, speak to his expendability. Michael Brown was left face down on the pavement rather than in the weeds, as was the case with Richard Henry. Notwithstanding Lesley McSpadden's desire for her son's corpse to be removed from the scorching Ferguson asphalt, he remained a spectacle for four hours—a mere hypervisible yet invisible mass of disposable "raw material." Comparatively, as an "animal," Mbembe (2001, 27) argues that in the colony, the "corpse remained on the ground . . . a material mass and mere inert object, consigned to the role of that which is there for nothing." The difference, however, is that in the Ferguson, Missouri, twenty-first-century context, Brown's body served the justificatory agenda of the white power structure. For the repressive state apparatus at the scene, similar to Richard's body, Brown's body was reduced to a (black) mass of evidence needed to legitimize white impunity, and to evidence of what happens when a Black body attempts to evade the confines of non-alterity.

Conclusion

I have offered a complex but in no way exhaustive answer to the question, Why are Black males targeted and killed by racist factions? Emmett Till, the fictional Richard Henry, Rodney King, Laquan McDonald, Michael Brown, and many others are brutalized because their knowledge of self as men is silenced in the face of dehumanizing constructions of "blackness" emanating from privileged white-supremacist "knowers." Black men have had their subjective identities "confiscated," to echo philosopher George Yancy (2008, 1–2), by the unchanging racist episteme of every era, and returned to them as nonhuman. But to securely and indefinitely deny Black males their humanity/subjectivity, white agents of power bar them from the domain of otherness insofar as they construct Black men as monsters or predatory animals and as perpetual objects entrapped in a racialized Self-Other dialectic. This imprisonment persists after death, as they are reduced to a mass of excess materiality that is sometimes dumped in the weeds or left exposed in a public street, and the testimonies of their murderers often reveal Black males to be phantasms in racist imaginations. Their murders are therefore warranted, if they have no human value and are viewed as threatening to the social order, or to the exclusionary tribe of the white Western man. In fact, they suffer a double killing if their pre-death, communicative performances of personhood remain unintelligible posthumously, for, as Fricker (2007, 44) posits, degrading a person as a knower entails a further symbolic dehumanization.

Moreover, I show that it is necessary to understand the mechanisms that maintain the non-alterity designation of young Black males, which necessitates a clear understanding of the epistemic dimensions of the "racial contract." I have used Baldwin's fiction as an epistemic resource to illuminate Black-male injustice in real life, since the epistemic violence that Richard Henry suffers and the white-supremacist world in which he exists directly parallel real-life cases of Black-male killings—namely, the killing of Michael Brown. In both cases, the racist epistemes rest upon misrepresentations of young Black males, which are realities agreed upon by those who endeavor to maintain the "white polity" (Mills 1997, 20). It is no coincidence that Jo Britten's testimony is analogous to Darren Wilson's, insofar as both depict the young men in question as predators and monsters. In addition, the juries did not consider the hallucinatory and so exaggerated perceptions of events from both Britten and Wilson as grounds for mistrust and probable cause to convict. Their acquittals suggest that at least many jury members of such racist communities as the fictional Plaguetown and Ferguson abide by the "contractual" agreement that "*white misunderstanding, misrepresentation, evasion, and self-deception*" (Mills 1997, 19; emphasis in original) where race construction is concerned is an "officially sanctioned reality" (18) in the world that whites themselves have engineered. And if this was so in both cases, as well as in the Rodney King case, the only sui generis component of the white narratives offered is the extent of the phantasmagoric recounting deemed credible to the grand jury.

These consensual mistaken perceptions are the result of an epistemology of ignorance defined by consistent cognitive lapses in perceptual judgments. The imprisonment of the Black body in the realm of non-alterity is facilitated by reliable manifestations of ignorance, structurally embedded in our society through practices of silencing oppressed bodies and refusing them self-representation, which can have deadly consequences. So long as Michael Brown could not define himself as an aspiring teen rap star or as a role model to his younger brother, Andre—as a human being—before or after death, there was no counternarrative available to undermine his dehumanizing construction by Darren Wilson, a proxy for the larger epistemic community in Ferguson. Kristie Dotson (2011, 241) suggests that reliable ignorance denotes "counterfactual incompetence," or the refusal of epistemic agents to ascertain the truth concerning a given proposition. It stands to reason that the way to combat the epistemology of ignorance is to force our voices, which communicate our self-defined identities, upon our oppressors, cementing them in the discursive terrains in which we exist. While this is the task before us, we must also weep, or sing the "blues," for those bodies that are currently silenced and those that have been destroyed.

Notes

1. This phrase derives from race philosopher Charles Mills's oft-cited work, *The Racial Contract* (1997, 18).

2. In "Richard Wright's Blues," Ralph Ellison (1999, 264) defines the blues as follows: "The blues is an impulse to keep the painful details alive in one's aching consciousness, to finger its jagged grain, and to transcend it, not by the consolation of philosophy, but by squeezing from it a near-tragic, near-comic lyricism."

3. In 1996, former Democratic presidential candidate Hillary Clinton spoke at Keene State College in New Hampshire in support of then-president Bill Clinton's 1994 Violent Crime Control and Law Enforcement Act. In her speech, she called Black gang members "superpredators" with "no conscience" who must be "brought to heel."

4. I employ Baldwin's drama as a litmus test, as it were, to make sense of the Michael Brown murder case. Fiction invites meditations on or critiques of societal structures or pervasive ideologies of real life. James Baldwin ([1955] 1998, 19–21) used literature, to a large degree, to offer a foray into the dehumanization of the Negro and the "myths perpetuat[ed] about him" as defining features of the white "American psychology" in the mid-twentieth century. To this end, tracing the narrative parallels between his dramatized account of a Black-male murder in the 1950s and a factual case of a Black-male killing in the twenty-first century establishes a framework to examine this epidemic as a historical stasis, and to better identify the epistemic violence that underwrites the modern American, white-supremacist social order in which Michael Brown was a victim.

5. The "being-for-others" concept emanates from Jean-Paul Sartre's *Being and Nothingness* ([1943] 1956). Modeled upon the Hegelian master-slave dialectic, one is made an object to instantiate the subjectivity of the other person, who never conceives of the opposite being as anything other than an object.

6. Other theorists and philosophers have expounded upon Fanon's conceptualization of non-alterity. See George Yancy's (2008, 20) *Black Bodies, White Gazes: The Continuing Significance of Race.* Also, see George Yancy's interview with Lewis Gordon in *African American Philosophers: 17 Conversations* (Gordon 1998, 107).

7. My argument is informed by the work of Afro-Caribbean essayist, literary critic, and postcolonial theorist Sylvia Wynter, who captures this consequence of

mobilizing nonhuman constructions of Black male bodies in her seminal essay "'No Humans Involved': An Open Letter to My Colleagues." She examines the 1991 videotaped beating of the twenty-six-year-old, Black male Los Angeles native Rodney King by four Los Angeles police officers. "By classifying [the social group of young, poor, Black males] as N.H.I. [no humans involved]," she reasons, "these public officials would have given the police of Los Angeles the green light to deal with its members in any way they pleased" (Wynter 1994, 42).

8. While Gail Bederman (1996, 15) argues in *Manliness and Civilization* that by 1890 white middle-class men had ascribed to a masculine ethos character-ized by an affinity for "powerful manhood" and aggression, since chattel slavery, the Negro man's gender identity and personhood were historically conflated. In *Scenes of Subjection*, Saidiya Hartman (1997, 177) argues that the ostensible "man" implied in postemancipation political and legal discourse where Black bodies were concerned often implicated the "masculinity of the [Negro] citizen-subject." She maintains that "sexual reverberations" lurked beneath the postslavery project of "transforming brutes into men" (177). Amy Louise Wood (2011) also underscores this conflation in *Lynching and Spectacle*, arguing that lynching at once evinced the dehumanization of the Negro man's body, given that it was typically dese-crated like that of an animal, as well as sexualized the body so as to render the victim culpable in said crimes. Hence, she posits that the lynched "figure of the 'black beast rapist' was both inhuman brute (a 'beast') and hypersexual man (a 'rapist')" (98). Given the historical conflation of Black manhood and masculinity, Black men who endeavor to assert or reclaim their manhood are simultaneously asserting and reclaiming their personhood.

9. Sylvia Wynter (1994) identified the social group of young, poor, Black males through the classification of "no humans involved," or "N.H.I." Wynter suggests that the acronym refers "to any case involving a breach of the rights of young Black males who belong to the jobless category of the inner city ghettoes" (42). This category is discursively established and typifies the misrecognition of young Black males who are said to be "of a different *species*" (45).

10. See Ben Casselman's (2014) "The Poorest Corner of Town."

11. Rachel Clarke and Christopher Lett (2014) disclose the witness accounts in the events that led to Michael Brown's murder in their article "What Happened When Michael Brown Met Officer Darren Wilson."

12. For the full text of volume 5 of the grand-jury transcription of Darren Wilson's testimony, see State of Missouri v. Darren Wilson (2014).

References

Baldwin, James. [1955] 1998. "Many Thousands Gone." *Notes of a Native Son*. In *Baldwin: Collected Essays*, 19–34. New York: Library of America.

————. [1964] 1995. *Blues for Mister Charlie: A Play*. New York: Vintage International.

Bederman, Gail. 1996. *Manliness and Civilization: A Cultural History of Gender and Race in the United States, 1880–1917*. Chicago: University of Chicago Press.

Butler, Judith. 1993. "Endangered/Endangering: Schematic Racism and White Paranoia." In *Reading Rodney King/Reading Urban Uprising*, edited by Robert Gooding-Williams, 15–22. New York: Routledge.

Casselman, Ben. 2014. "The Poorest Corner of Town." *FiveThirtyEight*, August 26, 2014. https://www.fivethirtyeight.com/features/ferguson-missouri/.

Clarke, Rachel, and Christopher Lett. 2014. "What Happened When Michael Brown Met Officer Darren Wilson." *CNN*, last modified November 11, 2014. https://www.cnn.com/interactive/2014/08/us/ferguson-brown-timeline/.

Collins, Patricia Hill. 2000. *Black Feminist Thought: Knowledge, Consciousness, and the Politics of Empowerment*. 2nd ed. New York: Routledge.

Dotson, Kristie. 2011. "Tracking Epistemic Violence, Tracking Practices of Silencing." *Hypatia* 26 (2): 236–57.

Eisler, Peter. 2014. "Ferguson Case: By the Numbers." *USA Today*, November 25, 2014. https://www.usatoday.com/story/news/nation/2014/11/25/ferguson-case-by-the-numbers/70110614/.

Ellison, Ralph. 1999. "Richard Wright's Blues." *The Antioch Review* 57 (3): 263–76.

Fanon, Frantz. [1952] 2008. *Black Skin, White Masks*. Translated by Richard Philcox. New York: Grove Press.

Fein, Helen. 1979. *Accounting for Genocide: National Responses and Jewish Victimization during the Holocaust*. New York: Free Press.

Foucault, Michel. 1980. *Power/Knowledge: Selected Interviews and Other Writings (1972–1977)*. Edited by Colin Gordon. New York: Pantheon.

Fricker, Miranda. 2007. *Epistemic Injustice: Power and the Ethics of Knowing*. New York: Oxford University Press.

Fuss, Diana. 1994. "Interior Colonies: Frantz Fanon and the Politics of Identification." *Diacritics* 24 (2/3): 19–42.

Gooding-Williams, Robert. 2006. *Look, a Negro! Philosophical Essays on Race, Culture, and Politics*. New York: Routledge.

Gordon, Lewis R. 1998. "Lewis R. Gordon." Interview in *African American Philosophers: 17 Conversations*, edited by George Yancy, 95–118. New York: Routledge.

Harris, Trudier. 2009. *The Scary Mason-Dixon Line: African American Writers and the South*. Baton Rouge: Louisiana State University Press.

Hartman, Saidiya.1997. *Scenes of Subjection: Terror, Slavery, and Self-Making in Nineteenth-Century America*. New York: Oxford University Press.

Hegel, G. W. F. 1998. *Phenomenology of Spirit*. Translated by A. V. Miller. Delhi, India: Motilal Banarsidass. First published 1807.

Mbembe, Achilles. 2001. *On the Postcolony*. Berkeley: University of California Press.

Mills, Charles W. 1997. *The Racial Contract*. Ithaca, NY: Cornell University Press.

NAACP (National Association for the Advancement of Colored People). 2018. "History of Lynchings." NAACP (website). Last modified 2018. https://www.naacp.org/history-of-lynchings/.

Otten, Liam. 2015. " 'Blues for Mr. Charlie' Runs Feb. 20 to March 1." *The Source*, February 12, 2015.https://www.source.wustl.edu/2015/02/blues-for-mr-charlie-runs-feb-20-to-march-1/.

Sanchez, Ray. 2017. "Laquan McDonald Death: Officer Indicted on 16 New Charges." *CNN*. Last modified June 27, 2017. https://www.cnn.com/2017/03/23/us/laquan-mcdonald-case-hearing/index.html.

Sartre, Jean Paul. [1943] 1956. *Being and Nothingness: A Phenomenological Essay on Ontology*. Translated by Hazel E. Barnes. New York: Washington Square Press.

Spivak, Gayatri. [1988] 1994. "Can the Subaltern Speak?" In *Colonial Discourse and Post-colonial Theory: A Reader*, edited by Patrick Williams and Laura Chrisman, 66–111. New York: Columbia University Press.

Missouri v. Darren Wilson. Circuit court of St. Louis County. Grand jury, vol. 5, September 16, 2014. http://www.archive.org/stream/grand-jury-transcript-Darren-Wilson-testimony-volume-5/grand-jury-transcript-Darren-Wilson-testimony-volume-5.

Thomas, Dexter. 2014. "Michael Brown Was Not a Boy, He Was a 'Demon.'" *Al Jazeera*, November 26, 2014. https://www.aljazeera.com/indepth/opinion/2014/11/michael-brown-demon-ferguson-2014112672358760344.html.

Thompson, Carlyle Van. 2004. *The Tragic Black Buck: Racial Masquerading in the American Literary Imagination*. New York: Peter Lang.

West, Kanye. 2016. *The Life of Pablo*. Recorded November 2013–February 2016. GOOD Music, compact disc.

Wood, Amy Louise. 2011. *Lynching and Spectacle: Witnessing Racial Violence in America, 1890–1940*. Chapel Hill: University of North Carolina Press.

Wynter, Sylvia. 1994. " 'No Humans Involved': An Open Letter to My Colleagues." *Forum N.H.I.* 1 (1): 42–71.

Yancy, George. 2008. *Black Bodies, White Gazes: The Continuing Significance of Race*. Lanham, MD: Rowman & Littlefield.

Chapter 8

Land(point) Epistemologies

Theorizing the Place of Epistemic Domination

ESME G. MURDOCK

The deployment and utilization of case studies have enriched both theoretical understandings and practical implications of philosophical scholarship. The inclusion and analyses of case studies have also broadened the purview of our epistemic considerations, urging knowers to contemplate spaces, places, peoples, and beings we might not encounter in our scholarship or everyday lives. While case studies can broaden our epistemic considerations, there is a worrying homogeneity present in the selection of case studies that reflects particular epistemic locations. The limited range of selection criteria, overdetermined by epistemically privileged selectors, presents a challenge to how inclusive our categories are of whom we consider as knowers and what we identify as knowledge, as well as how accurate and useful our knowledge is. Much of the scholarship that has placed critical attention on the homogeneity of epistemic locations represented in dominant discourse has been informed by the social identities of nondominantly or subordinately positioned knowers, emphasizing the importance of epistemic positionality to knowledge processes and production. For example, Patricia Hill Collins (1990, 225) discusses how Eurocentric, masculinist social-scientific analyses of family may be overdetermined by studies of the heteronormative nuclear family structure represented within white, male, elite social experiences and background assumptions. This has led to a lack of epistemic consideration and an underdevelopment of research agendas that explore familial structures more representative of those outside of the white, male, elite position, such as working-class people or people of color, and may lead to research findings ill suited to the complexity of differently situated peoples. The homogeneity of dominant epistemic locations and the limitations that exclusivity can produce are also addressed in the development of important research areas that examine the dangers of epistemic injustice, violence, oppression, and silencing within both feminist epistemologies and social epistemology (Medina 2013; Fricker 2007; Alcoff 2006; Pohlhaus 2012; Dotson 2011, 2014).

More broadly, the particular epistemic locations of the gatekeepers (dominantly situated knowers) of mainstream epistemological frameworks also influence the types of evidence presented as indicative of particular knowledge projects and claims, as well as the processes of knowledge validation. To refer back to the above example of dominant social-scientific research projects, the types of case studies included in Eurocentric, masculinist epistemologies may disproportionately represent situations exclusive to white, male positionalities. These dominant social positionalities influence dominant exclusive epistemological frameworks, which affect both what is presented as evidence and the interpretative context of that evidence. In this chapter, I argue that nondominant epistemic vantage points informed critically by subordinated social identities are useful for identifying worrisome epistemic exclusions in the selection and presentation of evidence and in how that evidence is interpreted. I will do this by orienting my analysis in nondominant epistemic positionalities and traditions, specifically by employing Black feminist method and engaging with Indigenous epistemologies as particularly important angles of vision on processes of domination—for the purposes of this chapter, epistemic domination. In the first section, I examine the ways in which dominant epistemological frameworks have been constructed from homogeneous places of privilege while presenting these positionalities as neutral and universal (e.g., generic man and generic knower). I do this through engaging with a foundational theoretical understanding of epistemic location and standpoint within Black feminist epistemology. I also examine implications that the dominant epistemological construction of generic knowers has for how we consider and interpret evidence. In the second section, I examine the ways in which knowing within particular standpoints or epistemic locations are always part of a hermeneutical or interpretive process that can be obscured in both dominant and nondominant epistemic standpoints. This section will also examine the ways in which particular hermeneutic contexts and processes can compromise epistemic standpoints by infusing perspectives with interpretative content that is simultaneously merged with and perceived as the object of knowledge itself. In this way, I assert that the epistemic vantage point of dominant epistemological frameworks is compromised in particularly colonial ways. In the third section, I argue that the interrogation of social identities of the knowers of dominant Western epistemological frameworks needs also to interrogate the physical, environmental *place* of epistemic domination because an interpretative distortion of a dominant settler-colonial epistemological framework is the construction and obfuscation of Indigenous land as possession and property. A settler-colonial epistemological framework is one that privileges the social location of settlers through the attempted erasure and displacement of Indigenous socioecological systems, for the purposes of constructing settler sovereignty as primary. This construction of land is sedimented into landscapes through the ecological violence of settler colonialism, particularly through landscape modifications, for example, colonial afforestation campaigns. In this way, the land is modified to signify it as the possession of settlers and knowers, who, within settler-colonial contexts, are taught to perceive land as non-Indigenous. Finally, in the fourth section, I examine the epistemic violence of settler-colonial epistemic prescriptions of relating to land as possession through a case study of Bedouin peoples in the Naqab Desert and their attempts to present evidence relevant to land claims within the settler legal/juridical structures of the State of Israel. I use this case as a way of illustrating the epistemic mismatching of evidence to differing standards and interpretative contexts across dominant and nondominant epistemic locations and epistemological frameworks. This case demonstrates how the land deeply informs epistemic horizons as hermeneutic contexts that can differ greatly between communities of knowers. Land and relation to land form the foundation of interpretative contexts of place and of location and can function as a site of both epistemic domination and epistemic decolonization.

Before I continue, I would like to address the specific methodological decisions I have made in the production of this scholarship, namely, the decision to include particular epistemologies and epistemic vantage points of nondominantly situated subjects and communities. In this chapter, I rely primarily on the work of people of color, specifically, Black and Indigenous women. This is a strategic and political decision that I own in the crafting of this scholarship. My argument draws attention to the histories of exclusion and epistemic domination that continuously leave out or leave unconsidered the epistemological contributions, labor, and scholarship of knowers who exist outside of those whom the Western dominant epistemological tradition identifies as knowers or indeed knowable, except, overwhelmingly, to present epistemic Others as *objects of inquiry*. I am particularly sensitive to not only theorizing these exclusions but also disrupting this continuous practice of epistemic violence by practicing what I preach in the production of my own scholarship. I write from this intentional position as a way of locating myself in the epistemic practices of knowledge production as a nondominantly situated knower, as a multiethnic Black woman and philosopher. I use my own nondominant positionality and standpoint as a way of understanding my particular angle of vision on domination and oppression, as well as to theorize how I am implicated and complicit in epistemic privilege, albeit differently from dominantly positioned knowers. In this way, I hope that through literally locating myself in my identity as a nondominantly situated knower I can encourage the positioning of ourselves as knowers as a more common practice that disrupts the functioning of Western colonial ways of knowing overrepresented in much Western academic scholarship. To write about the places and conditions that make knowledge possible, I must acknowledge my own. I write what I write because of who I am and my relations to others, especially the land, not in spite of it.

The Hermeneutic Context of Knowing

A major inheritance of the Eurocentric, Western, white epistemological tradition is a preoccupation with a hyperseparation of knower and known. While most knowers agree that we, as embodied beings, are in and of the world, epistemic aspirations toward decontextualization, detachment, and estrangement from the world and toward more "perfect" objectivity pervade Eurocentric, Western, white traditions of knowing. One such conceptual striving is found in the hauntings of both the generic man and the generic knower. Both the generic man and generic knower are idealized archetypes meant to be useful for their universalizable qualities, such as reason. However, both the generic man and the generic knower bear strikingly similar characteristics and qualities to the actual men in whose image they were created. The creation of the generic man and, consequently, the generic knower, by a particularly small and privileged group of elite, Western, white men, reveals an aspiration to escape or diminish attention to the particular contexts this colonial enlightenment project emerges from: largely, domination. In situations of domination, the generic also becomes the normative standard by which knowers and knowledge are measured. Black feminist thought has been central to the articulation of the particular qualities of dominant epistemic positionality (dis)embodied in the generic knower precisely because the positionality and consideration of Black women are strikingly absent from, and thus stand in stark contrast to, Eurocentric and masculinist epistemological frameworks overrepresented throughout the West. The relief of the generic knower as universal superior subject becomes possible through the construction of the particular subordinated Other. Hence, we can understand the thought produced and articulated from the Eurocentric, masculinist standpoint as a type of specialized construction of knowledge created by and for a particular dominant epistemic community and not one that can be universalized or generalized to all knowers or epistemic communities (Collins 1990).

The legacy of the generic knower has worked with processes of domination to construct nongeneric or nondominantly situated knowers in a visibilized specificity that accompanies practices of racialization and gendering. The Black woman is a nongeneric, or specific, knower precisely because of the ways her racialized and gendered identities depart from the dominantly existent yet invisibilized prescription of white, male identity. A key tenet of Black feminist thought is the importance of focusing on the interconnection of experience and knowledge. Part of what the Black feminist tradition and Black feminist intellectuals have stressed and continue to stress is how social identity and experience inform our epistemic standpoint, or the conditions that affect our particular angle of vision of the world. Including and embracing this crucial dimension of experience means that Black feminist thought is also foundational in arguing that in a power-unequal world that denigrates nondominant social identities, such as Black womanhood, various standpoints exist as dominant and subordinated. Standpoints steeped in the experiences and self-understandings of the dominant epistemic community are simultaneously constructed as superior through contexts of domination; they can and do produce and reproduce distorted understandings of the world and of others, which contribute to continued social subordination. If knowing through a dominant epistemological framework requires complicity in one's own subordination, then the development of nondominant, self-defined epistemic standpoints and traditions is paramount to projects of liberation. In this way, subordinated social identities can (but do not always) lead to the development of a critical consciousness aimed at understanding the particularity of the knower's situation that is excluded from dominant discourse. Patricia Hill Collins (1990) draws our attention to the fact that knowledge production and generation, when bounded exclusively within domains of privilege and domination where knowers belonging to a tradition or discipline are highly homogeneous in identity and social location, produces both knowledge traditions and knowledge that are biased and necessarily incomplete: "Black feminist thought, like all specialized thought, reflects the interests and standpoint of its creators. Tracing the origin and diffusion of any body of specialized thought reveals its affinity to the power of the group that created it (Mannheim 1936). Because elite white men and their representatives control structures of knowledge validation, white male interests pervade the thematic content of traditional scholarship. As a result, Black women's experiences with work, family, motherhood, political activism, and sexual politics have been routinely distorted in or excluded from traditional academic discourse" (201). Members of dominant epistemic communities and epistemic groupings may be less apt or skilled at identifying anomalies or problematic aspects of knowledge projects precisely because the knowledge articulated gels more or less perfectly with the social positions and identities represented therein. In this way, their positionality infuses the content of what they perceive as self-evident. Dominant epistemic communities who also benefit from unequal power structures that favor them have more incentive to preserve that structure. For example, a community of dominant knowers that is socially homogeneous and exclusive in membership as white, upper-class, cisgender men may import criteria into research design that does not adequately attend to marginalized standpoints, say of Black, lower-class, queer women. This can lead to inaccurate research results and knowledge production, since results tailored for a particular group are generalized to many or all others. It also plays an important role in how particular phenomena or evidence are presented and interpreted within an epistemic framework.

Knowledge as a social process and the outcome of relationships in community is an idea present in many epistemological frameworks and traditions. The generation and validation of knowledge have important implications for the presentation and acceptance of evidence within specific communities of knowers. For example, Black feminist thought has attended to the specialized knowledges emerging from the lived experiences of Black women's standpoints and has identified the ways in which all knowledge is situated in a community or standpoint of some kind (Collins 1990). In this way, standpoints emanating from particular epistemic groups or communities work together to take the background, everyday experiences of their knowers' social identities and make them intelligible through developing an epistemological framework for understanding them and validating them. However, in that social relations marked by power inequalities and the suppression of certain standpoints allow for the flourishing and overrepresentation of dominant epistemological frameworks, the validation of particular standpoints and situated knowledges can be withheld. This matters, especially for the purposes of this chapter, because it indicates that what is presented as evidence or fact from a particular subordinated standpoint is sometimes held to dominant epistemic standards ill suited to assess it. For example, if the standards for evidence are set in a Eurocentric, masculinist standpoint that draws the background assumptions of experience from the social location of elite white males, then evidence presented from a subordinated standpoint, such as that of Black women, may not satisfy those standards, leading dominant knowers to dismiss the knowledge claims they present as unintelligible or illegitimate. In contexts of domination, this is especially pernicious, because the Eurocentric, masculinist standpoint is presented not only as legitimate but as universal, such that the standards are applied to any and all knowledge claims emanating from power-unequal relations and epistemic positionalities. As Collins (1990, 204) argues, "Black women scholars may know that something is true but be unwilling or unable to legitimate our claims using Eurocentric, masculinist criteria for consistency with substantiated knowledge and criteria for methodological adequacy. For any body of knowledge, new knowledge claims must be consistent with an existing body of knowledge that the group controlling the interpretative context accepts as true. The methods used to validate knowledge claims must also be acceptable to the group controlling the knowledge validation process." It is important to note that the embedded nature of knowers in worlds necessitates nonneutral standpoints that situate knowledge in communal and social interpretative contexts. Not attending to the background, everyday assumptions that contribute to the way in which we frame and interpret knowledge does not erase those interpretative contexts or biases from our knowledge projects. So, a major issue with the proposal of the generic knower is that the interpretative context established by the homogeneous social locations of the dominant epistemic community it emanates from is obscured and, as such, taken to disappear. Subsequently, the standards fitted to a particular dominant epistemic community are universalized in ways that harm, ignore, and dismiss other situated knowledges (especially those that threaten the unequal power structure) not just as inconvenient but as unintelligible, as not knowledge. This process reproduces the homogeneous content and character of dominant discourse as emanating from the particular dominant epistemic community and situates knowers in particularly racialized, gendered, classed, and colonial ways.

Perception and Visibilized Knowers

Black feminist thought provides us with reasons for taking seriously the embeddedness of knowledge in the world and expands our attention to the social location and positionality of knowers. Black feminist thought also encourages us to challenge the dominant Eurocentric, masculinist epistemological frameworks that overdetermine relationships of stability and reification between clearly identifiable subjects and objects. Thus, it is not only that knowers are situated in a world with different relationships to unequal power structures but, importantly, that our entire knowledge-production processes and objects of knowledge are necessarily entangled within our worlds; our positionality is a part of our knowledge. This means that our own in-the-worldness is a part of our understanding and constitution of objects/subjects of knowledge (Code 2008; Harding 1993). As such, there is no purely decontextualized evidence, in the same sense that there is no generic knower. We can say perhaps, though, that there are more or less transparent knowers in the sense of acknowledging and accounting for the ways in which our social locations and positionality influence/affect our epistemic vantage point. This acknowledgment may be useful in identifying when epistemic standpoints and epistemic vantage points are compromised or colonized in salient ways.

One way of understanding the desire to decontextualize both subjects and objects of knowledge in Eurocentric, masculinist epistemological frameworks and traditions is to examine the role of epistemology in historical practices of Western domination itself. The emergence of particular forms of domination such as European colonialism and imperialism has been accompanied by particular epistemological projects such as scientific classification. For example, the historical emergence of projects of domination such as colonialism and the Western construction of the concept of visible race was steeped in classificatory epistemological frameworks (Goldberg 1993; Mignolo 1995; West 2002; Alcoff 2006; Mignolo 2007).

Difference was not only mapped or classified through projects of colonial cartography, literally classifying and superimposing order(s) onto lands and geographies, but physical bodily difference also became a racialized reality mapped onto the body that was signified and read in particular ways (Jhally 1997; hooks 2014; Alcoff 2006). Ways of knowing and understanding are necessarily discursive projects between embedded subjects and objects of knowledge, but ways of knowing and particular forms of domination can also compromise understanding. The legacy of Western epistemological frameworks that imbue particular visible realities with specific socially constructed meaning for the purposes of domination and subordination has led to naturalized ways of perceiving these objects of knowledge with their attendant socially constructed distortions as the truth itself (Jhally 1997; Alcoff 2006). Thus, in the same way that the generic knower aspires to decontextualization through obscuring or ignoring the literal conditions of epistemic vantage point, epistemological frameworks steeped in domination can also present interpretation of socially constructed meanings as simple, unadulterated perceptions of the objects perceived in themselves.

In addressing the ways in which race has been constructed as visible and taught to be perceived always already imbued with particular meanings, Linda Martín Alcoff (2006, 184) argues that the process of perception "represents sedimented contextual knowledges." Part of the "reality" of race and racialized perception in a racist society is that actual physical, embodied realities come to signify a range of meanings such as position in a racial hierarchy. Alcoff suggests that the contextual knowledge of racialized and racist interpretation becomes attenuated in the physical characteristics of difference (e.g., skin color, hair texture) themselves, and thus perceiving racialized features is taken as evidence of the existence of race itself. Race as constructed and signified through particular real physical characteristics on bodies becomes a self-evident feature of our racialized world. However, meaning always accompanies processes of perception, and it is directly informed by the hermeneutic or interpretative context of the knower, the known, and the process of perception. Hence, we *learn* how to perceive and pick out certain visible characteristics (such as skin color) as salient for the purposes of interpolating them with particular meanings, which are dependent on the discursive context and conditions we find ourselves in. In the case of living in a white-supremacist society, we learn to pick out racialized physical characteristics as meaningful for classifying persons in a racist hierarchy.

These ways of perceiving and interpreting in relationships of domination affect both dominator and dominated, albeit in different ways. These practices of compromised or colonized perception and knowing are learned as well as internalized by both colonizer and colonized, dominant and subordinated. Domination is not something achieved just by the external imposition of force; it is also importantly maintained through external habituation and internalized disciplining (Fanon 2008). Thus, processes of domination affect not only how we perceive the world but also how we perceive ourselves (Fanon 2008; hooks 2014). To learn to perceive and understand yourself through logics of domination, as a subordinated and oppressed subject, is to perceive yourself and know yourself with the attendant meanings the classificatory schemes of domination have imposed upon you. This can and does occur on a deeply epistemic level when we consider what orienting ourselves (people of color) within dominant Western, masculinist epistemologies that encourage knowledge and knowers as disembodied subjects does to the perception of our own particularity, which is constructed precisely as anti-universal, as inferior. The work done on the interpretative processes and context of knowing when it comes to things like racialized, visibilized identities is a useful framework with which to further understand how dominant Eurocentric epistemological frameworks have constructed the physical place of knowing: land itself.

The Landedness of Knowing

I will move now to examining how dominant Western Euro-descendent epistemological frameworks enact epistemic violence through ways of knowing and perceiving that obstruct and distort the literal site of knowing (land) through constructions of land as white possession and property. These conceptions within systems of domination and epistemic oppression discipline marginalized knowers by incorporating them within epistemological frameworks that prescribe perceiving and knowing land in particularly harmful ways, especially in the context of Indigenous communities. This particular context for knowing and perceiving land within processes of domination is naturalized and normalized in dominant discourse such that it is not often made a site of critical analysis; it is accepted as the universal way in which we know through dominating and distorting land and land relations. It is an invisibilized condition of generic (dominative) knowing.

Bringing the context of how dominant epistemological frameworks come to have the normative power of dominance is necessary to highlight historical and continuous processes of epistemic domination. For the purposes of this chapter, I will be exploring the primacy of dominant epistemological frameworks' reliance on historically oppressive structures through ongoing systems of settler colonialism. As addressed earlier, Black feminist thought gives us compelling reasons to believe that knowers are embedded in the world and social in important ways. The extent to which dominant epistemological frameworks obscure those relevant conditions is telling especially for the purposes of domination, oppression, colonialism, and settler colonialism. In this section, I will focus on how land and relations to land constitute an important part of epistemic standpoints through centering accounts that articulate nondominant Indigenous conceptions of land and land relating as informed by Indigenous epistemological frameworks and traditions.

The literal ground of epistemic positionality is land, is earth. The decontextualization of subjects, objects, and processes of knowing from land and earth are marked in Eurocentric, masculinist epistemological frameworks. However, the centrality of land and earth to projects of colonization bound up with the creation and expression of Eurocentric, masculinist epistemological frameworks is an epistemic tension worth exploring. I begin this section with a reframing, a reorientation necessary for the articulation of my argument, particularly in a Western academic context. I write this work from within a settler-colonial nation-state on currently ceded Muscogee lands, currently referred to as northeastern Georgia. While this acknowledgement may not seem particularly profound, it disrupts and draws attention to the ways in which the land and one's relationship to the land, in this case, the occupation of ceded Indigenous lands, can erase or obscure particular land relationships from our understandings, hermeneutic horizons, and literal possibilities for our being. In the same way that I have learned to perceive myself and others as racialized and gendered, I have learned to acknowledge and pay attention to landedness, or rather I have begun to unlearn constructing "land as possession" as that which uncritically belongs to, supports, and reflects me. I have begun to unlearn perceiving land as non-Indigenous. Knowers' conceptions of their relationship to land as structured in a settler-colonial state (dis)ordered by settler-colonial frameworks and values encourages them to perceive and know space, place, and land in particular ways that often involve racialization and violence. As knowers inculcated in particular epistemological traditions, taught to know or perceive in particular ways, we are formed by our lived contexts and the attendant meanings attached to them, but often we forget, or are discouraged from remembering, that the way in which we understand our context is dependent on the meanings imposed upon our literal bodies and landscapes. That we do not situate ourselves in relation to the literal land we occupy and that makes our actions possible is learned and further naturalized by continuous practice. The fact that I am writing about land and conceptions of land from occupied Indigenous territories in a settler-colonial state matters immensely for my argument, because the US settler-colonial context has narrated conceptions and interpretations of land in order to legitimate and maintain settler colonialism, the topic to which I now turn.

The possibility of the US as a settler-colonial state rests on the fact and attendant erasure of continuous Indigenous dispossession (Bang et al. 2014; Moreton-Robinson 2015; Murdock 2018). The formation of the settler colony and its transformation into settler-colonial nation-state relies on continuous processes of Indigenous dispossession and occupation of Indigenous lands. It also relies on a concomitant continuous process of construction of land and territories in what is currently called the US as possessions of the nation-state. As Kyle Whyte (2018, 349) states,

> Settler colonial domination occurs when several factors are present. First, at least one society secures its members' cultures, economies, health, and political sovereignty by permanently inhabiting the places in which one or more other societies already inhabit. . . . The original societies have already cultivated these places to suit their members' own cultures, economies, health, and political sovereignty. Second, the settler societies engage in settlement by erasing the capacities that the societies that were already there—Indigenous societies—rely on for the sake of exercising their own collective self-determination over their cultures, economies, health, and political order.

The construction of land within the settler state, imbued with meanings attached to the legitimacy of the very same settler society, is achieved through Indigenous dispossession and the cultivation of land and space to reflect particular meanings and interpretative contexts. This cultivation of place and land to reflect Eurocentric/settler values and settler-nation-state legitimacy is produced and reproduced through the disruption of Indigenous systems and institutions grounded in land and territory. This disruption is accompanied by the subsequent construction of settler systems and institutions that ground settler identity and meaning in place alongside the obfuscation, erasure, and inferiorization of Indigenous identities and meanings. This process of domination engages similar disciplining logics to those seen in the construction of visible race through the external force of physical/ecological violence and through the internalization of disciplinary tactics that distort ways of relating to self/land. In this way, settlers' identities and their relationship to place are signified and reinforced through constructions of the landscape that reflect settler meanings, while Indigenous identities are othered in racialized and violent ways to reflect and signify unbelonging; each of these processes are internalized to varying degrees.

The classificatory logics present in the emergence of global processes of domination such as settler colonialism have also been accompanied by possessive logics.[1] The naturalization and normativity prescribed to perceiving, knowing, and naming the US or any settler nation-state as the primary sovereign state in a geographical territory relies on the ways in which dominant Euro-descendent settler epistemological traditions have constructed land and territory of the settler space as a white possession. Aileen Moreton-Robinson (2015) identifies a core practice of settler-colonial domination as the permeation of white possessive logics that exist not only through the fact of Indigenous dispossession but also through the modification of landscapes to materially reflect land as possessed *by settlers*. This meaning and interpretation of Indigenous lands as unending white possession and property of the settler state through the erasure of Indigenous sovereignty is habituated, naturalized, and normalized through interaction with a landscape we are taught to see *not* as Indigenous but, rather, as proprietary, as belonging to the nation-state. In this way, land and landscape act as discursive and importantly contested sites or texts that can be, and are, interpreted in various ways, especially in relation to power. In the same way that the power or privilege of social location can be obscured for the creation of the mythic generic knower, the power of dispossession and possession can be obscured from the possibilities of knowing and interpreting. Many Western scholars can write and live on occupied land without ever making that fact an intentional object of their analysis, of their possibilities. However, for Indigenous peoples, Indigenous dispossession is not something that can be backgrounded, as it can be within other dominant epistemic standpoints that are made possible by the concomitant fact of Indigenous dispossession and the subsequent erasure of that fact for settler legitimacy. As Moreton-Robinson (2015, xiii) argues in *The White Possessive*,

> For Indigenous people, white possession is not unmarked, unnamed, or invisible; it is hypervisible. In our quotidian encounters, whether it is on the streets of Otago or Sydney, in the tourist shops in Vancouver or Waipahu, or sitting in a restaurant in New York, we experience ontologically the effects of white possession. These cities signify with every building and every street that this land is now possessed by others; signs of white possession are embedded everywhere in the landscape. The omnipresence of Indigenous sovereignties exists here too, but it is disavowed through the materiality of these significations, which are perceived as evidence of ownership by those who have taken possession. This is territory that has been marked by and through violence and race.

This marking is incredibly important for the maintenance and reproduction of settler colonialism and settler rule. In the same way that race is visibilized in a classificatory schema sedimented in real material phenomena such as physical characteristics of the body, settler belonging and white possession are materialized in the landscape to signify settler belonging and Indigenous otherness and unbelonging (if Indigenous peoples are figured at all). Thus, the constructed meaning and interpretation of settler states as legitimate, sovereign territories are taken to be demonstrable through the evidence of land modified to reflect settler rule via ownership/possession. I should also underscore quite explicitly the ways in which the obscuring of Indigenous sovereignty does not negate the continuous presence and power of Indigenous nations and sovereignties; however, domination works to obscure this knowledge and perception. In the same way that the context of social identity/positionality is obscured in attempts to render it nonexistent to legitimate the generic knower and to hypervisibilize the racialized, gendered, nongeneric knower as Other—outside the realm of knowledge/intelligibility—so, too, is the fact of Indigenous dispossession, foundational to the interpretative context of Euro-descendent Western settler epistemological frameworks, obscured. I should add here that the fact of Indigenous dispossession is also something that can be invisibilized and backgrounded in nondominant epistemic standpoints and so must also be visibilized and made an intentional object of analysis in the work of nondominantly situated knowers, as well. For example, rhetorical practices such as referring to the US nation-state as a "nation of immigrants" or a cultural "melting pot" can and do obscure the fact of Indigenous presence and continuous sovereignty and Indigenous dispossession as foundational to the formation of the US nation-state. These rhetorical practices also present cultural hegemony through incorporation, assimilation, or citizenship as the normative mode of belonging to this geographical space.

In discussing the ways in which interpretative contexts and content can be infused or mapped onto landscapes, Leroy Little Bear addresses the ways in which frameworks of understanding are systems superimposed upon that which is to be understood, such as natural phenomena. These systems of understanding are not a part of nature itself. He states, "It is like the land survey system: a grid framework of townships, sections, and acres superimposed on the land. These units, in turn, are used as the basis for dealing with the land, but they are not part of the nature of the land" (Little Bear 2016, ix). To return to the praxis of settler colonialism as expounded by Whyte, we can say that part of the violence of settler colonialism is the superimposition of settler frameworks upon Indigenous landscapes through dispossession that works to obscure/erase Indigenous sovereignty and land relating for the purposes of demonstrating, reflecting, and signifying settler belonging and possession. If, as Moreton-Robinson states, every city, street, and building of the settler state signifies Indigenous erasure through white possession, the ontology of settler place is materialized in land, but this product is constructed, not natural or self-evident. We can apply this directly to the context of evidence and practices of justification through the signification of land as possession and property of the settler state. This signification, within white possessive logics, requires Indigenous dispossession and landscape modification to gain traction.

The long history of ecological violence in the form of colonial dispossession and land expropriation in settler-colonial contexts is often accompanied by severe landscape alteration and modification. For example, historical and ongoing traumas such as genocide, removal, and relocation of Indigenous peoples from their ancestral homelands are a means of constructing "empty land" for the creation of natural preserves or property for settlers (Nash 1970; Spence 1999; Brockington and Igoe 2006; Dowie 2011). Here, ecological violence is enacted in several ways, but landscape modification and alteration also act as a way of obscuring

Indigenous land-use practices, land belonging, and continuance. The landscape is restructured to reflect settler values and land-use practices that create a relationality to place over and on top of Indigenous ones. The logic of white possession pervades the landscape and is signified everywhere, encouraging the perception and interpretation of the US as non-Indigenous. In this way, by reconstructing conceptions of land from a system of relations to inert material for profit or object to be possessed, one can also conceal different, competing land-use practices as well as traditional forms of belonging and land rights (Dunbar-Ortiz 2014). If land is constructed only to reflect the capacity to own and use it through dominative property ascriptions and Indigenous dispossession, there is no room for imagining different land uses, land belongings, histories, or memories—for perceiving the agency of land.

In discussing the history of landscape modification involved in settler colonialism in Shikaakwa (the currently ceded Indigenous territory commonly referred to as Chicago), Megan Bang et al. (2014) discuss processes of decolonizing place-based education practices through (re)storying ways of seeing, experiencing, and relating to Shikaakwa in Indigenous ways that disrupt and make visible settler-colonial violence as the normative mode of interaction. She states, "Chicago is a wetland that becomes part prairie and part oak savannah. It's hard to see with the *layers of colonial fill,* but actually it's hiding in plain sight (Brayboy 2004)" (Bang et al. 2014, 2). This quotation points to the constructed nature of the urban landscape of Shikaakwa and how it has changed as a result of settler colonialism (wetland to prairie and savannah). However, dominant Euro-descendent settler-colonial frameworks present the contextual and interpretative product of settler-colonial domination, the place and land of Chicago, as a natural and unchanged entity, which simultaneously articulates or demonstrates settler possession/belonging through superimposed and constructed material conditions of the landscape. In other words, as Little Bear teaches us, the superimposed system of understanding is taken up, uncritically and mistakenly, as the object of analysis or knowledge itself.

In this way, Bang et al. argue that we need to re-remember how to perceive land as Indigenous and reorient/reinhabit epistemological frameworks that articulate and interpret land differently than the dominant property/possession ascription of the settler state—to understand that just as land through settler domination has become other than what it was, land can also (re)become itself. The obstacles to doing this are apparent in the ways in which Indigenous ontologies and epistemologies have been a pronounced target of settler-colonial violence. A primary feature and means of settler colonialism is the rupturing, interrupting, erasure, and attempted destruction of the place-based land epistemologies of Indigenous peoples with the external (and yet also other place-based) epistemologies of settlers. Disrupting Indigenous epistemologies to refashion Indigenous lands as settler properties attempts to sever relationships to Indigenous lands and destroy Indigenous continuance/futurity. Land as Indigenous can only (re)become itself through the relations, memory, and praxis of Indigenous sovereignty, through Indigenous being-in-the-world. Epistemic domination is also often accompanied by the internalizing of disciplinary logics that coerce dominated others to perceive themselves with borrowed or "Western eyes" (Mohanty 1984), to eliminate Indigenous peoples through assimilation by attempting to destroy the difference of Indigeneity. Bang et al. (2014, 4) state, "The reification of western intellectual traditions is often made possible by the denial or erasure of 'Indigenous points of reference,' which, as Marker (2006) points out, is a form of epistemic violence." The epistemic violence of denial or erasure of Indigenous points of reference functions as a foreclosure or disinclination to the possibility of perceiving or relating to Indigenous lands in ways that identify the fact of Indigenous dispossession necessary for settler occupation, the possibility of perceiving or identifying lands as Indigenous. These Indigenous points of reference, however, are not destroyed through obscuration or attempted erasure.

The fact that settler institutions are made possible primarily through the enactment of ecological violence and through the epistemic violence of reorienting belonging to place and governance structures in epistemological frameworks geared towards the legibility, legitimacy, and futurity of settler traditions and understandings has implications for what evidence is and how it is interpreted in settler-colonial legal/juridical frameworks. If evidence of Indigenous dispossession and settler-state possession of land is always already embedded in landscape in ways that signify materially, through reified dominant epistemological frameworks, that the land is settler property in its actual perceived facticity, then how are divergent interpretations meant to emerge or be taken into account? One way to begin to answer this question is precisely to acknowledge the construction of the dominant Western Euro-descendent epistemological tradition as a historical artifact forged in the fires of domination and wedded to interpretative schemas that invisibilize its whiteness, hypervisibilize that which is different as inferior, and materialize difference in ways that are perceived as marked.

The presentation and reliance on conceptions of land/landscape as possession/property prescribe processes of knowledge validation that exclude other conceptions and their accompanying forms of evidence, or indeed disparate meanings and interpretations ascribed to the same evidence. In this way, Indigenous evidence claims are always already out of bounds by the interpretatively compromised process of perceiving within a settler epistemological standpoint that conflates the constructed evidence of settler possessive logics with the straightforward perception of land itself. One example is language used to describe Indigenous nations as cultural minorities *within* the settler state. The misrepresentation of sovereign Indigenous nations as cultural minorities within the settler state already positions the relationship to the land as ownership, as white-settler possession, making the perception of land as Indigenous always already epistemically out of bounds. Since settler belonging is naturalized and embedded in land, alternative interpretations of those material signifiers are understood as indemonstrable, as anti-fact, as fiction. Any evidence presented within dominant settler epistemological frameworks is always already perceived in interpretive contexts that read land as settler possession to endlessly fulfill the continuation of settler colonialism.

Settler Horizons, Evidence, and Erasure

Now I transition to a case study in which we can clearly identify the ways in which evidence presented to signify the landed ecological violence settler colonialism enacts, erases, and denies is misread and misinterpreted in dominant settler frameworks ill suited to perceive it or perceive it well. It is a case that demonstrates how even when evidence of landscape modification exists, it is still interpreted through frameworks that continue to ignore or deny the ecological violence of settler domination for the continuance, proliferation, and futurity of settler colonialism. This case reveals the pervasiveness of processes of epistemic violence through dominative perceptual processes that refuse to see land or landscape as Indigenous, that always already position the possibility of land as Indigenous as out of epistemic bounds.

I examine a case of settler colonialism in the Middle East, assessing the ways in which Bedouin peoples in the Naqab (Negev) Desert are attempting to challenge Israeli seizure and occupation of their homelands. The Naqab, as it is traditionally named, is a desert largely referred to now in a Hebraicized form, *Negev*, that lies between Egypt and Jordan, within Palestine and Israel, south of both the West Bank and the Gaza Strip. It is worth stating that it is hard to even express in language where this desert is without invoking colonial logics or using colonial cartography and bounding to locate it. The eastern and western borders of the triangular Naqab are marked by the straight, fixed international/political borders of Jordan and Egypt; however, the Naqab's northern border "is defined by the aridity line, which over centuries has shifted continually" (Weizman 2015, 10). However, this northern-border aridity line is drafted as a fixed cartographic line, which has serious implications for political processes that happen along it as it moves and changes, expanding or shrinking the actual boundaries of the desert. The meteorological line of the desert ebbs in times of drought and flows in rainy seasons and, as such, is sometimes analogized to a shoreline. This line of demarcation, with its attendant changes with increasing anthropogenic climate change, has historically functioned and continues to function as an important juridical and colonial marker (10). In *The Conflict Shoreline*, Weizman (2015, 10) states, "Since the threshold of the desert marked a border beyond which permanent agricultural cultivation and settlement was deemed impossible, Israeli jurists argued that the area was not cultivated in practice and therefore no Bedouin property rights could be respected there. The threshold of aridity thereafter marked the border of a zone of expropriation within which the Bedouins were put completely at the mercy of the state and tolerated only as a matter of charity. It was an act of cartographic and territorial violence." Thus the more the line of aridity moves, making Bedouin cultivation and inhabitation impossible by Israeli-settler legal/juridical standards, the more territory opens up to be expropriated and occupied by Israeli settlers and institutions, such as the military. In this way, the State of Israel has invoked what is called the Dead Negev Doctrine, a legal/juridical apparatus that functions similarly to the doctrine of terra nullius. *Terra nullius* translates literally to "empty land" and was a doctrine of land expropriation invoked in settler colonies in Australia, North America, and throughout the colonial world to legally declare territories as uninhabited and thus belonging to no one while also relying on racist constructions of Indigenous peoples as part of the land/environment itself (Pateman 2007, 36; Lindqvist 2007). Legal/juridical doctrines such as terra nullius are well-worn means of Indigenous dispossession, and "scholars of settler colonialism have argued that the conceptual construction of uninhabited land, a form of Indigenous absence, opens the space for settler majorities to establish their ways of knowing, doing, and being as normative and morally superior and begin attempts to indigenize settler majority identities (Veracini 2011)" (Bang et al. 2014, 5). In other words, if the cultivation of the desert by inhabitants predating Israeli occupation (Bedouin peoples) is deemed impossible by Israeli legal/juridical standards, then cultivation becomes understood as an Israeli interaction/relation enacted through their superior cultivation abilities, demonstrating an affiliation to the Naqab as homeland. The citing of Israeli cultivation of the Naqab as the first instance of such cultivation of an arid region works to indigenize Israeli settlers to the Naqab while erasing or obscuring Bedouin cultivation and land-use histories.

The Dead Negev Doctrine led to very particular ecological land-scape-modification campaigns on the part of the Israeli government, such as large and historic campaigns of colonial afforestation of the Naqab. Weizman details the planting of the largest forest in Israel, Yatir, and the ways this project was conceptualized as jointly ecological and security driven, as it would both cultivate the desert and create an ecological barrier or security zone for Israelis. Additionally, projects of Israeli colonial afforestation were deployed to literally cover up the remains of Palestinian villages destroyed during and after the formation of the State of Israel in 1948, to preempt claims or possibilities of return. Weizman (2015, 25) chronicles how colonial afforestation campaigns continue presently in the Naqab as a means of Bedouin erasure and prevention of Bedouin return to resettle their lands.

Thus, colonial campaigns of landscape modification and climate change were construed as ecological necessities to make the desert habitable for settlers but also functioned to obscure the traces of previous Bedouin cultivation and thus claims to those lands as well as possibility of return through socioecological as well as epistemic attachments and belonging to those places. The language used to characterize these ecological modifications to landscapes in the form of colonial afforestation campaigns is also telling. Colonial afforestation of the desert was often referred to by euphemisms such as "making the desert bloom" (Weizman 2015, 23). This language is important because it constructs these practices as positive in terms that signal particular epistemically dominant positionalities. "Making the desert bloom" supports the Dead Negev Doctrine as a factual, apolitical accounting of the space of the desert in which cultivation by Bedouin peoples is deemed impossible and absent. By cultivating the desert through afforestation to "improve" it, making it productive in a colonial sense, evidence of prior sites of cultivation that exist in the allegedly "dead Negev" are also obscured, erased, and potentially made irretrievable.

In addition, engineers and proponents of colonial afforestation campaigns in the Naqab spoke quite explicitly of the relationship between these campaigns and projects of legitimizing Israeli sovereignty through colonial dispossession of Bedouin lands. The colonial campaigns of afforestation were often accompanied by language and logic of Europeanizing or Judaizing the Naqab to create climates more hospitable to Israeli settlers. The introduction of plant species from other geographical territories, such as Europe, attempted to signify the non-Bedouin nature of desert cultivation, to encourage the perception of the Naqab as demonstrably, evidently non-Bedouin. However, climate change was not the only aim of these afforestation campaigns, as evinced through the words of Yosef Weitz, which identified these landscape modifications as "a biological declaration of Jewish sovereignty" and integral for "setting up geopolitical facts" (Weizman 2015, 24). Again, the connection between the erasure of certain ecological facts and the development of different ecological contexts through colonial projects of ecological modification of landscapes is explicit. The development of socioecological systems that inscribe settler belonging and settler futurity over and on top of Bedouin ones is both an ecological and an epistemological project. These colonial afforestation campaigns changed landscapes in ways that modified the land as a discursive site to encourage forms of perception that legitimize sovereignty structures for Israelis to the destruction or erasure of traces of other evidence and interpretative contexts that tell different stories. The land was modified in ways intended to construct the meaning of the Naqab and its perception as Israeli and not Bedouin.

However, the traces of alternative and competing forms of evidence are still embedded within the landscapes, just as the presence and continuance of Bedouin/Indigenous sovereignty remain within the land. Reading historic aerial photographs and the more recent photographing of the Naqab by artist Fazal Sheikh, during autumn when underlying topographies not seen when the desert is in bloom are visible, demonstrates the discursiveness and existence of evidence that has different interpretations and meanings than the dominant narrative of the Israeli settler state. These aerial photographs record the traces and presences of cultivation the land remembers and demonstrates. These aerial photographs, both from the past and taken more recently, constitute evidence that some Bedouin peoples are using and relying on to enter their claims in the Israeli-settler juridical arena in attempts to recover their land and have their land claims seen, acknowledged, and respected by the State of Israel. These constitute efforts to survive, to survive in culturally appropriate ways, and to return home. These efforts constitute acts of resistance in articulating a truth the Israeli state would rather not acknowledge.

Instances of epistemic violence and domination of the Bedouin abound in the legal/juridical proceedings of the Israeli state regarding Bedouin land claims. For example, the testimony of Bedouin peoples on histories of land cultivation and presence has been thrown out as hearsay because of the denigration of oral histories within the settler juridical framework (Weizman 2015, 55). However, at the same time, written testimonies of colonial European travelers passing through the Naqab are relied upon by the State of Israel as factual, objective representations supporting the Dead Negev Doctrine through constructing racist and untrue depictions of Bedouin peoples as nomadic and thus incapable of sustained cultivation or depicting Bedouin belonging to place as always already transient and impermanent (Weizman 2015, 51). This reliance on racist, colonial "knowledges" relates to the ways in which colonialism relies on racialized categories and violence to construct epistemological frameworks that perceive Bedouin peoples in racialized ways, visibilizing and naturalizing their unbelonging while upholding the accounts of white European colonial travelers as superior knowledge. Additionally, the State of Israel presented colonial-era maps as evidence of Bedouin absence from the Naqab, maps in which colonial cartographers literally left blank spots on sites of Bedouin settlements, effectively "whiting out" Bedouin presence, which "led to the wiping out of entire native cultures"(Weizman 2015, 83). Hence the refusal of colonial cartographers to construct maps that reflected Bedouin presence acted as a means of figurative and literal erasure that normalized Bedouin absence and was used to justify the literal elimination of Bedouin peoples and cultures. Thus, colonial maps became a representation, memorialized as fact, of Bedouin absence and nonexistence.

Even the seemingly straightforward aerial photographs presented documenting land use and cultivation were subject to the power pathologies and contradictions of settler-colonial reproduction and futurity. Ostensibly, these aerial photographs should have been given more weight, by the colonial epistemological frameworks' own standards. However, in the same way that colonial cartographers erased Bedouin presence through their cartographic "whiting outs," perception of the aerial photographs of the Naqab were accompanied by interpretative mechanisms that refused to perceive representations of Bedouin cultivation outside of settler possessive logics. The "whiting outs" on colonial maps align with terra nullius and the Dead Negev Doctrine, which construct Bedouin peoples as a part of the environment incapable of civilization. The Bedouin peoples are figured in the colonial maps, through colonial afforestation campaigns, as not there, as not capable of being perceived; their absence is literally manufactured. Thus, in historical colonial fashion, the State of Israel openly violates its own Enlightenment epistemological standards for the purposes of continued domination. While the land via the photographs demonstrated an alternative narrative, the hermeneutic perceptual practices of settler domination were still "whiting out" Bedouin presence, desiring to attend to the material significations of land as settler possession. This way of perceiving is reinforced through an orientation toward land and landscape that has been internalized through continuously relating to constructed material signifiers that demonstrate settler possession and belonging. In this sense, Israeli settlers in the legal/juridical arena are reading the land in colonial ways that read out Bedouin peoples; the possibility of perceiving the Naqab as Bedouin is already epistemically out of bounds.

Here, we have a compelling case that highlights the ways in which dominant epistemological frameworks can impart colonized and compromised perception but still represent these ways of perceiving as objective, neutral, and normative. Not only is the evidence contextualized in specific dominant, colonial ways, but also the evidence itself represents particular colonial affectations: "whiting out"/reading out. The possessive logic is added to the interpretative context and backgrounded into the perceptual project, such that the colonial logic is not seen as separate from the object of perception but rather appears materially as evidence of land demonstrably as settler possession. As Gaile Pohlhaus Jr. (2012) eloquently argues, it is not only the case that some knowers experience injustice because they are not believed; dominantly situated knowers sometimes enact "willful hermeneutical ignorance." Willful hermeneutical ignorance for Pohlhaus is "more than an act of 'not seeing' parts of the world"; rather, "it can manifest in a systematic and coordinated misinterpretation of the world" (731). Thus, it is necessary when considering evidence and presentations of evidence to both understand the social identities of knowers and the ways in which the interdependence of knowledge and the world is constituted in particular arrangements that produce and reproduce willful hermeneutical ignorance. Willful hermeneutical ignorance in the case of the erasure of the ecological violence of colonial land seizures stands as an immense obstacle to justice for Bedouin peoples and Indigenous peoples globally.

Thus, while creating the space of perceiving differently is a necessary step toward dismantling settler-colonial systems, it is insufficient by itself because evidence presented is still read in ways that enforce and select particular evidentiary claims in ways that erase, manipulate, and cover over. It is not just that justice for Indigenous peoples lies outside of the horizon of settler juridical frameworks but also that even when it is perceived it is subject to denial and willful hermeneutical ignorance in a manner that manifests erasure all over again. Therefore, we need to be particularly attendant to the ways in which power pathologies can incorporate themselves into the construction of knowers and knowledge as well as how constructions of what is taken or understood as evidence are subject to the same formations of domination and power as any other dimension of epistemological processes. Land is the ground upon which we all stand, upon which we all are and become, but it is also subject to colonial distortions that not only cause it to recede into the background of our understanding and knowledge possibilities but can do so in a particularly compromised configurations. Subjects, objects, evidence, and processes of knowledge are all worlded, all landed, and the place of knowing as land must become a site of our critical analysis and must be decolonized for justice, especially for Indigenous peoples and Indigenous futurity.

Conclusion

In this chapter, I argue that an area of epistemology and epistemological frameworks often underexamined in dominant philosophical literature, especially in relation to forms of epistemic domination, is the selection, presentation, and interpretation of evidence. Specifically, I argue that the interpretation of evidence in the form of the case study of Bedouin land claims in the Naqab Desert is subject to important distortions resulting from dominant Euro-descendent, settler-colonial commitments built into and invisibilized within dominant Western epistemological frameworks, which are rooted in the historical and ongoing projects of white supremacy, gender oppression, and colonialism. In the first section, I examine a key tenet of Black-feminist-standpoint epistemology, which relies on the understanding that knowers are thoroughly embedded in worlds that are power unequal.

The pervasiveness of this power inequality in the world is drawn out in Black-feminist-standpoint epistemology by the understanding that episte-mologies are specialized forms of knowledge that implicate their creators' affinities to power and that the specificities of creators' positionalities are made knowable through the exclusion of others who are simultaneously constructed as outsiders or nonbelongers to traditional universal, generic knowledge. The second section of this chapter builds on this understand-ing of worlded and specific epistemological frameworks by exploring the epistemological projects of perceiving visibilized race and gender. Race and gender are visibilized in ways that attach meaning to and perceive visible realities as one and the same with that constructed meaning (a meaning that is birthed in relations of domination and unequal power dynamics) such that race and gender appear to become or are perceived to be evidence or self-evident features of the existence of race and gender themselves, whereas, in fact, race and gender exist as naturalized social power/social constructions. In this way, meaning becomes sedimented into visible physical realities that take the appearance of the visible reality as the meaning imposed upon it.

The second and third sections are conceptually related in that they both expose the ways in which dominant Western epistemological frame-works construct both knowers' standpoints and visibilized particularity in relation to other particular dominant constructs: whiteness, center, Europe, nation-state, masculinity, and so on. The third section builds on the contributions of the first two sections by examining the ways in which the construction of Otherness in relation to dominance is also achieved through the dominant construction of land, the place of knowing or that upon which all knowers stand, as always already non-Indigenous or always already colonial. Thus, the default or normative place of dominant Western epistemological frameworks is land as settler-colonial belonging or white possession materialized in the landscape to signify settler belonging and Indigenous otherness and unbelonging. Land, then, as the place of know-ing, can also be understood as a backgrounded and fundamental condition of epistemology subject to the same distortions of meaning and interpreta-tion that race and gender are in the construction of nondominantly situ-ated knowers. Just as race and gender become self-evident by the selected physical realities of difference infused with dominant Western meanings informed by coloniality, so, too, are lands modified to reflect settler mean-ing, interpretation, rule, and ownership/possession. In the same way that the context of social identity/positionality is obscured in attempts to render it nonexistent to legitimate the generic knower and to hypervisibilize the racialized, gendered, nongeneric knower as Other—outside the realm of knowledge/intelligibility—so, too, is the fact of Indigenous dispossession, foundational to the interpretative context of Euro-descendent, Western, settler epistemological frameworks, obscured. Put another way, the fact of Indigenous dispossession during the formation of the conditions of our possibility of knowing and knowledge production is rarely acknowledged or, indeed, made an intentional object of our conscious reflection or ways of knowing: our epistemologies. In the same manner that Black feminist thought draws our critical awareness to the specificity of the generic knower, I encourage us to go further by examining and becoming critically aware of not just the standpoint or social context of our knowing but also the land(point) that informs our knowing.

The insights of the first three sections of this chapter are connected to the selection, presentation, and interpretation of the Naqab Desert case study. The Naqab case presents the attempted universalization of a particular dominant group's positionality and social context (Israeli settlement) as the generic epistemological framework, the framework that counts. The Naqab case also presents the modification of landscapes to reflect the belonging of Israeli settlers and the racialized othering of the Bedouin, as well as how a colonial land conceptualization and perception is built into the dominant epistemological framework. Finally, the Naqab case presents epistemic standards ill suited for interpreting evidence because of the invisibilization of power presented as objectivity or truth. The land(point) in this case is always already compromised in colonial ways, such that evidence will be interpreted to fit that landed way of knowing, which is not a natural, eternal quality of nature itself but a social construction. I argue that nondominantly positioned knowers are excluded and invisibilized in instances of epistemic domination such as those examined in the Naqab Desert, that nondominant points of reference in and on the land can and are similarly erased or obscured to contribute to the perception of land as always already non-Indigenous, and that this must become a conscious reflection of our awareness and our knowing. So, not only do we need to pay careful and critical attention to the ways in which our processes of knowing can be colonized in evidence selection, presentation, and interpretation, but, most importantly, we need to do the necessary work of decolonizing our understanding and interpretations of the very land and earth we stand on and know within and that makes our knowledge projects both possible and more or less subject to colonial distortions or decolonial transformations.

Notes

1. Throughout this chapter, I describe various practices as logics, e.g., disciplinary logics, classificatory logics, and possessive logics. I am using *logic/logics* conceptually to describe the ways in which various practices of domination are enacted through a construction of domination as natural or normative. I am thinking with Val Plumwood here when she describes a Western logic of domination emergent since at least the Enlightenment period that conceptually links forms of domination through various oppositional dualisms, primarily focusing on the reason-versus-nature dualism. Plumwood argues that, historically and currently, the dominative category of reason, in exclusive opposition to nature, has been used to present reason as superior to inferior nature. Furthermore, racism, colonialism, and sexism have "drawn their conceptual strength from casting sexual, racial and ethnic difference as closer to the animal and the body construed as a sphere of inferiority, as a lesser form of humanity lacking the full measure of rationality and culture" (Plumwood 2003, 4). *Disciplinary logics* refer to processes of disciplining particular bodies, knowers, persons, communities to a dominative standard constructed for the purposes of power, domination, and oppression (Foucault 1995; Million 2014). *Classificatory logics* refer to processes of classifying the world into discrete, exclusive, and oppositional categories and orders, as well as to the characterization of these processes as superior science or knowledge (Mignolo 1995; Plumwood 2002; Alcoff 2006). Finally, I use *possessive logics* by relying on Aileen Moreton-Robinson's (2015, xii) concept of white possessive logics, which she uses to "denote a mode of rationalization . . . that is underpinned by an excessive desire to invest in reproducing and reaffirming the nation-state's ownership, control, and domination." I rely on the language of *logic/logics* to highlight the constructed nature of these processes and the attendant meanings as they become naturalized into an expectation of experience within the context of domination and contact with dominant cultures/societies.

References

Alcoff, Linda Martín. 2006. *Visible Identities: Race, Gender, and the Self*. New York: Oxford University Press.

Bang, Megan, Lawrence Curley, Adam Kessel, Ananda Marin, Eli S. Suzukovich III, and George Strack. 2014. "Muskrat Theories, Tobacco in the Streets, and Living Chicago as Indigenous Land." *Environmental Education Research* 20 (1): 37–55. https://www.doi.org/10.1080/13504622.2013.865113.

Brockington, Daniel, and James Igoe. 2006. "Eviction for Conservation: A Global Overview." *Conservation and Society* 4 (3): 424–70.

Code, Lorraine. 2008. "Taking Subjectivity into Account." In *The Feminist Philosophy Reader*, edited by Alison Bailey and Chris J. Cuomo, 718–40. Boston: McGraw Hill.

Collins, Patricia Hill. 1990. *Black Feminist Thought, Knowledge, Consciousness and the Politics of Empowerment*. 1st ed. Boston: Unwin Hyman.

Dotson, Kristie. 2011. "Tracking Epistemic Violence, Tracking Practices of Silencing." *Hypatia* 26 (2): 236–57.

———. 2014. "Conceptualizing Epistemic Oppression." *Social Epistemology* 28 (2): 115–38. https://www.doi.org/10.1080/02691728.2013.782585.

Dowie, Mark. 2011. *Conservation Refugees: The Hundred-Year Conflict between Global Conservation and Native Peoples*. Cambridge, MA: MIT Press.

Dunbar-Ortiz, Roxanne. 2014. *An Indigenous Peoples' History of the United States*. Boston: Beacon Press.

Fanon, Frantz. 2008. *Black Skin, White Masks*. Translated by Richard Philcox. New York: Grove Press.

Foucault, Michel. 1995. *Discipline and Punish: The Birth of the Prison*. Translated by Alan Sheridan. New York: Vintage Books.

Fricker, Miranda. 2007. *Epistemic Injustice: Power and the Ethics of Knowing*. New York: Oxford University Press.

Goldberg, David Theo. 1993. *Racist Culture: Philosophy and the Politics of Meaning*. Malden, MA: Blackwell.

Harding, Sandra. 1993. "Rethinking Standpoint Epistemology: What is 'Strong Objectivity'?" In *Feminist Epistemologies*, edited by Linda Alcoff and Elizabeth Potter, 49–82. New York: Routledge.

hooks, bell. 2014. *Black Looks: Race and Representation*. 2nd ed. New York: Routledge.

Jhally, Sut, dir. 1997. *Race, the Floating Signifier: A Lecture with Stuart Hall*. Media Education Foundation. DVD.

Lindqvist, Sven. 2007. *Terra Nullius: A Journey Through No One's Land*. Translated by Sarah Death. New York: New Press.

Little Bear, Leroy. 2016. Introduction to *Native Science: Natural Laws of Interdependence*, by Gregory Cajete. 2nd ed. Santa Fe, NM: Clear Light.

Medina, José. 2013. *The Epistemology of Resistance: Gender and Racial Oppression, Epistemic Injustice, and Resistant Imaginations*. New York: Oxford University Press.

Mignolo, Walter D. 1995. *The Darker Side of the Renaissance: Literacy, Territoriality, and Colonization*. Ann Arbor: University of Michigan Press.

———. 2007. "Delinking." *Cultural Studies* 21 (2–3): 449–514. https://www.doi.org/10.1080/09502380601162647.

Million, Dian. 2014. *Therapeutic Nations: Healing in an Age of Indigenous Human Rights*. Reprint ed. Tucson: University of Arizona Press.

Mohanty, Chandra Talpade. 1984. "Under Western Eyes: Feminist Scholarship and Colonial Discourses." *boundary 2* 12 (3)/13 (1): 333–58. https://www.doi.org/10.2307/302821.

Moreton-Robinson, Aileen. 2015. *The White Possessive: Property, Power, and Indigenous Sovereignty*. Minneapolis: University of Minnesota Press.

Murdock, Esme G. 2018. "Unsettling Reconciliation: Decolonial Methods for Transforming Social-Ecological Systems." *Environmental Values* 27 (5): 513–33.

Nash, Roderick. 1970. "The American Invention of National Parks." *American Quarterly* 22 (3): 726–35. https://www.doi.org/10.2307/2711623.

Pateman, Carole. 2007. "The Settler Contract." In *Contract and Domination*, by Carole Pateman and Charles W. Mills, 35–78. Cambridge: Polity.

Plumwood, Val. 2003. *Feminism and the Mastery of Nature*. New York: Taylor & Francis / Routledge.

Pohlhaus, Gaile, Jr. 2012. "Relational Knowing and Epistemic Injustice: Toward a Theory of *Willful Hermeneutical Ignorance*." *Hypatia* 27 (4): 715–35. https://www.doi.org/10.1111/j.1527-2001.2011.01222.x.

Spence, Mark David. 1999. *Dispossessing the Wilderness: Indian Removal and the Making of the National Parks*. New York: Oxford University Press.

Weizman, Eyal. 2015. *The Conflict Shoreline: Colonialism as Climate Change in the Negev Desert*. Photography by Fazal Sheikh. Göttingen, Germany: Steidl.

West, Cornel. 2002. *Prophesy Deliverance! An Afro-American Revolutionary Christianity*. Anniversary ed. Louisville, KY: Westminster John Knox Press.

Whyte, Kyle Powys. 2018. "Food Sovereignty, Justice, and Indigenous Peoples: An Essay on Settler Colonialism and Collective Continuance." In *The Oxford Handbook of Food Ethics*, edited by Anne Barnhill, Mark Budolfson, and Tyler Doggett, 345–66. New York: Oxford University Press.

Chapter 9

Epistemology and HIV Transmission

Privilege and Marginalization in the Dissemination of Knowledge

LACEY J. DAVIDSON AND MARK SATTA

Theory, Cases, and HIV-Risk Intuitions

The philosophical work of feminists and critical race theorists has resulted in the formation and development of important epistemological concepts and theories. Many of these, such as theories of epistemic injustice, have been remarkably effective in confronting issues resulting from current, wide-sweeping power imbalances between and among the intersections of race, gender, socioeconomic status, and sexual orientation, among others. In this chapter, we apply some of the lessons from feminist and critical race epistemology to an area where philosophers have traditionally had less to say—namely, epistemic issues related to HIV and HIV transmission risk. More specifically, we bring together a broad swath of empirical work conducted in a range of disciplines alongside recent work in feminist and critical race epistemology to highlight and address these issues.

We identify ways in which popular social perceptions about HIV do not properly align with empirical findings, and we develop a framework for explaining this incongruency. Central to our discussion are the identification of epistemic harms related to HIV and some of the normative implications of the presence of these harms. By *epistemic harm* we mean damage done to an individual in their capacity as a knower (or harm done to a group in their capacities as knowers). We use the term *epistemic harm* as a general category that encompasses, among other things, both epistemic injustice and epistemic oppression (cf. Fricker 2007; Dotson 2014). Epistemic injustice is "a *wrong* done to someone specifically in their capacity as a knower" (Fricker 2007, 1; emphasis added). Epistemic oppression "refers to persistent epistemic exclusion that hinders one's contribution to knowledge production" (Dotson 2014, 115).

We identify these epistemic harms by examining case studies and research findings through the lens of feminist and critical race epistemology. Some of these harms, like Miranda Fricker's hermeneutical injustice and Kristie Dotson's contributory injustice, are previously identified harms that we are identifying in a new context. In looking at how these injustices arise and how they are (in some cases) being addressed, we identify patterns of marginalization and privilege among communities significantly affected by HIV and the combinations of knowledge and ignorance to which these patterns give rise. Because applying theories of epistemic harm in an extensive manner to issues pertaining to HIV is new terrain, our treatment is somewhat general. We hope this work will spur further discussion about how feminist and critical race epistemology can inform our understanding of the epistemic conditions of HIV-positive people and of those at risk of contracting HIV. To help frame our discussion, we open with four scenarios that will help us take stock of the epistemic landscape and provide reference points for our analysis:

Scenario 1

Adam is a gay, cisgender man living in the US. Adam has had five different male sexual partners in the past year. Adam asked each of his partners before having sex with them for the first time whether or not they were HIV positive. Each one told Adam that they were HIV negative and had been tested recently. Adam has good reason to think that each of the partners was being honest with him. Adam usually uses condoms when he has sex, but not always. Adam's last HIV test was about a month ago. He tested negative, and he has not had sex since.

Scenario 2

Ben is also a gay, cisgender man living in the US. Ben has also had five different male sexual partners in the past year. Unlike Adam, Ben did not discuss matters related to HIV with his partners, but he thinks it is likely that if any of his partners were HIV positive, they would have said something. Unlike Adam, Ben does not usually use a condom when he has sex. Ben's last HIV test was about three months ago. He tested negative for HIV and has only had sex a few times since.

Scenario 3

Carrie is a straight, cisgender woman living in the US. Carrie has also had five different male sexual partners in the past year. Like Ben, Carrie did not discuss matters related to HIV with her partners, but she thinks it is likely that if any of her partners were HIV positive, they would have said something. Like Ben, Carrie does not usually use a condom when she has sex (although she uses birth control). Carrie's last HIV test was about three months ago. She tested negative for HIV and has only had sex a few times since.

Scenario 4

Dan is a gay, cisgender man living in the US. Dan has been in a monogamous sexual relationship with an HIV-positive male partner for the past year. Dan's partner was diagnosed with HIV five years ago and faithfully adheres to the treatment prescribed by his doctor, whom he meets with every three to six months. Dan and his partner have sex on a regular basis and do not use condoms. Dan gets tested for HIV twice a year. Dan's last HIV test was six months ago, and he tested negative for HIV.

When juxtaposed, these scenarios raise interesting questions concerning perceptions of individual risk and understanding of risk. Many will confidently judge that Dan, the man having sex regularly with his HIV-positive male partner, has the greatest risk of contracting HIV and that either Adam, the gay man whose partners all identify as HIV negative and who uses condoms regularly, or Carrie, the straight woman, has the lowest risk of contraction. Many will also think that Carrie and Adam should have a fairly good understanding of their risk levels being low. Others might think that Dan has a less accurate understanding because it has been longer since his last HIV-negative test and because he has had sex regularly with an HIV-positive person since his last test.

Such judgments result from certain common assumptions about some of the major contributing factors in HIV transmission. Such assumptions include that the risk of sexual transmission from an HIV-positive to an HIV-negative partner is always relatively high (or at least never negligibly low), that heterosexual sex comes with a low risk of HIV transmission, and that condom use is the most salient (or only) preventative measure to pay attention to in assessing risk levels for sexual transmission of HIV between serodiscordant couples (i.e., couples with different HIV statuses). Assumptions like these are problematic in at least two ways. First, they fail to acknowledge how radically undetermined the above scenarios are— that is to say, such responses fail to identify the significance of a whole host of other factors relevant to knowledge of risk levels. People making such assumptions are working with a very simplified understanding of HIV transmission and risk. The empirical data we present will reveal the inadequacies of this simplified understanding. Second, once these additional factors are taken into account, it turns out that there are good reasons to think that Dan has the lowest level of risk of HIV infection and the most accurate understanding of his own low risk level. As we shall show, these outcomes are plausible upshots of recent epidemiological and sociological findings.

HIV Research Findings and Initial Epistemic Implications

BASIC EPIDEMIOLOGY OF HIV

HIV (human immunodeficiency virus) is a virus that attacks the body's immune system and spreads through transmission of certain bodily fluids. The typical progression of the virus, when left untreated, is divided into three stages. The first stage, primary (or acute) infection, lasts for roughly three to six months. During this stage, the HIV-positive person's viral load (the amount of virus present in the blood) is very high, making the person much more infectious compared to the second stage. During this stage, many but not all of those infected experience flu-like symptoms or other maladies.

The second stage, asymptomatic HIV infection, begins when primary infection ends. During the asymptomatic stage, the virus remains active and continues to replicate, but at a much slower rate. For those not on treatment, the length of this stage varies, although it is a matter of years, sometimes a decade or longer, before the virus progresses to the third stage. In this second stage, HIV-positive persons may not experience any symptoms but remain capable of infecting others. How long this period lasts and how infectious a person is both depend on whether they are on proper medical treatment. (Current standard treatment consists of regular checkups with physicians and taking a pill or set of pills daily. This daily pill regimen to treat HIV is known as antiretroviral therapy—ART, for short.)

Those that reach the final stage of the infection develop AIDS (acquired immunodeficiency syndrome). By this stage, the virus has caused substantial damage to the HIV-positive person's immune system (in the form of a very low CD4 T cell count), leaving them vulnerable to many opportunistic infections, which can prove fatal for someone in their immunocompromised condition. The viral load of a person with AIDS is high, leading to increased infectivity. Without treatment, people typically survive about three years with AIDS.[1]

Thankfully, in the forty years since HIV/AIDS first came into cultural consciousness in the United States and around the globe, remarkable medical advances have been made in our understanding of and ability to treat HIV. Successful use of ART can help persons living with HIV or AIDS stay or become healthy, such that "with these treatment regimens, survival rates among HIV-infected adults who are retained in care can approach those of uninfected adults" (Günthard et al. 2016, 191). ART can also dramatically decrease or eliminate completely the possibility of infecting others (McCray and Mermin 2017). While not a cure, ART has been very successful in increasing quality of life and prolonging the life expectancy of persons living with HIV or AIDS and has led to a reclassification of HIV from a fatal disease to a chronic, treatable condition.

IGNORANCE OF HIV-POSITIVE STATUS

One method to avoid contracting HIV—i.e., seroconverting—is to avoid contact with the virus completely. Common-sense thinking like this leads some people (many of them men who have sex with other men, or MSM) to engage in serosorting. Serosorting is the practice of intentionally selecting sexual partners who identify as having the same HIV status as you.[2] But serosorting is based on the serostatus reported (or perceived to be reported) by potential partners. Such reports are effective only to the extent that the status reported matches the status those potential partners actually have, epidemiologically speaking.

Some HIV-positive individuals may be dishonest or give unclear responses that could be misinterpreted by others (Dodds, Bourne, and Weait 2009, 142). Alternatively, serosorters may make incorrect assumptions about what constitutes an indication that a prospective partner is HIV negative. For example, one might assume that silence on the topic is a tacit way of indicating that one is HIV negative. But research shows that, among HIV-positive MSM, clear reports of HIV-positive status are relatively infrequent, occurring perhaps less than half the time, and even in cases where disclosure does occur the disclosure frequently fails to be explicit (Dodds, Bourne, and Weait 2009, 142; Koblin et al. 2006, 735). Even when casting these issues aside, effective serosorting requires that those reporting their status know whether they are infected. Estimates suggest that roughly 13% to 20% of HIV-positive people in the United States do not know they are positive (Chou et al. 2012; Hall et al. 2015; McNulty, Cifu, and Pitrak 2016). In some communities in the US, those numbers are much higher. Research suggests that as many as nearly half of all HIV-positive people in certain communities may be unaware that they are HIV positive (Koblin et al. 2006, 735; Millett et al. 2006, 1010). An estimated 20,000 new HIV infections occur annually in the United States due to transmission from persons who are unaware that they are infected (Chou et al. 2012), and over 30% of new infections are transmitted from those with undiagnosed HIV, according to the Centers for Disease Control and Prevention (CDC).[3] Thus, there are significant limits to one's ability to knowingly avoid contact with HIV solely by relying on the reported HIV status of others.

HIV TESTING, THE WINDOW PERIOD, AND EPISTEMIC LIMITS

An obvious reason why many HIV-positive people do not know that they are positive is because they have not been tested. Increasing the percentage of at-risk individuals getting tested and the frequency with which they get tested is widely recognized as an important way to decrease the percentage of HIV-positive people unaware that they have the virus (McNulty, Cifu, and Pitrak 2016). There is also another factor at play here—namely, the window period between contraction of HIV and the ability of an HIV screening to accurately render an HIV-positive result. For a highly informed population, this window period might prove minimally problematic. But part of the problem here is epistemic; in other words, those tested may not understand the window period.

The time period between contracting HIV and testing positive for HIV is dependent on several factors, including the strain of HIV one has contracted and the type of HIV test being administered. The most common type of HIV test given is an antibody test, which identifies the presence of HIV by testing for the antibodies our bodies make in response to the virus. Because it takes time for these antibodies to be produced, currently, the quickest a person will test positive for HIV given a standard antibody test is two weeks, but evidence suggests it sometimes may take up to three months or longer to develop the necessary antibodies to test positive.[4]

If we think back to our four scenarios in the first part of this chapter, of Adam, Ben, Carrie, and Dan, given their regular sexual activity, any of them could have been infected with HIV when they last tested negative. Furthermore, for Adam and Carrie, even though their partners disclosed HIV-negative statuses, for all Adam and Carrie know, any of their partners could have been in a similar situation of having contracted the virus too recently at the time of their last HIV screening to have tested positive. This is not to deny the important epistemic advantage gained by HIV-negative screenings but rather to recognize the limits of that advantage. Our purpose here is to survey the epistemic landscape of HIV while also being careful not to create an overinflated sense of risk.

These epistemic limits have very real practical effects. In 2006 the results published from a longitudinal study run with over 4,000 HIV-negative MSM conducted in six US cities found that over one-fifth (21.6%) of the seroconversions that occurred were "accounted for by unprotected receptive anal intercourse with partners believed to be HIV negative" (Koblin et al. 2006, 735). This number was in fact higher than the percentage of seroconversions accounted for by unprotected receptive anal intercourse with partners believed to be HIV positive (18.6%). Crucially, in this study, partners were classified as HIV negative when "a partner told the participant they were negative and the partner had no reason to doubt it" (Koblin et al. 2006, 731), meaning that the seroconversion rate of 21.6% does not account for the cases of seroconversion due to contact with sexual partners whose status was classified as unknown. Seroconversions from partners with unknown status accounted for an additional 28.4%. Findings like these, along with a lack of awareness of the full window period for positive HIV results from HIV screenings, call into question the effectiveness of things like serosorting or assumptions about the low risk level of HIV contraction during sexual contact with self-identified HIV-negative individuals.

VIRAL LOADS AND INFECTIVITY

Misperceptions cut both ways. Many who do not see relevant differences in risk levels for sexual contact among partners labeled as HIV negative also fail to see relevant differences in risk levels for sexual contact among HIV-positive individuals. One of these relevant differences among HIV-positive persons is the HIV-positive person's viral load. Viral load is important when considering risk of infection because higher viral loads are strongly linked to greater infectivity (McNulty, Cifu, and Pitrak 2016).

A person's viral load is particularly high during primary HIV infection. The high level of virus in the blood and semen leads to elevated infectivity during primary HIV infection (Pilcher et al. 2004, 2789–90). A 2008 study found that primary infection was twenty-six times more infectious than the second asymptomatic stage (Hollingsworth, Anderson, and Fraser 2008, 687). Thus, for biological reasons, primary infection is a time in which transmission is more likely. This is compounded by the epistemic factor that many people in the primary-infection stage are unaware of their infection (Pao et al. 2005, 89; Koblin et al. 2006; 735, Chou et al. 2012). As a result, these individuals may be less apt to take precautions and may unintentionally disclose a status that does not accurately reflect the presence of infection. Such biological, behavioral, and social elements combined have led to primary infection serving as a particularly potent factor in the ongoing spread of HIV (Cates, Chesney, and Cohen 1997; Koopman et al. 1997, 249; Brenner et al. 2007). Studies estimate that between one-quarter and one-half of new infections occur during primary infection (Pao et al. 2005, 86). One study estimated that in 2010 infection from undiagnosed HIV-positive men, the majority of whom were in the primary-infection stage, accounted for 82% of new infections in the UK (Phillips et al. 2013).

ART AND SUPPRESSED VIRAL LOADS

While research has shown the high infectivity of primary HIV infection, it has also shown that with proper treatment infectivity is very low or nonexistent for many HIV-positive people. A noteworthy case of such findings occurred in 2014 when a group of European researchers reported their initial findings on HIV-transmission risk through condomless sex between serodiscordant couples in which one partner was HIV positive, on ART, and had a low viral load (less than 200 copies/ml) and the other partner was HIV negative (Rodger et al. 2012, 2016).[5] The study, known as the PARTNER study (referring to partners of people on ART), revealed that, over a two-year period, an estimated over 40,000 occasions of condomless vaginal or anal sex (comprised of roughly 16,400 instances of sex between men and 28,000 instances of sex between men and women) within a sample of 767 couples resulted in zero cases of transmission of HIV from the positive partner to the negative partner (Rodger et al. 2014, 2016).[6] This result is congruent with results from previous studies (notably, Cohen et al. 2011), although PARTNER represented a significant advancement over previous studies due to the larger sample size of MSM couples. The researchers in PARTNER concluded that risk of sexual transmission for those on ART with a highly suppressed viral load was very low and that their best estimate was there being zero risk (Cairns 2014; Rodger et al. 2014, 2016).

ART has proven highly effective for the vast majority of those who faithfully adhere to the treatment and can lead to viral loads significantly more suppressed than even the less than 200 copies/ml required for participation in PARTNER. In fact, ART allows many people's viral loads to get so low that the presence of the virus cannot currently be detected, which, depending on the test, typically requires a viral load of less than 40 to less than 75 copies/ml. During periods in which they achieve such low viral loads, individuals are referred to as *undetectable*. This is a term that many HIV-positive people use to convey information about their viral load, adherence to treatment, and identity (Grace et al. 2015, 333).

Since the release of the PARTNER-study results, numerous medical providers and organizations have publicly endorsed the view that those with undetectable viral loads are incapable of transmitting HIV (Prevention Access Campaign 2017). This view is often encapsulated by proponents as "undetectable = untransmissible" (see, for example, King 2016). On September 27, 2017, the CDC joined this consensus in a public letter stating that "people who take ART daily as prescribed and achieve and maintain an undetectable viral load have effectively no risk of sexually transmitting the virus to an HIV-negative partner" (McCray and Mermin 2017).

DEVELOPMENTS IN PROPHYLAXIS

Recent developments have also provided new means for HIV-negative individuals to decrease their likelihood of infection independent of the precautions that may or may not be taken by their partners. In 2012, a new means became available in the United States with the Food and Drug Administration's approval of Truvada (emtricitabine/tenofovir diso-proxil fumarate) for the purpose of HIV pre-exposure prophylaxis (PrEP; Jefferson 2012). Such prophylaxis consists in HIV-negative persons at higher-than-average risk of HIV contraction taking Truvada on a daily basis. Clinical studies have shown that Truvada, when taken consistently, reduces the risk of HIV transmission via sex by more than 90% and of transmission via injection-drug use by more than 70% (CDC 2015c). And PrEP usage in combination with other forms of prophylaxis, like condoms, further reduces the risk of HIV transmission.[7] Between 2008 and 2014, there was an 18% drop in the number of annual HIV infections in the United States, and the CDC has suggested that this may be due in part to usage of PrEP (NCHHSTP 2017).

REVIEWING THE EPISTEMIC IMPLICATIONS

Reflecting on this research, we can revisit our four scenarios. Dan, who regularly has condomless sex with his HIV-positive male partner, may have initially appeared to have the highest risk of contracting HIV. But recall that Dan's partner faithfully adheres to ART and meets with his doctor regularly. These regular visits include measurements of Dan's partner's viral load. Given Dan's partner's adherence to ART, Dan's partner has a high chance of having a very low viral load. If Dan's partner's viral load is undetectable, research like PARTNER shows that this makes Dan's chance of contraction of HIV from his partner effectively nonexistent. In addition, even if a minuscule risk remains, Dan can further reduce any remaining risk by going on PrEP. Thus, if Dan is on PrEP and his partner has a low viral load, not only is the likelihood of Dan contracting HIV effectively nonexistent, Dan also has a high degree of knowledge about his risk level given the information Dan's partner gets from his regular doctor visits and given the information Dan gets during his own visits to the doctor because he is on PrEP. In contrast, Adam, Ben, and Carrie all have a variety of unaccounted-for variables that influence their risk levels (e.g., when their partners were last tested, whether any of their partners use injection drugs, whether any of their partners are in primary infection), which certainly influences how clearly they understand their own level of risk. Adam, Ben, and Carrie are also in a more precarious position when it comes to assessing the honesty of their potential partners' reports on HIV status and risk. And, as will be discussed more in the following section, their partners may be incentivized to be dishonest. But the communication of wrong information is not limited to cases of dishonesty. Issues can arise when someone reports a status without having been tested at all or when tested at a time that doesn't account for a window period—something of which the person being tested may not have known to be mindful.

As concern about the HIV/AIDS epidemic has receded from the forefront of the general population's consciousness in much of the United States, Canada, and Western Europe, many advances in our understanding of and ability to treat HIV, along with their implications for how to avoid contraction of HIV, have failed to become widely known or well understood across the public as a whole. In 2013 and 2014, only 21% of adults in the United States were aware that ART could reduce the risk of an HIV-positive person infecting a partner, and only 14% were aware of PrEP and its ability to lower risk of contracting HIV (Firth et al. 2016).[8] The extent to which a person is apt to be well informed about advancements in HIV treatment and to have thought through the implications of those advances for personal health and/or risk management is correlated with their perception of their likelihood of being at risk of contracting HIV or of knowing others who are HIV positive or at higher-than-average risk of becoming so.[9] In turn, the likelihood of being at higher risk is correlated with many aspects of one's social situation. For example, MSM, Black people, and intravenous-drug users (among other populations) continue to account for a highly disproportionate amount of new infections in the United States (CDC 2016b).[10] Given the ways in which these groups are already marginalized and stigmatized, the further marginalization and stigmatization of being HIV positive has led to complex patterns of risk management, methods of knowledge collection and dissemination, and forms of communication (or communication avoidance) concerning HIV.[11]

Epistemic Harm, Epistemic Injustice, and HIV

We are now in a position to identify some of the epistemic harms related to HIV and HIV transmission. Much more could be said on the topic than we have space for, but we hope to offer a sampling of the sorts of issues that arise in what follows. We first argue that two previously identified types of epistemic harm affect HIV-positive people: hermeneutical injustice (Fricker 2007) and contributory injustice (Dotson 2012). We then examine the state of social knowledge and linguistic practices concerning HIV and, to an extent, sexually transmitted infections (STIs) more broadly to identify a different type of epistemic harm that we call *structural-linguistic epistemic harm.*

Hermeneutical Injustice, Contributory Injustice, and the Epistemic Resources of HIV-Positive MSM

Miranda Fricker (2007, 1) writes, "Hermeneutical injustice occurs . . . when a gap in collective interpretive resources puts someone at an unfair disadvantage when it comes to making sense of their social experiences." Members of dominant communities, who frequently control the development of collective interpretive resources, due to their lack of interest in or awareness of certain salient experiences of those in nondominant groups, often prevent the development of the resources needed to explain or understand the experiences of the marginalized. On Fricker's account, the unfair disadvantages that the marginalized face due to an inability to explain, or even understand, their own experiences constitute hermeneutical injustice.

At least implicitly, this characterization of collective interpretive resources seems to assume that there is a single shared set of resources. Following Rebecca Mason (2011), we argue that although the collective resources are often insufficient to provide understanding of certain experiences within broader knowledge communities, nondominant groups are often very successful in developing their own additional resources, which may not be part of the collective resources of the larger community, to understand their experienced world. Thus, Mason asserts, and we concur, that "marginalized groups can be silenced relative to dominant discourses without being prevented from understanding or expressing their own social experiences" (301). In this latter sort of circumstance, rather than being mystified by an experience that does not yet have robust epistemic discourse, the marginalized are unfairly disadvantaged because those in power fail to understand or to make use of the hermeneutical resources developed by the marginalized. When this failure is willful, Gaile Pohlhaus (2012) calls this *willful hermeneutical ignorance.* This unwillingness of the powerful to learn about or make use of the hermeneutical resources developed by the marginalized leads to an avoidable and epistemically unjust gap in understanding between the powerful and the marginalized.

Mason's distinction between different types of discourse communities and Pohlhaus's identification of willful hermeneutical ignorance point to a second type of epistemic injustice that arises when the dominant engage in willful hermeneutical ignorance in a way that disadvantages nondominant populations. Kristie Dotson (2011) calls this *contributory injustice*. In the case of contributory injustice, the injustice of being unfairly silenced and/ or misunderstood by the dominant constitutes the epistemic wrong. This is contrasted with Fricker's understanding of hermeneutical injustice in which there is the separate wrong of the marginalized being robbed of the ability to understand or explain their own experiences due to a lack of adequate hermeneutical resources. In what follows, we argue that both forms of injustice are present for HIV-positive MSM. We think these injustices apply to HIV-positive people generally, but, by way of example, we focus here on MSM.

To see how these injustices arise, it will be useful to take stock of several different, sometimes overlapping, communities with differing levels of marginalization. Sexually active adult males can be separated into a dominant community, those who engage in exclusively heteronormative sexual activity, and a nondominant community, those who engage in forms of nonheteronormative sex, including MSM. Another distinction can be made: HIV-negative MSM constitute a comparatively dominant community, and HIV-positive MSM constitute an additionally marginalized community. This puts HIV-positive MSM in a doubly marginalized position and HIV-negative MSM in an intersectional position in which they are both marginalized as part of a broader group and dominant within a specific community. In the remainder of this section, we first describe ways in which many HIV-positive MSM have developed resources to understand their world (as well as looking at those who do not have such resources). We then identify hermeneutical and contributory injustices in light of these knowledge- and discourse-community distinctions.

Two areas of discourse relevant to understanding the world as HIV-positive MSM are medical/health discourse and social/relationship interaction discourse. The former refers to understanding HIV as a virus, as well as to precautionary measures and treatment. The latter refers to social processes such as the stigmatization and isolation that may occur as a result of one's status and the perceptions of HIV-positive people by HIV-negative people.[12] As we will show, both these areas of discourse have important epistemic components.

Many HIV-positive MSM develop epistemic resources relevant to understanding the virus and its potential health impacts. As we learn more about HIV and new treatments are developed, these epistemic resources expand, but they are limited by the pace and focus of medical and scientific research. Fricker acknowledges the complexity of trying to understand one's own experiences living with medical conditions that are not fully understood or diagnosable. In situations where little is understood about a disease but this lack of understanding is not due to any kind of willful ignorance or prejudice, the lack of collective cognitive resources is a case of "circumstantial epistemic bad luck" and not a case of hermeneutical injustice for those suffering from the disease (Fricker 2007, 152). When HIV/AIDS first began to spread and impact MSM living in the United States, their own and others' inability to understand the virus or how it affected social practices was limited by the state of knowledge in the medical community at large. Thus, initially, HIV-positive MSM may have encountered a state of circumstantial epistemic bad luck. (Although to the extent that bias against MSM may have influenced initial diagnoses, treatment, and research, this period in which the harm to HIV-positive people was merely circumstantial epistemic bad luck may have been very short or nonexistent.)

As we have learned more about HIV and as affected communities have developed modes of communication that allow for an increased understanding, contributory and hermeneutical injustices have replaced any circumstantial epistemic bad luck that may have obtained initially. This is because there are many epistemic resources currently available to help explain the experiences of HIV-positive MSM, which many HIV-negative people, including many HIV-negative MSM, fail to recognize or use. Focusing on the developing discourse around serostatus, communication, and safe-sex practices, we can see the ways in which dominant HIV-negative MSM commit epistemic injustices against nondominant HIV-positive MSM.

As the biomedical research on viral loads and transmission rates expanded, the new term *undetectable* emerged, referring to HIV-positive individuals with low viral loads associated with decreased transmission risk. In a longitudinal study, Grace et al. (2015) found that viral-load information impacts communication and sexual activity. First, they found that many HIV-positive MSM report abstaining from sex during the period shortly after diagnosis, in part in order to avoid transmitting the virus (338). This period of abstinence typically ended when viral loads decreased, especially for those labeled *undetectable* (340–41). As this label is increasingly used in medical discourse, it translates into social discourse. *HIV positive* alone does not fully reflect the relevant experiences of many undetectable MSM. And when our experience of the world cannot be expressed by our current epistemic resources, we develop new ways of understanding our lives so that we can understand our world and, in some circumstances, explain it to relevant others (Pohlhaus 2012, 719). As one participant in Grace et al.'s (2015, 341) study notes, "Most guys, they put 'undetectable,' actually, instead of that they're positive" when discussing online dating and sexual partnering.[13] Several HIV-negative MSM participants noted that knowledge about HIV and *undetectable* status was an important factor in their decision to engage in sexual activity with an HIV-positive partner (Grace et al. 2015, 343). HIV-positive MSM have constructed a set of epistemic tools to understand their own experiences and transmission risks, and the willingness of HIV-negative MSM to use these tools impacts sexual decision-making and can decrease stigmatization of HIV-positive MSM (and HIV-positive persons generally).

When HIV-negative individuals refuse to acknowledge, educate themselves about, or use the terms and practices around *undetectable*, a contributory injustice occurs, often as the result of willful hermeneutical ignorance. For example, a disclosed positive serostatus frequently is sufficient for HIV-negative individuals to cease pursuing any relations with an HIV-positive individual, even if the HIV-positive individual's viral load is undetectable and the developing discourse is used to communicate this information. This is part of a general tendency in which HIV-positive men report "that they sense fear among HIV negative men regarding HIV/AIDS and that many men avoid the topic of HIV and will avoid potential sex partners if the topic does arise" (Courtenay-Quirk et al. 2006, 62). Such responses from HIV-negative individuals fail to account for or attend to salient aspects relating to the health or infectivity of HIV-positive MSM and indicate a distrust of health-based self-knowledge reports by HIV-positive MSM. Recall our character Ben, who assumes that silence about status indicates safety. Any discussion of HIV status often leads to avoidance, despite open discussion of status typically being a sign of diligent research and commitment to not transmitting HIV. We are not claiming that concern about contracting HIV constitutes an injustice, but an unwillingness to investigate and understand the current research on HIV-transmission risk unjustly results in the further marginalization of HIV-positive people, even among communities where risk is high overall and understanding these identities is relevant to the health of the broader MSM community.

Additionally, this willful hermeneutical ignorance results in an increase of risk for HIV-negative participants by limiting conversations about HIV prevention and decreasing the likelihood that an HIV-positive partner will disclose their status. Due to the high level of stigmatization of HIV, MSM may not be willing to discuss HIV prevention for fear that others will think they have HIV (Ramallo et al. 2015, 308). The hesitancy to mention HIV in any capacity radically undermines the development of epistemic resources around sexual health and HIV prevention. In addition, Ramallo et al. (2015, 300) note that HIV-positive MSM might not discuss their HIV status with potential partners online prior to engaging in high-risk sexual activities. They write, "The HIV-positive participants expressed conflict in whether to be forthright by disclosing their status on social networking hook up sites, and the potential consequences of men being uninterested in them" (305). In cases where HIV-positive MSM avoid disclosing—for any of a variety of reasons including fear of rejection, nervousness, shame, or discomfort being honest—they may further do something epistemically unjust to their potential partners—leading to a cycle of reciprocal epistemic injustice.

Ramallo et al. attribute serosorting by HIV-negative individuals to HIV stigma. Not only does the popularity of serosorting result in a decreased chance of HIV disclosure, but utilizing serosorting as the primary tool for sexual safety also emphasizes a dichotomy between those that *know* they are positive and those that *believe* (including those who falsely believe they know) they are negative. However, due to window periods, infrequent testing, and other risky sexual behavior, decisions made utilizing this distinction are unreliable; reinforcing this dichotomy harms the MSM community as a whole.

Additionally, because of society's slow uptake of the new hermeneutical resources developed to explain and understand the medical and social aspects of living with HIV, many HIV-positive people themselves lack any sort of exposure to hermeneutical resources that can be used to describe their own experiences and identities. As a result, hermeneutical injustice still obtains in the portions of society where HIV-positive people lack the hermeneutical resources needed to explain or understand their own experiences. This occurs in addition to the contributory injustice experienced in other segments of society where HIV-positive individuals are marginalized and silenced because others fail to recognize or make use of the hermeneutical resources those HIV-positive individuals possess and use in explaining their own experiences and identities.

In summary, willful hermeneutical ignorance on the part of HIV-negative MSM leads to both contributory and hermeneutical injustices for HIV-positive MSM, further marginalizing this group in the MSM community. In addition, the further stigmatization and unwillingness to learn about current HIV research decreases the likelihood of fruitful conversations between serodiscordant individuals that may engage in sexual relations. These epistemic injustices hurt the MSM community. Acceptance of epistemic resources aimed at helping explain the experiences of HIV-positive MSM by the MSM community at large (as well as other communities) is an important step toward epistemic justice, decreased marginalization, and lower seroconversion risk.

STRUCTURAL-LINGUISTIC EPISTEMIC INJUSTICES AND TALKING ABOUT HIV

Elizabeth Anderson (2012) distinguishes between transactional and structural injustices. Transactional injustices are violations of justice in particular interactions, while structural injustices are derived from global properties of a system of rules governing transactions. Anderson points out that this distinction applies to epistemic injustices. A similar distinction between harms arising from specific interactions and harms derived from global properties of the rule systems governing transactions also applies in considering epistemic harms more generally. In viewing language practices as having a rule-governed type of structure, we see that certain language practices, which currently govern discourse about how HIV status operates, generate systemic epistemic harm by covering over some of the risk factors and knowledge gaps relevant to risk management for HIV exposure.

Ben has been seeing a guy, Joe, and the two are considering becoming sexually active. In discussing this possibility, Joe asks Ben, "Are you negative?" (meaning HIV negative). Carrie recently met a man on a business trip. Before inviting her up to his room, he asked, "Are you clean?" (referring to being "clean" of [without] STIs). Adam uses the MSM dating and hookup app, Grindr, to meet guys. A guy he's considering meeting sends him a message reading "ddf?" (short for "[are you] drug and [sexually transmitted] disease free?").

On the surface, once translated, these questions may seem relatively straightforward. But there are underlying epistemic problems with the structure of these questions. First, these questions conflate an epidemiological status with an epistemic status. Presumably, when one asks "Are you clean?" or "Are you negative?" they're asking about what diseases you do or do not have. Interest in your test results is implied because such test results are the primary means by which you can secure information about your epidemiological status. But when the two statuses (epidemiological and epistemic) are woven so tightly together in conversation, the distinction between them is minimized, if not lost. Due to this conflation, a respondent may mistakenly take his knowledge about his test results to constitute knowledge about viral status, or, even in cases where this conflation hasn't been made internally, a respondent's language may allow an interlocutor to draw mistaken conclusions about the level of information had by the respondent.

In addition to the epistemic problems with such language, there are also other important ways in which such language problematically contributes to the stigmatization of HIV, HIV-positive people, and those with other STIs. For example, the argument has been made that the phrase "ddf" is problematic because "it puts HIV status on the same level as drug use" (Humburg 2016). And many of those fighting to end HIV stigmatization have pointed out the stigmatizing effect of framing HIV status in terms of being "clean" or "dirty" (e.g., King 2012).

Concerning the epistemic issues, one could try to address the epistemic problems with the language by giving a nuanced response that pulls the epistemic and epidemiological statuses apart, but the linguistic and social rules governing such interactions often provide disincentives for doing so. On the linguistic level, the syntax of these questions encourages yes or no answers and can render responses of other forms infelicitous. Thus, these responses imply (and perhaps even require) a level of trust that is unwarranted. Furthermore, if whenever one makes an assertion, one is claiming knowledge (as those who have defended the view that knowledge is "the norm of assertion" have argued, e.g., DeRose 2002), such yes or no responses constitute knowledge claims despite factors that frequently prevent one from knowing the answer to that question (factors like outdated test results, having never been tested, or not taking into account the window period). Socially, someone who gives a nuanced response is often viewed with suspicion. Nuance can suggest that one is untrustworthy or has something to hide. For example, it probably will not go over well for Adam if he types back "probably" or "it depends on what you mean" or anything along those lines.[14] Thus, the current structure of such linguistic practices harms on two levels: (1) it distracts from the gap between one's epistemic state concerning HIV status and one's epidemiological condition, and (2) it disincentivizes more honest or nuanced expressions that try to make clear the epistemic gaps.

We call this type of epistemic injustice a *structural-linguistic epistemic injustice* because it is the structure of the language and the accompanying social practices that create the epistemic harm. This situation harms askers because they are less apt to receive the best information with which to make an informed risk assessment, and it harms those asked because it encourages either giving epistemically suspect answers or risking social consequences by providing a more informative response.

This cycle of harm is perpetuated by, and in turn contributes to, other forms of epistemic injustice. Where a systematic absence of understanding of the harm of current social and linguistic practices surrounding discussions of HIV and STIs prevails, hermeneutical injustice occurs. For HIV-positive people, the hermeneutical injustice occurs via sociolinguistic practices that harm them and contribute to their stigmatization and isolation and that stunt the development of other sociolinguistic practices that may make clearer their epistemic reality and stigmatized condition. For HIV-negative people, the hermeneutical injustice occurs via sociolinguistic practices that hide the epistemically salient factors to their own risk. And contributory injustice occurs in cases where some parties recognize the epistemic and social issues of current sociolinguistic practices but are negatively affected when they attempt to break these practices with more honest and nuanced responses. Furthermore, those who avoid deviating from current social or linguistic practices because of fear of negative consequences encounter a type of epistemic harm, which Dotson calls epistemic smothering. Epistemic smothering is "the truncating of one's own testimony in order to ensure that the testimony contains only content for which one's audience demonstrates testimonial competence" (Dotson 2011, 249). Testimonial smothering often occurs when one chooses to suppress their own testimony because they perceive the testimony to be risky or unsafe (249–50). If one avoids giving nuanced and helpful responses about HIV status because of a perceived risk from doing so, one's testimony is smothered, and a coerced silence occurs. Thus, the structural-linguistic epistemic injustice present in the discourse regarding HIV has the potential to lead to testimonial smothering and coerced silence.

These structural-linguistic epistemic harms, and the epistemic injustices both caused by and resulting from them, can be addressed via the promotion of alternative language that makes the epistemic reality clearer.

These harms and injustices can also be addressed via the promotion of other means such as education, which may help people come to properly understand the epistemic reality even if the social language norms, for a time, remain unchanged. These remedies can be implemented both on a transactional level (e.g., a personal commitment to responding in an epistemically forthright way despite social consequences) and on a structural level (e.g., a public-health initiative to educate people about the social realities of HIV transmission). In addition, given the way language communities work, amassed transactional remedies have the power to become a structural remedy.

To some extent, such remedies have occurred in the MSM community. For example, many users of MSM dating apps have changed the dialectic by posting things like "last tested HIV negative on [month/day/ year]" or "on PrEP" on their profiles. And, in recent years, the developers of many of these apps have added areas to profiles dedicated to providing a place for users to share information about status, testing, and other preventative measures (Staley 2015). Such actions result in a movement toward the normalization and encouragement of disclosing this kind of information. By posting information explicitly about testing dates, one highlights the epistemic intermediary, and by posting about prophylactic practices, one highlights steps being taken to minimize risk. These new phrases come with their own problems, but they still seem to represent a marked improvement in bringing epistemic limits to the fore. Cases like these show ways in which our language and understanding can be used to obscure or illuminate our epistemic situations and create or rectify epistemic injustices for those at risk for contracting HIV.

Conclusion and Additional Steps

The prevalence of HIV and the drastic changes in understanding and treatment of HIV in the past forty years have given rise to complex patterns of knowledge and ignorance among different communities. In this chapter, we've brought together empirical, epidemiological, and sociocultural research about HIV with discussions of epistemic injustice to develop a framework for identifying and potentially addressing harms done to individuals and groups in their capacities as knowers in relation to their sexual activity, health, and identity. In our discussion, we have addressed the hermeneutical and contributory injustices committed against

HIV-positive MSM in the quest to both understand and communicate transmission-risk levels and the structural-linguistic epistemic injustices that arise out of sexual-health communication patterns. These discussions not only highlight the types of epistemic injustices committed against MSM but also point to strategies for decreasing the potential risks associated with sexual activity.

Though we believe this discussion moves the conversation in a useful direction, there are other important, related topics that must be explored further to give a more complete theory of epistemic harms in relation to HIV. Just as sexual orientation and HIV status interact to produce varying levels of marginalization and privilege, so do other factors such as gender, race, and socioeconomic status. For example, the evidence regarding the racialized development of HIV-criminalization laws highlights the importance of race in both the perception of HIV-positive individuals and their epistemic situations. Anthony Lemelle (2003, 275) argues that HIV-specific "laws are available to profile and arrest African Americans, in much the same way that powder and crack cocaine federal status were used to unevenly prosecute African Americans." Furthermore, Black women account for nearly two-thirds of women newly diagnosed with HIV (CDC 2016a), and 44% of Black trans women have HIV (Black Women's Health Imperative 2019). This rise of HIV prevalence among Black people in the United States is often left invisible in mainstream discussions of HIV and prevention.

Finally, we've left out of our account the often-justified lack of trust in government and public-health authorities found among many members of communities where HIV acquisition is prevalent (for example, communities that have been harmed by "public health" initiatives in the past) (Davidson and Satta, forthcoming). Though our discussion of epistemic harms can certainly explain some aspects of these cases, we acknowledge and emphasize that more work must be done to provide a fully intersectional account. A fully developed account of epistemic harms is not reached without taking issues related to gender and race into account. We hope that our work here is a starting point for continued work in this area.

Notes

1. For more information on HIV and the stages of infection, see the CDC's (2015a) "About HIV/AIDS." For another quick overview of HIV, see Malani (2016).

2. Serosorting is also a practice engaged in by HIV-positive persons for various reasons. See Adams et al. (2014, 45).

3. For more information, see CDC (2016c).

4. For more information on the HIV-testing window period, see Department of Health and Human Services (2015) and CDC (2016c).

5. In addition, the HIV-negative partner could not be on PrEP or PEP (prophylactic methods for HIV prevention) at any point in the study.

6. For an accessible discussion of the preliminary results from the PARTNER study, see Cairns (2014).

7. For more information on PrEP, see CDC (2015b, 2015c).

8. The ramifications stemming from such a lack of awareness about the realities of HIV range from the legal to the political to the social for HIV-positive individuals. Over thirty states in the United States still have laws geared specifically toward the criminalizing of certain activities by HIV-positive people, including eleven states where activities like spitting and biting that have virtually no risk of transmission are criminalized (Lehman et al. 2014). In October 2017, Betty Price, a Georgia state legislator, anesthesiologist, and wife of former Health and Human Services Director Tom Price, asked during a public hearing if it was legal to quarantine HIV-positive people (Tinker 2017). And, earlier in 2017, the gay dating app DaddyBear, which self-identifies as the "No. 1 gay sugar-daddy dating app," created waves by not allowing HIV-positive members to join, citing as reasons that "most mature gay daddies grew up under the macro environment of AIDS epidemic and scare, so they know how to protect themselves and you, and enjoy safe sex with you" and that, in the words of DaddyBear's CEO, "No one would like to date people living with HIV unless he is living with it. Most gay sugar daddies are not living with HIV, so they don't want to bring home any unwanted souvenirs" (Koff 2017).

9. Firth et al. (2016) provides confirmatory evidence showing that Black adults in the US and gay and bisexual adult males in the US are better informed about the benefits of ART and PrEP—although these differences are quite small.

10. For demographic information broken down by race, ethnicity, and "risk groups," see the CDC's (2016b) "HIV in the United States: At a Glance."

11. Our chapter focuses on the United States. The reason we have limited our scope despite the notable impact of HIV/AIDS on many other parts of the world, particularly the African continent, is because the epistemic circumstances are not unified geographically, and to try and take cross-cultural issues into account in addition to intracultural issues in the United States would not be doable in a single chapter of this length. That said, we recognize the need for and encourage the additional development of work in this area that addresses the epistemic circumstances of other parts of the world.

12. This is not to say there isn't important overlap between the medical and social realms, but for our purposes it will be useful to talk about these areas as two things that, at the very least, are not identical to one another.

13. It is important to note that not all members of the HIV-positive MSM community endorse the adoption of these epistemic resources and some suggest that these terms should not be used in relational negotiations on social media, though this view is not particularly pervasive (Ramallo et al. 2015, 305).

14. The reasons why this may not go over well are varied, and we don't have the space to lay out any kind of complex psychological account as to the different reasons why a questioner may not respond well to a nuanced response. But among the reasons why one may not want a nuanced response are a desire to avoid the discomfort of having to consider as a more likely option that a partner may have HIV or an STI, that the question asker may never have really wanted to know the answer (but rather only wanted to discharge the duty of asking a responsible question), and the desire to avoid the distrust that one may associate with nuanced responses.

References

Adams, Barry D., Richard Elliott, Patrice Corriveau, and Ken English. 2014. "Impacts of Criminalization on the Everyday Lives of People Living with HIV in Canada." *Sex Research Social Policy* 11: 39–49.

Anderson, Elizabeth. 2012. "Epistemic Justice as a Virtue of Social Institutions." *Social Epistemology* 26 (2): 163–73.

Black Women's Health Imperative. 2019. "HIV/AIDS Policy Agenda for Black Women." Black Women's Health Imperative. Accessed August 5, 2020. https://bwhi.org/wp-content/uploads/2019/12/BWHI_HIV-AIDS-Policy-Agenda_v17_Final.pdf.

Brenner, Bluma G., Michel Roger, Jean-Pierre Routy, Daniela Moisil, Michel Ntemgwal, Claudine Matte, Jean-Guy Baril, Reiean Thomas, Danielle Rouleau, Julie Bruneau, et al. 2007. "High Rates of Forward Transmission Events after Acute/Early HIV-1 Infection." *Journal of Infectious Diseases* 195 (7): 951–59.

Cairns, Gus. 2014. "No-one with an Undetectable Viral Load, Gay or Heterosexual, Transmits HIV in First Two Years of PARTNER Study." NAM aidsmap, March 4, 2014. https://www.aidsmap.com/No-one-with-an-undetectable-viral-load-gay-or-heterosexual-transmits-HIV-in-first-two-years-of-PARTNER-study/page/2832748.

Cates, Willard, Jr., Margaret A. Chesney, and Myron S. Cohen. 1997. "Primary HIV Infection—A Public Health Opportunity." *American Journal of Public Health* 87 (12): 1928–30.

CDC (Centers for Disease Control and Prevention). 2015a. "About HIV/AIDS." CDC. Last modified December 6, 2015. https://www.cdc.gov/hiv/basics/whatishiv.html.

———. 2015b. "Pre-Exposure Prophylaxis (PrEP)." CDC. Last modified October 28, 2015. Accessed January 15, 2016. https://www.cdc.gov/hiv/prevention/research/prep/.

———. 2015c. "PrEP." CDC. Last modified December 15, 2015. Accessed January 15, 2016. https://www.cdc.gov/hiv/basics/prep.html.

———. 2016a. "HIV among Women." CDC. Last modified September 26, 2016. Accessed January 23, 2017. https://www.cdc.gov/hiv/group/gender/women/.

———. 2016b. "HIV in the United States: At a Glance." CDC. Last modified December 2, 2016. Accessed Janurary 7, 2017. https://www.cdc.gov/hiv/statistics/overview/ataglance.html.

———. 2016c. "HIV Testing." CDC. Last modified June 20, 2016. Accessed July 20, 2016. https://www.cdc.gov/hiv/testing/.

Chen, Aria Hangyu. 2016. "Should Dating Apps Have HIV Filters?" CNN Health, last modified September 15, 2016. https://www.cnn.com/2016/09/15/health/online-dating-app-hiv-std-filter/.

Chou, Roger, Shelley Selph, Tracy Dana, Christina Gougatsos, Bernadette Zakher, Ian Blazina, and P. Todd Korthuis. 2012. Screening for HIV: Systematic Review to Update the U.S. Preventive Services Task Force Recommendation. Evidence Synthesis no. 95. Agency for Healthcare Research and Quality (AHRQ) publication no. 12-05173-EF-1. Rockville, MD: AHRQ. NCBI Bookshelf. https://www.ncbi.nlm.nih.gov/books/NBK114872/pdf/Bookshelf_NBK114872.pdf.

Cohen, Myron S., Ying Q. Chen, Marybeth McCauley, Theresa Gamble, Mina C. Hosseinipour, Nagalingeswaran Kumarasamy, James G. Hakim, Johnstone Kumwenda, Beatriz Grinsztejn, Jose H. S. Pilotto, et al. 2011. "Prevention of HIV-1 Infection with Early Antiretroviral Therapy." New England Journal of Medicine 365 (6): 493–505.

Courtenay-Quirk, Cari, Richard J. Wolitski, Jeffrey T. Parsons, Cynthia A. Gómez, and Seropositive Urban Men's Study Team. 2006. "Is HIV/AIDS Stigma Dividing the Gay Community? Perceptions of HIV-Positive Men Who Have Sex with Men." AIDS Education and Prevention 18 (1): 56–67.

Davidson, Lacey J., and Mark Satta. Forthcoming. "Justified Social Distrust." In Social Trust, edited by Kevin Vallier and Michael Weber. Routledge.

Department of Health and Human Services. 2020. "HIV Testing Overview." HIV.gov. Last modified June 15, 2020. Accessed August 5, 2020. https://www.hiv.gov/hiv-basics/hiv-testing/learn-about-hiv-testing/hiv-testing-overview.

DeRose, Keith. 2002. "Assertion, Knowledge, and Context." Philosophical Review 111 (2): 167–203.

Dodds, Catherine, Adam Bourne, and Matthew Weait. 2009. "Responses to Criminal Prosecutions for HIV Transmission among Gay Men with HIV in England and Wales." Reproductive Health Matters 17 (34): 135–45.

Dotson, Kristie. 2011. "Tracking Epistemic Violence, Tracking Practices of Silencing." Hypatia 26 (2): 236–57.

————. 2012. "A Cautionary Tale: On Limiting Epistemic Oppression." *Frontiers* 31 (1): 24–47.

————. 2014. "Conceptualizing Epistemic Oppression." *Social Epistemology* 28 (2): 115–38.

Firth, Jamie, Liz Hamel, Jennifer Kates, Anne Jankiewicz, and David Rousseau, for the Kaiser Family Foundation. 2016. "HIV Awareness and Testing, 2013 and 2014." *Journal of the American Medical Association* 316 (2): 139.

Fricker, Miranda. 2007. *Epistemic Injustice: Power and the Ethics of Knowing.* New York: Oxford University Press.

Grace, Daniel, Sarah A. Chown, Michael Kwag, Malcolm Steinberg, Elgin Lim, and Mark Gilbert. 2015. "Becoming 'Undetectable': Longitudinal Narratives of Gay Men's Sex Lives after a Recent HIV Diagnosis." *AIDS Education and Prevention* 27 (4): 333–49.

Günthard, Huldrych F., Michael S. Saag, Constance A. Benson, Carlos del Rio, Joseph J. Eron, Joel E. Gallant, Jennifer F. Hoy, Michael J. Mugavero, Paul E. Sax, Melanie A. Thompson, et al. 2016. "Antiretroviral Drugs for Treatment and Prevention of HIV Infection in Adults: 2016 Recommendations of the International Antiviral Society–USA Panel." *Journal of the American Medical Association* 316 (2): 191–210.

Hall, H. Irene, Qian An, Tian Tang, Ruiguang Song, Mi Chen, Timothy Green, and Jian Kang. 2015. "Prevalence of Diagnosed and Undiagnosed HIV Infection—United States, 2008–2012." *Morbidity and Mortality Weekly Report* 64, no. 24 (June 26): 657–62. https://www.cdc.gov/mmwr/preview/mmwrhtml/mm6424a2.htm?s_cid+mm6424a2_e.

Hollingsworth, T. Déirdre, Roy M. Anderson, and Christophe Fraser. 2008. "HIV-1 Transmission, by Stage of Infection." *Journal of Infectious Diseases* 198 (5): 687–93.

Humburg, Burt. 2016. "Unclean: The Removal of HIV Stigma and Discrimination." *Left Magazine*, last modified January 12, 2016. https://www.liveleft.com/unclean/.

Jefferson, Erica. 2012. "FDA Approves First Drug for Reducing the Risk of Sexually Acquired HIV Infection." U.S. Food and Drug Administration News and Events. https://www.fda.gov/NewsEvents/Newsroom/PressAnnouncements/ucm312210.htm.

King, Mark S. 2012. "The Stupid Question: 'Are You Clean?' " *My Fabulous Disease* (blog), June 21, 2012. Accessed January 1, 2017. https://www.marksking.com/my-fabulous-disease/the-stupid-question-are-you-clean/.

————. 2016. "Five Reasons 'HIV Undetectable' Must Equal 'Untransmittable.' " *My Fabulous Disease* (blog), December 15, 2016. Accessed October 17, 2017. https://www.marksking.com/my-fabulous-disease/five-reasons-hiv-undetectable-must-equal-untransmittable.

Koblin, Beryl A., Marla J. Husnik, Grant Colfax, Yijan Huang, Maria Madison, Kenneth Mayer, Patrick J. Barresi, Thomas J. Coates, Margaret A. Chesney, and Susan Buchbinder. 2006. "Risk Factors for HIV Infection among Men Who Have Sex with Men." *AIDS* 20 (5): 731–39.

Koff, Derek de. 2017. "Looking for a Sugar Daddy? Join the New Dating App Daddybear—Unless You're HIV-Positive." *Queerty*, August 25, 2017. https://www.queerty.com/looking-sugar-daddy-join-new-dating-app-daddybear-unless-youre-hiv-positive-20170825.

Koopman, James S., Adam A. Jacquez, Gavin W. Welch, Carl P. Simon, Betsy Foxman, Stephen M. Pollock, Daniel Barth-Jones, Andrew L. Adams, and Kenneth Lange. 1997. "The Role of Early HIV Infection in the Spread of HIV through Populations." *Journal of Acquired Immune Deficiency Syndromes and Human Retrovirology* 14 (3): 249–58.

Lehman, J. Stan, Meredith H. Carr, Allison J. Nichol, Alberto Ruisanchez, David W. Knight, Anne E. Langford, Simone C. Gray, and Jonathan H. Mermin. 2014. "Prevalence and Public Health Implications of State Law that Criminalize Potential HIV Exposure in the United States." *AIDS and Behavior* 18 (6): 997–1006.

Lemelle, Anthony J., Jr. 2003. "Linking the Structure of African American Criminalization to the Spread of HIV/AIDS." *Journal of Contemporary Criminal Justice* 19 (3): 270–92.

Malani, Preeti N. 2016. "Human Immunodeficiency Virus." *Journal of the American Medical Association* 316 (2): 238.

Mason, Rebecca. 2011. "Two Kinds of Unknowing." *Hypatia* 26 (2): 294–307.

McNulty, Moira, Adam S. Cifu, and David Pitrak. 2016. "HIV Screening." *Journal of the American Medical Association* 316 (2): 213–14.

Mermin, Jonathan H., and Eugene McCray. 2017. "National Gay Men's HIV/AIDS Awareness Day." CDC, September 27, 2017. https://www.cdc.gov/nchhstp/dear_colleague/2017/dcl-092717-National-Gay-Mens-HIV-AIDS-Awareness-Day.html.

Millett, Gregorio A., John L. Peterson, Richard J. Wolitski, and Ron Stall. 2006. "Greater Risk for HIV Infection of Black Men Who Have Sex with Men: A Critical Literature Review." *American Journal of Public Health* 96 (6): 1007–19.

NCHHSTP (National Center for HIV/AIDS, Viral Hepatitis, STD, and TB Prevention). 2017. "New HIV Infections Drop 18 Percent in Six Years." HIV.gov blog, February 14, 2017. https://www.hiv.gov/blog/new-hiv-infections-drop-18-percent-in-six-years.

Pao, David, Martin Fisher, Stephane Hué, Gillian Dean, Gary Murphy, Patricia A. Cane, Caroline A. Sabin, and Deenan Pillay. 2005. "Transmission of HIV-1 during Primary Infection: Relationship to Sexual Risk and Sexually Transmitted Infections." *AIDS* 19 (1): 85–90.

Phillips, Andrew N., Valentina Cambiano, Fumiyo Nakagawa, Alison E. Brown, Fiona Lampe, Alison Rodger, Alec Miners, Jonathan Elford, Graham Hart,

Anne M. Adamson, et al. 2013. "Increased HIV Incidence in Men Who Have Sex with Men Despite High Levels of ART-Induced Viral Suppression: Analysis of an Extensively Documented Epidemic." *PloS One* 8 (2): e55312.

Pilcher, Christopher D., Hsiao Chuan Tien, Joseph J. Eron Jr., Pietro L. Vernazza, Szu-Yun Leu, Paul W. Stewart, Li-Ean Goh, Myron S. Cohen, Quest Study, and Duke-UNC-Emory Acute HIV Consortium. 2004. "Brief but Efficient: Acute HIV Infection and the Sexual Transmission of HIV." *Journal of Infectious Diseases* 189 (10): 1785–92.

Pohlhaus, Gaile, Jr. 2012. "Relational Knowing and Epistemic Injustice: Toward a Theory of *Willful Hermeneutical Ignornace*." *Hypatia* 27 (4): 715–35.

Prevention Access Campaign. 2017. *Risk of Sexual Transmission of HIV from a Person Living with HIV Who Has an Undetectable Viral Load: Messaging Primer and Consensus Statement.* Issued July 21, 2016. Endorsements updated October 15, 2017. Accessed October 30, 2017. https://www.docs.wixstatic.com/ugd/de0404_331d89073852464aa7f798957e882a2d.pdf.

Ramallo, Jorge, Thomas Kidder, Tashuna Albritton, Gary Blick, Adam Pachankis, Valen Grandeleski, and Trace Kershaw. 2015. "Exploring Social Networking Technologies as Tools for HIV Prevention for Men Who Have Sex with Men." *AIDS Education and Prevention* 27 (4): 298–311.

Rodger, Alison, Tina Bruun, Matthew Weait, Pietro Vernazza, Simon Collins, Vincente Estrada, Jan Van Lunzen, Giulio Maria Corbelli, Fiona Lampe, Andrew Phillips, et al. 2012. "Partners of People on ART—A New Evaluation of the Risks (The PARTNER Study): Design and Methods." *BMC Public Health* 12: 296–302.

Rodger, Alison, Tina Bruun, Valentina Cambiano, Pietro Vernazza, Vicente Estrada, Jan van Lunzen, Simon Collins, Anna Maria Geretti, Andrew Phillips, and Jens Lundgren. 2014. "HIV Transmission Risk through Condomless Sex if HIV+ Partner on Suppressive ART: PARTNER Study." Paper presented at the 21st Conference on Retroviruses and Opportunistic Infections, Boston, March 2014. Abstract 153LB.

Rodger, Alison J., Valentina Cambiano, Tina Bruun, Pietro Vernazza, Simon Collins, Jan van Lunzen, Giulio Maria Corbelli, Vicente Estrada, Anna Maria Geretti, Apostolos Beloukas, et al. 2016. "Sexual Activity without Condoms and Risk of HIV Transmission in Serodifferent Couples When the HIV-Positive Partner Is Using Suppressive Antiretroviral Therapy." *Journal of the American Medical Association* 316 (2): 171–81.

Staley, Oliver. 2015. "Gay Dating Apps Become Messengers for Warnings on HIV." *Bloomberg Technology*, February 12, 2015. https://www.bloomberg.com/news/articles/2015-02-13/gay-dating-apps-become-messengers-for-warnings-on-hiv-health.

Tinker, Ben. 2017. "Georgia Lawmaker: Can People with HIV Be 'Legally' Quarantined?" *CNN Health*. Last modified October 22, 2017. https://www.cnn.com/2017/10/20/health/betty-price-hiv-aids-quarantine/index.html.

Chapter 10

Mestizaje as an Epistemology of Ignorance
The Case of the Mexican Genome Diversity Project

SERGIO ARMANDO GALLEGOS-ORDORICA

I

One of the key claims that Charles W. Mills (1997, 3) proposes in his classic book *The Racial Contract* is that social contract theory (either in its classic or contemporary versions) is a poor lens for studying properly the nature and functioning of contemporary Western polities since "in its obfuscation of the ugly realities of group power and domination, it is, if unsupplemented, a profoundly misleading account of how the actual world is and came to be." To address this shortcoming, Mills proposes another lens, which he calls the "racial contract," that aims to illuminate the origin and the persistence of the deep racial injustices that permeate contemporary polities. Through the use of this lens, Mills argues that part of the reason that racial injustices systematically endure is that large portions of the populations of contemporary Western polities embrace what he describes as "an inverted epistemology, an epistemology of ignorance, a particular pattern of localized and global cognitive dysfunctions (which are psychologically and socially functional), producing the ironic outcome that whites will be unable to understand the world they have made" (18). Thus, an epistemology of ignorance involves a series of epistemic practices that, while being psychologically and socially functional, are cognitively dysfunctional since they are geared toward the production and perpetuation of ignorance.

Building on Mills's work, Linda Alcoff (2007) has refined the notion of an epistemology of ignorance by showing how the different economic and social structures we are subject to and the various social positions we occupy may work in tandem to create epistemologies of ignorance. To be specific, Alcoff has shown how the claims that Sandra Harding (1991) and Lorraine Code (1993) have made concerning the positionality of all knowers can be connected to Mills's view in a unifying way by appealing to Horkheimer's critique of instrumental rationality. The key idea behind the critique is this: since our modes of belief formation and justification are always shaped by the various social and economic forces that we face as well as by the social positions that we occupy, both the product and the process of knowing are systematically dependent on history and context. In virtue of this, Alcoff contends that relying on instrumental rationality, which is a form of reasoning that dehistoricizes and naturalizes both the product and the process of knowing by reducing them to a simple end-means relation, is conducive to the production of ignorance, as it blinds us to the fact that the epistemic and social norms we adopt reflect often the ugly realities of power group and domination.

In consequence, ignorance is often not an accidental gap but rather something that is actively produced and perpetuated by following certain epistemic norms (e.g., norms about what one should remember or forget) that are deeply intertwined with certain social norms (e.g., norms about what one should celebrate or disparage). To illustrate this, consider the fact that the annual celebration on March 2 of Texas Independence Day, which commemorates the heroism of Texians such as Stephen F. Austin and Samuel Houston rising against Mexican oppression, omits that the interference of the Mexican government in the early 1830s in the affairs of Texians was aimed at eradicating their slavery practices, since slavery had been abolished in Mexico in 1829.[1] This example shows clearly how social norms and epistemic norms can map onto and reinforce each other, thus giving rise to an epistemology of ignorance that creates and perpetuates a distorted account of history for modern Texans (and Americans in general).

Though the abovementioned case shows how the interplay between certain epistemic and social norms can generate an epistemology of igno-rance that affects privileged groups by distorting or omitting historical facts, in other cases, the interplay between epistemic and social norms can generate instances of what Kristie Dotson (2011, 238) calls *pernicious ignorance*, a notion she characterizes in the following terms: "Pernicious ignorance should be understood to refer to any reliable ignorance that, in a given context, harms another person (or set of persons). Reliable ignorance is ignorance that is consistent or follows from a predictable epistemic gap in cognitive resources." Thus, the establishment of an epistemology of ignorance often affects not only those who are its primary promoters by trapping them in what Mills (1997, 18) dubs "a consensual hallucination" but also others who are harmed in different ways (e.g., by being silenced when they attempt to speak from marginalized positions).

Now, since forms of pernicious ignorance can be particularly damaging, some authors such as José Medina (2013, 50) have proposed potential remedies to them by developing an epistemology of resistance, which involves a form of "beneficial epistemic friction" by "forcing one to be self-critical, to compare and contrast one's beliefs, to meet justificatory demands, to recognize cognitive gaps and so on." According to Medina, this form of friction has been used effectively by certain historical figures (e.g., the Novohispanic nun Sor Juana Inés de la Cruz) to fight back against structural forms of pernicious ignorance. Indeed, though Sor Juana was born and lived in the seventeenth century in a colonial society that aimed to control women by denying or severely restricting their right to education, she was able through beneficial epistemic friction to force some of her critics to acknowledge the internal tensions of their positions.

Given that a great deal of current work about epistemologies of ignorance has focused on their development and impact in the anglophone world (specifically, in the US) and has tended to leave aside the rest of the world, my general goal in this chapter is to analyze how an epistemology of ignorance that progressively emerged in Mexico as a result of a nation-building project impacted a project of genomic research undertaken by Mexican scientists in the last decade—the Mexican Genome Diversity Project (MGDP). In my analysis, I first argue that the program of *mestizaje* (or race mixing), which was adopted by the Mexican government throughout most of the twentieth century as part of a nation-building project, functioned as an epistemology of ignorance that, in addition of influencing different governmental policies that harmed specific groups, shaped also the planning and the realization of the MGDP. I argue, too, that it is possible to resist (at least partially) this epistemology through the development of beneficial epistemic friction by undertaking and promoting some practices that constitute a form of what Medina (2013) has called, drawing on Foucault's work, an "insurrectionary genealogy." This type of epistemic friction involves "interrogating and contesting any settlement, making the past come undone at the seams . . . so that it does not appear anymore as a single past that has already been made, but rather as a heterogeneous array of converging and diverging struggles that are still ongoing" (287). If my arguments here are correct, my work has two upshots: (1) showing how the program of *mestizaje* was connected in Mexico to the development of an epistemology of ignorance that impacted a recent scientific project and (2) illustrating how some of the deleterious effects of this epistemology can be combated.

Here is a roadmap. I offer in section II an extensive review of the notion of *mestizo* in Mexican history that highlights how it was understood during colonial times and how it gave rise to the notion of *mestizaje*, which was used after the Mexican Revolution as the basis of a unifying and homogeneous Mexican identity. Subsequently, I provide in section III an account of how the program of *mestizaje* functioned as an epistemology of ignorance by rehearsing its impact on diverse scientific projects, and I focus in particular on the case of the MGDP, which was carried out by scientists of the National Institute of Genomic Medicine (INMEGEN). Indeed, since Mexican genomic scientists used the notion of *mestizo* in the collection of samples and in the interpretation of results, I maintain that the MGDP led to a biological reification of socioracial categories. In addition, I show that this reification supported a racialized picture of the Mexican population that helped to perpetuate the myth of a homogeneous nation. In section IV, I argue, using Medina's work, that it is possible to resist this epistemology of ignorance by developing insurrectionary genealogies. To be specific, I argue that the development of some insurrectionary genealogies could be carried out through forms of art that, despite being products of the mestizo identity, also resist this construction. Finally, I offer in section V a brief conclusion and outline a couple of lines of future research.

II

The notion of *mestizo* has had a crucial importance in Mexican history. However, in order to understand properly its impact, it is important to notice that it has not always been employed in a uniform way; its connotations have shifted through time. In particular, though the notion has today a clear racial connotation, this was not always the case. Indeed, María Elena Martínez (2008) argues that, though the notion began to surface in church and administrative records in New Spain in the 1540s to refer to the offspring of Spaniards and non-Europeans (mostly Amerindians),[2] it initially lacked racial connotations since "in the early period what seems to have mattered was the status of the father and legitimacy or illegitimacy of the child" (144). However, even if the notion initially lacked racial connotations, it had nonetheless a negative one given that, as Moisés González Navarro (1970, 145) observes, "since most of these unions [between Spaniards and non-Europeans] were illegitimate, the term 'mestizo' became synonymous with bastard."

As the number of mixed-race individuals progressively grew in New Spain, Spanish colonial authorities sought ways to control this population, and one of the ways in which this was done was to racialize the notion of *mestizo*. This racialization took place through the articulation of a caste system in which the notion of *limpieza de sangre* (i.e., purity of blood), which had been developed in the Iberian Peninsula in the fifteenth century as a mechanism to block the access of Jewish and Muslim converts (and their offspring) to religious and government offices, was progressively modified and adapted to the colonial context to hierarchize individuals on the basis of their *raza* (lineage).[3] As mixed-race individuals (or *castas*), mestizos had more-limited rights and privileges than individuals born in Spain (*peninsulares*) or those born in the colony of Spanish parents (*criollos*), but their lot was in certain cases better than that of Amerindians[4] (and was clearly superior to that of Black slaves). One important point to keep in mind is that, even if racial identities came to regulate (especially in the middle and late colonial periods) all aspects of individual life, the notion of *mestizo* did not have a clear, stable meaning despite being extremely widely used—a fact which, as Kuznesof (1995, 165) has argued, led to its being "constantly negotiated and redefined in colonial courts."[5]

After Mexican independence in 1821, the caste system was abolished and racial designations were eliminated from official documents in a deliberate effort to make all Mexicans legally equal regardless of their lineage and of any phenotypical or cultural markers. However, in spite of this, the old socioracial categories (and, in particular, the notion of *mestizo*) continued to play an important role in debates concerning the best way to forge a strong and homogeneous nation. One common assumption that virtually all nineteenth-century Mexican politicians and intellectuals participating in these debates accepted consisted in the fact that, in order to become a modern and unified nation, Mexico had to address its "Indian problem," which required forging a national identity and a common culture for a great number of different groups that were divided along linguistic and racial lines and bringing these groups into modernity by integrating them into a capitalist economic system.

Since these two goals were deemed to be inconsistent with the recovery and the adoption of the Mesoamerican past, politicians and intellectuals then argued that the key to Mexico's future resided not in its Amerindian groups but rather in its mestizo population that had steadily grown since colonial times. But there were serious discrepancies about the role that mestizos had to play. In particular, Mexican elites throughout the nineteenth century were split into two currents of thought. One viewpoint, which was championed by historians such as José María Luis Mora (1794–1850) and Francisco Pimentel (1832–1893), closely reproduced the hierarchy of the colonial caste system, as it defended a project in which the government should endeavor to eventually turn Mexico into a criollo (i.e., white) nation. In this project, the mestizos, who were still inferior to the whites, had nevertheless a certain value because of their role to facilitate the progressive assimilation and, in the long run, the disappearance of the Amerindian population. In this sense, the mestizo population was seen as a bridge that could help Mexico become a unified, modern, and wealthy nation, without the mestizos being part of this utopic future.[6]

A second viewpoint, endorsed by writers and politicians such as Vicente Riva Palacio (1832–1896) and Justo Sierra (1848–1912), rejected the primacy of the criollos (while admitting the existence of a certain hierarchical racial order) and instead contended that the mestizos were valuable not as a bridge to Mexico's future but as the very essence of that future. In the words of the contemporary political scientist Agustín Basave Benítez (2002, 32), "The mestizo is no longer a means but an end; it is a being that becomes desirable not because of its proximity to the white but insofar as he is himself."[7] In particular, in the case of Justo Sierra, an inversion of the traditional negative connotations of the notion of *mestizo* began to take place. Indeed, while Sierra (1948) acknowledged openly the traditional connotation of *mestizo* as "bastard" when he wrote that the War of Independence and the War of Reform were "actions of immense energy of Mexico's *bastard race*" (129–30),[8] he suggested that this illegitimate status was precisely what made the mestizo population "the dynamic factor of our history" (131),[9] as this drove mestizos to spearhead the fight for the abolition of caste distinctions and for legal equality throughout the nineteenth century. In virtue of this, the figure of the mestizo was recast by Sierra as the courageous patriot that was responsible for Mexico's political progress, while the criollos were now considered conservative parasites whose real allegiance was to the colonial order given that they constituted "a passive class, wherein the political dogma has been the radical incapacity of the Mexican people to self-govern" (1948, 130).[10]

In parallel to the political recasting of the figure of the mestizo as the quintessential patriot, Sierra and his intellectual successors such as the sociologist Andrés Molina Enríquez (1868–1940) also introduced two other important positive connotations to the notion of *mestizo*, an economic one and a moral one. For Sierra, not only was the mestizo the main protagonist of Mexico's political struggles, but he was also considered to be the foundation of a modern capitalist economy, because "the indigenous, just as the rich criollo, hoard, which is an unproductive form of thriftiness that certainly does not give rise to capital" (1948, 145).[11] And, insofar as the mestizo was taken to be a racial hybrid, he was also considered to embody, notwithstanding the profound influence of figures such as Herbert Spencer on Mexican intellectuals at the end of the nineteenth century and in the first two decades of the twentieth century,[12] the best character traits of his progenitors. In particular, for Molina Enríquez (1909, 331–32), the mestizos provided the best possible moral foundation for the Mexican nation because "the taciturnity of Indians and the joviality of the Spaniards are neutralized in them, thus yielding a balanced austere and noble dignity of which our great men have given magnificent examples."[13]

Once the notion of *mestizo* was associated with these positive connotations during the long presidency of the mestizo Porfirio Díaz (1876–1911), the ground was set for the program of *mestizaje* to emerge. As the chaos of the Mexican Revolution (1910–1920) laid bare a series of social, geographic, and racial fractures that threatened the viability of the nation, intellectuals during the revolution and in the immediate postrevolutionary period advocated a project that rested not only on a glorification of the mestizo population (which became identified with the Mexican population) but also on a series of immigration, educational, and public-health policies that were aimed at fusing all the different groups inhabiting the national territory into a single, homogeneous whole. The key goal of this project was, in the words of the anthropologist Manuel Gamio (1883–1960), one of its main architects, to forge "a powerful *patria* (fatherland)" through "fusion of races, convergence and fusion of manifestations of culture, linguistic unification and the economic equilibrium of social elements" ([1916] 2010, 164). Thus, once the mestizo was enthroned as the figure of the ideal Mexican, *mestizaje* emerged as a multifaceted political project that involved using what had originally been a vague socioracial notion to define an archetype whose physical and cultural features provided the norm of Mexicanhood and to devise and execute policies that pursued the progressive transformation of the population in accordance with this ideal.

To be more specific, these policies included severe restrictions on which individuals could immigrate to Mexico and settle;[14] public-health campaigns aimed at identifying and isolating individuals whose antecedents, habits, or pathologies constituted a threat to the racial hygiene of the nation;[15] and educational drives to set up schools in rural areas with important Amerindian concentrations that taught only Spanish and basic mathematics.[16] Considering this, various scholars such as Guillermo Zermeño who have studied the rise and the flourishing of *mestizaje* in Mexico have pointed out that there was a mismatch between the project's ideals and its actual consequences. Indeed, though the program of *mestizaje* and its concomitant policies were officially touted as positive since they were deemed to pave the way for the elimination of the old racial divisions and inequalities, the consequences were often deeply negative: "One of the problematic aspects of this modern notion resides in the fact that its construction was realized at the expense of the devaluation and the reclusion of indigenous populations. At the same time that the image of the mestizo was magnified as a metaphor for a progressive and enterprising nation, the construction of the image of the 'really existing' Indian as a 'race' in a process of degradation was undertaken" (Zermeño 2011, 311).[17]

In fact, the consequences of the adoption of *mestizaje* as a political project were even more problematic than Zermeño describes. Not only did *mestizaje* entail the devaluation of Amerindian communities, but, as Gerardo Rénique (2001) and Jason Chang (2017) have shown, it also involved a state-sponsored eugenics program in the 1930s that carried out the persecution and deportation of undesirable groups, such as Chinese immigrants along with their Mexican spouses and children, since they were considered disease vectors that could potentially undermine the health of the Mexican population and undermine its racial integrity.[18] Though the virulent racial nationalism that underpinned the political project of *mestizaje* in Mexico reached its peak in the first half of the twentieth century and subsequently subsided as other mechanisms of mass control emerged, the core ideas behind the project (and, to be precise, the racialized picture of the Mexican population that came along with it) have continued to be influential in many aspects of Mexican life. In particular, I show in the next section that the program of *mestizaje* functioned as an epistemology of ignorance that shaped, throughout the twentieth century, the design and the implementation of various scientific projects in Mexico (including the genomic project that I discuss in detail).

III

Having explained how the notion of *mestizaje* emerged and came to play a crucial role in the construction of a modern racialized Mexican identity, I now consider the influence of *mestizaje* in the production of genomic knowledge in Mexico. However, before doing this, it is important to bear in mind how scientific knowledge about the Mexican population was produced during the twentieth century by focusing on specific examples, paying attention to the key assumptions that scientists made. Virtually all scientists in this period endorsed two central tenets: (1) the Mexican population is a nationally homogeneous whole given that it is the result of pervasive racial admixture between different groups and (2) there are differences between various regional subpopulations, which are located somewhere in a spectrum in which the two extremes are the mestizo and the *indio*. In virtue of this, just as the construction of the postrevolutionary Mexican society unfolded in accordance with the political project of *mestizaje*, both the mestizo and the *indio* became central objects of inquiry for Mexican scientists throughout the twentieth century.[19]

One particular concern for the early pioneers (who were mostly anthropologists and physicians) was to produce an accurate anthropological and medical picture of the Mexican population that could be used to design and implement development policies and that would stand in opposition to racist techniques used in the United States and Europe.[20] To do this, anthropologists studied regional populations in the 1920s and 1930s through the lens of provided by the works of Franz Boaz, a prominent anthropologist who contended that racial differences among various human populations stemmed from environmental and cultural factors, not from biological innate characteristics.[21] Subsequently, physicians in the 1940s and 1950s aimed to classify individuals in accordance to specific biotypes, which were characterized not in terms of the traditional socioracial categories but in terms of abstract statistical means for features such as height, cardiovascular function, and memory capacity. However, as some contemporary authors have remarked (e.g., Stern 2003), while both anthropologists and physicians held that their scientific practices were impartial and geared to end racism, their work in fact relied on the two aforementioned assumptions (homogeneity of the Mexican population at the national level and heterogeneity between different Mexican subgroups at the regional level) and thus helped perpetuate a racialized picture of the Mexican population as divided between a core growing majority (the mestizos) and a dwindling periphery (the indios), the latter of which had to be integrated for its own sake. In particular, these assumptions were implicitly invoked in the articulation and the implementation of pacification policies after the Mexican Revolution, when the Mexican government under Emilio Portes Gil (1928–1930) sought to quell social unrest in certain regions of the country with Amerindian groups (e.g., Sonora) by deporting a portion of the groups (specifically, Yaquis) to other regions of the country to force them to assimilate and to become mestizos.[22] As this example shows, the program of *mestizaje* generated a pernicious ignorance that harmed Amerindian groups.

These two assumptions about national homogeneity and regional heterogeneity were subsequently also adopted by human geneticists and population biologists, as these sciences began to develop in Mexico in the 1960s and beyond, who used imported techniques such as immunoassays and electrophoresis.[23] The use of these techniques, which allowed the marking of molecular variants in hemoglobin and the study of polymorphisms in immune identity antigens, promised to yield a much-finer-grained look at human diversity by enabling scientists to quantify more precisely than their predecessors the contributions made by different ancestral groups to the Mexican population. However, though these techniques were progressively refined and yielded larger amounts of information as time passed, their incorporation and use within research projects aimed at the analysis of the admixture still rested on the two aforementioned assumptions. Consequently, even though the data supported a far more complex picture than the received one (which emphasized the admixture between European and Amerindian groups), the scientific research was used to bolster, as Carlos López Beltrán, Vivette García Deister, and Mariana Ríos Sandoval (2014, 94) pointed out, a picture in which "local narratives of differential admixture in each region feed on and reinforce the national narrative of Mexican admixed homogeneity, and vice versa."

Just as the program of *mestizaje* influenced the production of scientific knowledge in Mexico in fields such as anthropology and medicine in the early to mid-twentieth century, it also has had a more recent impact in the development of genomic research. As the Human Genome Project was carried out throughout the 1990s, mostly by institutions in the United States, Europe, and other developed countries, a group of Mexican scientists and politicians grew concerned that future scientific research about the Mexican population, which had been done mostly by Mexicans throughout the twentieth century, would be done abroad in the future. In virtue of this, this group successfully lobbied the Mexican government to create and generously fund INMEGEN in 2004 to undertake genomic research. During the tenure of its first director, Gerardo Jiménez Sánchez (2004–2010), the flagship project of the institution—the Mexican Genome Diversity Project (MGDP)—was to study the genetic variability of the Mexican population.

Though this project was seen as a positive illustration of how cutting-edge scientific knowledge could be produced by Mexicans and for Mexicans,[24] the ways in which it was motivated, characterized, and carried out were problematic. First, though there were (and still are) very real concerns about the risk of unscrupulous "safari research" being carried out by private corporations and even foreign academics, the MGDP was motivated by a notion of "genomic sovereignty" that involved treating certain genetic sequences containing single-nucleotide polymorphisms as objects belonging to the national patrimony (in line with earlier nationalistic stances), which is troubling given that, as López Beltrán and Vergara Silva (2011) observe, they are "molecular variants that are shared and dispersed throughout the globe."[25] Moreover, another problematic motive underpinning the project consisted in linking the production of knowledge to the future development of a personalized genomic medicine that promised attractive business opportunities for pharmaceutical companies interested in developing and commercializing drugs specifically tailored to conditions prevalent in the Mexican population. Indeed, the production of genomic knowledge was justified not only as a way to improve the health of the Mexican population but also as a means to generate revenue from it.[26]

In addition to these motivations, the politicians that initially supported the project and the institutions that advertised its results characterized the MGDP in misleading ways that revealed a deeply racialized view of the Mexican population lurking in the background. Indeed, since the project was characterized by some politicians as aiming to decipher "the genome of the Mexicans," people were led to believe that, in spite of the fact that all human populations are overwhelmingly similar at the genetic level, there is a set of characteristics that single out a particular "Mexican genome" as distinct from others.[27] Moreover, in the first publication that it produced, the project offered a very problematic description of the different Mexican regional subpopulations that it studied. Indeed, after the authors of the publication singled out in their study eighty-nine alleles that were absent in all HapMap populations but present in a least one Mexican regional subpopulation and then established that eighty-six of these alleles were present in a group of Zapotec Amerindians that was taken as proxy for the pre-Columbian Amerindian population, they stated that "all alleles private to the Zapotecs were private to [Mexican] Mestizos" (Silva-Zolezzi et al. 2009, 8613). This way of characterizing Mexican regional subpopulations is troublesome, since it suggests that the vague socioracial descriptor *mestizo* has in fact a specific genetic basis, thus biologically reifying the socioracial category.

Finally, some researchers considered the sampling protocol to be problematic. For instance, when collecting samples for genomic study, scientists at INMEGEN relied on self-identified mestizo donors who were students at public universities in different states located in geographically distant regions of the country. The rationale for undertaking this sampling was that, since public universities have traditionally been open to all, this sampling would then be representative of the whole Mexican population since "most attendees come equally from rural and urban areas and belong to a wide range of socio-economic strata" (Silva-Zolezzi et al. 2009, 8615). However, as López Beltrán and Vergara Silva (2011, 129) point out, this rationale ignores that "powerful socioeconomic forces operate against the access of peasants and the working class to education, particularly at the college level."[28] In light of this biased sampling[29] and of other problems that led to increasing dissatisfaction with the tenure of Jiménez Sánchez at the head of INMEGEN,[30] the project lost support. And, when Jiménez Sánchez was replaced in 2010, his successor Xavier Soberón purposefully de-emphasized the MGDP in order to focus the resources of INMEGEN on other projects such as the investigation of the genomics of infectious diseases and of preterm labor.[31]

Though the MGDP has ceased to be a priority for INMEGEN, a number of very pressing questions remain about how a scientific project of this magnitude[32] with the abovementioned problems could be carried out. In particular, López Beltrán, García Deister, and Ríos Sandoval (2014, 99) have wondered how "a recent but powerful scientific institution like INMEGEN could brandish the strongly racialized category of mestizo in the public space and make it the defining element of its gauging of the Mexican population" while raising very few questions from scientists who "seemed to inhabit the same collective common sense within which most Mexicans found themselves."

In response, I contend that INMEGEN was able to use the socioracial notion of *mestizo* as a bona fide biological category in genomic research because the program of *mestizaje* functioned as an epistemology of ignorance that distorted the cognitive functions of scientists engaged in the MGDP. Indeed, in the case of the MGDP, the two traditional assumptions made with respect to the Mexican population (both homogeneous at the national level and heterogeneous between different regions) clearly induced a series of cognitive dysfunctions in scientists and politicians that influenced them in ways that obscured certain key issues. Let me illustrate this with two examples. First, insofar as the public education system was developed after the Mexican Revolution precisely as a homogenizing mechanism aimed at "mexicanizing" the population, scientists who designed the protocols for collecting samples for the MGDP mistakenly believed that they would get a representative sample of the Mexican population by focusing on students from state universities, without considering that these often did not include working-class Mexicans. Second, insofar as the mestizos have traditionally been considered to be the economic pillar of Mexico, various scientists and politicians justified the project by appealing to the possibility of developing a fine-tuned genomic medicine that would address diseases such as diabetes, hypertension, and obesity that are on the rise among the majority of Mexicans. However, the emphasis on the potential development of individualized genomic medicine led them to ignore (or at least downplay) evidence that shows that the increased prevalence of these diseases is due in good part to the adoption of sedentary lifestyles and to changes in nutrition habits.[33] Thus, as we can see, these two examples show how the program of *mestizaje* operated within the framework of the MGDP to create forms of pernicious ignorance that harmed working-class Mexicans as well as other groups of Mexicans particularly vulnerable to metabolic diseases.

To be more specific, my contention is that, in the case of the MGDP, the efforts to map the genome of the Mexicans were driven by the blurring of national identity and genetic particularity and that this conflation was promoted by the program of *mestizaje* and also supported by market incentives. To appreciate this, it is important to bear in mind that, as López Beltrán and Vergara Silva (2011, 141) have stressed, the carrying out of the MGDP was accompanied by a powerful media campaign in which "in every occasion the same themes were emphasized: the Mexican genomic singularity, the need to control the genomic knowledge (of Mexicans), and the savings in public-health costs that the use of individualized drugs would generate in the future."[34] When we consider the insistence on these themes to justify the MGDP to the public, one of the most plausible accounts for this insistence is that the project was underscored by what Alcoff (2007), following Horkheimer, calls an "instrumental rationality." In her analysis of Horkheimer (who was one of the first authors to examine the social production of ignorance), Alcoff argues that Horkheimer showed that reliance on what he called "instrumental rationality" often generates epistemologies of ignorance since it operates as "a kind of a dysfunctional cognitive norm, functional within very narrow parameters of capital accumulation and the maintenance of ideology" (50). In the case of the MGDP, it seems that the program of *mestizaje* operated as a form of instrumental rationality in at least two ways that created forms of pernicious ignorance. On one hand, it created a framework in which both politicians and scientists were inclined to ignore the relevance of diet changes and sedentary lifestyles for the health of Mexicans and to divert their efforts to the production of genomic knowledge since this was seen as a source of revenue. On the other hand, it obscured for them the fact that the very notions (e.g., *mestizo*) that were used in the production of genomic knowledge were not scientific concepts but pieces of a political ideology that had been previously deployed for nation-building purposes. Thus, nonepistemic (i.e., economic and political) motivations combined with epistemic forces in order to create a persuasive but ultimately false narrative about the needs, goals, and outcomes of the MGDP.

IV

I have argued that the program of *mestizaje*, in conjunction with other motivations, operated as an epistemology of ignorance that impacted the design and the carrying out of the MGDP. Though the MGDP was eventually put aside, the shift away was not accompanied by a change in the racialized conceptual framework underpinning the social imaginary of Mexican society—a framework in which the notions of *mestizo* and *indio* continue to play key organizing roles. In virtue of this, a pressing question arises: Is it possible to resist (even partially) the epistemology of ignorance that shaped the MGDP and that continues to distort the vision that Mexicans have of themselves and to harm those most vulnerable among them?

In response to this question, I suggest, using José Medina's work as a basis, that it is possible to develop an epistemology of resistance that may enable us to partially combat the effects of the aforementioned epistemology of ignorance. As I mentioned previously, one of the ways in which Medina suggests that this can be done is through the production of a "beneficial epistemic friction" that forces one to be self-critical and to compare and contrast one's beliefs. To be more specific, Medina proposes that the production of a beneficial epistemic friction can occur within the framework of a practice that he calls, following Foucault, an "insurrectionary genealogy." What is crucial to this practice is that, as Medina (2013, 286) indicates, it is "not only a way of refreshing or reviving our past in light of the present; it is the more radical attempt to make our present and our past alien to us . . . [through] the unearthing of the radical differences that lie within our practices and within ourselves, but which have been silenced, marginalized, stigmatized, excluded, or forgotten." Hence, undertaking insurrectionary genealogies enables us to question the very idea that our past is settled once and for all, because these practices provide, as Medina argues, "new venues for imaginative appropriations of a heterogeneous past, which in turn opens new paths for projections into the future" (292).

Let me be more precise. In the case of Mexico, I propose that one possible path to develop insurrectionary genealogies that could produce beneficial epistemic friction against social practices that result in pernicious forms of ignorance is provided by the reappraisal and retelling of Mexican history that has been accomplished in the last few decades by several Mexican artists and writers. In this reappraisal and retelling, various artists and writers have indeed produced works that challenge the Mexican *mestizo* identity and that, in so doing, have contributed to promoting what Medina (2013, 299) refers to as a "resistant imagination" that "is ready to confront relational possibilities that have been lost, ignored, or that remain to be discovered or invented." One very prominent example is the case of the writer Carlos Fuentes, who imagines in his novella "The Two Shores" (published in *The Orange Tree*) a scenario in which Amerindians take over the Iberian Peninsula.

Now, the purpose of imagining this scenario within the novella is not to remake the past, given that, as Medina (2013, 303–4) acknowledges, "a community of resistant memories cannot be formed if people simply make up the facts and choose whatever revisionary history is convenient for them." Rather, a better way to read Fuentes is as proposing an alternate reality that enables us to appreciate things that we did not consider before about our own world. In particular, one of the things that Fuentes (1994, 44) stresses in his description of how Amerindians conquer Spain is that, as this process unfolds, "the ultimate result was a mixing of bloods—Indian and Spanish but also Arab and Jew." In doing so, Fuentes brings attention to the fact that the Spanish population was (and still is) the product of different mixtures—thus challenging the myth of Spanish whiteness. Because of this, Fuentes's novella does three important things: (1) it points to a truth that the MGDP filtered out (namely, that the Spaniards were already a genetically mixed population, with important North African contributions),[35] (2) it suggests that the Mexican *mestizo* is much more complex than what was popularly and scientifically proposed (as it embodies cultural and genetic elements from different populations that stem from different geographical regions), and (3) it reveals the contingency of certain categories (such as *mestizo* or *indio*) that have been used scientifically but that also have an ideological origin.[36]

Once we realize that these categories are contingent, this opens up space for developing knowledge on the basis of new categories. For instance, rather than deploying the old socioracial categories, one could use a series of regional categories in the production of genomic knowledge. And, in fact, in a recent project of genomic research, an international team of scientists with which INMEGEN staff was associated has shown that, when this shift in categories is undertaken, Mexico's different subpopulations turn out to have a huge degree of genetic diversity that varies in accordance with the geographical locations that they inhabit (and not with the socioracial categories that have been attributed to them), as they acknowledge when they write that "the distribution of each Native American component across Mexico demonstrates a high correlation of individual admixture proportions with *geography, even in individuals of mixed ancestry*" (Moreno-Estrada et al. 2014, 1283; my emphasis). As we can appreciate, this passage clearly suggests that, if we leave aside the old socioracial categories of *criollo, mestizo,* and *indio* (since they are of rather questionable value, as Fuentes hints in his fiction) and use instead regional categories, we can then obtain better knowledge of the genetic variability existing across the Mexican population, since the socioracial categories fail to track any significant differences between different admixed Mexican subpopulations. Now, as I have argued (using the example of Carlos Fuentes's novella) that it is possible for Mexican artists to contest the traditional conception of Mexican identity through their works, art seems to have the ability to be used to develop "insurrectionary genealogies" that enable us to question the categories we use to produce knowledge (as well as ignorance). Thus, art could function as a tool to develop an epistemology of resistance against collective forms of pernicious ignorance.

V

I have argued that the program of *mestizaje* (which was developed and used as a nation-building tool in Mexico) functioned as an epistemology of ignorance that shaped the justification, the design, and the carrying out of the MGDP and that it is possible to develop a series of insurrectionary genealogies to challenge, at least partially, this epistemology of ignorance through art (in particular, through literature). If what I have argued for here is correct, there are at least two interesting lines of research that are worth pursuing. First, given that *mestizaje* flourished not only in Mexico but also in the rest of Latin America, as several authors (e.g., Miller 2004) have pointed out, it would be interesting to determine whether the program has also shaped other scientific projects in the region. Second, if *mestizaje* operated (perhaps in unison with other incentives and forces) as an epistemology of ignorance in other Latin American countries, it would be interesting to assess if there have been actions throughout the region that could be considered as contributing to an epistemology of resistance. I intend to tackle these two issues in future work.[37]

Notes

1. For a more thorough discussion of this, see Martha Menchaca (2001), chapter 7.

2. Though *mestizo* was initially used refer to any individual of mixed descent, the proliferation of mixed individuals during the colonial period as well as the Spanish need to control them led to the term being used to refer to the offspring of Spaniards (who were primarily men) and Amerindians (who were primarily women), while other terms (e.g., *lobo, coyote, cambujo, torna atrás*) were used to refer to other mixes.

3. It is crucial to keep in mind that, though the notion of *raza* (understood as lineage) came to dominate all facets of individual existence, this notion was quite different from the scientific notion of race that emerged in the nineteenth century. For a detailed account of the emergence of the scientific notion of race, see Jackson and Weidman (2006), chapters 2 and 3.

4. In particular, even though Amerindians had a legal status that mestizos lacked and were guaranteed certain protections, the social status of mestizos was often superior because they had closer contact with the ruling classes and spoke their language. For further discussion of this mismatch, see Mörner (1967, 60–61).

5. The absence of a fixed, stable meaning for the notion of *mestizo* can be appreciated by reflecting on the fact that its scope was constantly debated in colonial courts by people seeking to climb the social ladder. In particular, certain mestizos (and even mulattoes) were able to purchase *gracias al sacar* (i.e., certificates of whiteness) from the Spanish colonial government under certain circumstances. For further discussion of this, see Ann Twinam (2015).

6. Though this project may seem counterintuitive to US readers, it is important to keep in mind here that the one-drop rule did not exist in either New Spain or Mexico. Rather, the opposite was deemed to be the case: the addition of white blood was considered to improve the national stock. Thus, *mestizaje* was seen as a vehicle to whiten the population.

7. Agustín Basave Benítez (2002, 32): "El mestizo ya no es un medio sino un fin; es un ser que se vuelve deseable no por su cercanía al blanco sino en la medida en que se asemeja a sí mismo."

8. Justo Sierra (1948, 129–30): "Si se estudiase nuestra historia se vería que la Independencia y la Reforma no son más que actos de inmensa energía de la *raza bastarda* de México."

9. Justo Sierra (1948, 131): "La familia mestiza, llamada a absorber en su seno a los elementos que la engendraron . . . ha constituído el factor dinámico en nuestra historia."

10. Justo Sierra (1948, 130): "Los criollos ricos han constituído una clase pasiva, en donde el dogma político ha sido la incapacidad radical del pueblo mexicano para gobernarse a sí mismo."

11. Justo Sierra (1948, 145): "El indígena, lo mismo que el criollo rico, atesoraban, forma improductiva del ahorro improductivo, que no es por cierto la que da origen al capital."

12. Though the impact of Spencer was very deep in Latin America, it is important to remark that his views were both adopted and subverted, in the sense that while most Latin American intellectuals between 1850 and 1930 rejected his claims about the degeneration of mixed races, they accepted the existence of a hierarchy of races in which the order was reversed. This led to internal tensions in the thought of advocates of mestizaje because, though they claimed the program was geared to end racism, it was built on a hierarchical picture of racialized populations. For discussion of these tensions, see Alan Knight (1990).

13. Andrés Molina Enríquez (1909, 331–32): "Los mestizos . . . son generalmente serios, porque en ellos se neutralizan la taciturnidad de los indios y la alegría de los españoles, dando un término medio de dignidad austera y noble, de la cual nuestros grandes hombres han dado magníficos ejemplos."

14. To give a measure of how the ideology of *mestizaje* shaped immigration policy in Mexico, we just need to consider article 37 of the Mexican Law of Population of 1974 (which was only repealed in 2011): "The Secretariat of the Interior can deny entry to foreigners . . . when the national demographic balance demands it" (Gobierno Constitucional de los Estados Unidos Mexicanos 1974, 4).

15. These public-health campaigns were closely associated with antivice policing (which targeted mostly the poor) and a strict control of the labor force. For a thorough analysis of one of these campaigns in Veracruz between 1928 and 1932, see Alexandra Stern (2011).

16. These schools were designed with the goal of interrupting the transmission of culture (in particular, of language) from parents to children in Amerindian communities. For a discussion of the impact of these schools, see Courtney Jung (2008, 96).

17. Guillermo Zermeño (2011, 311): "Uno de los aspectos de esta noción moderna radica en que su construcción se hizo a costa de la desvalorización y reclusión de las poblaciones indígenas. Al tiempo que se magnificó la imagen del mestizo como metáfora de una nación progresista y emprendedora, se produjo una fabricación de una imagen del indio 'realmente existente' como una 'raza' en proceso de degradación."

18. The implementation of the mestizaje program was intimately connected to the development of a vigorous eugenics movement that flourished in the 1920s and 1930s in Mexico. For a detailed analysis of the link between mestizaje and eugenic practices in Mexico, see Laura Suárez y López Guazo (2001).

19. This is clearly shown by Carlos López-Beltrán and Vivette García Deister (2013).

20. Though Mexican anthropologists intended to demarcate themselves as clearly as possible from practitioners of racial science in the US and Europe, their views and practices still assumed a hierarchical conception of human populations framed in terms of culture.

21. Franz Boaz's (1969, 27) views about the influence of environmental and cultural factors on human diversity are expressed in this passage: "No convincing proof has ever been given of the hereditary character of complex functions that are found prevailing among a given people at the present time. We rather see that all racial strains, when subjected to the same social environment, develop the same functional tendencies."

22. In the case of the Yaquis, the Mexican Revolution did not change significantly their treatment by Mexican authorities, since the internal deportation policies carried out under Emilio Portes Gil had also been carried out previously at a larger scale under Porfirio Díaz (1877–1911). The Yaquis were allowed to return to their lands under Lázaro Cardenas (1934–1940), but attempts to "mexicanize" them by less violent means continued. For further discussion, see Gouy-Gilbert (1985).

23. For more details on the labor of Mexican human geneticists in the 1960s (and, in particular, of the pioneering work of Rubén Lisker), see Edna Suárez-Díaz (2014).

24. For a more detailed discussion of this motive, see Carlos López Beltrán, Vivette García Deister, and Mariana Ríos Sandoval (2014, 96).

25. Carlos López Beltrán and Francisco Vergara Silva (2011, 118): "Produce, sin embargo, cierto pasmo el traslado de conceptos emanados de la tradicional patrimonialización de objetos (arqueológicos, por ejemplo) o de recursos geológicos naturales a variantes moleculares que se reparten y se dispersan por toda la orbe."

26. In addition, another problematic aspect of the MGDP is that it seemed to be motivated by a need to follow the footsteps of scientific research projects in developed nations, as this replication gave Mexican scientific production a kind of legitimacy. This tendency to replicate research, as Goonatilake (1993) has argued, is problematic because it often prevents the creation of new modes of knowledge gathering in developing nations (I thank Nancy McHugh for this observation).

27. It is important to stress that this assumption is not specific to Mexican genomic research, but that scientists in other countries that are also engaged in cataloging and studying human genetic diversity share it. In particular, see Taussig (2009) for a thorough analysis of genomic research in the Netherlands.

28. Carlos López Beltrán and Francisco Vergara Silva (2011, 129): "poderosas fuerzas socioeconómicas actúan contra el acceso a la educación de los campesinos y de la clase trabajadora, especialmente en los niveles universitarios más altos."

29. In an opinion piece published in the newspaper La Crónica de Hoy, Fabrizzio Guerrero McManus (2009) severely criticized the socioeconomic bias in the sampling methodology used by INMEGEN (as well as other aspects of the project). In the months that followed the publication of this piece, there was increased public scrutiny of INMEGEN.

30. In particular, journalist Ángeles Cruz Martínez (2009) divulged to the public, in an article published in the newspaper La Jornada, that there were several instances of budget mismanagement during the tenure of Jiménez Sánchez, some of which raised suspicions of embezzlement during the construction of the building that houses INMEGEN.

31. This point is emphasized by Carlos López Beltrán, Vivette García Deister, and Mariana Ríos Sandoval (2014, 100).

32. In 2005, INMEGEN received a budget of Mex$298,666,300 (of which, Mex$164,299,872 was spent in the construction of the building). From 2005 to 2013, INMEGEN received Mex$2,700,939,900. I am extremely grateful to Vivette García Deister, Carlos López Beltrán, and the other members of their team who obtained these figures (and kindly shared them with me) after toiling for years to obtain public records and to comb through the information in them.

33. See, in particular, Gustavo Olaiz-Fernández et al. (2007, S333).

34. Carlos López Beltrán and Francisco Vergara Silva (2011, 141): "En cada ocasión se insistía en los mismos temas: la singularidad genómica mexicana, la necesidad de controlar el conocimiento genómico (del mexicano) y el ahorro en gastos de salud pública que eventualmente generarían en el futuro el uso de fármacos individualizados."

35. Indeed, in order to analyze degrees of admixture in the Mexican mestizo population, Silva-Zolezzi et al. (2009, 1811) used for comparative purposes data sets from other HapMap populations such as Northern Europeans (CEU). This specific use was, I think, problematic since it ignored the facts that the largest influx of European immigrants to Mexico came from the Iberian Peninsula (which is located in Southern Europe) and that this group was genetically admixed with significant contributions from North Africa. For more details on the genetic legacy of North Africa in the Iberian Peninsula, see Plaza et al. (2003).

36. In a private communication, Linda Martín Alcoff has wondered whether the analysis that I present here supports the claim that the *mestizo* category is more complicated than it is typically presented as or the claim that it should not be racialized at all. My view is that we should either completely dispense with the *mestizo* category (and this is my first preference) or, if we want to preserve it, we should at least acknowledge the very deep cultural and genetic complexity that lies behind it.

37. Several persons read prior versions of this essay and provided extremely valuable comments and suggestions that have improved it. In particular, I am grateful to Vivette García Deister, Carlos López Beltrán, Linda Martín Alcoff, José Medina, and the students in my Philosophy of Race course during the fall 2016 semester (especially Laurie Bohne, Alexa Brown, Danai Cruz, Alessandra Ragussin, Adam Marquez, Peter Schroeder, James Rose, and Jorge Proa). Last, but not least, I thank warmly Nancy McHugh and Heidi Grasswick for their generous dedication, strong encouragement, and long-lasting patience as they pushed me to clarify the ideas expressed here.

References

Alcoff, Linda Martín. 2007. "Epistemologies of Ignorance: Three Types." In *Race and epistemologies of ignorance*, edited by Shannon Sullivan and Nancy Tuana, 39–58. Albany: State University of New York Press.

Basave Benítez, Agustín. 2002. *México mestizo: Análisis del nacionalismo mexicano en torno a la mestizofilia de Andrés Molina Enríquez*. 2nd ed. Mexico City: Fondo de Cultura Económica.

Boaz, Franz. 1969. *Race and Democratic Society*. New York: Biblo and Tannen.

Chang, Jason. 2017. *Chino: Anti-Chinese Racism in Mexico, 1880–1940*. Champaign: University of Illinois Press.

Code, Lorraine. 1993. "Taking Subjectivity into Account." In *Feminist Epistemologies*, edited by Linda Alcoff and Elizabeth Potter, 15–48. New York: Routledge.

Cruz Martínez, Ángeles. 2009. "Sede del INMEGEN, inconclusa ante sinfín de anomalías en las obras." *La Jornada*, June 1, 2009. https://www.jornada.unam.mx/2009/06/01/sociedad/042n1soc.

Dotson, Kristie. 2011. "Tracking Epistemic Violence, Tracking Practices of Silencing." *Hypatia* 26 (2): 236–57.

Fuentes, Carlos. 1994. *The Orange Tree*. Translated by Alfred MacAdam. New York: Farrar, Straus and Giroux.

Gamio, Manuel. [1916] 2010. *Forjando patria, pro-nacionalismo (Forging a Nation)*. Translated by Fernando Armstrong-Fumero. Boulder: University of Colorado Press.

Gobierno Constitucional de los Estados Unidos Mexicanos. 1974. "Ley General de Población." *Diario Oficial de la Federación* 322 (4): 1–10. http://www.diputados.gob.mx/LeyesBiblio/ref/lgp/LGP_orig_07ene74_ima.pdf.

González Navarro, Moisés. 1970. "*Mestizaje* in Mexico during the National Period." In *Race and Class in Latin America*, edited by Magnus Mörner, 145–69. New York: Columbia University Press.

Goonatilake, Susantha. 1993. "Modern Science and the Periphery: The Characteristics of Dependent Knowledge." In *The "Racial" Economy of Science: Toward a Democratic Future*, edited by Sandra Harding, 259–68. Bloomington: Indiana University Press.

Gouy-Gilbert, Cécile. 1985. *Una resistencia india: Los Yaquis*. Mexico City: Instituto Nacional Indigenista.

Guerrero McManus, Fabrizzio. 2009. "Del Genoma mexicano, la dislexia genética y otros males postmodernos." *La Crónica de Hoy*, June 23, 2009. https://www.cronica.com.mx/notas/2009/440764.html.

Harding, Sandra. 1991. *Whose Science? Whose Knowledge? Thinking from Women's Lives*. Ithaca, NY: Cornell University Press.

Jackson, John P., Jr., and Nadine M. Weidman. 2006. *Race, Racism, and Science: Social Impact and Interaction*. New Brunswick, NJ: Rutgers University Press.

Jung, Courtney. 2008. *The Moral Force of Indigenous Politics: Critical Liberalism and the Zapatistas*. New York: Oxford University Press.

Knight, Alan. 1990. "Racism, Revolution, and *Indigenismo*: Mexico, 1910–1940." In *The Idea of Race in Latin America, 1870–1940*, edited by Richard Graham, 71–113. Austin: University of Texas Press.

Kuznesof, Elizabeth Anne. 1995. "Ethnic and Gender Influences on 'Spanish' Creole Society in Colonial Spanish America." *Colonial Latin American Review*, 4 (1): 153–76.

López Beltrán, Carlos, and Vivette García Deister. 2013. "Aproximaciones científicas al mestizo mexicano." *História, Ciências, Saúde-Manguinhos* 20 (2): 391–410.

López Beltrán, Carlos, Vivette García Deister, and Mariana Ríos Sandoval. 2014. "Neogtiating the Mexican Mestizo: On the Possibility of a National

Genomics." In *Mestizo Genomics. Race Mixture, Nation, and Science in Latin America*, edited by Peter Wade, Carlos López Beltrán, Eduardo Restrepo, and Ricardo Ventura Santos, 85–106. Durham, NC: Duke University Press.

López Beltrán, Carlos, and Francisco Vergara Silva. 2011. "Genómica nacional: El INMEGEN y el genoma del mestizo." In *Genes & Mestizos: Genómica y raza en la biomedicina mexicana*, edited by Carlos López Beltrán, 99–142. Mexico City: Ficticia.

Martínez, María Elena. 2008. *Geneological Fictions: Limpieza de Sangre, Religion, and Gender in Colonial Mexico*. Stanford, CA: Stanford University Press.

Medina, José. 2013. *The Epistemology of Resistance: Gender and Racial Oppression, Epistemic Injustice, and Resistant Imaginations*. New York: Oxford University Press.

Menchaca, Martha. 2001. *Recovering History, Constructing Race: The Indian, Black, and White Roots of Mexican Americans*. Austin: University of Texas Press.

Miller, Marilyn Grace. 2004. *Rise and Fall of the Cosmic Race: The Cult of Mestizaje in Latin America*. Austin: University of Texas Press.

Mills, Charles W. 1997. *The Racial Contract*. Ithaca, NY: Cornell University Press.

Molina Enríquez, Andrés. 1909. *Los grandes problemas nacionales*. Mexico City: Carranza e Hijos.

Moreno-Estrada, Andrés, Christopher R. Gignoux, Juan Carlos Fernández-López, Fouad Zakharia, Martin Sikora, Alejandra V. Contreras, Victor Acuña-Alonzo, Karla Sandoval, Celeste Eng, Sandra Romero-Hidalgo, et al. 2014. "The Genetics of Mexico Recapitulates Native American Substructure and Affects Biomedical Traits." *Science* 344 (6189): 1280–85.

Mörner, Magnus. 1967. *Race Mixture in the History of Latin America*. Boston: Little, Brown.

Olaiz-Fernández, Gustavo, Rosalba Rojas, Carlos A. Aguilar-Salinas, Juan Rauda, and Salvador Villalpando. 2007. "Diabetes mellitus en adultos mexicanos: Resultados de la Encuesta Nacional de Salud 2000." *Salud Pública de México* 49 (S3): S331–37.

Plaza, Stéphanie, Francesc Calafell, Ahmed Helal, N. Bouzerna, Gérard Lefranc, Jaume Bertranpetit, and David Comas. 2003. "Joining the Pillars of Hercules: mtDNA Sequences Show Multidirectional Gene Flow in the Western Mediterranean." *Annals of Human Genetics* 67 (4): 312–28.

Rénique, Gerardo. 2001. "Anti-Chinese Racism, Nationalism, and State Formation in Post-revolutionary Mexico, 1920s–1930s." *Political Power and Social Theory* 14: 91–140.

Sierra, Justo. 1948. "México social y político." 1889. In *Obras completas del maestro Justo Sierra*, vol. 9, edited by Agustín Yáñez, 125–69. Mexico City: Universidad Nacional Autónoma de México.

Silva-Zolezzi, Irma, Alfredo Hidalgo-Miranda, Jesus Estrada-Gil, Juan Carlos Fernandez-Lopez, Laura Uribe-Figueroa, Alejandra Contreras, Eros Balam-Ortiz, Laura del Bosque-Plata, David Velazquez-Fernandez, Cesar Lara, et al. 2009. "Analysis of Genomic Diversity in Mexican Mestizo Populations to Develop Genomic Medicine in Mexico." *PNAS* 106 (21): 8611–16.

Stern, Alexandra Minna. 2003. "From Mestizophilia to Biotypology: Racialization and Science in Mexico, 1920–1960." In *Race and Nation in Modern Latin America*, edited by Nancy P. Appelbaum, Anne S. Macpherson, and Karin Alejandra Rosemblatt, 187–210. Chapel Hill: University of North Carolina Press.

———. 2011. " 'The Hour of Eugenics' in Veracruz, Mexico: Radical Politics, Public Health, and Latin America's Only Sterilization Law." *Hispanic American Historical Review* 91 (3): 431–43.

Suárez-Díaz, Edna. 2014. "Indigenous Populations in Mexico: Medical Anthropology in the work of Ruben Lisker in the 1960s." *Studies in History and Philosophy of Biological and Biomedical Sciences* 47: 108–17.

Suárez y López Guazo, Laura. 2001. "The Mexican Eugenics Society: Racial Selection and Improvement." In *The Reception of Darwinism in the Iberian World: Spain, Spanish America and Brazil*, edited by Thomas F. Glick, Miguel Ángel Puig-Samper, and Rosaura Ruiz, 143–51. Dordrecht, Netherlands: Kluwer Academic.

Taussig, Karen-Sue. 2009. *Ordinary Genomes. Science, Citizenship, and Genetic Identities*. Durham, NC: Duke University Press.

Twinam, Ann. 2015. *Purchasing Whiteness: Pardos, Mulattos, and the Quest for Social Mobility in the Spanish Indies*. Stanford, CA: Stanford University Press.

Zermeño, Guillermo. 2011. "Del mestizo al mestizaje: Arqueología de un concepto." In *El peso de la sangre: Limpios, mestizos y nobles en el mundo hispánico*, edited by Nikolaus Böttcher, Brend Hausberger, and Max S. Hering Torres, 283–318. Mexico City: Colegio de México.

Chapter 11

Epistemic Activism and the Politics of Credibility

Testimonial Injustice Inside/Outside a North Carolina Jail

José Medina and Matt S. Whitt

Introduction

Over the last decade, the general public has become increasingly aware of the problems inherent in the United States' rampant use of incarceration. Often called "mass incarceration," the skyrocketing rate of punitive confinement has been analyzed across academic disciplines and the political spectrum. Nevertheless, carceral institutions remain largely invisible—spaces that are represented and imagined, but not known, to many Americans. Thus, carceral institutions present unique knowledge problems for the communities that they purportedly serve. These problems are simultaneously epistemic and political: correctional institutions are accountable to local publics that do not know—and may be actively discouraged from knowing—how they affect the individuals detained within them.

In this chapter we focus on one part of the carceral system, the jail: a facility primarily designed to house those who have not been convicted of a crime and who are legally presumed innocent while awaiting trial. Beyond the general invisibility/inaudibility of carceral institutions, the jail involves a peculiarly paradoxical epistemic injustice. While the public is required to treat (most) jail detainees as legally innocent, it subjects them to the stigma of presumed criminality and treats them as guilty in an epistemic sense—as untrustworthy narrators of experience and knowledge.

Thus, although detainee testimony could be a powerful source for public knowledge about the jail, the voices of detainees are rarely allowed to reach publics outside jails, and when such testimony becomes possible, it is typically discredited or ignored precisely because it is *detainee* testimony, and the detainees themselves are unfairly disqualified from speaking about the conditions of their own lives. This kind of epistemic injustice, we argue, can only be appreciated through the detailed analysis of a case study, because the injustice occurs not merely in the transactions between a testifier and an audience but in specific relations between epistemic contexts and patterns of communicative interaction.

While jails are invisible and unknown to much of the general public, the communities most directly affected by the criminal justice system have different perspectives. In particular, incarcerated detainees themselves have concrete, firsthand experience of the conditions within jails, and they know a good deal about how these institutions work. They know the official policies of particular facilities, and they know how informal practices deviate from these policies. Most of all, they know how incarceration impacts detainees, their families, and communities. This knowledge would be greatly beneficial to the publics that are presumably served by and purportedly oversee local jails. However, detainees are often rendered invisible and inaudible (or precariously visible and audible) by the conditions of their incarceration. Additionally, they are subject to stigmas of criminality and untrustworthiness that public discourses attach to all persons deemed offenders by the criminal justice system, regardless of their guilt or innocence. Silenced and stigmatized in these ways, jail detainees are subject to particular forms of epistemic injustice. They are harmed in their capacities as epistemic subjects when their voices are silenced, their experiences are obscured, and their testimonies are distorted by the conditions of their incarceration.[1] And this, in turn, reinforces wider public ignorance about the operations and effects of carceral institutions.

In this chapter, we argue that jail detainees face particular credibility challenges and testimonial injustices that can only be properly diagnosed by looking at the specific epistemic context of jail and the communicative practices within and around that institution. To this end, we build on Karen Jones's (2002) powerful arguments for a "politics of credibility." Drawing on decades of research in feminist epistemology, Jones argues that epistemic matters are practical, interpersonal matters. As such, they cannot be analyzed simply in terms of abstract rules that agents follow (155). Rather, they must also be analyzed in terms of norms embedded in concrete interactions between epistemic agents, as well as the specific capacities that agents may cultivate and exercise through these interactions (170–72). While we affirm Jones's core insight that social epistemology must proceed case by case, by considering concrete interactions and the norms governing them, we nonetheless argue that Jones's approach is limited when it comes to diagnosing the testimonial injustices faced by jail detainees. Her framework rightly calls attention to the immediate context of inter-personal epistemic exchanges; however, it does not adequately account for the wider social and institutional contexts and patterns of interaction that structure not only the acts of giving and receiving testimony but also the norms that guide these acts. Thus, in the end, Jones diagnoses testimonial injustice as an *ethical* problem—the failure of a listener to follow certain rules and practice certain virtues when ascribing credibility to a speaker's testimony (159, 164–65, 172). We argue that unjust credibility assessments involve much more than this: they involve a *political* problem.

Beyond the normative attitudes and interpersonal relations of par-ticular epistemic actors, testimonial injustice also involves wider contests for knowledge. These contests are shaped by the positions, power, and agency of their participants and also the wider social context in which the contests are fought, as well as the patterns of social action that impact the effectiveness of any particular epistemic "move" within these contests. Turning to our central example, jail detainees face testimonial injustices that cannot be adequately diagnosed as the general public's refusal or failure to be good listeners when detainees speak on particular matters. Rather, the institutional context of the jail, the limited means of communi-cating from inside to outside, and the wider patterns of social interaction that routinely position detainees as "criminal" all shape how different audiences receive detainee testimony. More still, detainee testimonies are subject to contestation, silencing, and undermining by other speakers who offer explicit countertestimonies or implicitly discredit the stories of those held in jail. In other words, with regard to detainee testimony at least, credibility assessments involve contests over social, political, and epistemic power. Thus, to make good on Jones's promise of a "politics of credibility," we take her practical shift in epistemology a step further, from the norms governing interpersonal interactions to the wider social contexts and practices through which differently situated agents give tes-timony and ascribe credibility. Put simply, our analysis locates epistemic injustice in the *polis* and not only in the *ethos* of epistemic actors. This enables us to highlight forms of epistemic resistance and activism that might disrupt both the normative attitudes and interpersonal relations that discredit detainee testimonies, and the wider contexts and patterns of interaction that prevent detainees from effectively speaking about the conditions of their own lives.

To this end, we use a case study of one particular jail, the Durham County Detention Facility (hereafter DCDF) in Durham, North Carolina, to explore social, political, and epistemic contests for knowledge of carceral institutions. DCDF is the subject of controversy within the surrounding community, as reports of neglect, abuse, and death in the facility have for years captured public attention. These reports come primarily from firsthand accounts of individuals currently or previously incarcerated in the jail, although many have been corroborated by community activists and investigative journalists. While many in the general public are inclined to discount or disregard the testimonies of prisoners, DCDF detainees have found innovative ways to get the word out, including allying with Inside-Outside Alliance, a group of incarcerated and unincarcerated organizers that seeks to "amplify" the voices of detainees.[2] By studying this contest for public knowledge about the jail, we will expand Jones's framework to better account for both the social contexts in which credibility assessments are made and the social practices (or patterns of interactions) that connect testimony givers and their audiences. We will argue that only through a social contextualist and social interactionist shift can practical epistemology gain the conceptual resources to offer a politics (and not just an ethics) of credibility.

Jail and the Politics of Credibility

Recently, much attention has been given to the social and political significance of confining individuals in state and federal prisons. Less attention has been paid to jails, the city- or county-level facilities where individuals are typically detained for shorter periods while they await trial or serve out misdemeanor sentences.[3] This oversight is unfortunate. Jails instantiate the same problems as prisons, including overcrowding, unsanitary conditions, seemingly arbitrary administrative policies, violence, neglect, and abuse. Moreover, individuals are spending more and more time locked up in jails, which function for many as the front door of the prison system. However, jails are perhaps even more invisible and less well known to the general public than prisons. This has nothing to do with their literal visibility—jails are often sited in city centers, in full view of the public, while prisons are increasingly removed to rural areas—but rather with the higher rate of population turnover in jails. Because prisons are designed for long-term detention, they typically host a variety of durable relationships to the outside world. Through these relationships, family members, educators, social workers, religious leaders, reporters, lawyers, state- and national-level supervisors, academic observers, and visitors such as school groups and even tourists can gain some knowledge of carceral facilities. Conversely, due to their higher turnover rate, jails typically lack these durable relationships. Thus, they remain relatively unknown to persons who have neither been detained nor worked within their walls. Moreover, given the uneven social distribution of policing, surveillance, arrest, detention, and conviction, some segments of society—notably whiter, more affluent, and more politically powerful segments—have little secondhand information of local jails, even as the news media flood with stories about state and federal prisons. In short, local jails are blank spots on many residents' cognitive maps of their own cities and counties. As such, they are sites of unique epistemic problems, with high stakes for both prisoners and outside residents.

For years, detainees have reported inadequate conditions in DCDF, as well as inappropriate treatment by correctional staff. They have consistently reported day-to-day problems like unsanitary sleeping mats and food trays, cold cells and inadequate blankets, hikes in fees for medical attention coupled with routine medical neglect, inflated prices for commissary items that are standard in other correctional facilities (such as shower shoes) or specifically necessary in DCDF (thicker blankets or thermal underwear), and limited recreation and visitation time.[4] Detainees have also reported more severe problems. These include the seemingly arbitrary use of jail-wide "lock-back," or punitive confinement, for several months in 2015, at the height of which all prisoners were confined to their cells 95 percent of the time, with only two hours every two days in which to shower, exercise, call loved ones or legal help, purchase items in the commissary, exercise, or access writing instruments and educational resources. Other severe problems include assaults by correctional officers, which led to the firing of two staff members in 2015, and inattention to prisoners' emergency calls, which resulted in the death of at least one detainee, Matthew McCain, in January 2016.[5]

In their attempts to report on these conditions, DCDF detainees face testimonial difficulties that constitute epistemic injustices: they are mistreated as subjects of knowledge and understanding. But these epistemic injustices also facilitate the production and perpetuation of nonepistemic harms, including even death. Thus, epistemic injustices are deeply intertwined with social and political injustices. As our analysis will show, the testimonial difficulties faced by jail detainees are of three kinds: (1) difficulties in reporting at all, in getting the word out about their experiences and the conditions of their incarceration; (2) difficulties in being understood in their own terms, without being coopted, reinterpreted, or misinterpreted; and (3) difficulties in being believed, in being trusted and treated fairly as reliable informants. The first kind of difficulty concerns silencing, while the second concerns hermeneutical distortions. This chapter focuses on the third kind of testimonial difficulty, which concerns credibility deficits. Nevertheless, it is important to keep in mind that testimonial injustices rooted in credibility deficits are compounded by (often systematic forms of) silencing and misinterpretation.[6]

These testimonial difficulties have high stakes, not only for detainees themselves but also for wider publics that depend, whether or not they know it, on detainees for important knowledge. In Durham, detainee reports are the primary avenue of information regarding the problems within DCDF, as both the local media and the sheriff's office only comment once the reports circulate beyond the jail walls. The recent death of Matthew McCain offers an illuminating example. According to his loved ones, McCain had reported months of insufficient and inconsistent medical treatment for his diabetes and epilepsy while incarcerated in DCDF.[7] Then, early on January 19, 2016, McCain suffered a seizure while detainees in his pod repeatedly pressed emergency call buttons and yelled for help. According to detainee witnesses, these calls were not answered by the detention officer on duty, and McCain died without assistance. The Durham sheriff's office does not publicly announce in-custody deaths, except to oversight officials and the deceased's registered next of kin, so previous deaths in the jail have garnered no press coverage and little public attention. This time, however, detainee witnesses immediately reached out through intermediaries to the community organizers of Inside-Outside Alliance. Convinced that McCain's death was a direct result of medical neglect and unresponsiveness by detention officers, detainee witnesses wanted to alert McCain's loved ones and draw attention to conditions in the jail. Together with McCain's family, Inside-Outside Alliance broke the story to local news media and published reports on its own website, Amplify Voices Inside. In turn, inquiries from journalists prompted the sheriff's office and the Durham County Department of Public Health to release public statements on McCain's death and to acknowledge two other recent deaths in the jail.[8]

In this case, the testimonies of incarcerated individuals were essential to public knowledge of three recent deaths in a public institution. Moreover, they provided information that official sources are unlikely to reveal, including the fact that emergency calls went unanswered. In these ways, prisoner testimonies enabled more comprehensive knowledge of the jail and provided counterweight to official reports that emphasized the professionalism and responsiveness of jail administrators.

However, jail-detainee testimonies often go unheard in public discourse. This is in part because of patterns of silencing that are enforced structurally (by the institutional design of detention facilities) and agentially (by the action or inaction of detention staff and administrators). But more than this, even when they are not actively silenced, detainees are subject to unfair credibility deficits that can undermine their testimony. Disbelief and disregard are widely accepted ways to treat individuals who are presumed to be uncivil, self-serving, untrustworthy, infamous, or otherwise "criminal." The sociologist Victor Rios (2011, xiv) defines criminalization as "the processes by which styles and behaviors are rendered deviant and are treated with shame, exclusion, punishment, and incarceration." Criminalized individuals are also treated, we might add, with disbelief or disregard; they are viewed as unreliable in many senses, including in their capacities as truth-tellers and narrators of their own experiences. As Rios (2011, xiv) emphasizes, criminalization is a social process that happens "beyond the law," interpellating individuals as criminal, regardless of their guilt or innocence, by symbolically associating them with real or imagined deviance in the eyes of many members of the public (Butler 2004, 71, 76). This is the sense in which most DCDF detainees are criminalized. As in most jails, the vast majority of DCDF detainees are pretrial detainees who are legally presumed innocent, and most of them are not deemed dangerous. Rather, they are incarcerated because they cannot afford to pay the bonds that ensure their appearance in court.[9] Among other things, this means that individual detainees may be no more deviant, untrustworthy, volatile, or criminal than many of us who walk and speak freely.[10] Nevertheless, because they are incarcerated, their testimonies are *detainee* testimonies. Thus, they are subjected to the negative credibility assessments that accompany criminalization, even when their testimonies are mere descriptions of their own surroundings. In short, the conditions of possibility of their firsthand, concrete knowledge of the jail are precisely what disqualifies that knowledge in the eyes of the general public.

Credibility deficits are relational—that is, comparative and contrastive—and detainee testimonies can be especially vulnerable to disbelief and disregard when they are opposed by the countertestimonies of other agents.[11] In many respects, jail staff members and detainees may be similarly situated, especially when they share the same class, race, geographic, and sometimes even family connections. However, when their testimonies diverge, staff members are much better positioned to be regarded as trustworthy and knowledgeable than detainees. In particular, detention officers and administrators may benefit from ascriptions of professionalism, officialdom, and expertise in much the same way that prisoners are disadvantaged by ascriptions of criminality. Moreover, officers and administrators can cooperate and share information with one another, while prisoners may be discouraged or prohibited from doing so; they also have better access to "legitimate" avenues of information and communication, such as official reports, press conferences, and partnerships with other governmental institutions, which may help them seem credible in ways that prisoners do not. These patterns of credibility excesses and deficits do not necessarily track truthfulness or epistemic reliability in any traditional philosophical sense; nor do they necessarily reflect the differently situated speakers' interests in knowing or telling the truth. Consequently, they create dysfunctional testimonial dynamics in which some voices (those of correctional officers) are systematically and disproportionally trusted, while other voices (those of detainees) are systematically and disproportionally distrusted, especially by audiences who believe or assume that the criminal justice system functions efficiently and fairly for all. These unfair credibility assessments can bias potential audiences even before they look into the truth of conflicting reports. Worse still, they can preclude independent investigation and corroboration altogether.[12]

As a result, detainee testimonies about jail conditions are much like the "astonishing reports" that Karen Jones (2002, 154) analyzes in her foundational work on "the politics of credibility": these reports face systematic incredulity, in part because they conflict with what audiences take themselves to know. According to Jones, when it comes to astonishing reports, grounds of credibility pull in multiple directions as we are forced to reconcile the competence and veracity of informants on the one hand with the incredibility of astonishing claims, vis-à-vis our accepted background knowledge, on the other hand (156–58). For example, if a climate scientist reports that the sea level is rising, while all the time I've lived at the beach I have not noticed any change and have paid no attention to debates in climate science, I am forced to weigh my view of the scientist's competence and veracity (i.e, her trustworthiness) on this particular topic against my confidence in my own relevant background beliefs. As Jones emphasizes, this is a practical, domain-specific, and case-by-case endeavor. It is practical in the sense that it involves "concrete, contested, epistemological questions" requiring situated acts of interpretation and judgment, rather than abstract or formal puzzles (154). It is domain-specific insofar as my assessment of the report's credibility should reflect the informant's trustworthiness "with regard to this exchange of information regarding p" (e.g., rising sea levels), even if her competence is different in other areas, for example, in projecting stock market trends (156). Finally, assessing the credibility of astonishing reports is a case-by-case endeavor insofar as each astonishing report is different, requiring credibility assessments that take into account the specifics of the informant, the topic, the particular testimonial exchange, and the audience's beliefs (162–63).

By approaching testimonial exchanges in a practical, domain-specific, and case-by-case way, we are better attuned to social and political dynamics at work between the givers and receivers of testimony. These dynamics are especially apt to influence credibility assessments in situations like our case study, in which informants are regarded as incompetent or untrustworthy from the start. Jones writes: "Testifiers who belong to 'suspect' social groups and who are bearers of strange tales can thus suffer a double disadvantage. They risk being doubly deauthorized as knowers on account of who they are and what they claim to know. If we operate with norms of credibility that do not take into account the influence of background beliefs and of prejudice on our credibility judgments, there is a very real risk of committing epistemic injustice" (158). Incarcerated individuals who report abuse and neglect behind bars are indeed, in the eyes of many, "suspect" bearers of strange tales that conflict with background assumptions about the criminal justice system. And yet, the very basis of their suspiciousness is also the basis of their knowledge. *Because they are in the jail, they know the jail; but because they are in the jail, their knowledge is viewed as untrustworthy.* In the eyes of many potential audiences, the detainees in DCDF are "doubly deauthorized," as Jones puts it. They are at special risk for testimonial injustice.

To respond to situations like this, Jones proposes three rules for guiding how audiences should receive astonishing reports, especially when

302 | José Medina and Matt S. Whitt

they are given by presumably suspect informants. First, separately assess the trustworthiness of the informant and the plausibility of their report; then, and only then, assess the credibility of the report in light of the fact that it is given by that informant (159). Second, when it is reasonable to distrust one's own distrust or judgments of implausibility, let this rebut the presumption against accepting astonishing reports (164). Third, let the burden of seeking corroborating evidence vary inversely with how reasonable it is to trust one's own tendency to trust this type of informant and one's confidence in the background knowledge weighed against this kind of report (165). Taken together, these rules ask us to "investigate our tendencies to trust and distrust" so that we might assess the credibility of astonishing reports with better judgment and less prejudice (168). Jones acknowledges that rules alone cannot ameliorate dysfunctions in testimonial dynamics, especially if audiences are not apt to follow the rules well. However, developing "affective and perhaps even moral capacities," such as empathy, kindness, and respect, can help (155, 171–72). All told, Jones advocates an ethical-epistemic shift, at the personal and interpersonal level, so that individuals may ameliorate testimonial injustices when they encounter astonishing, unexpected, or heterodox testimony from "suspect" informants.

Although we fully agree with Jones that the study of credibility in practical epistemology must proceed case by case, we argue that such an approach cannot only center on ethical-epistemic norms and capacities without also accounting for particular social-institutional contexts and patterns of interaction. Indeed, the case study of jail is particularly well suited for showing this. If we focus only on ethical-epistemic norms and capacities, then we risk reinscribing the epistemic injustices that detainees face, because these norms and capacities are already stacked against them. Detainees, in particular, are widely presumed to be undeserving of the very ethical-epistemic capacities, like empathy, that Jones highlights as being necessary for combatting epistemic injustice (171–72). But, as we will argue, this presumption is itself an effect of the social-institutional contexts and patterns of interaction in contests for knowledge; jail detainees are viewed as undeserving of empathy because they are criminalized. Thus, for a politics of credibility that can diagnose—and perhaps even resist—the particular testimonial injustices that arise in a setting like jail, it is not enough to take into account particular subjects' relations to particular topics, or their particular ethical-epistemic capacities, or those of potential audiences, because these operate differently, and are qualified or disqualified differently, for different subjects in different contexts and different patterns of interaction. To understand the systemic silencing and credibility deficits that detainees suffer, we need to take into account the specific epistemic features of the social-institutional contexts of the jail, its various relations to other contexts, and the patterns of interaction that take place within and between relevant contexts.

Thus, besides the practical shift in epistemology that Jones forcefully argues for (and on which we build), we propose two additional shifts: a social-contextualist shift and a social-interactionist shift. By deepening Jones's practical shift through wider forms of social contextualism and social interactionism, we aim to make practical epistemology more socially alive and socially engaged. In particular, we highlight the roles that audiences as well as informants and their allies play in confronting testimonial injustice. To this end, we theorize forms of epistemic activism that seek to ameliorate the social-epistemic contexts and practices that structure testimonial interactions, rather than just the individual norms and capacities that guide credibility assessments. Besides better describing the risks of testimonial injustice, our expanded framework highlights something that Jones does not explicitly acknowledge, namely, the agency of marginalized informants in combatting the injustices they face. For Jones, ameliorating testimonial injustice requires audiences to become better listeners when considering the reports of marginalized or suspect informants. For us, it is also a matter of suspect informants, perhaps together with their allies, actively resisting or subverting the contexts, practices, and conditions that work against their reports. In short, we believe that responding to testimonial injustice requires more than the *ethics* of credibility that Jones, in the end, advocates. To make good on her exciting promise of a *politics* of credibility, we need to consider not only the interpersonal interactions of informant and audience but also the multiple social and institutional terrains on which contests for knowledge, belief, and voice are fought.

The Social-Contextualist Shift: Jail and Its Surrounding Contexts

Credibility does not exist in a vacuum, nor merely in particular interpersonal exchanges between an informant and an audience. Rather, it is gained and lost in social contexts of interaction; and the details of the wider, preexisting context matter deeply for understanding why particular subjects are perceived as having or lacking credibility within particular exchanges. What is the positionality of the relevant subjects (speaking and knowing subjects as well as the ascribers of credibility) within that context? What set of relations bind them together or set them apart? A subject's utterance or contribution may be appraised quite differently across contexts and by differently situated subjects within the same context. For this reason, it becomes essential to explore social contexts in a pluralistic and heterogeneous way. We must pay attention to how a given social context is differently inhabited, understood, and navigated by differently positioned subjects, as well as how that social context relates or fails to relate to other contexts in which the epistemic dynamics are different. These contextualist and intercontextualist modes of examination are both crucial for identifying possibilities for critique, resistance, and subversion that can ameliorate epistemic contexts and correct dysfunctional dynamics within and between them.

Within a given social context, different subjects occupy different positions and negotiate epistemic, ethical, and sociopolitical relations differently. The contexts themselves are established and maintained structurally and agentially, that is, by structural conditions and designs and also by the way they are inhabited, by the attitudes and relations that epistemic agents express, and by the patterns of epistemic actions and reactions produced in that context.[13] However, social contexts are not static; they are constantly negotiated, and their boundaries are fluid, which is why they should be conceived not as fully formed entities with sharp and definitive edges but as (often tentative, fragile, and fluid) social constructions that are always in the making and always relative to other contexts. Moreover, social contexts are not fully insulated or sealed off from one another. Rather, they intersect, overlap, and interact in all kinds of ways, and the interrelations among them are essential to understanding how any given context is formed, operates, and can be transformed. Thus, we need to investigate their interrelations in order to understand the dynamics within them. For these reasons, we examine social contexts in terms of how they are multiply constructed from the inside by those who inhabit them and also in terms of how they relate (or fail to relate) to the wider social terrain (that is, to neighboring—and sometimes also far-away—contexts, to other social constructions of the same kind). In our view, the trust and distrust cultivated within a certain social context create presumptions of credibility or incredulity that attach to particular subject positions and to particular testimonial contents, both within that context and across multiple contexts.[14] So, once we begin to analyze testimonial injustices in terms of the wider social context in which they are situated, the contextual analysis must immediately become an *inter*contextual analysis.

Within the context of the Durham County Detention Facility, an important source of epistemic dysfunction is found in the pattern of distrust that jail detainees face: their testimonies are received with systematic suspicion by guards and administrators, and this creates an unfair credibility deficit for detainees that disadvantages their voices in testimonial dynamics. This situation is passively aggravated by the fact that some guards and administrators enjoy credibility excesses granted by other jail staff members. It is actively aggravated, moreover, by the way correctional officers are explicitly and implicitly trained to not trust, fraternize with, or empathize with incarcerated persons. Consequently, within the jail, the voices of guards and administrators can easily overpower those of detainees. Indeed, in hundreds of detainee letters collected by Inside-Outside Alliance, there is a repeated theme of jail staff members verbally minimizing, dismissing, or doubting detainee complaints and requests out of hand. A computerized system now enables detainees to file grievances and monitor their status, and this ostensibly makes the grievance process more efficient and transparent. However, the grievances are routed to over one hundred potentially responsible parties, and detainees report that grievances are not resolved, progress is not updated, or that complaints and requests fall into gaps in the system.[15] In this way, the computerized system reinforces a social-epistemic context in which detainee voices are systematically disadvantaged within the jail, even as it provides the appearance of technological impartiality and efficiency. This adds to the unfair epistemic advantage of jail staff and administrators so that, when reports conflict, detainee reports are already suspect, regardless of whether they are true.

These testimonial dysfunctions within the jail interact with other testimonial dysfunctions that take place in the relationships between the jail and other local epistemic contexts. Hence, we need to adopt an *inter*contextual analysis that might seem, at first, inappropriate for our case study. DCDF is, like most carceral facilities, a deliberately isolated space, in which detainees are largely cut off from outsiders. For this reason, the jail may seem like a self-contained and fully separate context for epistemic exchanges. But appearances are indeed deceiving. Separation is itself a relation, and this is more obvious when separation is maintained by principle and cultivated practice. Even contexts purposefully insulated from each other are in fact intrinsically connected and must be analyzed in their intercontextual relations. Just as others have emphasized the social porosity of carceral facilities (Davis and Dent 2001; Whitt 2015), we emphasize the epistemic porosity of the jail. In this case, the stark contrast between the "inside" and the "outside" of a context of epistemic action makes the question of intercontextuality even more pressing. To address how jail detainees are epistemically appraised by outside publics, we need to interrogate the apparent contextual separations between *inside* and *outside*, *lawlessness* and *lawfulness*, *untrustworthy* and *trustworthy*.

Relations between epistemic contexts can escalate testimonial injustices. The local community often does not hear the detainees within the DCDF, because many within that community inhabit a different, seemingly separate epistemic context from the one located behind jail doors. This is due in part to the detainees' confinement within a concrete building that only selectively grants access to the public. Speaking outward from the context of the jail, prisoner voices are mainly carried over phone calls, through the mail, via visiting hours, and in court appearances—all of which can be slow, expensive, restrictive, intermittent, obstructed, and subject to surveillance and censorship. Transmitted by these means, it is rare that prisoner voices are heard by anyone who is not intentionally seeking them out and listening, so they make little connection with the public at large, or the officials who command municipal power.

But beyond this silencing, prisoners are often ignored or disregarded by the wider public, even when they are heard, because discursive contexts stigmatize prisoners and encourage outside audiences to discount their testimonies. In the media, especially, prisoners are positioned as inherently unlike the presumed speakers and listeners of public discourse, a quarantined group that neither speaks nor is spoken to but is only spoken about. For instance, news coverage frequently lists the charges against detainees even when the charges are irrelevant, as in coverage of the conditions within carceral facilities. In much the same way that news coverage identifies unincarcerated subjects by their professions (e.g., local teacher, line cook), it identifies incarcerated subjects by their charges, even when they have not been convicted of those charges (e.g., narcotics possession, burglary). This rhetorically separates detainees from the (presumedly law-abiding) audience, so that even when detainee voices are present in news stories, they speak from the other side of an implicit them/us divide. This is the case, for example, in some of the news coverage of Matthew McCain's death in DCDF, which listed his charges toward the beginning of news stories, identifying him as criminal even before identifying him as epileptic and diabetic although the latter were far more germane to the breaking news.[16]

More generally, a series of oppositions structures relations between the context of the jail and the context of the wider local public. Detainees are often regarded as a collective "them," defined by their position inside the jail, which suggests their criminality and therefore their untrustworthiness. Conversely, the presumed speakers and listeners of public discourse are a collective "us," defined by our position outside, which suggests our lawfulness and therefore our trustworthiness. But these discursive oppositions artificially distinguish detainees and free persons in terms of credibility, essentializing their subject positions in a way that presents a bright line between an untrustworthy "them" and an epistemically reliable "us." The distinction should itself be regarded with suspicion. The vast majority of jail detainees have not been found guilty of a crime, while many persons who are not detained have indeed committed illegal acts and other violations of trust that call into question their own trustworthiness. There are many factors that determine who goes to jail and who does not; consequently, the fact of jail incarceration (or the fact of walking freely) is not a reliable indicator of credibility. Nevertheless, because much of the free public puts faith in the proper functioning of the criminal justice system—in particular, the white, middle-class people who have relatively little antagonistic contact with that system—the artificial opposition between untrustworthy detainee and trustworthy outsider becomes taken for granted.[17] Thus it appears that detainees inhabit a discursive (epistemic, social, political) context defined by its (apparent) separation from the context that "trustworthy" subjects inhabit. The relation between these contexts matters deeply—here, testimonial injustice is intercontextual.

To see this, consider the ways in which jail detainees are discredited through intercontextual forms of criminalization. At a 2016 public forum on conditions within the Durham County Detention Facility, a community member spoke about the abusive and exploitative treatment he received while awaiting trial in DCDF and likened the jail's disproportionate impact on Black residents to the Ku Klux Klan. In response, Major Paul Martin of the Durham County Sheriff's Office ignored the community member's testimony about abuse and seized on the metaphorical reference to the KKK, saying that "people are overblowing and distorting the truth." After the moderator called for more respect in the room, Major Martin's next remarks attempted to bury the community member's testimony under the stigma of criminality: "Law enforcement needs some respect too. . . . You're not going to call us out like that. *Why were you in jail?*" ("Child support.") "Ok, who put you there? *We did not put you there.*"[18] The question "*Why were you in jail?*" rhetorically recriminalized the community member and, in contrast to Major Martin's call for respect for law enforcement, reinforced the assumed divide between trustworthy and untrustworthy reporters on "the truth" about conditions in the jail. Notably, Major Martin did not engage the testifier's claims that he received threats of electrocution from jail staff members and that he "gave them 960 hours of free labor. . . . It's not voluntary."[19] In a public forum designed to connect carceral and civic contexts, the jail's representative did not rebut the content of this testimony but instead relied on the stigma of (re)criminalization to undermine the trustworthiness of the testifier and thus the credibility of his claims.

As Victor Rios (2011, xiv) argues, criminalization occurs "beyond the law"; consequently, criminalizing discourses can mark individuals as socially sanctioned targets of "shame, exclusion, punishment, and incarceration" regardless of whether they have been, or would ever be, found guilty. Lisa Cacho (2012) highlights an affective element of criminalization that is directly relevant to the media's portrayal of McCain: criminalization present targets as "ineligible for sympathy and compassion" (37) and "forecloses empathy" (82). This affective aspect of criminalization is inseparable from its epistemic aspect. As social epistemologists, including Karen Jones, have argued, speakers and their audiences can adopt certain norms, such as meta-level self-distrust, and practice certain epistemic and moral capacities, such as empathy, in order to ameliorate epistemic dysfunction (Code 1987; Jones 2002). But criminalization designates certain individuals as inappropriate recipients of this epistemic and moral work, marking them as ineligible not only for empathy but also for the forms of listening, verifying, trusting, and corroborating with which we typically receive other speakers. In short, the criminalization inherent in existing relations between "inside" and "outside" contexts does not simply mark detainees as "other." It also undermines their status as epistemic subjects. It bears repeating that this criminalization does not track violations of the law. Many of us who are not criminalized have violated the law, and many who are criminalized are in fact law abiding.

If epistemic injustice occurs not only within specific contexts but also intercontextually, then resistance and amelioration must also happen within and between contexts. In Durham, struggles against epistemic injustice (and injustice more generally!) have usually involved intercontextual strategies, in which activists inside and outside the jail work to correct the dysfunctional dynamics between epistemic contexts. For Inside-Outside Alliance (hereafter IOA), this has involved disrupting the dichotomies of inside/outside, them/us, criminal/lawful, and trustworthy/untrustworthy that purportedly separate the jail's detainees from their neighbors. Describing the jail as a "revolving door" capable of moving anyone into and out of incarceration at a moment's notice, a statement on IOA's website challenges the presumption that persons housed within the jail are more guilty, criminal, or dangerous than persons who walk free outside of it.[20] And, in direct response to the media's tendency to paint detainees like McCain as always already and always only criminals, IOA statements describe McCain as "a loving son, boyfriend, and father," feature pictures of him with his loved ones, and emphasize his leadership and volunteering in the local community.[21] These depictions do not cause the reader to judge McCain differently so much as they ask the reader to see McCain as something more than simply an object of judgment: a person, a community member, and a voice—a potential recipient of empathy and trust. In this way, IOA challenges the presumption of physical, moral, and social differentiation between the jail and the wider Durham community and also the criminalization inherent in that particular intercontextual relation.

Changing intercontextual dynamics often requires repeated interventions to denounce and disrupt patterns of epistemic neglect and dysfunction. This is what we call *epistemic activism*, transgressive forms of epistemic interaction that call attention to, and potentially disrupt, contexts, intercontextual relations, and patterns of interaction that contribute to epistemic injustice. Specifically, epistemic activism can augment the epistemic agency of unfairly disadvantaged subjects, amplifying their voices and facilitating the development and exercise of their epistemic capacities. It can also wake up potential audiences from their epistemic slumbers, inviting them to attend to contexts of epistemic marginalization and to the voices that come from those contexts, stimulating new and improved epistemic attitudes and habits across contexts, potentially leading to more-just dynamics. As we have argued in this section, the normative dimension of practical epistemology springs from and leads to socially situated epistemic *actions* where we can properly diagnose epistemic dysfunctions and where problems cry out for interventions and transformative practice—that is, for epistemic activism. This has been recently argued in forceful ways in feminist theory and disability studies, where the expressions *activist epistemology* and *epistemic activism* have been developed

(Hamraie 2015). Calls for epistemic subversions and transformations have also been issued by intersectional approaches to racial, gender, and sexual oppression. This literature contains a broad and rich repertoire of strategies for epistemic activism, such as epistemic disobedience (Mignolo 2009), disorientating/tricking (Ahmed 2006, Lugones 2003), and resistant logics/languages/imaginations (Lugones 2003; Ortega 2006; Medina 2013). It is not accidental that these activist perspectives in social epistemology have been developed by theorists who study the unfair treatment of intersecting identities in particular contexts and practices. It is only through the theoretical and practical engagement of case studies in situ, as they unfold in our actual social and epistemic lives, that we can properly diagnose epistemic injustices and identify effective ways to fight them.

When there are epistemic dysfunctions across contexts, when one epistemic context is systemically distorted by another, as happens when a group (such as jail detainees) is ascribed unfair credibility deficits, it is crucial to understand how intercontextual relations malfunction, how they can be improved, and thus how contexts and their relations can be ameliorated. For that, we need interaction, and not just any interaction but transformative social interactions both within and across contexts. Hence our second, interactionist shift beyond Jones's framework.

The Social-Interactionist Shift: Interacting Inside and Outside Jail

Credibility is not only socially contextual; it is also socially interactive. In order to understand how and why some subjects perceive others as having or lacking credibility, we need to pay attention not just to communicative contexts but also to specific patterns of interaction and the epistemic dynamics that unfold in those interactions. In particular, it is important to consider whether the epistemic interactions that take place within a given context admit of "epistemic friction" (Medina 2013). Beneficial epistemic friction occurs when epistemic perspectives and standpoints challenge and resist one another for their mutual enrichment (for the sake of learning, understanding, identifying, and correcting epistemic limitations, etc.). Detrimental epistemic friction occurs when an epistemic perspective monopolizes or skews the epistemic dynamics in order to stifle dissent, neutralize alternatives, silence dissonant voices, or block resistance.

Whenever there are good reasons to believe that epistemic appraisals have been unfairly distorted or skewed by dysfunctional patterns of interaction, we need to identify (and uproot) the detrimental epistemic friction in those dysfunctional patterns and diagnose the absence of beneficial epistemic friction, or else we acquiesce to epistemic injustice. Once we admit that credibility is not a static property of individual subjects, nor simply a static property impersonally allocated by contexts, but rather an advantage that is achieved or lost contextually and intercontextually in specific patterns of social interaction, then we should see credibility assessments as socially normative rather than descriptive and, in fact, as deeply political—that is, as concerning social norms, normative structures, and relations within the polis. Our normative assessments of patterns of epistemic interaction, and of the functional and dysfunctional dynamics within them, concern more than the ethos of particular individuals; they also concern communities, publics, institutions, and structures that empower or disempower subjects as they interact with each other. These evaluations call into question our entire social lives as well as our membership in and agency within communities.

As discussed in the previous section, detainees are subject to systematic disbelief and disregard by officers and administrators within the jail. However, this is not simply the result of being located in a particular context but, rather, the result of being subject to dysfunctional social patterns of epistemic interaction within and between contexts, patterns in which detainees systematically encounter detrimental epistemic friction in their interactions with staff members. As DCDF detainees report it, detention officers frequently assume that detainees needlessly complain about conditions that officers believe they see in a more neutral and disinterested way. In interviews, the partner of the late Matthew McCain relates how McCain's requests for medical attention were regularly minimized by detention officers who antagonized him for being a "crybaby."[22] Letters collected by Inside-Outside Alliance contain many examples of similar interactions, in which prisoners testifying to their own experience (often regarding medical care) are met with disbelief or disregard by officers and staff members. These patterns of interaction, in which testimonies are delivered by one party and undermined by the other, can become self-reinforcing when detainees' failed attempts to garner credibility—and thereby convey knowledge—are written off by staff members as frivolous whining or attention seeking.[23] They can also lead to coerced self-silencing and what Kristie Dotson (2011, 244–51) calls testimonial "smothering."

How can this interactive form of testimonial injustice be resisted? With epistemic action—more specifically, with epistemic interventions—that might change the course of dynamics and correct dysfunctions in patterns of interaction, both inside and outside the jail. We need epistemic activism to unmask and fight against unfair patterns of credibility ascriptions, to disrupt and disarm detrimental epistemic friction, and to disable the dysfunctional patterns of epistemic interaction that have led to distorted credibility assessments (Hamraie 2015). Of course, the strategies and tactics of epistemic activism will differ depending on who engages in it, in what contexts, and against what patterns of interaction. Oppressed subjects can become epistemic activists—sometimes by necessity, if not by choice—when they actively fight against their epistemic marginalization and work toward forms of self-empowerment that can achieve the epistemic agency they are unjustly denied. But nonoppressed subjects can also become epistemic activists when they actively and systematically disrupt their complicity with the epistemic mistreatment in question and work as allies for the empowerment of epistemically oppressed subjects (by echoing or amplifying oppressed voices, helping them to break silences, undoing unjust ways of discrediting and distorting oppressed voices, etc.). Differently situated subjects, oppressed and nonoppresed, can become social and epistemic advocates and help to disrupt complicity with social and epistemic injustices. As prominent feminist theorists such as Lorraine Code (2006) and Iris Marion Young (2013) have argued, advocacy is required to call attention to our complicity with ongoing injustices and to mobilize publics to fight against them. Advocacy is indeed a key component of epistemic activism and can bring together differently situated subjects and organizations across contexts (see especially chapter 5 of Code 2006).

Within the contexts of incarceration, prisoners can develop ways to work together, increase their voices, and hold correctional officers and administrators accountable in order to alter dysfunctional patterns of interaction. They are in a vulnerable position, and their epistemic agency can be limited and precarious. But they are certainly still agents, and, especially through collective (epistemic) action, detainees as a group can have a powerful voice. Together, they can collectively denounce conditions, call attention to unfair patterns of disbelief or disregard, and back up one another's testimonies, thereby mitigating some of the harmful consequences that individual acts of protest can have.[24] For instance, in the contest for knowledge about conditions in DCDF, an unknown number of detainees recently organized the First Five Grieving Committee, a "non-violent" and "non-gang affiliated" cooperative that anonymizes and amplifies the grievances of individual detainees.[25] By working together, the members of the Committee have successfully directed their concerns to the Durham

County sheriff, whereas individual grievances are typically heard—if they are heard at all—by subordinate staff members. This is an instance of epistemic activism, within the context of the jail, starting to ameliorate the testimonial disadvantage that detainees face. However, the Committee is clear that its actions within the jail need corresponding outside actions in order to be most effective. Indeed, in its founding communique, the Committee commits to "always seek help from outside sources and enterprises, including radio, television and film." More generally, in social contexts and institutional settings where the voices of oppressed subjects are systematically discredited or distorted, the mitigation of epistemic injustices sometimes requires the interventions of allies who have more voice, epistemic capital, or agency.

Not only detainees but also their allies outside of jail can engage in epistemic activism to redirect patterns of interaction and improve testimonial dynamics. Activists, scholars, journalists, family members, political leaders, social-media participants, and, in short, the general public can join forces with jail detainees to help ensure that their voices are heard and their concerns are addressed.[26] In the Durham County jail, administrators receive over thirty thousand grievances a year, which must be routed to a network of over one hundred potentially responsible parties. Detainees sometimes report that their unaddressed grievances seem to disappear in this system, and when their complaints have been especially urgent, they have worked with Inside-Outside Alliance to put external pressure on jail administrators. For instance, in November 2014, the activist group organized call-ins to overwhelm administrators' phone lines when evening meals were reduced to two cold sandwiches. They adopted similar tactics in September 2015, when jail staff would not grant emergency medical transfer to a detainee in severe pain.[27] In these actions, phone calls from diverse community members—many of whom do not consider themselves to be activists—echoed detainee grievances in ways that made them more difficult to disregard or disbelieve. Additionally, the phone calls reminded jail staff of their accountability to the local community. In these ways, the actions temporarily disrupted typical patterns of interaction inside and outside of the jail and indicated the possibility for alternative, less dysfunctional patterns. For alternative patterns to take hold, however, it may take repeated activist interventions.

While the voices of outside community members can penetrate the jail to disrupt patterns of interaction within it, it is much more difficult for the voices of detainees to move outward. In particular, detainees' voices rarely reach places of political authority without being distorted, translated into other idioms or discourses, or ventriloquized by others. For this reason, it is important to have forms of epistemic activism in which outside allies lend their voices as instruments or extensions of the detainees' own, without interpreting or translating them, but nonetheless making explicit their different social positions and relations.[28] IOA members practice this by reading detainees' letters in city council meetings and county commissioners meetings, disrupting "business as usual" with the testimonies of individuals who have been excluded from the sites of official power. This forces authorities to display their epistemic stance—to explicitly regard, or disregard, detainee testimonies—in public and on the record. At one recent forum on conditions in the jail, county officials referenced written-in comments from detainees, and activists read detainee letters, in order to bring the perspectives of incarcerated persons into the conversation. Major Paul Martin, who oversees operations in the jail, repeatedly objected to these testimonies on principle, saying, "Just because someone writes a letter doesn't mean it's true. Who wrote the letter? . . . I can't even authenticate that it's real. . . . Some of these letters are rigged; they've not been authenticated. And I don't believe them because I know the jail."[29] These objections to detainee testimony gave forum participants a clear indication of wider patterns of epistemic interaction—specifically, acts of discrediting inmate testimony while crediting official perspectives—that are at work both inside the jail and in the relations between "inside" and "outside" contexts. And once those patterns become evident, they can be called out.[30]

In addition to transporting detainee testimony into settings like these, Inside-Outside Alliance seeks to amplify detainee voices by publishing their letters verbatim, usually without context or commentary, on the website Amplify Voices Inside. Through the site, detainee voices reach outside readers—and not only local ones—in ways that challenge typical patterns of epistemic interaction. Moreover, IOA publishes detainee letters and artwork in a print zine called *Feedback*, which is mailed back into the jail and distributed on the outside. These forms of activism create new circuits of epistemic interaction that challenge typical patterns. This, potentially, can ameliorate some of the epistemic injustice faced by detainees and amplify resistance within the jail.

Inside-Outside Alliance is committed to amplifying and circulating the voices of detainees without speaking *for* them, although this can be a delicate line to negotiate, especially because some members of IOA *are* detainees. To supplement our account of epistemic activism, we note that when relatively powerful allies engage in activism on behalf of others, it does not have to—and usually should not—take the form of speaking *for* others, which risks ventriloquizing oppressed subjectivities and co-opting or instrumentalizing their voices, if only inadvertently. Rather, allies who engage in epistemic activism would do well to follow the example of IOA by speaking *with* others (i.e., engaging with oppressed voices in visible ways so that their voices are heard in their own terms), positioning themselves as media for disadvantaged others to speak *through* (e.g., reading statements written by informants who cannot speak right here, right now), or doing whatever preparatory work is necessary for empowering others to speak (e.g., removing obstacles or creating opportunities for oppressed subjects to speak in new circumstances or ways).

There have been vibrant discussions of the problems associated with acting as an ally of oppressed subjects and, especially, with speaking on their behalf (Spivak 1988; Alcoff 1991; Zurn and Dilts 2016; McKinnon 2017). Of special importance here is Linda Alcoff's (1991) influential essay "The Problem of Speaking for Others." Alcoff addresses the issue of connecting communicative contexts for the sake of liberating those subjects who inhabit them and empowering their voices, bringing to the fore the problem of speaking for those who have no voice or whose voice is not adequately heard. Alcoff's arguments also converge with our argument for alliances that can give visibility to those who are ignored or unseen by some segments of society. Sometimes it is necessary to use the voices, the visibility, and the cultural capital of allies to empower those who have more precarious voices, visibility, or cultural capital. But, as Alcoff argues, what becomes key is how to speak for others responsibly. This is how Alcoff articulates contextualist and interactionist conditions for doing so:

> We must . . . interrogate the bearing of our location and context on what it is we are saying, and this should be an explicit part of every serious discursive practice we engage in. Constructing hypotheses about the possible connections between our location and our words is one way to begin. This procedure would be most successful if engaged in collectively with others, by which aspects of our location less highlighted in our own minds might be revealed to us. . . . In order to evaluate attempts to speak for others in particular instances, . . . one cannot simply look at the location of the speaker or her credentials to speak,

nor can one look merely at the propositional content of the speech; one must also look at where the speech goes and what it does there. (25–26)

We take inspiration from Alcoff's remarks and see in them a useful supplement to Jones's (2002) reminders that audiences should adopt better norms and cultivate better capacities when receiving "suspect" testimony. When audiences want to do more than become better listeners, when they want to become epistemic activists by amplifying unfairly discredited voices, they ought to assess their own propensities to trust and distrust, as Jones argues, as well as the performative aspects of their activist speech, as Alcoff maintains.

Epistemic activism not only raises awareness but also demands that publics become self-critical about patterns of distrust and exclusion that unjustly harm the epistemic agency of some subjects while unfairly benefitting the agency of others.[31] The politics of credibility should call attention to testimonial injustices and the epistemic activism that engages it by analyzing credibility not solely in terms of audiences' norms and capacities but also in terms of the contexts, intercontextual relations, and prevalent patterns of interaction that are the terrains of epistemic contest. It often takes decades of persistent work by social movements and the slow transformation of epistemic habits before an epistemic injustice is mitigated or eventually eradicated. In other words, progress toward epistemic justice requires repeated interventions and sustained transformative practice, within and across patterns of epistemic interaction, in order to facilitate beneficial epistemic friction and reduce detrimental friction. An *activist* politics of credibility aims to contribute to this progress.

Summary: A Robust Politics of Credibility and Epistemic Activism

In this chapter, we have tried to deepen the practical shift in epistemology—and specifically the epistemology of testimony—by bringing social-institutional contexts and social practices to the fore. We have argued that social contextualism and social interactionism provide analytic and critical tools that are essential for diagnosing and resisting normative problems of epistemic injustice that can appear in testimonial dynamics within particular contexts of action.[32] Moving beyond Karen

Jones's foundational work, we have argued for a practical approach to epistemology that is not only domain-specific and case-specific but also social-contextualist (proceeding by elucidating the normative structures and relations within and across contexts) and social-interactionist (proceeding by elucidating the patterns of interaction within which particular testimonial dynamics are embedded). Through the case study of jail as a knowledge problem, we have argued that only a social-contextualist and social-interactionist analysis of testimonial dynamics can properly diagnose the forms of silencing and credibility deficits that are at the core of the epistemic injustices suffered by detainees. Moreover, social-contextualist and social-interactionist analyses directly connect with ways of resisting those injustices through sustained transformative epistemic action, that is, *epistemic activism*. With a social-contextualist and social-interactionist approach, practical epistemology becomes socially awake and engaged, and it can offer a robust *politics* of credibility that does not confine itself to the (ethical-epistemic) capacities of individual subjects but addresses also the (sociopolitical-epistemic) relations between subjects in institutional contexts and social practices. With the case study of the jail as a knowledge problem, we hope to have shown that practical epistemology can—and perhaps should—be continuous with activism, for social-contextualist and social-interactionist diagnoses and analyses, far from being mere descriptions, are sociopolitical indictments and calls for action.[33]

Notes

1. See Fricker (2007) for a definition of epistemic injustice and the subcategories of testimonial and hermeneutical injustices. In this chapter we focus on testimonial injustices as they appear in the context of a jail. A contextualist account of epistemic injustice can be found in Medina (2013).

2. See Amplify Voices Inside, accessed September 16, 2016, https://www.amplifyvoices.com. Inside-Outside Alliance worked closely with an ally organization, the Durham Jail Investigation Team, which sought to learn about conditions inside DCDF and publicize this information. One of us, Matt Whitt, was a member of the Investigation Team. His role in that organization informed and shaped the central case study of this chapter.

3. Jails are understudied in academic literature, but see Walsh (2013), Jeffreys (2018), and Lippke (2018) for important exceptions. Notably, although jails are primarily designed as temporary, nonpunitive detention centers for detainees awaiting trial, they are increasingly used to house convicted offenders

serving relatively short sentences. This is partly a response to prison overcrowding. Additionally, as courts have become backlogged with hearings, detainees spend increasingly long periods confined to jail as they await trial. This blurs the line between punitive and nonpunitive detention and presents urgent problems, since jails often lack the medical, recreational, and educational facilities of prisons. Throughout this chapter, we use the language of *detainees* or *prisoners* when talking about individuals confined to jail, following the chosen terminology of some current and former DCDF detainees.

4. For exemplary reports, see the letters collected at amplifyvoices.com, especially "Top Ten Problems at Durham County Jail," accessed September 16, 2016, https://www.amplifyvoices.com/2015/11/20/top-ten-problems-at-durham-county-jail/.

5. For local news coverage of these events, see the *Raleigh News and Observer* article "Questions Surround Durham Jail Detainee's Death," by Natalie Ritchie, January 27, 2016, 1:58 p.m. EST. See also "Family Says Dad Who Died at Durham County Jail Was 'Neglected,'" by Rodney Overton, *CBS 17*, January 26, 2016, 8:10 p.m. EST.

6. As has been discussed in the recent literature on epistemic injustice, testimonial and hermeneutical difficulties often intersect and compound each other. The obstacles one faces as a knowledge giver in testimonial exchanges and the obstacles one faces as a meaning maker in expressive practices cannot be sharply separated. For a discussion of the complex relations between testimonial and hermeneutical marginalization, see Fricker (2016) and Medina (2012, 2017).

7. Interview with Ashley Canady, February 16, 2016, interviewed by Matt Whitt.

8. In 2015, Dennis McMurray and Raphael Bennett also died in DCDF. For Inside-Outside Alliance reports on all three cases, see the following posts on Amplify Voices Inside: "Inmate Dies in Durham County Jail after Medical Neglect by Detention Staff," January 21, 2016 (https://www.amplifyvoices.com/2016/01/21/inmate-dies-in-durham-county-jail-after-medical-neglect-by-detention-staff/); "Inmates and Family Foil Jail's Attempted Cover-Up of Death," January 22, 2016 (https://www.amplifyvoices.com/2016/01/22/inmates-and-family-foil-jails-attempted-cover-up-of-death/); "They Covered Up My Dad's Death, and They Got Away With It," January 27, 2016 (https://www.amplifyvoices.com/2016/01/27/they-covered-up-my-dads-death-and-they-got-away-with-it/).

9. At a September 15, 2016, forum on the conditions and operations of DCDF, Chief District Court Judge Marcia Morey reported that 73 percent of DCDF detainees are awaiting trial, and some wait for multiple years (1:32:32). Human Relations Commissioner Felicia Arriaga reported that approximately 75 percent of the detainees are considered nonviolent, according to the jail's own classification system (53:48). See "Public Town Hall Forum on the Impact of the Durham County Jail on Durham City Residents," presented by the Durham

Human Relations Commission, https://www.youtube.com/watch?v=wZJEyYggrNA &feature=youtu.be. On the relations between the bail system, jail overcrowding, and racialized criminalization, see Cynthia Jones (2013).

10. In saying this, we do not naively attribute innocence to individuals incarcerated in jails. However, we acknowledge that many unincarcerated individuals—including those who have avoided arrest, paid bonds, had sentences reduced, been exonerated, been convicted in more lenient jurisdictions, or served out their sentences, as well as those who are subject to noncarceral disciplinary mechanisms like college honor councils—are no more innocent than many people currently awaiting trial in jail. We emphasize, moreover, that while roughly one in three American adults has a police record, race and class are strong determinants of who goes to jail and who does not. Finally, we want to underscore that people serving time in jails or prisons, even if convicted of criminal offenses, are often trustworthy and reliable narrators of their own experiences.

11. Medina (2011) offers a relational account of credibility assessments in terms of implicit comparisons and contrasts. See Medina (2011) for a contextualist and interactionist analysis of how credibility deficits and credibility excesses go together and contribute to the perpetuation of testimonial injustice.

12. Indeed, if outside audiences typically hear only the reports of officials and administrators without also hearing divergent reports from detainees, then they may be more likely to attribute credibility to official reports and to discredit any detainee reports they finally do hear. We thank Heidi Grasswick for pressing us to consider this. Another Durham civil-society group, the Durham Jail Investigation Team, challenged this dynamic by starting with the reports of prisoners and corroborating them when possible, thereby constructing an accurate view of the jail that centers on prisoners' knowledge. The Jail Investigation Team allied with Inside-Outside Alliance but was a distinct organization with different goals and tactics.

13. For this reason, the contextual shift discussed in this section is inextricable from the interactionist shift of the next section.

14. Testimonial dynamics also change, of course, with the content or topic of testimony. Although here we are emphasizing the contextual, intercontextual, and interactionist aspects of testimonial dynamics, traditionally recognized aspects, especially content, still matter. For instance, within the context of jail, prisoner testimonies about abuse and neglect might be discounted by guards and administrators, while testimonies that cast suspicion on other prisoners (i.e., snitching) may be granted more credibility. Here, not only the content but also the particular contexts and interactions (e.g., being asked or pressured to supply evidence about others' actions) result in localized credibility assessments that may be contrary to the general credibility deficits imposed on prisoners. In fact, the presumed criminality of the detainee may entail the presumption

of authority or expert knowledge in some areas, especially those that pertain to criminal life, such as gang activity, drug dealing, etc. But even when detainees are stereotypically presumed to know about criminal activities, the domain-specific epistemic authority ascribed to them does not always result in an ascription of credibility. That is, they may be suspected of lying (for complex reasons) even when knowledge is available to them.

15. *Initial Report of Grievances, Rules Backgrounder*, internal report by the Durham Jail Investigation Team, prepared May 2016; and *Durham Jail Investigation Team Infopack for Human Relations Commission*, report prepared September 2016. Both reports are based on Durham County public records, detainee letters, news coverage, and information provided by DCDF public-information officers.

16. See, for instance, the *Raleigh News and Observer* article "Questions Surround Durham Jail Detainee's Death," by Natalie Ritchie, January 27, 2016, 1:58 p.m. EST.

17. See notes 9 and 10 above.

18. "Public Town Hall Forum on the Impact of the Durham County Jail on Durham City Residents"; see note 9 for more information and to access the video. Remarks are at 1:25:05–1:25:55. Accessed September 16, 2016.

19. See "Public Town Hall Forum" cited in note 9, remarks at 1:22:22–1:24:30. For related news coverage, see "Major: Complaints about Durham County Jail Are 'Overblown Distorted Lies,' " *WRAL News*, September 15, 2016 (https://www.wral.com/major-complaints-about-durham-county-jail-are-overblown-distorted-lies-/16018494/).

20. See https://www.amplifyvoices.com/about/.

21. See "Inmates and Family Foil Jail's Attempted Cover-Up of Death," Amplify Voices Inside, January 22, 2016.

22. Interview with Ashley Canady, February 16, 2016. Canady reports discussing this with McCain and, on occasion, hearing remarks like these in the background of phone calls.

23. Although we are focusing on testimonial injustice, our discussion here is informed by Andrea Pitts's (2014) important work on hermeneutical injustice in the context of correctional health care. In light of specific hermeneutical injustices in contemporary correctional health care, Pitts argues that legal oversight mechanisms focusing on intentional or wanton treatment of prisoners (in particular, Eighth Amendment challenges to prisoner treatment) are insufficient.

24. For example, in 2013, prisoners held in solitary confinement in California's Pelican Bay State Prison coordinated a hunger strike that involved thirty thousand prisoners in facilities across the state. This form of activism had distinctly epistemic effects: it amplified the voices of prisoners held in solitary confinement, thereby disrupting typical patterns of (non)interaction. See Guenther (2015). Speaking more generally about epistemic resistance within contexts of incarceration, the members of the LoCI-Wittenberg University Writing Group (2016) examine how

detainees can work together to overcome epistemic obstacles and to "construct knowledge on the inside."

25. The First Five Grieving Committee's founding document, "The First Five Grieving Committee: Who We Are, What We Stand For" (March 18, 2016), is available at https://www.amplifyvoices.com/2016/03/28/the-first-five-grieving-committee-who-we-are-what-we-stand-for/. Evidence of the impact of their epistemic activism, including gaining the attention of the Durham County sheriff directly instead of his subordinates, is archived at https://www.amplifyvoices.com.

26. Indeed, community members may bear ethical, political, and epistemic responsibility for becoming allies, or at least for working independently to ameliorate injustices that detainees face. We thank Lisa Guenther for pressing this point, which we cannot develop here.

27. See "Call-In to the Durham Jail—Demand Dignity for Hungry Prisoners!" (Amplify Voices Inside, November 13, 2014, https://www.amplifyvoices.com/2014/11/23/call-in-to-the-durham-jail-demand-dignity-for-hungry-prisoners/); and "Call In to the Jail to End Criminal Medical Neglect" (Amplify Voices Inside, September 13, 2015, https://www.amplifyvoices.com/2015/09/13/call-in-to-the-jail-to-end-criminal-medical-neglect/).

28. For excellent suggestions as to how one can responsibly navigate the problems involved in "speaking for others," see Alcoff (1991). We return to this issue below.

29. "Public Town Hall Forum on the Impact of the Durham County Jail on Durham City Residents"; see note 9 for more information and to access the video. Remarks are at 1:19:30–1:20:00, 2:02:55–2:03:17, and 2:06:33–2:06:45.

30. At the same public forum, another community member called critical attention to Major Martin's dismissal of "people's truths" and the "lived experiences" of detainees and former detainees. We view her remarks, starting at 2:01:10 in the video, as an exemplary form of epistemic activism.

31. For a related discussion of the limitations of awareness-raising strategies, see Whitt (2016, 437).

32. In making this argument through the examination of our case study, we have drawn from, and hope to contribute to, discussions of epistemic injustice at the intersections of social epistemology (Jones 2002; Fricker 2007; Dotson 2011; Medina 2013), prison studies (Rios 2011; Cacho 2012; Guenther 2013; Whitt 2015), race and gender theory (Lugones 2003; Sullivan and Tuana 2007), decolonial theory (Alcoff 1991; Spivak 2003; Mignolo 2009), and disability studies (Hamraie 2015; Tremain 2017).

33. For their helpful comments—and especially their intellectual and material work toward justice—the authors would like to thank Nancy McHugh, Heidi Grasswick, Lisa Guenther, Ashley Canady, Matt Hartman, Nolan Bennett, Nora Hanagan, Eli Meyerhoff, Sergio Armando Gallegos-Ordorica, Inside-Outside Alliance, and Andrea Pitts.

References

Ahmed, Sara. 2006. *Queer Phenomenology: Orientations, Objects, Others.* Durham, NC: Duke University Press.

Alcoff, Linda. 1991. "The Problem of Speaking for Others." *Cultural Critique* 20: 5–32.

Butler, Judith. 2004. *Precarious Life: The Powers of Mourning and Violence.* London: Verso.

Cacho, Lisa M. 2012. *Social Death: Racialized Rightlessness and the Criminalization of the Unprotected.* New York: New York University Press.

Code, Lorraine. 1987. *Epistemic Responsibility.* Hanover, NH: University Press of New England.

———. 2006. *Ecological Thinking: The Politics of Epistemic Location.* New York: Oxford University Press.

Davis, Angela, and Gina Dent. 2001. "Prison as a Border: A Conversation on Gender, Globalization, and Punishment." *Signs* 26 (4): 1235–41.

Dotson, Kristie. 2011. "Tracking Epistemic Violence, Tracking Practices of Silencing." *Hypatia* 26 (2): 236–57.

Fricker, Miranda. 2007. *Epistemic Injustice: Power and the Ethics of Knowing.* New York: Oxford University Press.

———. 2016. "Epistemic Injustice and the Preservation of Ignorance." In *The Epistemic Dimensions of Ignorance*, edited by Rik Peels and Martijn Blaauw, 160–77. Cambridge: Cambridge University Press.

Guenther, Lisa. 2013. *Solitary Confinement: Social Death and its Afterlives.* Minneapolis: Minnesota University Press.

———. 2015. "Political Action at the End of the World: Hannah Arendt and the California Prison Hunger Strikes." *Canadian Journal of Human Rights* 4 (1): 33–56.

Hamraie, Aimi. 2015. "Cripping Feminist Technoscience." *Hypatia* 30 (1): 307–13.

Jeffreys, Derek S. 2018. *America's Jails: The Search for Human Dignity in an Age of Mass Incarceration.* New York: New York University Press.

Jones, Cynthia. 2013. " 'Give Us Free': Addressing Racial Disparities in Bail Determinations." *Legislation and Public Policy* 16 (4): 919–61.

Jones, Karen. 2002. "The Politics of Credibility." In *A Mind of One's Own: Feminist Essays on Reason and Objectivity*, edited by Louise M. Antony and Charlotte E. Witt, 154–76. New York: Westview Press.

Lippke, Richard L. 2018. "The Case Against Jails." In *The Ethics of Policing and Imprisonment*, edited by Molly Gardner and Michael Weber, 109–28. Cham, Switzerland: Palgrave Macmillan.

LoCI-Wittenberg University Writing Group. 2016. "An Epistemology of Incarceration: Constructing Knowing on the Inside." *philoSOPHIA* 6 (1): 9–26.

Lugones, María. 2003. *Pilgrimages/Peregrinajes: Theorizing Coalition against Multiple Oppressions*. Lanham, MD: Rowman & Littlefield.

McKinnon, Rachel. 2017. "Allies Behaving Badly: Gaslighting as Epistemic Injustice." In *The Routledge Handbook of Epistemic Injustice*, edited by Ian James Kidd, José Medina, and Gaile Pohlhaus Jr., 167–74. London: Routledge.

Medina, José. 2011. "The Relevance of Credibility Excess in a Proportional View of Epistemic Injustice: Differential Epistemic Authority and the Social Imaginary." *Social Epistemology* 25 (1): 15–35.

———. 2012. "Hermeneutical Injustice and Polyphonic Contextualism: Social Silences and Shared Hermeneutical Responsibilities." *Social Epistemology* 26 (2): 201–20.

———. 2013. *The Epistemology of Resistance: Gender and Racial Oppression, Epistemic Injustice, and Resistant Imaginations*. New York: Oxford University Press.

———. 2017. "Varieties of Hermeneutical Injustice." In *The Routledge Handbook of Epistemic Injustice*, edited by Ian James Kidd, José Medina, and Gaile Pohlhausn Jr., 41–52. London: Routledge.

Mignolo, Walter. 2009. "Epistemic Disobedience, Independent Thought and Decolonial Freedom." *Theory, Culture and Society* 26 (7–8): 159–81.

Ortega, Mariana. 2006. "Being Lovingly, Knowingly Ignorant: White Feminism and Women of Color." *Hypatia* 21 (3): 56–74.

Pitts, Andrea. 2014. "Cruel and Unusual Care and Punishment: Epistemic Injustices in Correctional Health Care." *APA Newsletter on Philosophy and Medicine* 14 (1): 6–9.

Rios, Victor. 2011. *Punished: Policing the Lives of Black and Latino Boys*. New York: New York University Press.

Spivak, Gayatri. 1988. "Can the Subaltern Speak?" In *Marxism and the Interpretation of Culture*, edited by Cary Nelson and Lawrence Grossberg, 271–313. Urbana: University of Illinois Press.

Sullivan, Shannon, and Nancy Tuana, eds. 2007. *Race and Epistemologies of Ignorance*. Albany: State University of New York Press.

Tremain, Shelley. 2017. "Knowing Disability, Differently." In *The Routledge Handbook of Epistemic Injustice*, edited by Ian James Kidd, José Medina, and Gaile Pohlhaus Jr., 175–83. London: Routledge.

Walsh, John P. 2013. *The Culture of Urban Control: Jail Overcrowding in the Crime Control Era*. Lanham, MD: Lexington Books.

Whitt, Matt S. 2015. "Sovereignty, Community, and the Incarceration of Immigrants." In *Death and Other Penalties: Philosophy in a Time of Mass Incarceration*, edited by Geoffrey Adelsberg, Lisa Guenther, and Scott Zeman, 174–92. New York: Fordham University Press.

———. 2016. "Other People's Problems: Student Distancing, Epistemic Responsibility, and Injustice." *Studies in Philosophy and Education* 35 (5): 427–44.

Young, Iris Marion. 2013. *Responsibility for Justice*. New York: Oxford University Press.

Zurn, Perry, and Andrew Dilts, eds. 2016. *Active Intolerance: Michel Foucault, the Prisons Information Group, and the Future of Abolition*. New York: Palgrave Macmillan.

Contributors

Corwin Aragon is an assistant professor of philosophy at California State Polytechnic University, Pomona (Cal Poly Pomona). His research focuses on questions of individual responsibility to remedy structural injustices, both material and epistemic, and he works primarily in the fields of contemporary social and political philosophy, feminist philosophy, critical philosophy of race, and global justice. He has additional research interests in philosophy of humor and comedy. Currently, he is preparing a book-length manuscript titled *Seeking Justice in an Unjust World*.

ShaDawn Battle is an assistant professor of gender and diversity studies at Xavier University. Her research interests include African American literature, Afro-diasporic studies, Black feminist/womanist studies, critical race epistemology, and hip-hop studies. She writes on anti-Black politics and Black masculine and feminine politics, intersecting hip-hop, anticolonial theories, critical race theory, and literature that spans the Black diaspora. She has published essays examining the epistemological and psychosocial underpinnings of Black-male shootings, the hypermasculinity of Kanye West, and the trajectory of Jay-Z as an artist through a philosophical and an anticolonial theoretical lens. Battle's current research projects—a documentary and manuscript—explore Chicago Footwork, which she considers an embodied vernacular language of resistance, as a subject of inquiry into the question of biopolitics, race construction, and the politics of a Black diasporic "homeplace."

Lorraine Code's philosophical biography mirrors a trajectory of thought that led to the possibility of thinking and writing about knowledge issues that depart from such standard, faceless analyses as dominated

English-language empiricist practices through the twentieth century. Code's engagement with knowledge and subjectivity in her doctoral dissertation, and her engagement with both continental and Anglo-American sources, prompted investigations not just of subjects but of subjectivities in the silent part they had hitherto played in "real" epistemology. Hence, in 1987, she posed a previously outrageous question: Is the sex of the knower epistemologically significant? Thanks also to a rapprochement between Anglo-American and continental philosophy in the final decades of the twentieth century, the hermeneutic dimension of knowing and being came also to inform her thinking. As it slowly became clear that human subjects, together and separately, were to be celebrated, not condemned, for their diverse ways of knowing, feminist and postcolonial epistemology came into its own. Code's work has gone on to follow and shape it. Her recent work includes *Ecological Thinking: The Politics of Epistemic Location* (2006) and *Manufactured Uncertainty: Implications for Climate Change Skepticism* (2020, SUNY Press).

Sharon Crasnow is a distinguished professor of philosophy emerita at Norco College and an associate researcher at the Centre for Humanities Engaging Science and Society (CHESS) at Durham University, Durham, United Kingdom. She was a fellow at the Center for Philosophy of Science, University of Pittsburgh, in spring 2017 and a visiting professor at the London School of Economics and Political Science (LSE) Department of Gender Studies in spring 2019. She has published in *Philosophy of Science*, *Hypatia*, and *Philosophy of the Social Sciences*. She is coeditor with Anita M. Superson of *Out from the Shadows: Analytic Feminist Contributions to Traditional Philosophy* (2012). She is also coeditor (with Joanne Waugh) of the Lexington Books series *Feminist Strategies* and (with Kristen Intemann) of *The Routledge Handbook of Feminist Philosophy of Science* (2020).

Lacey J. Davidson is currently a visiting assistant professor at California Lutheran University. Her research and teaching focus on the intersections of philosophy of race, social epistemology, and philosophy of mind. Davidson is interested in using philosophy as a tool of and for liberation. Her work is published in *Overcoming Epistemic Injustice* and *An Introduction to Implicit Bias* as well as the *Journal of Applied Philosophy*, *Fat Studies*, and *Teoria*. Currently, Davidson is focused on the ontology of racism and exploring interventions focused on changing epistemic landscapes and social norms. In addition, she and her coauthor in this volume, Mark

Satta, hope to continue their work in examining the epistemic features of public health and health-care access.

Carla Fehr holds the Wolfe Chair in Scientific and Technological Literacy in the philosophy department at the University of Waterloo and conducts research in socially relevant philosophy of science, feminist epistemology and philosophy of science, and philosophy of biology. She also conducts interdisciplinary research on equity and diversity in STEM. Her scholarship explores the coupled ethical and scientific benefits arising from just and supportive research communities. Fehr's work can be found in journals including *Molecular Ecology*, *Philosophy of Science*, *Biology and Philosophy*, *Hypatia*, and the *National Women's Studies Association Journal* and has been funded by the Natural Sciences and Engineering Research Council and the Social Sciences and Humanities Research Council in Canada and the National Science Foundation and National Endowment for the Humanities in the US. She is a cofounder of the Association for Feminist Epistemologies, Methodologies, Metaphysics, and Science Studies; the Consortium for Socially Relevant Philosophy of/in Science and Engineering; the American Philosophical Association Committee on the Status of Women site-visit program; and the journal *Feminist Philosophy Quarterly*.

Sergio Armando Gallegos-Ordorica is an assistant professor in the Department of Philosophy of John Jay College of Criminal Justice. His research and teaching interests lie in Latin American philosophy (with a special focus on Mexican philosophy), philosophy of science, philosophy of race, and US pragmatism and feminist philosophy (particularly, Indigenous feminism). His work has appeared in *Synthese*, *Studies in History and Philosophy of Science Part A*, *Hypatia*, *Transactions of the Charles S. Peirce Society*, *Critical Philosophy of Race*, and the *Inter-American Journal of Philosophy*.

Heidi Grasswick is the George Nye and Anne Walker Boardman Professor of Mental and Moral Science at Middlebury College in Vermont, where she teaches in the philosophy department and is a regular contributor to the Feminist, Sexuality, and Gender Studies Program and the Environmental Studies Program. She holds a PhD from the University of Minnesota. Grasswick's research interests include feminist understandings of the social production of knowledge and the relationship between individuals and communities in responsible inquiry. Her recent work has focused on analyzing the important role of trust relations between knowers, particularly between lay communities and scientific communities. Her edited volume titled *Feminist Epistemology and Philosophy of Science: Power in Knowledge* was published in 2011.

Nancy Arden McHugh is professor and chair of philosophy at Wittenberg University and the director of the Wittenberg Institute for Public Humanities and Sciences. She was the president of the Public Philosophy Network from 2018–2020, which "promotes philosophy that engages issues of public concern and works collaboratively with civic and professional communities." McHugh is the author of *The Limits of Knowledge: Generating Pragmatist Feminist Cases for Situated Knowing* (2015, SUNY Press), the research for which was funded by the National Science Foundation, and *Feminist Philosophies A–Z* (2007). She is also the author of articles in feminist philosophy of science and epistemology. McHugh teaches philosophy courses in juvenile detention centers and in adult prisons, and she also partners with reentry programs for women who were incarcerated. Her work with the Kettering Foundation to develop deliberative conversations to rethink reentry from prisons intersects with her work in the carceral system. Her website is http://www.nancyamchugh.org.

José Medina is the Walter Dill Scott Professor of Philosophy at Northwestern University and works in critical race theory, gender/queer theory, social epistemology, and political philosophy. His latest book is *The Epistemology of Resistance: Gender and Racial Oppression, Epistemic Injustice, and Resistant Imaginations*, which received the 2012 North American Society for Social Philosophy Book Award. He is currently working on issues concerning epistemic injustice and epistemic activism in relation to race, gender, and sexuality. His current projects in critical race theory, decolonial theory, and gender and queer theory focus on how social perception and the social imagination contribute to the formation of vulnerabilities to different kinds of violence and oppression. These projects also explore the social movements and kinds of activism (including epistemic activism) that can be mobilized to resist racial and sexual violence and oppression in local and global contexts.

Esme G. Murdock is an assistant professor of philosophy at San Diego State University. Her research explores the intersections of social/political relations and environmental health, integrity, and agency. Specifically, her work troubles the purported stability of dominant, largely Euro-descendant, and settler-colonial philosophies through centering conceptions of land and relating to land found within African American, Afro-diasporic, and Indigenous eco-philosophies. Her work has been published in *Environmental Values*, *Journal of Global Ethics*, and *Hypatia*.

Gaile Pohlhaus Jr. is an associate professor of philosophy and faculty affiliate in women's, gender, and sexuality studies at Miami University (Ohio). She is coeditor of *The Routledge Handbook of Epistemic Injustice* and has published articles in critical epistemology, feminist philosophy, and the later Wittgenstein.

Mark Satta is an assistant professor of philosophy at Wayne State University in Detroit, Michigan. He has published articles in *Philosophical Studies*, *Analysis*, *Synthese*, and *Episteme*, among other journals. His philosophical interests span epistemology, philosophy of language, philosophy of law, bioethics, and immigration law, among other areas. Satta is particularly interested in using philosophy to address practical social and political issues. Currently, Satta is working on a paper in which he uses misguided HIV-criminalization laws to argue that legislators have obligations to update laws in accordance with new developments in science. He and his coauthor in this volume, Lacey J. Davidson, are also examining the conditions under which members of society with marginalized identities are justified in exhibiting social distrust.

Sean A. Valles is an associate professor with an appointment in the Michigan State University Lyman Briggs College and the Department of Philosophy. His research explores the ethical and evidentiary questions underlying scientific research on the health of human populations: What does it mean to be healthy? How can we make sense of the ways that racism and other social injustices affect health? How can we more justly distribute health benefits and harms in diverse societies? He is author of the 2018 book *Philosophy of Population Health: Philosophy for a New Public Health Era*. He is also coeditor (with Quill R. Kukla) of the book series *Bioethics for Social Justice*.

Matt S. Whitt earned his philosophy PhD in 2010. For a decade, he taught a variety of philosophy courses, including two classes in men's prisons, and published articles in political philosophy and critical pedagogy. He is now earning a master of social work degree, with the aim of working as a trauma-informed therapist.

Index

feminism *(continued)*
  and feminist evolutionary
    psychology, 155
  and feminist method and
    methodology, 43n3, 47–48, 50
  and feminist philosophers, 108,
    112, 131, 140
  and feminist philosophy of science,
    77, 94n3, 95n5
  and *Feminist Philosophy Quarterly*,
    175n8
  and feminist science studies, 9–10,
    52, 73, 75–77, 94
  and feminist values, 82, 92
  and gender bias, 75–76, 91
  and oppression, 52
  and philosophy of science, 47, 48,
    50–51, 52–53, 67–68, 73, 75–77
  and situated knowledge, 105
  and values, 47, 48, 75, 76, 81, 82–
    83, 87, 90, 91
  See also Collins, Patricia Hill;
    Crasnow, Sharon; Fehr, Carla;
    philosophy; science; theory
Fricker, Miranda, 38, 184, 188, 194–
  95, 204, 242, 252–53
Fuentes, Carlos, 283–84

Gallegos-Ordorica, Sergio Armando,
  3, 16–17, 321n33
Garner, Eric, 180
gender:
  and androcentric and sexist bias,
    89, 167
  and background assumptions, 211
  and Black male identity, 207n8
  and Black women, 114–15
  and cisgender people, 242–43
  and epistemic injustice, 241
  and epistemology, 112, 115
  and familial structure, 211–12
  and family roles, 81

  and female orgasm, 88
  and feminist evolutionary
    psychology, 155
  and feminist values, 91
  and heteronormative family, 211
  and knowledge, 118, 215, 218,
    235
  and language, 75
  and marginalization, 261
  and masculinity, 189, 235
  and methodology, 75
  and oppression, 234, 310
  and philosophy, 128, 129
  and power relations, 81
  and race, 67
  and science, 67, 73–77, 155
  and scientific knowledge, 73
  and sex chromosomes, 155
  and sexism, 121, 123
  and sexual harassment, 128
  and stereotypes, 155
  and stratification, 61
  and systemic biases, 33
  and visible reality, 235–36
Grasswick, Heidi, 43, 148n29, 174n3,
  175n10, 289n37, 319n12, 321n33
Guenther, Lisa, 321n26, 321n33

Haraway, Donna, 105, 123
Harding, Sandra, 43n3, 94n3, 270
Haslanger, Sally:
  and the abstract subject or
    observer, 27
  and ameliorative philosophical
    analysis, 8, 26–27
  and good theories, 25
Hemmings, Claire:
  and "Affective Solidarity: Feminist
    Reflexivity and Political
    Transformation," 120
  and affect's importance, 121
  and importance of stories, 104

sexuality *(continued)*
  and HIV scenarios, 242–43, 263n14
  and HIV transmission, 243–44,
    250, 254–55
  and human reproduction, 95n5,
    96n13
  and LGBT people, 147n26
  and male orgasm, 96n15
  and marginalization, 261
  and *mestizo* notion, 272–73
  and oppression, 310
  and PARTNER study, 249
  and pregnancy, 135
  and prophylaxis, 262n9
  and race, 191
  and safe-sex practices, 254, 262n8
  and serosorting practice, 245–46,
    256
  and sexual orientation, 241
  and violation of white woman, 189
  See also HIV
Shrader-Frechette, Kristin, 157, 158,
  168, 172
Solomon, Miriam, 91
Spivak, Gayatri, 7, 180
Stewart, Abigail, 74, 78, 81, 82, 83,
  86, 87, 92
Symons, Donald, 88, 89–90, 91, 92

theory:
  abstract theory, 4, 5, 28
  and anticolonial theory, 181
  and case studies, 36–37, 41, 78
  and civic duty, 34–35
  critical race theory, 14, 18n1, 67
  critical social theory, 23, 24, 27–28,
    35–36
  and disability studies, 309–10
  and epistemic injustice, 241
  and epistemic violence, 214
  and ethical issues, 25

evidential support for, 88–89, 90,
  92
and evolution, 89
and feminist theory, 7, 14, 18n1,
  309–10, 312
and gender bias, 75
ideal theory, 8, 23, 28–29, 30,
  31–35, 37, 42
intersectional theory, 67–68
and justice, 26, 27, 28–29, 30, 31,
  32–33, 37
and knowledge, 25, 33, 104
and lived experiences, 104
and marginalization, 9
and method, 25, 26, 29
and moral thinking, 34, 35, 36
and narrative and literary
  theorizing, 3
nonideal theory, 2, 8, 9, 23–25, 26,
  27–28, 29, 34, 35–42, 43n3
and philosophy, 25, 26–28
and Rawl's principles of justice,
  33–34
and scientific theories, 79–80
and social-contract theory, 269
and social epistemology, 26, 27,
  35–36, 42
and social justice, 23, 26–27, 33,
  35–36
and social morality, 26, 27, 33–35,
  42
and social ontology, 26, 27, 29–31,
  35, 42
and US criminal justice system, 30
and work of Diana Fuss, 183
See also philosophy; Spivak,
  Gayatri
Theory of Justice, A (Rawls), 28–29
Till, Emmett, 180
Tuana, Nancy:
  and climate science, 167, 168

www.ingramcontent.com/pod-product-compliance
Lightning Source LLC
Chambersburg PA
CBHW021111270326
41929CB00009B/826